MARGARET FORSTER

The Rash Adventurer

The Rise and Fall of Charles Edward Stuart

GRAFTON BOOKS
A Division of the Collins Publishing Group

LONDON GLASGOW
TORONTO SYDNEY AUCKLAND

Grafton Books
A Division of the Collins Publishing Group
8 Grafton Street, London W1X 3LA

Published by Grafton Books 1975
Reprinted 1986

First published in Great Britain by
Martin Secker & Warburg Ltd 1973

ISBN 0-586-04062-5

Printed and bound in Great Britain by
Collins, Glasgow

Set in Linotype Fournier

For my own Flora

By the same author

Charles Edward Stuart is one of those characters that cannot be portrayed at a single sketch but have so greatly altered as to require a new delineation at different periods.

Lord Mahon

Contents

LIST OF ILLUSTRATIONS

Acknowledgments

I am indebted to Mr D. T. Richnell, Director of the University of London Library and Goldsmiths' Librarian, for affording me the facilities to study the microfilmed Stuart Papers, given to this library in 1966, and available by gracious permission of Her Majesty The Queen; to Miss Joan Gibbs, the University of London Library Archivist, who made me most welcome and introduced me to the mysteries of the Stuart Papers Index, not to mention the horrors of the microfilms themselves; to Mr Peter Slater who patiently put the microfilm reading machine right every time I wrecked it; to Mr Robert Mackworth-Young, the Royal Librarian at Windsor Castle, and his archivist Miss Lang for kindly allowing me to have photostat copies of some of the more indecipherable letters; to Mr Kenneth Smith of Carlisle Library for help beyond the call of duty, and in particular for allowing me to study the manuscript of Baron Clarke's Notebook; to Mr Jones at the Record Office, Carlisle Castle, for suggesting I might look at the diaries of George Williamson, Curate of Arthuret, and making these fascinating notebooks available; to my great friend Margaret Maddern for heroically translating some excruciatingly badly written letters of the Princesse de Talmond; to Marion Leyland, who typed so immaculately my handwritten manuscript with all its sellotaped gummed-on additions; but not to my husband and children who have had a lovely time enjoying themselves in Scotland, Italy and Switzerland on the excuse that they were helping me work.

My publishers and I are also most grateful to the following for their permission to reproduce pictures and letters: Her Majesty The Queen, Revd J. G. Antrobus, Ashmolean Museum, Oxford, The Duke of Atholl, The Duke of Buccleuch, PC, KT, D. H. Cameron of Lochiel, The Mansell Collection, National Portrait Gallery, London, The National Trust for Scotland, The Lord Primrose, Scottish National Portrait Gallery, Stonyhurst College, The Earl of Wemyss and March, KT, LLD.

Note on the Title

I thought I had discovered the perfect title for this book when I came across a reference to Charles as 'the Rash Adventurer' in a letter from the Provost of Dumfries to the Dean of Carlisle. It seemed that the Provost, being of a cautious nature, did not want to commit himself in writing to calling Charles either 'Prince' or 'Pretender'. (It became a popular custom to think of ways of getting round this problem and some very fancy titles were dreamed up.) Later, however, I found that I had been beaten to it by Winifred Duke who used this title twenty years ago for her account of Charles' journey into England. I hope that extending the title to cover the whole of Charles' life – which was at all times both rash and adventurous – is some justification for re-using it.

Preface

———————

Whenever I have been unable to sleep during the last three years I've succumbed not to 4 a.m. cancer but 4 a.m. preface writing. There seems so much that is interesting to comment on about the process of writing a biography that I could not resist indulging myself.

To start with, it had never occurred to me that writing a biography about any well-known historical character was a matter for apologies of the most abject kind. When I began reading for this one, I was worried and puzzled to discover that almost every author began with an embarrassed justification for his work. I also noticed that the critics who slaughtered novels as hackneyed were as lambs compared to those who heaped their contempt on 'yet another book' on, say, Dickens or Henry VIII – or Bonnie Prince Charlie. Now why? The stock answer seems to be that the research involved, and the very print and paper of the book itself, would be better spent on a period or person that has been neglected. This seems to me like telling a man to marry not the woman he loves but the woman who needs his love. All very praiseworthy, but not likely to prove a lasting marriage.

In fact, I am far from being obsessed by Charles Edward Stuart. What made me settle on him after close scrutiny of many other possibles was the symbolic nature of his life. Here was a man groomed for stardom who performed in blazing limelight for two short years and then was yanked off the stage protesting all the way. What does this kind of rejection do to a man? Nobody who had written about him seemed interested in finding out – since after 1745 he was of no historical importance they couldn't close doors, pull curtains and avert their eyes fast enough. The rest of his life was 'sordid' and 'squalid' and not worth recording. It was this fate that finally made him irresistible to me.

I began, like all innocents, with the highest possible standards. Since I'd moved from novels to biography with a puritanical zeal for the work involved, what I intended to do was use only manuscript and printed contemporary sources. Nothing anybody had written about Charles was to be taken on trust. The chief manuscript source for Charles was obviously his letters. These letters, I discovered, belong to the Queen and are housed in the Royal Archives at Windsor Castle. They are part of the seven-hundred-odd volumes of the Stuart Papers. With happy thoughts of gruelling days ahead, I wrote to the Librarian asking how I set about applying for permission to study the relevant documents.

What followed was an object lesson of several kinds. To begin with, I was strongly discouraged from applying for permission at all. It would, I was assured, only lead to a long wait and inevitable disappointment. I was expected to be sympathetic to the difficulties involved, for these were letters of 'a former member of the Royal Family', a phrase I liked. I roped in everyone I could think of to help but after a lot of telephone calls it emerged that there really was a rigid rule that nobody got to see those papers without having written two works of historical value and without references from a couple of bishops and assorted ilk. I find this shattering. At a time when files only thirty years old are being opened for inspection at the Public Record Office, how can access to papers two hundred years old be made so difficult? I remember it particularly annoyed me to read, not long after, that at a cocktail party the Queen had had laid out a selection of Bonnie Prince Charlie's letters (among other goodies) as a side attraction for guests who probably wouldn't have known them from the Highway Code.

However, there was no point in sulking. The question was, to give up before I'd begun or not? The Librarian at Windsor had mentioned that all the papers had been microfilmed and as I could easily get permission to see these films I really had nothing to complain about. I thought I'd give them a try. They are housed in Senate House (in the Library of the University of London), and everybody there resents the space they take up. They are also scathing about the quality of the films, made in a hurry in the war. After a test-run through several I saw why. Some are so blurred that even using the most powerful machine they are indecipherable, and others have been photographed at such strange angles, or held by such shaking hands, that one imagines the bombers overhead were very close. But I decided to use them. It was laborious work, not just the actual reading but all the threading in and out of films. I soon developed a magnificent squint which I swear will be with me for ever. Her Majesty has a lot to answer for. Luckily, it was worth it. There is nothing quite like finding a letter, however trivial, that nobody has ever used or referred to, even if they have read it. But then reading other people's letters is surely one of the most fascinating of occupations on any level.

Reading contemporary accounts of the 1745 rising – though I was determined to keep the '45 to a minimum – was also interesting. Again, I had thought collecting these books might be expensive but certainly not too difficult. That shows how little I know about rare books. I never managed to buy a single one, to my great sorrow, though in the process of trying I struck up intimate acquaintance with some score of booksellers. These are not the booksellers you and I know about, with their smart shops in high streets. These men don't have shops. They operate from home, hide their books in back rooms and sometimes take a malicious pleasure in assuring you they have the book but don't feel like selling it. I was fortunate to have the London Library to fall back on – doubly fortunate, for not only did they supply me with every text I needed (except one, which luckily Carlisle Castle had), but they supplied me *by post*. O joy! I have always dreaded libraries. Going into the Bodleian or the Camera at Oxford was always a source of the greatest misery to me, and I would do anything to avoid it. The very atmosphere that others find so conducive to work repels me – I feel stifled, restless, self-conscious and insatiably curious about everyone else there so that I can't concentrate. To have all the books at home was bliss and I am eternally grateful for such a marvellous institution.

It remains only to say that there can be no more absorbing task than attempting to write a biography. With a character like Charles Edward the accumulation of knowledge is so slow that one is hooked while still ignorant. As ignorance fades a little, and one feels the first urge to join in the academic bitchery by challenging some point with a pencil-written note in the margin of some well-known historian's book, a kind of panic sets in. Where will it all end? Can one possibly cope with all there is to learn? I learnt to respect and deeply admire those who have spent their lives patiently laying bare some small part of Jacobite history. Beside them, it is sheer impudence to presume to know anything at all. It is one of these dedicated handful, R. C. Jarvis, who in his introduction to Volume 1 of *Collected Papers of the Jacobite Risings* put the problem so succinctly:

... many a sober devotee of history has approached this particular field with an honest intention to truthful inquiry and impartial investigation only to be lured away to fall victim to the well-known magic spell. He has been seduced from history to romance: he has, perhaps all unwillingly or possibly quite unwittingly, been converted – corrupted – from historian to romancer.

I hope I have not fallen victim. I wanted to write about Charles Edward, not Jacobite history. It is his dilemma as a man, not his place in history, that attracts me. I would not claim that one iota of what I offer is of importance, but I find it of interest, and hope others will too.

THE STUART SUCCESSION

Years in bold are the dates of succession

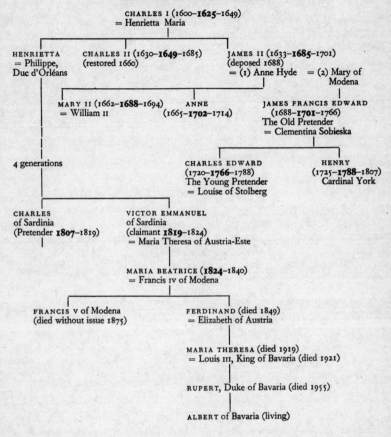

CHARLES I (1600–**1625**–1649)
= Henrietta Maria

HENRIETTA
= Philippe,
Duc d'Orléans

CHARLES II (1630–**1649**–1685)
(restored 1660)

JAMES II (1633–**1685**–1701)
(deposed 1688)
= (1) Anne Hyde = (2) Mary of
                               Modena

MARY II (1662–**1688**–1694)
= William II

ANNE
(1665–**1702**–1714)

JAMES FRANCIS EDWARD
(1688–**1701**–1766)
The Old Pretender
= Clementina Sobieska

4 generations

CHARLES EDWARD
(1720–**1766**–1788)
The Young Pretender
= Louise of Stolberg

HENRY
(1725–**1788**–1807)
Cardinal York

CHARLES
of Sardinia
(Pretender **1807**–1819)

VICTOR EMMANUEL
of Sardinia
(claimant **1819**–1824)
= Maria Theresa of Austria-Este

MARIA BEATRICE (**1824**–1840)
= Francis IV of Modena

FRANCIS V of Modena
(died without issue 1875)

FERDINAND (died 1849)
= Elizabeth of Austria

MARIA THERESA (died 1919)
= Louis III, King of Bavaria (died 1921)

RUPERT, Duke of Bavaria (died 1955)

ALBERT of Bavaria (living)

PART I

The Inheritance 1688-1744

Flight into Exile

On the morning of 10th June 1688, 'when most if not all the Protestant ladies were at church', a son was born to Mary of Modena, the second wife of the Catholic King James II of England. The Protestant ladies had only themselves to blame, for Mary and James had done their best to make sure no one missed the event and thereby forestall accusations that the birth was not genuine.

Mary Beatrice had married James II in 1673 at the age of fifteen, when he was still Duke of York. Since then she had had four children, all of whom had died in infancy, and four miscarriages. It seemed that James' two daughters by his first marriage, Mary and Anne, both Protestants, would be his heirs, for his wife had not been pregnant since 1684. When she realised in the autumn of 1687 that she was, she could hardly believe it, and delayed the announcement till Christmas.

Instantly, doubts were cast both on her pregnancy and on the father of her child. Her catty stepdaughter Anne, to whom she had always been extraordinarily kind, maintained that Mary would have nobody about when she was in her shift and that her belly might indeed be false. The rumours and innuendoes of suspicion which circulated at the time distressed Mary deeply. She was in any case not well – her previous pregnancies and miscarriages had weakened her – and she almost lost her baby three times. She approached the birth with dread, but also with a strong determination that there should be no doubts in anyone's mind that whatever baby arrived it was indisputably hers. It took courage for a naturally shy and modest woman to prepare to make a spectacle of herself at such an intimate moment but that is what Mary did, as though anticipating the warming-pan myth before it was ever thought of.

The birth was arranged to take place in Whitehall and not at Windsor where the Royal couple were living. Everyone of importance was invited well ahead of time to attend. Mary's first thought when labour began and she realised that she was going to have her baby a month early was to make sure that witnesses as well as doctors were summoned. Luckily, she was in London and had herself carried through the streets on a litter to her new apartments. Once there she asked James anxiously if he had remembered to send for the Queen Dowager. He replied, wearily, 'I have sent for everyone.'

From the crowds in her bedroom on the morning of 10th June Mary could tell this was true, but she regretted that Anne had not returned from Bath. She lay on the great bed with its high canopy and rich curtains, decorated with fruit and flowers, averting her face from the officials who pressed in on her at James' insistence. She hid her face in his periwig and held his hand tightly. Just before ten o'clock when the air in the room was heavy after the long, hot night with so many people present, the baby was delivered. It was a fine, strong boy, but James did not at first realise. He had arranged that one of the women should give him a signal according to the sex, but such was his confusion he failed to recognise it and had to ask, 'What is it?' It took several seconds for 'What your Majesty desires' to sink in.

It seemed to James on that June morning that at last the Catholic succession to the throne of England was assured. Five months later, he and Mary were in exile and his Protestant son-in-law, William of Orange, and his daughter by his first marriage, Mary, ruled in his place.

Thirty-two years later, on the last day of December 1720, another and almost equally public birth took place in the Palazzo Muti in Rome. Clementina Sobieska, wife of the man all the city knew as King James III, was delivered of a son.

The Palazzo Muti is a dull, unattractive building cramped into a corner of a small narrow street off the busy Corso. It is easy to miss, surrounded as it is by vast edifices, each one larger and grander than the last. Rome seems a crowded stage upon which too many brilliant scenic designers have been let loose. In 1720 this Palazzo looked exactly the same – even then shabby, undistinguished, pushed aside – and this made it particularly suitable to be the centre of a refugee world, which is what it was. Inside, it seethed with the families, friends and servants who had for thirty-two years been with James Stuart in exile. It had all the hopeless activity of a busy transit camp, all the solidarity and yet furious jealousies of a house of outcasts. Into this strange, intense world of make-believe came a baby who arrived with an inheritance so onerous and inescapable that no amount of merrymaking could lighten the load.

Charles was conceived and born for a definite purpose: to inherit the throne of England, lost in 1688 by his grandfather, James II. From the moment he was old enough to understand anything at all he understood that this was his object in life. To reject it – which he never for one moment thought of doing – would have been to reject everything he was brought up to hold sacred. He was never the son and heir of a man who might one day be King of England, always of a man who *was* King. He absorbed throughout his childhood a tale of suffering that went back forty years. All the people round him had sacrificed their homes, lands, and sometimes their wealth, in order to follow his grandfather and now his father. It was a story of heroism and cowardice, of loyalty and betrayal, of missed chances and lost opportunities, a story hard to follow for anyone except Charles who absorbed it effortlessly from his earliest days.

No man has ever been more in sympathy with a son's problems than James Francis Edward was with Charles'. He had been through it all himself. He, too, had been born the son of a king, he too had had much expected of him, he too had fought and struggled to fulfil what everyone around him saw as his responsibilities. The first act, as it were, had been performed – Charles only came on after the interval.

Since 1688 the fight to regain the throne had never stopped. Once James II had set up his court at St Germain-en-Laye, graciously provided by his self-interested host Louis XIV, his attention was turned to winning back his kingdom. Never for one minute did the contemporary world think he had lost it for good. Even after James lost the Battle of the Boyne in 1690 and his own hopes were shattered, he was still reckoned to be in with a good chance. He died in 1701 leaving to his thirteen-year-old son, James Francis Edward, the momentous task of regaining his rightful inheritance.

The new James tried. His chances seemed even better than his father's had done, for his half-sister Anne now sat on the throne. Blood was surely thicker than water and Anne had no surviving issue. James might well succeed without lifting a finger. But that would mean waiting and no certainty of the final reward. His youthful impatience – for he was a far more warlike character than has ever been generally thought – was catered for by Louis XIV who in 1708 announced he would back a campaign.

Louis badly needed a diversion to offset Marlborough's victories at Blenheim and in the Low Countries. An expedition was fitted out, consisting of the formidable force of six French regiments, five French men-of-war, twenty transports, and thirteen thousand stand of arms. James proceeded in high spirits to Dunkirk. But the venture ended in ignominy. The French pilots miscalculated and the fleet reached the wrong part of the Scottish coast, hotly pursued by the English. The French Admiral Forbin turned tail and fled back to Dunkirk. Opportunity had been missed – perhaps as good an opportunity as was to come the Jacobite way, for Scotland was seething over the Act of Union with England passed the previous year; and soon James' hopes were further dampened by news of impending peace between England and France. It was a condition of the Peace of Aix-la-Chapelle, signed in 1712, that James should leave France; he and his dejected and mutually quarrelling court moved to Bar-le-Duc in Lorraine.

Two years later Queen Anne died. In the interim many people told James that, if only he would become a Protestant, the throne of England was his. In March 1714 he gave his unequivocal reply: 'I neither want counsel nor advice to remain unalterable in my first resolution of never dissembling any religion, but rather to abandon all than act against my conscience and honour, cost what it will.' So it was with the Catholic millstone round his neck that he determined to make his second attempt to recover his father's kingdom. Confident of French support, he set out for Paris, only to receive a message on the way from the Foreign Minister that no help from France would be forthcoming and that, if he didn't return at once to Lorraine, his mother's pension would be stopped. Afraid of risking bloodshed, without adequate backing, and unsure of the depth of English support, James did the sensible but disastrous thing: he decided to wait. For two months the throne of England remained empty, though George, Elector of Hanover, had been proclaimed King. It was another perfect opportunity let slip.

However, even after the arrival of George I all seemed far from lost. On James' birthday, 10th June 1715, there were enough riots in his favour to reveal a considerable resentment against the new king who did not even speak English and took no trouble to ingratiate himself. Always encouraged by his mother to believe that the English people would in the end see right triumph over wrong, James was excited and cautiously optimistic. One of his chief supporters who had now joined him, Henry St John, Viscount Bolingbroke, wrote – a little contemptuously – 'He talked to me like a man who expected every moment to set out for England or Scotland but did not very well know for which.' That he did not know was symbolic of the muddle James was in. Instead of being at the centre of operations, he was on the fringe, waiting to be told what to do. In the South of England the rising of 1715 was crushed before it properly began, while in the North Thomas Forster struggled inefficiently to keep going what had become an isolated insurrection. The Earl of Mar, in Scotland – with no instructions from James – raised the standard on 6th September.

It was not until 29th October that James left Lorraine, confident at last that it was worth going.

His journey proved hazardous. It was not until 2nd January 1716 that James arrived in Scotland – after the fatal battle of Sherriffmuir had already been fought. This bad news that greeted him, the sickness he had endured and the terrible cold that prevailed could not destroy his satisfaction that at long last he had set foot in his own kingdom. Keeping sight of James, rather than what was happening around him, a strangely happy picture emerges. Whatever others thought, James himself found his welcome beyond all expectations. He wrote: 'My prescence has had and will have I hope a good effect. The affection of the people is beyond all expression.' Now, for a while, he was inspired. It did him little good. His forces had been driven into a position of retreat before his arrival. Argyll, the Government leader, advanced relentlessly. James wrote '... I have plainly seen that nothing but a considerable succour of arms, ammunition and money could enable us to maintain ourselves here. We look upon you [France] as our only hope, we earnestly claim your instant help ...'

It was not forthcoming. On 15th February James and Mar embarked at Montrose for France. They were at St Germain by the 22nd. There followed a brief burst of activity with James frantically rushing round Paris trying to organise help for his followers, still fighting to the last ditch in Scotland. When he failed to produce any, he rode off to Avignon, full of guilt and bitterness, his high hopes again dashed.

From 1716 to February 1717 James lived at Avignon, the guest of Pope Clement XI. It was a time of ill health for him. He believed, not without reason, that misfortune dogged him. It seemed to him that his bad luck this time had begun on 1st September 1715 when Louis XIV had died and was succeeded by his young grandson. The Regent, the Duc d'Orléans, had never been a friend of the Stuarts: if only Louis had lived, James persuaded himself, help would have been forthcoming. He bore France a grudge – but, paradoxically, had more respect for her strength and power than ever before. He had seen himself weak and helpless: never again would he attempt anything without men, money and arms at his disposal. It was a lesson he felt he had learnt the hard way and he was determined to profit by it. From now on internal risings depending on local support were definitely not on.

In the spring of 1717 James moved, reluctantly, to Urbino. Here, with his fortunes at their lowest ebb, he turned his thoughts to marriage. What hopes could his loyal – and disloyal – supporters have of an eventual

Stuart restoration if there were no prospect of a son and heir? James realised that marriage was essential to his cause. He approached the prospect with no joy but complete dedication. But the search for a suitable bride was not easy. Reigning kings and princes were far from eager to entrust their daughters to a king in exile, whose prospects of regaining his throne had grown dimmer with the years. His choice fell finally on the sixteen-year-old Maria Clementina Sobieska, the granddaughter of King John of Poland. Convinced that he was always to be unfortunate, James was not surprised when not even marriage with a willing bride proved easy. England objected, naturally, to him marrying anyone at all. Clementina was imprisoned by the Holy Roman Emperor, Charles, at England's request, on her way through his dominions to meet James in Italy. Only her own courage and daring – amazing in a young girl who had led a protected life until then – and the resourcefulness of one Charles Wogan, a devoted follower of James, succeeded in organising her dramatic escape.

James and Clementina were married, to the rage of King George of England, in the cathedral of Montefiascone, in September 1719. Thence they proceeded to Rome, where they settled down in the Palazzo Muti.

CHAPTER ONE

Rome

Rome, where James Francis Edward Stuart and Clementina Sobieska, the newly married pair, settled down, was at that time the city all men of society wished to live in. French taste might be the arbiter of the world, but even Frenchmen acknowledged the superiority of Rome as a place to live.

Rome was not, in 1719, a cosmopolitan city within the usual sense of the phrase. It was more countrified than urbanised, lacking any real industry and with the most haphazard of governments.

People treated the place as though it was the country, peeing behind every statue or column as they would behind a bush or tree, but since it was not the country the stone did not respond like the grass: Rome stank. Apart from the pigs, gardeners took some of the excrement for manuring the box hedges so much more admired than flowers, and the rain had to do the rest in the winter. Yet Rome had good country air – the eighteenth century there was healthy, far healthier than in any other major city.

As far as diversions went, Rome was a good place to be. Both James and Clementina took pleasure from the musical activity of the time. Rome had the best music, the best musicians and the best audiences. The crowds were insatiable in their love of new operas and musical plays. Tickets were sold *inside* the theatres and the price varied alarmingly and most democratically according to the success of the piece then being performed. This love of music was so intense that it actually led to the castrating of boys of seven or eight so that a sufficient number of sopranos would always be available. Women were not allowed to perform so could not, less painfully, fill the breach. These boys, known as the 'castrati', were a privileged class and openly approved of. They at least served a double purpose, for not only did they sing, they satisfied the homosexual tastes of some sections of Rome. This 'vice', so hated by Louis XIV and never condoned in France, was generally regarded with indulgence – a wise viewpoint considering the greatest entertainers of the castrati were certain cardinals, out of whom a good living was made. Apart from musical evenings, very definitely the star attraction, Romans also loved all forms of gambling, from card-playing to the lottery, and dancing. They did not go in for physical exercise, though the nobility hunted and went riding on their country estates. Swimming was practically unheard of, even though Rome was so near the sea and the climate in the summer was so hot. Yet they loved water – Rome had plenty of it and fountains played everywhere. Entertaining was a matter of conversing, not of sumptuous dinners, which the French found odd. Certain families held open house for 'conversazioni', and not feasting at public dinners. The only food distributed lavishly on every conceivable occasion was ice-cream, especially water-ices.

The most extraordinary thing about Rome, apart from its beauty, was the lack of social distinction observed. English and French travellers, used to the maintenance of rigid divisions, were astonished to find that in Rome there was a free intermingling between classes. Louis Madelin, who wrote a book about Rome at the end of the century, described '... the palaces standing open to any menial's distant cousin, the great cardinal's snuff box offered naturally to the unassuming "fratone", the jesting between Prince and Artisan'. This was not to say that high and low did not exist: they did, but no pride was taken in separating them. The nobility had as many codes of etiquette as that of any other country, but they were internal. The class James and Clementina settled among was not as powerful as elsewhere. They had few political rights – the Pope had these – and their power was that of birth and possessions. Because of this rôle they were called upon to play, they were not educated to anything else. All a Roman youth had in the way of education was a little Latin, a grounding in church history and heraldry, and musical appreciation. He did not travel like the Parisian and Londoner. Honour was more important than knowledge, chivalry than experience. Since he was not interested in displaying any kind of intellectual superiority, the Roman aristocrat placed great emphasis on appearance. He had scores of lackeys beautifully dressed, and lived in magnificent palaces. Carriages were incredibly important, prestige going to the largest and most ornamental, the Rolls-Royces of the future.

Yet, all this gay living aside – and Rome was never thought of as a licentious city – this was a papal state. Religion was a daily commodity of life. It was the only aspect of the city that truly appealed to Clementina, but even then it was different from anything she had either known or expected. Steeped as they were in it, the Romans' attitude to religion appeared casual. There was no misery in their devotion. James had been brought up by his mother to think of religion as a happy thing, but happy in the sense that it made one content inside. The Romans were content outside too. Even confession, where they had a very great deal to confess, was a cheerful affair, never approached with dread. One confessed, one was shriven, one started again: there was nothing to be upset about. This attitude was encouraged by the celebration of a hundred and fifty festivals each year, when no work was done and everyone paraded and made merry. Church itself was not a place of deathly hush. Quiet chapels could be found at the right time of day, but most churches were crowded, noisy places with everyone jostling each other and shrieking greetings to their friends – not to Clementina's taste at all. Even the music was not what it should have been. Sacred music was all right, but too dreary for the Romans' taste who preferred a more worldly selection. Gilbert and Sullivan would have gone down well. It took visitors time to adjust to this scene, but when they realised that it all sprang from the deepest devotion imaginable, and not irreverence, they usually approved and liked it. They had to admit, after all, that if the Pope liked it this way who were they to disapprove. And the Pope did. The papal court itself could bristle with solemnity when it chose, but on the whole it was an informal place. All the popes James was to encounter were good men and each, with the possible exception of Clement XI, liked a relaxed, carefree atmosphere around him. Next in power to the Pope were the cardinals, between sixty and seventy of them, who were supposed to be chosen for their religious and intellectual excellence and on the whole were up to standard. A cardinal at that date did not have to be a priest first, but could start, as it were, at the top. They had tremendous influence and played an active part in every branch of Roman life.

As foreigners, James and Clementina were welcome in Rome, especially since Clementina at least was reputed to have plenty of money. The numbers of visitors to Rome was never-ending and the number of foreign residents high. There was no cold shoulder offered – the Romans were delighted to have anyone, especially anyone under the wing of the Pope. Strangers were welcomed and accepted in a way that would have been unthinkable in Paris or London. Cafés, restaurants and inns all sprang up to cater for these tourists, and the Romans worked hard to earn their city's place as number one tourist attraction. Hostility was rare, politeness and helpfulness the rule.

This, then, was the city that James and Clementina came to live in during the autumn of 1719. The Pope had graciously given them one of his houses to live in, the Palazzo Muti. Palazzo makes it sound grander than it is but every building over a certain size in Rome was always a

palazzo. It was not what either of them had been used to, though James
had by that date occupied so many houses that it was not quite the
shock to him that it was to Clementina, fresh from the grandeur of her
father's palace at Ohlau. The best thing about the Palazzo Muti was its
nearness to the Corso, a bare hundred yards away up a narrow side-
street. Coming down that street, the Palazzo Muti is easily passed since
it is on a corner, at the end of what is more a wide street than a piazza,
and is dwarfed by the Church of the Apostles. It is a four-storey building
of yellow stone with an arched entrance in the middle to a courtyard. Most
of the windows face into this courtyard, which is barely large enough for
a carriage and horses to turn round in. A wide, stone staircase leads up
it to the numerous small, high-ceilinged rooms. There are no views
available from them except of the gigantic church across the road. It is a
gloomy place, not at all splendid or imposing, particularly viewed in its
context where beautiful buildings are everywhere. It was, however, a
prestige residence in that it was very near the Quirinale where the Pope
presided, as well as to the Corso. Since prestige mattered more than
comfort or elegance to James, he at least was pleased. Their country
house, also given to them (temporarily – everything was always temporary) by the Pope, was much more attractive. This was the Palazzo
Savelli at Albano, up in the hills about eighteen miles from Rome. Whereas
in Rome the Palazzo Muti was a poor relation, in Albano – a small but
bustling hill-town – the Palazzo Savelli set the tone. It stands in the middle
of the town, on a slope, and its large, airy rooms command fine views
over the town. There is a certain elegance about the building with its
arched portico and marble stairs, and it must have been a relief to come to
it from the Palazzo Muti. It must also have been a relief to exchange the
noise of the nearby Corso for the quiet of the hills, and the dust of the
streets for the breezes from the nearby lake of Albano. There is always
a sense of surprise at finding such magnificent countryside so near
to a crowded, almost green-less city. The lake has thickly wooded
sides and hills encircle the huge amphitheatre of water so that, looking
down from near Albano, it is not unlike a Scottish loch. The wild life
and vegetation are also very reminiscent of loch sides in Scotland.
Only the quality of the blue sky makes an essential difference, but
presumably when the snow falls in winter the grey above changes
everything.

Naturally, Clementina found the composition of her court confusing.
Apart from getting to know everyone, which was in itself an exhausting
business since her English was still not fluent and many of the Scots and
Irish had strange accents, she had to accustom herself to the surprising

fact that her husband put in a long working day. Used to the indolence of her own father and his court, Clementina was amazed to find that James shut himself up with his secretary James Edgar for three or four hours every day while they attended to The Correspondence. James never stopped writing letters, nor did people stop writing to him. There are literally thousands and thousands of letters written by him, most of them lengthy and detailed. Such polished epistles took time, James' time. Edgar – another exile after the '15 – was invaluable to his master, but it was never a case of James simply adding his signature to a letter, or dictating what he wanted Edgar to say. If he dictated at all, it was line by line, all the words his own. Clementina could not comprehend that there could be so much in the world to write about. After James had finished this office work, his time was still not necessarily hers. There were always people to be seen, wanting him to give them money or a place at his court, or else visitors simply wanting to pay their respects to him. With this the case, Clementina had to find her own amusements, so it was fortunate that her musical tastes and abilities were well catered for in Rome. Fortunate, too, that she was deeply religious and could spend so much time in prayer. It formed an escape from the tensions of the court, so little understood by her, and yet so inevitable. The court was divided into factions that split several ways: there was the Catholic–Protestant axis, the Scots–Irish rivalry, and the opposing sides on what line James ought to take. The jealousy and instability inherent in such a situation bored and irritated Clementina, though James was endlessly patient and good-tempered if rather depressed by it all. It was a state of affairs he had been used to since birth and had long since resigned himself to.

Life was not as dull as it had been at Urbino and most Jacobites at this court were as satisfied as any exile can be. James Edgar described Rome aptly as 'a place nobody can be weary in', and thought one could wear out a pair of shoes in a fortnight just gadding about. The movements of James' court were watched day and night by English spies, who reported back to the government of the day all the trivia they could think of as well as events of significance. This scrutiny was never let up. Baron Philipp Stosch, whose pen name was John Walton, was the principal British agent in Rome and made it his business to know literally everything that went on in the Palazzo Muti. There was nothing he would not stoop to, however sordid, in his efforts to titillate his employers. It became, at one time, almost a full-time job going through Clementina's dirty laundry in his efforts to discover whether she might be pregnant – there was hardly a maid he could not bribe, even if the ladies-in-waiting were above corruption.

If James and Clementina were pleased with Rome, Rome was pleased with them. The Romans were as fascinated by this King and Queen of England as the French had been more than thirty years before. The pair had youth and beauty on their side and people crowded to look at them. Their best opportunity came during the fêtes and festivals that were at least weekly occurrences in the city. Then the carriages of the nobility, including James' and Clementina's, would file round the piazza in question and the occupants settled down on a balcony to watch the proceedings and be watched themselves. With these kinds of amusements and outings to Albano the time passed pleasantly. Clementina had not yet fully appreciated the hollowness of her title 'Queen' for in Rome she was treated as such and had not had time to grow tired of it. Besides, James and the whole court lived in daily expectation of restoration and who was she to question their faith?

In the spring of 1720, six months after their marriage, Clementina became pregnant. Since she had been closely watched right from the first month, nobody could claim to be stunned, but there had throughout this time been so many rumours every month that the announcement of her condition did create quite a sensation. Walton, who almost took it as a personal insult that he had not been asked to witness the conception, was confident that Clementina would never carry the child. She was too young, too small, too delicate. He expected her to miscarry quite soon. But Clementina did not. James formally announced the pregnancy to the courts of Europe and invited well ahead of time all the chief persons in Rome to be present at the birth. Clementina was prominently displayed for all to see, and since she shared none of Mary of Modena's reticence there was nothing Walton's spies could do but confirm the authenticity of her belly.

There was some doubt as to when the birth would be. James wrote with some embarrassment to the Duke of Ormonde at the beginning of November: 'The Queen ... continues very well. It is indeed a little singular to have mistaken so much as three or four months in her reckoning but the great mind everybody had she should be with child made several people think that they felt it move at a time when it was not natural to think her in that condition, but she has enjoyed a perfect health during the whole time and so mistakes and delays need give [no anxiety].' It looked as if he had announced his wife's pregnancy before she was actually pregnant, which was mortifying to say the least. The only advantage was that, unlike his own premature birth, the mistake was on the right side. By the end of November James' philosophical outlook was giving way to exasperation. He wrote to Dillon: 'We are still in doubt as to the time of the Queen's lying in. It is very possible that may happen in a fortnight but the last reckoning was a month longer.' Even the last reckoning was too optimistic. The month came and went and still nothing happened. James was frantic and Clementina exhausted. He could not even find solace in his correspondence, writing 'the condition the Queen is in does not allow me to enlarge unnecessarily on anything'. It was the only time he ever wrote short, curt letters.

On the evening of 27th December 1720 Clementina began to feel unwell during a rehearsal before her of an opera. Since her baby was now daily expected, the cardinals, prelates, the magistrate of Rome and everyone else who had been asked to the party, were invited to come to the Palazzo Muti. They came, then they went. Clementina's 'unwellness' had abated. On the 30th they were all summoned again, and sent away, only to be brought back on Tuesday the 31st. All this time poor Clementina was in intermittent labour and it did not help to have something on a hundred people trooping in and out to inspect her. At last, forty-two minutes after the sun had set, she gave birth to a fine, healthy boy and confounded the sceptics. Witnesses were numerous and their credentials impeccable. There were cardinals in plenty, a dozen princesses, several ambassadors. The child's father had after all, on the death of James II, been recognised as the lawful King of England by France, Spain, Modena, Savoy and the Holy See. The baby was baptised an hour after his birth and given the names Charles Edward Louis John Casimir Silvester Severino Maria. The Pope sent round his best relics as well as ten thousand scudi as a present for the triumphant mother. The next day, the cannons of Castello St Angelo boomed out and people in the street shouted 'Viva' to each other. There were displays of fireworks, the fountains ran with wine and everyone was delirious with happiness. Never had a New Year been more enthusiastically celebrated. The significance of the date knocked the portent-loving Romans between the eyes, and was not lost on the world in general (though in Scotland it was still, at that time, only 20th December for the New Calendar had not been adopted). At St Germain a bonfire was lit by the few remaining Jacobites there, and Louis XV is said to have clapped his hands for joy.

James sat down at his desk on the morning of Wednesday 1st January 1721 to the pleasurable task of spreading the good news. He spent the day writing letters announcing the birth, eleven in all. His joy came through unmistakably – these were the letters of a man transported beyond his usual caution and reserve. Three days later he had written to all the important people and was now giving the glad tidings to lesser mortals.

His enthusiasm had still not abated, as can be seen in this letter to Harry Stratton.

H. Stratton   January 4th 1721

    This is to direct *you* to aquaint *my friends* with you that on *Tuesday night* last *the Queen was safely delivered of a son* whom I have *called Charles* both one & t'other are I thank God in perfect good health and I trust in providence that this *great blessing* will soon be followed with others, in the mean time let *this* keep *up* your *hearts* and *Courage* for better *days*. I am labouring to *hasten* all I can, I have not time to *write* particular *letters* to *my friends* on this *occasion* but you may assure them, that tho' it be natural for me to be pleased at the *increase* of my family, yet I am it full as much on their account as my own, their *welfare* is what I have chiefly *at heart* and I chiefly desire to see *better days* that they may be shares of them *with me*.

Throughout the next few weeks congratulations poured in from all over Europe, much to James' satisfaction. The glow remained with him for months. Apart from the more formal messages from heads of state, there were letters from his adherents that meant even more to him. John Menzies referred to 'this time of Jubilee', and James Hamilton wrote 'May I have the joy, Sir, of congratulating you on the 2, 14, 28, 31, 12, 49, 50 of a 26, 28, 14, 22, 4, 7.' The words 'arrival' or 'Prince' were apparently too secret and dangerous to use. The 26, 28, 14, 22, 4, 7 was coyly referred to by Mar as the 'Young Gentleman' who had 'put a good end to the old year and a good beginning to the new'. The baby continued well, as did his mother, who was recovered enough to go to the opera on 3rd February and bask in the applause. Gratified though he was, James had one wish. He wrote to Lansdowne: 'I shall be impatient to know what effect this news will have in our own country.'

It had exactly the effect he would have wished – open rejoicing on the part of his supporters, and consternation in the Government camp. The news could not have come at a better time for his cause, since 1720 had been the year of the South Sea Crisis which had plunged England into apparent economic disaster – apparent because though it was disaster for many individuals it was not for the country. Those ruined by it, Jacobites and others alike, wanted revenge and were in a mood to distrust their comparatively new King and his ministers. Politically, the scene was no more stable. At the time James overflowed with love for his newborn son, George I seethed with rage and hatred towards his. The Prince of Wales had his own court at Leicester House, a natural centre for discontented politicians, or those thinking of the future rather than the present (the King was sixty). There was as yet no settled party enjoying any measure of power: Walpole still fought it out with Stanhope and

Sunderland. It was an atmosphere in which anything could happen and when opportunities came in plenty for action. Charles Edward's birth simply added to the excitement.

James was unaware of how short a time this promising state of affairs was to last. By April 1722 Robert Walpole was in a position to create a political system strong enough to keep the Stuarts out. The crushing of Jacobitism became part of his security measures. No plot could survive his vigilance and, as prosperity slowly increased, plots did not have the same appeal. Peace was essential to his plans, and while there was peace Jacobite hopes were slim. Furthermore, with every year that slipped by more true Jacobites died. It was becoming the cause of anyone who disliked the Hanoverians rather than of those who regarded James as King by divine right.

But in 1720, when Charles Edward was born, the possibility of restoration was still real.

CHAPTER TWO

'This Pretty Young Prince'

There were few rôles in his life that fitted James better than fatherhood. He relished it. Not only was his love total and consuming, but he regarded being a father as a job of work to which he was particularly suited. He had thought deeply and carefully about how his son should be brought up. His own childhood had been happy and he was determined that Charles' should also be happy. At the same time he wanted him to be brought up as an Englishman and treated, as he himself had been treated, like a prince. He wrote to Ormonde that his 'brave, lusty boy shall be dressed and looked after as much as the climate will allow in the English Way; for though I can't help his being born in Italy, yet as much as in me lyes he shall be English for the rest over'. It was a bold promise, considering James had never set foot in England.

Before Charles was born, James had given much consideration to the question of who should be his governess for the first few years. He wanted an Englishwoman of good birth and proven loyalty. Those at his court in Rome already had appointments, so he looked elsewhere, to Paris, where there were many such exiled ladies. The woman he finally settled on was a Miss Sheldon, daughter of one Ralph Sheldon who had been equerry to James II, and sister-in-law of General Dillon, who was one of James' most trusted friends. James had known the Sheldons all his life. There were at least a dozen of them at St Germain-en-Laye during his childhood and he knew their devotion to be absolute. Accordingly, Miss Sheldon was sent for to assist at the birth and afterwards to take care of the baby and look after its household.

It is hard to get any clear impression of this woman who had charge of Charles during his so-called formative years. Clementina certainly took to her, preferring her to either Lady Nithsdale or Marjorie Hay, the ladies of her household. There are only two letters from Miss Sheldon, which reveal that she was sensible enough and spirited enough to deal firmly with James' fussing. It appeared that Charles was a fat toddler, slow to walk. By the time he was twenty months, James was taking medical advice and passed on to Miss Sheldon the opinion that drugs – presumably stimulants – should be given to him. Miss Sheldon was respectful but scornful and put James in his place:

> ... as far as the advice sent by the famous doctor is concerned, I have the honour of informing you, Sire, that I do not consider that his Royal Highness is in need of any of his remedies ... I have no doubt that once this hot spell is over he will walk very well ... it is only the heat and his habit of leaning on his reins which hinder him. His knees are still rather weak and as this bothers him somewhat he doesn't like putting his weight on them. He is eating and sleeping well & is plumper than when Your Majesty went away ... Truly, Sire, it is far better that His Royal Highness should not walk very well for another few months than risk making him ill ... the only thing to do is to be very careful that he doesn't eat heavy food.

Three weeks later, in spite of a light diet, she wrote that Charles 'is putting on weight and grows more lovable every day ... now that the weather is cooler, His Royal Highness won't be so lazy and will soon want to walk'.

James liked daily reports on his son's welfare if he was not there to see himself. Clementina does not seem to have had the same interest. By the time Charles could run around, he did so with such violence that he gave her headaches and had to be taken away. She was one of those pale, pretty mothers who reclined on sofas and liked children to be decorative and decorous, whereas James, for all his sober ways, was much more indulgent, at least in the early years. Clementina, having produced an heir, was more interested in marital than filial love, and she was finding married life increasingly unsatisfactory as the first gloss wore off. It became obvious to her that she was Queen in name only and, without James' faith, she saw no chance of things changing. This, together with the inordinate amount of time James spent working, made her discontented. They had scenes and quarrels in which she said he didn't care about her and he said she didn't understand: it was a classic situation. As John Hay put it: 'Their tempers are so very different that though in the greatest trifles they are never of the same opinion the one won't yield an inch to the other.' But the feeling was still there. While taking the Baths at Lucca in 1722, Clementina could still send James a present of a dog and write: 'I should envy the happiness this dog will have of being near all I hold most dear in the world ... you know very well that I love you beyond all expression.' She seems to have been ashamed of her bad temper and at least at a distance wanted to apologise: 'I am trying to overcome my naughty temper, so as to appear to you the best girl in the world.'

Mollified, James rushed to Lucca to join her, but within days they were at each other's throats again.

None of these squabbles affected Charles, safely left behind with the solid Miss Sheldon. What did affect him was the birth of a brother on 6th March 1725 when he was four years old. Henry Benedict arrived just in time to be of any use to Charles as a companion, for though four years at first seemed a big gap, Henry was so quick to develop and so advanced where Charles had been slow that they became real friends. James, remembering how much his sister Louise had meant to him, was delighted. He was pleased that the two boys played so well together without any apparent rivalry or jealousy. He was pleased, too, to have another son, a double insurance for the throne of England.

It was now time, James thought, to begin his elder son's education. For that, Miss Sheldon would not do. Apart from the fact that she was a woman, which meant she could not possibly undertake such an onerous task, however brilliant her learning, it was clear to James that Charles, approaching five, was going to be difficult to handle. A man must be appointed equal to the job. James had several interesting ideas about this appointment. One of these was the Chevalier Ramsay, brought to Rome by Hay in 1724, when James was beginning to consider replacing Miss Sheldon. Ramsay was a disciple and former pupil of Fénelon, the French archbishop, philosopher, writer and educationalist and one-time admirer of James himself. Fénelon's theories were for the time revolutionary, and though he himself had died in 1715 his ideas had not died with him. Briefly, they consisted of paying more attention to stimulating the pupil to want to learn than forcibly ramming facts down his throat. Learning should be attractive and not fearsome. James was drawn to Fénelon's theories.

Fénelon had had a chance to put his theories into practice when he became tutor to the Duc de Bourgogne, Louis XIV's grandson. According to Saint-Simon, the Duc de Bourgogne was born terrible and during his early years terrorised everyone he came into contact with. He had a violent temper which he let rip at the slightest suggestion of being thwarted and was interested only in pleasure. Lacking any concentration, and being very highly strung, he found learning impossible. His sole talent seemed to be musical. Fénelon transformed this unattractive brat into a kind, thoughtful, well-read, knowledgeable young man and James must have remembered being as impressed as everyone else. He may also have seen strong parallels with Charles and the young Duc de Bourgogne. But for some unexplained reason Ramsay did not prove suitable and returned to Paris (he later became Chancellor of the Grand Lodge of France).

A pity, for Charles needed some approach other than the conventional one.

In the autumn of 1725 James appointed James Murray, now titular Earl of Dunbar, as governor to Prince Charles, and Sir Thomas Sheridan as sub-governor. Murray, the second of the fourteen children of the Lord Stormont, was thirty-seven, two years younger than James. He was a Protestant, Sheridan a Catholic, which was supposed to make it quite fair and pleasing to everyone. They were both bad appointments. Murray was not the stuff of which good teachers are made for personality rather than intellectual reasons. Academically, he was gifted, certainly more gifted than James' own governor had been. He had been called to the Bar in 1710, at the age of twenty, and had then gone on to be a Member of Parliament for Dumfries and later for the Elgin boroughs. He had joined the Stuart cause in 1715, was imprisoned in Newgate, and eventually joined James at Avignon where his cheerfulness heartened his gloomy master. His handwriting is one of the clearest to read among all the many hands in the Stuart papers and his spelling much better than most of his contemporaries'. But Murray's air of superiority with everyone except James did not endear him to the young Charles. He nagged the boy and had no sense of humour – essential, for Charles was developing a liking for jokes. Sheridan was a more sympathetic character, and more relaxed in his attitude, but he was an old man. He came from an Irish family of unquestioned loyalty and had been educated at the Collège Louis-le-Grand. Between them, with many misgivings, they began the herculean task of educating a lively, high-spirited little boy who did not want to be educated.

Their job was not begun without objections. Clementina was furious. She saw no reason why her friend Miss Sheldon should be replaced. This was silly of her, but even more silly was her assertion that since Murray was a Protestant her son would not be brought up as a true Catholic. It is hard to understand Clementina's attitude. She knew perfectly well that James was a sincere Catholic, and indeed had been put to the test many times. Furthermore, the Pope approved the appointment and if the head of the Church sanctioned it, who was Clementina to object? What she was in fact suffering from was jealousy. She was jealous of James' friends who all the time seemed to get nearer to him than she did. Not only was Murray now Earl of Dunbar and Governor to Charles, but Hay was Earl of Inverness and Secretary of State. Where, Clementina stormed, did that leave her? Not only were Murray and Hay even more important, but Marjorie Hay, the new Lady Inverness, was carried along on the tide of popularity and given, Clementina thought, undue prominence. It looked to her like a conspiracy to exclude her. So strong did her persecution complex become that, after failing to get the Hays dismissed and Murray removed, she took the disastrous step of leaving the Palazzo Muti for a convent in November 1725.

Her departure caused a sensation. James was shattered. He knew himself to be entirely innocent of Clementina's accusations, varied as they were. Both Hay and Murray were good, loyal men, and Marjorie Hay nothing more than the wife of his friend. Some said that Clementina accused James of taking Mrs Hay as his mistress, but all she actually did accuse him of in this respect was allowing both the Hays to come between them. There was not a scrap of evidence that James either had a mistress or that he wanted his son brought up anything but a good Catholic. But the personal blow his wife had dealt him was as nothing compared to the disgrace she had brought on his family. This was what James could not forgive. To have no sense of higher duty was beyond his comprehension and later he was to write: '... I cannot answer for myself that I may not finally take some violent step to release myself from the infamous tyranny of a wife ... who knows how to cover her true dispositions to the public by the finest dissimulation & hypocrisy.' The ammunition she provided his enemies with was obvious. Until then, James and his little family had led exemplary lives compared to the Hanoverians. Now it was a case of the pot calling the kettle black. Enormous capital was made out of the whole thing and the disgrace made James ill. But he behaved with an admirable calm and courage, writing that 'I am at each moment more convinced that the malice and the finesse of our enemies have imposed themselves on your youth & the follies of your sex'.

During this separation, James took his sons to Bologna for part of the time, where they enjoyed themselves so much it put everything else out of their heads. Charles' sixth birthday was celebrated with a magnificent ball, and in February, during the local carnival season, there were endless feasts and dances which the two small, dazzled boys attended. They lived in a rented house far more sumptuous in style than the Palazzo Muti, which made the hard winter that year more endurable. Part of the charm of their disrupted routine was the new affability of their father, who seemed determined to be seen to be happy. They enjoyed his company even more than they usually did and were sad when he left to go on a mysterious journey. He was away six months, during which time their mother came to see them and wept copiously all over them.

The affair had dragged on for two years with the whole of Europe taking sides. In the end, James temporarily dismissed John Hay (who, to his credit, begged him to), but kept Murray. Clementina was glad to accept the compromise. Her sojourn in the convent, like her outing to Lucca, had given her time to reflect and she was genuinely anxious to return. In January 1728 they were reunited at Bologna, neither side having gained anything from this sordid matrimonial dispute. Since Hay had rejoined James, James had in a sense shown he was master, but he knew better than anyone how much he had lost. It pained him to have constantly before him the memory of his own mother, of his own parents' marriage. Clementina was no Mary of Modena, to his everlasting regret.

The separation of his mother and father and the comings and goings of Miss Sheldon were not good for Charles. The normal pattern of his education, which had only just begun, was broken and during the time he spent without his mother he ran wild in the sense that no disciplined period of daily study was imposed on him. It seems amazing that James should not have insisted on this but presumably his preoccupation with other matters – George I died in 1727 – prevented his overseeing of Charles' day. But in 1728, when the family were reunited under one roof at the Palazzo Muti, there was no excuse. Charles was expected to settle down to acquiring the learning James had himself and expected his sons to have. It proved a dreadful struggle. Murray moaned nonstop: 'It is impossible to get him to apply to any study as he ought to do.' Study, in fact, was beyond Charles since he was still trying to read and write fluently. When he finally mastered these essential skills he still had to be driven to using them, but too much has been made of his poor writing and spelling. More important – though neither historians nor James seem to have thought so – are the sentiments expressed in these painfully written epistles. There was something very endearing about Charles' messages. Apart from his first letter at seven, often quoted, there is another in April 1729 when he was eight that is very natural and engaging:

Dear Papa

I am mighty glad to hear that you are so wel, and that I shall soon have the happiness to see you. I shall endeavour to be good that you may be all-ways pleased with me. My Brother is grown well again and my Cough is almost gone. I bugg your blessing for us both.

And another in June:

I am glad you find the good weather at Albano so favorable to your health tho it hinders me so much longer from the happiness of seeing you. Whether absent or present I hope you will always continue your love to me. My brother is very well and so i is.

James was not impressed. Though he always wrote back very affectionately he never missed an opportunity to correct. Things like 'bugg' for 'beg' and 'i is' for 'I am' enraged him, knowing that at the same age he would never have been guilty of such common grammatical errors. Murray and Sheridan were taken to task and ordered to give Charles extra work. Miserably, they lectured Charles but he would take nothing seriously. His Latin, basis of all learning to them, was dreadful. Charles had neither the patience nor the incentive to tackle it, nor any natural application.

The interesting thing was that there were subjects he would apply himself to which were not necessarily easy. He was, for example, a good linguist. He spoke French and Italian fluently, as well as English (though with a strange Irish-Scots accent). It was true that these he picked up by ear from the people around him, but he learnt how to read and write in both languages which showed a certain intelligence and interest as well as native ability. Then, in addition, he was an accomplished musician by the time he was nine. Again, this was a talent he was born with rather than had acquired, but mastering the viola still required a good degree of hard work as well as skill. It was, in fact, too easy to dismiss Charles as stupid and lazy. He was neither. The knowledge that he was neither was what goaded his tutors and his father beyond endurance. If only, they wailed, he would devote his energies to the things he did not like as well as those he did – particularly as the former included all the important things and the latter the trivial.

Charles did, however, have teachers who had nothing but praise for his industry. His riding master had never had such a pupil. By the time he was eight he could ride large horses meant for fully grown men with ease; by the time he was nine he was an accurate shot. Any game appealed to him, whether it was golf or shuttlecock. To be such a good sportsman he had to be strong, which he was. He loved anything out of doors and could endure heat and cold alike far better than most of his contemporaries. When at Albano he was often out hunting at dawn and did not return till dusk, and that was before his teens. Naturally, all this made him something of a showpiece, far more so than if he had been a bookworm. The Jacobites and Italians alike doted on him: what it was to have a Prince who could not only hunt and shoot with the best, but in the evening play music that melted your heart! James had known such adulation himself, and rated it accordingly, but he was nevertheless proud of Charles and glad that his son had the gaiety and liveliness he had always lacked. But he worried constantly about him, knowing only too well his character needed moulding.

In spite of his worries, James enjoyed the company of his children and could write with real feeling, 'my children give me a great deal of comfort'.

He liked to be with them, whether it was walking along the lake Albano while they boated on it, or accompanying them to festivals in Rome and supplying them with a never-ending supply of ice-creams. He had a sense of excitement that comes as a surprise, ordering his carriage to take them all out for a midnight spin when they had officially been put to bed. Walton thought it disgraceful, particularly as it made his job of keeping tabs on them all very difficult, but the children adored it. In accordance with his own promise, James always talked and wrote to them in English, saw that they ate English food (meaning roast beef, exotic in Rome), and wore English clothes. As he had been, they were brought up to believe they were heirs to the throne of England, and to be conscious of a deep sense of responsibility. Charles seems to have responded instinctively to this and, instead of being weighed down by his destiny, as James had been, he was exhilarated by it. He announced that all his sporting activities were training for the future. It needed James to point out that the future also called for a well-educated King, not a semi-illiterate.

It is to James' credit – or perhaps to Murray's – that Charles was never seriously punished or forced to learn by any vicious beatings. The rod certainly ruled the child at that time and there were many princes in Europe, brutally coerced into learning, who would gladly have swopped places. He was also fortunate in having tutors who at least did their best and did not encourage his laziness as those of Louis XV did. But he was most fortunate of all in having a younger brother who was cleverer and more academically inclined than he was, for this acted as a spur to Charles, though it might just as easily have made him into a 'don't care'. Henry was a swot, to James' pleasure. He loved to study, and this had a steadying influence on Charles who found he could not be the leader in everything. Very quickly Henry could write and spell better than Charles who was four years older, and from the time this started to happen Charles made better progress. At ten Henry was fluent:

> My dear Papa, the impatience I am in to see you makes me write this letter which I hope will be acceptable being writ without any assistance by your most dutiful son
>
> Henry

By the same post James got, from Charles, in greatly improved hand-writing:

> Dear Papa, I cannot be so long without assuring you of my Duty and letting you know that my brother and I are, God be praised, in perfect health. We long very much to hear that you are so and more to see it. In the mean time we humbly begg your blessing.

James, though pleased at the improvement in the spelling of 'beg', could not resist casting up Henry as an example, always rubbing it in that he was four and a quarter years younger. Charles took the rebukes good-naturedly.

It was clear to all that James was the main influence in the lives of his sons and that their mother counted for very little. They adored her in a distant kind of way as someone to be spoken of with reverence and respect, someone whose presence made you feel honoured, someone not quite real. She had no part in their ordinary activities beyond enjoying their music, which was their one link with her. Clementina, for her part, was equally distant from her sons. They disturbed the repose she had striven so hard for. During these years of Charles' and Henry's childhood she became almost a religious recluse, finding rest and satisfaction in prayer and fasting. This devotion was without doubt both an escape and a substitute for the married bliss she had expected. With all the intensity she was capable of she threw herself into religious life. James was distressed but, beyond accurately describing her state, did nothing to halt this mania. He wrote: 'She leads a most singular life, takes no manner of amusement, not even taking the air, and when she is not at church or at Table, is locked up in her room & sees no mortal but her maids or so; she ... fasts to that degree that I believe no married woman that pretends to have children ever did; I am very little with her, I let her do what she will ... She has quite left off dressing and parure.' There were occasional false alarms when Clementina believed herself pregnant, but it was a case of menstruation ceasing because of malnutrition. This was also the cause of the scurvy that she finally contracted and suffered from until her death.

So for Charles and Henry their mother was a thin, grave lady in black, with a crucifix or rosary beads ever in her hands, her head bowed in permanent prayer. This shadow that was their mother would disappear for weeks on end only to reappear, briefly, looking even more ghastly than before. She inspired them with awe and a little dread rather than love and they had only the most tenuous relationship with her. The sight of them more often than not moved her to tears and neither of them ever had any happy memories of her. All that they were aware of was her goodness. Slightly to their bewilderment, and not altogether with James' approval, this goodness took on a concrete form from 1730 when a Friar, Leonard of Port Maurice, came on a mission to Rome. Inspired by him Clementina visited hospitals, helped look after the sick, distributed alms among the poor and so forth. Naturally, it wore her out but she was pleased to be so worn out. But it was a strain too much for her fast-weakening body and James worried.

1730 proved altogether a worrying year for James. Charles caught smallpox in July of that year. It was natural that James should expect the worst. He remembered his sister's death vividly and his own serious illness. But in fact Charles not only survived but got off very lightly so that James was able to write on 11th July: 'I thank God my Son is in a very good way of recovery of the smallpox which broke out upon him on Saturday morning and since Sunday he has been without fever. All goes mighty wel & hitherto there has not been the least appearance of danger ... He has a good many spots on his face but very few on the rest of his body & the weather is mighty favourable.' That kind of attack was in reality no more than an inoculation and served Charles better than a vaccination would have done. Only the Hanoverians were advanced enough to believe in that: George II led the way in this field by having, in 1726, the Duke of Cumberland and his other children vaccinated, which was considered very daring. When they did not drop dead on the spot many followed this courageous example and it became quite the rage.

In 1735, when Charles was fifteen and Henry eleven, Clementina finally died. The Pope ordered a state funeral with every honour, and burial of her embalmed body in St Peter's. James was desolate. Murray wrote: 'I thought he would have fainted ... the princes are almost sick with weeping and want of sleep & on all sides there is nothing but lamentation.' It was a sad end to a chapter of James' life, and it was as well that at the time he was aware other chapters were opening: the axis had shifted from him to Charles. It was a movement barely perceptible at first but some time in the decade following 1730 attention became fixed on his son and, without ever at that stage admitting it, James was beginning to relinquish his own hopes and find them reborn in Charles. Partly his own failing health was to blame but it was also a matter of energy: Charles exuded energy. His very presence revitalised those who came into contact with it. James knew it must be used.

CHAPTER THREE

Apprentice to a Cause

In the 1730s, how exactly to harness this energy of Charles' was a problem. James could remember vividly his own desire to go off and try to win back his kingdom by fighting for it. Charles' impatience was nothing new to him. But in a way it was even more difficult to satisfy his son's lust for active service than it had been to satisfy his own. In the first decade of the century, when James had yearned to test himself in war, there had been plenty of war about. Now, in the fourth decade, the only area where there was any fighting was in Naples where Spain struggled to regain these principalities lost under the Treaty of Utrecht. There was, as yet, no chance of any power supporting a bid to regain the English throne and though in constant touch with many loyalists in Scotland, James would never risk his son on any venture that was purely internal – not, that is, unless he was formally invited back by the Government, something James never entirely ruled out. So how could he let Charles go on a campaign that did not exist?

Fortunately, in the summer of 1734, the Duke of Liria wrote to James suggesting that Charles might be allowed to join him at the siege of Gaeta. Liria was the son of the Duke of Berwick (James II's illegitimate son by Arabella Churchill and therefore James' own half-brother) and had only just succeeded him. James was interested in the suggestion but by no means sure that it was a good idea. Rather foolishly, he told Charles of what was in the air and brought upon himself constant, tremendous pressure from his ardent fourteen-year-old son which finally wore him down. Charles could go – under certain conditions. First, he was to be incognito, under the title of the Chevalier de St George, which he himself had once used with much pleasure at the freedom it gave him. Secondly, he was not to be exposed to any real danger but was to keep well in the background at all times. Thirdly, he was to be accompanied by both Murray and Sheridan. Charles heard the last condition with about as much enthusiasm as the tutors themselves. Sheridan did not relish a sea voyage and then weeks of roughing it in camp. He thought he was too old for such junketings. Murray, for different reasons, was equally reluctant. He needed no imagination to see what Charles would be like in these circumstances: it would all go to his head and he would be more uncontrollable than ever. Furthermore, his cousin Liria would be a bad influence on him and encourage him to show off. Though the Prince was supposed to continue his studies on the campaign, that would be a farce. But James was adamant: where Charles went his governors must go. Furthermore, Gaeta had the advantage of being very near Rome. It was about the most boring place in Italy to have a siege, situated as it was on the west coast midway between Rome and Naples. The country between this small port and Rome was flat and swampy and dull, and had about as much to offer in the way of excitement as Gaeta itself. For a first trip from home it was a good place to send a young lad.

They set off on 27th July 1734 with Charles in a high state of excitement and Henry, who was left behind, furious with envy. His excitement abated slightly on the first leg of the trip, for he was sick all the way to Naples. However, once on dry land his spirits revived under the welcome he received and he quickly made an impact on those who saw him. Some French officers who had been about to embark for home stayed on for two more days to satisfy their curiosity and were not disappointed. Liria, who had always doted on Charles and indulged him shamelessly, saw to it that he had a good time. Naturally, Charles tried to take advantage of this to get himself into the trenches but Liria was not so foolish, though it became daily more of a struggle to hold Charles back. Murray and Sheridan watched with smug satisfaction. By accident rather than design Charles was once very near some action and behaved very calmly. Praise was lavished on him for his coolness but in fact he had done nothing but not have hysterics.

Back in Rome, James and Henry waited impatiently to share Charles' adventure vicariously. They ought to have known him better. He was a youth of action, not of letters. The few letters that came were insulting: 'I have been very good and umbly ask your blessing,' and, 'My Lord Dunbar has excused me for not having write to you hitherto. I have been very good and umbly ask your blessing.' James was angry and hurt, remembering the long detailed accounts he had always written back to his mother whenever anything interesting happened and he was away from her. This time he was not prepared to make allowances. Charles was ordered to copy out correctly his disgracefully short letters three times each. He was told, at length, that this could not go on and he must learn to apply himself. 'I am sensible,' James wrote, 'these ommissions proceed from your too natural aversion to all application & that if you do not get the better of yourself & endeavour to cultivate the Talents which Providence has given you, you will soon lose that good character which your present behaviour is beginning to gain you.' It is doubtful whether Charles ever read the letters to the end. He had Murray and Sheridan forever on at him to write home and that was enough. Besides, he knew perfectly well that they both wrote copious accounts of every tiny thing he did so why should he bother. He was having far too good a time to want to write letters and indeed considered it grossly unfair that he should be expected to. Wandering about talking to the soldiers was much more fun, and for their part the soldiers were more than willing to be diverted by this pretty young Prince who spoke Spanish to the Spaniards among them, and Italian to the Italians, as well as English, French and even a little German. Always a show-off, Charles was in his element. Egged on by the soldiers, he tried his hand at drinking with them, which had Murray dashing off imploring letters to James. James duly replied ordering Charles to stop it. Only Liria spoke in his praise, saying how brave Charles was and how popular. James was pleased but not deceived: he knew how to value his nephew's estimate.

On 12th September Charles returned from his summer camp. James and Henry met him at Albano, where he arrived with a guard of fifty men and two Spanish horses given to him as a present. Murray and Sheridan collapsed with exhaustion but Charles was more energetic than ever, and also more conceited. The compliments he had received had given him a very good opinion of himself and James saw at once that the experience might have done him more harm than good. He spoke sharply to him and Charles responded with fury to what he considered an ungracious reception. He was now, he felt, a man, and ought to be treated as such. Whatever happened he was not prepared to go back to kicking his heels in the Palazzo Muti. His appetite was whetted, and he wanted to go on another campaign. He sulked and was discontented, and if it had not been for his mother's illness and then her death things would have come to a head much more quickly than they in fact did.

For two long years after Clementina's death James was so melancholy that he could not bring himself to think of what he was going to do with Charles. He wrote and read letters as usual but the rest of the time he shut himself up and prayed, emerging only to entertain Church dignitaries. Charles and Henry were left to their own devices. For Henry this was no hardship. He enjoyed study and profited from the period of mourning. But for Charles it was irksome. Murray and Sheridan had virtually given up trying to teach him anything. He rode and hunted harder than ever but all the time he longed for action.

In the spring of 1737 James finally pulled himself out of his apathy and turned his attention to Charles. He must see something of the world. At first he thought of sending him to Poland to see the land of his dead mother's family, but in the end he decided to restrict his travels to Italy. Charles would go under the title of Count of Albany and would make a tour of the northern Italian cities – Florence, Venice, Genoa. But he could not go alone – the albatross must be firmly tied round his neck. Sheridan begged to be excused, but James would not allow him to default, and Murray was again called to the mast. To help him he had two new companions – Francis Strickland and Henry Goring. Both these young men came from old Jacobite families and James felt that was sufficient guarantee of their conduct. As far as Goring went he was right, but Strickland was a different matter, and Charles found in him an unexpected ally for any wild living. His actual job was to keep the accounts, which he did very well, and to look after the writing box. Since one of Charles' permanent excuses for not writing to his father this time was that the writing box had not arrived in the baggage he was clearly aided and abetted by Strickland. His other excuses were that he was in a hurry to go to church, and that his hand was unsteady because the road they had been travelling over was rough and stony.

Murray, however, as usual filled in the gaps. Charles was having much too good a time. Drinking with soldiers was as nothing compared to dancing himself into a stupor every night. He wrote: 'H.R.H. cannot enjoy the diversion of dancing with moderation but overheats himself monstrously ... the later he comes home the more he wants to sleep ... it is not possible to get him to bed till near three in the morning.'

But there was some good to report for a change. Charles, it seemed, sat through interminable speeches of staggering dreariness with an animated expression as though he was entranced. Murray, who could hardly keep awake from boredom, grudgingly admired his charge's acting ability. He also noted that Charles could be both kind and tactful, especially to older people (except Murray). To one old duchess who spoke atrocious Italian without her teeth in, Charles was polite and charming. All this was not lost on the Italians, who fêted the young Prince royally, even to the extent of annoying the powerful English ambassadors. The Doge of Venice assured his English representative that he had no intention of taking any notice of Charles, but then he went ahead and accorded him every honour. The Venetian ambassador in England was forthwith ordered to get out within three days. As a public relations exercise Charles' tour was becoming far too successful. He attracted unstinted admiration wherever he went for his good looks and impeccable social behaviour.

James had followed his progress with his usual keen interest. Charles must have written better letters to him this time (though they do not seem to have survived) for on 7th June James was remarking, 'I am pleased with your writing', but the sting was in the tail: 'a little custom & application will soon make you write well both for Spelling & Sense.' The highlight of the tour, from James' point of view, had been Charles' meeting with the Elector of Bavaria in Venice, which James thought of some political significance. He waited eagerly for Murray's account of it, and it duly came, all fourteen close-written pages of it, completed and dispatched before Charles was awake the next morning. Charles and the Elector, reported Murray, had talked for about a quarter of an hour in front of a hundred people. He had acquitted himself very well, particularly when the Elector complimented him on his bravery at Gaeta. Murray evidently considered the compliment not a little tinged with mockery and in any case a trick question for Charles. To his amazement Charles dealt with it with great aplomb, giving them 'a fair account' of what had actually happened and firmly disclaiming any acts of bravery. He was quite prepared that it should be known Gaeta was a routine affair in which he played a routine part. The Elector was impressed by his unnecessary honesty. Murray was dumbfounded. Was this the same boy who was cheeky to every one of his servants, 'particularly me who go in the chair with him'? James was pleased. He was also pleased that as well as dancing and feasting Charles used his eyes and his feet. He was an indefatigable sightseer. In Venice the heat was dreadful that summer, but Charles when he went to visit the Arsenal spent the entire day there and 'walked it all over which in this heat was a tour of some fatigue'. For Murray, but not Charles. It served as Charles' Grand Tour which his English counterparts undertook at the time and even if he did not get very far afield it broadened his experience far more than Gaeta had done.

But, inevitably, the tour had to come to an end, and at the end of July Charles returned to Rome, where Henry had been recovering from the after-effects of measles. There was now a giant question mark over his future. Charles was perfectly aware of the state of the Cause, as it were, having from the age of ten been allowed to share in his father's confidence. One of his good points, according to Murray, was his ability to keep his own counsel and not betray any secrets. At that time – the end of 1737 – there were few secrets to betray. If Charles read his father's correspondence assiduously, he knew that since his own birth in 1720 and the events of the first few years following, nothing exciting had happened to justify

James' hopes of restoration. The brief burst of activity in the 1720s produced a plot which came to nothing. This was the Layer plot, led by a barrister called Christopher Layer, who planned to seize the Tower of London. He was executed in 1722. Except that James grieved for every man who died in his cause, the loss of Layer was no tragedy. Far more important was the use to which the fast-ascending Robert Walpole put the plot. He managed, because of it, to get the Bishop of Atterbury to flee the country. Atterbury, who had been implicated, was one of the few important 'inside' men James had and it deprived the cause of a much needed internal anchorman. Furthermore, the revelation of this plot helped Walpole to threaten that the realm was in danger and confusion might follow. In the insecure days of the end of George I's reign nobody wanted confusion if it could possibly be avoided. Walpole showed them how to avoid it: stick to the existing régime and stamp out conspiracy.

By 1737 there had been ten years of stable government in England. George II ascended, peacefully, in 1727 and with Walpole to help him made a better impression than his father. During all this time James kept up close contact with his agents in Paris and Scotland, constantly looking for straws to blow in a wind which did not exist. His 'friends' for their part watched too. The Hanoverians never relaxed, believing, like their rivals, that there might be something to watch for. In 1729 the Duke of Newcastle, feeling nervous, wrote to Duncan Forbes (who had been appointed Lord Advocate in Scotland in 1725) while the King was in Hanover:

> My Lord
> Her Ma^ty having received private intelligence, that there was reason to believe some design was carrying on in Scotland in favour of the Pretender and that several of his Adherents were lately gone thither from Rome for that purpose ... Your Lop will paticularly inquir whether any of the Pretenders followers are lately come from abroad & on what account.

A mystified Forbes replied that he did not know what the noble Duke referred to and that the Highlands had never been quieter, but that in any case he would not relax his vigilance. Forbes had been invaluable to the Government. He loved his country but hated Jacobitism and believed that its only future lay in the strengthening of the union between the two countries. He did everything he could to further the development of industry, especially in the poorer areas of Scotland. In 1737 he was appointed Lord President of the Court of Session. He had the sense to see that Jacobitism would only appeal as a solution to discontent because of other than political causes, and he did his best to eradicate these causes.

But the threat remained real and on all sides there was vigilance even when England was prosperous and peaceful. It is easy to forget that as far as contemporaries were concerned the Stuarts were still a power to be reckoned with, in certain circumstances. These circumstances were discontent at home and war with France abroad.

Charles, during his late teens, showed that he shared with his father a strong, unshakeable belief that he would be restored to his rightful kingdom. It was a question of when everyone would recognise their *duty* to restore his family: there was never any hint that he, any more than James, had the honesty to admit that the family would only get back if it suited France's convenience. He had been indoctrinated by his father to believe that no attempt could be made without the help of a foreign army. Upon this, James was unshakeable. Any foreign army would do, but there must be one. The best bet was still, as it always had been, France. But France was at peace with Walpole's England. What everyone in Rome watched for was a crack in this unnatural friendship. At the end of the 1730s, as Charles reached his majority, it came. By October 1739 Walpole had been forced, very much against his will, into war with Spain, with whom British merchants were at loggerheads in the Caribbean and America. Spain expected help from France and seemed likely to get it. What excited everyone in Rome most of all, however, was not Anglo-Spanish enmity but the outbreak of the War of the Austrian Succession in 1740. Without going into the details of this complex situation, only one thing mattered to the Jacobites: France and England took opposite sides. The daily trickle of letters into the Palazzo Muti became a positive avalanche as Jacobites everywhere speculated on the exploitation of this state of affairs.

James behaved with his customary cool. He had on the one hand a son of nearly twenty who for the last three years had been straining at the leash. His hair had been formally cut, his majority attained, a glorious future eagerly awaited. He knew his son's character. In a similar position himself, back in 1708, his temperament had enabled him to overcome his disappointment and employ himself usefully. Charles had not the emotional reserves this required. He could not turn to study or prayer but indulged in violent physical exercise which lasted from dawn to dusk. As yet, this soaked up his frustration but James knew that the time when it would not was near. On the other hand, he had 'friends' in Scotland who assured him that the time was now ripe and a blow must be struck. James never for one minute thought of putting two such elements together. The friends in Scotland, the son at his side – both must be kept fettered until foreign aid was assured. Charles would only leave Rome to head a properly mounted campaign, or else he would not leave at all. The invitation must come from France.

During the seemingly interminable time that it took to come Charles continued with his sporting activities and showed interest in what was going on: he awaited as eagerly as anyone news from the theatre of war in Germany and read the letters that came from Scotland with news of plots and plans on his behalf. With a lifetime of such goings-on before him, James was blasé, but Charles was not. In 1741 he wrote to 'The Clans' (a magnificently vague address): 'I have received yours with a great deal of pleasure and see by the Plan which came with it the zeal and affection of those who propose it. I have examined and compared it with the map in the best manner I could and as far as I can judge it seems very rational. I cannot without rashness say mor but you may easily believe I long very much for the execution.'

What map could he possibly have been using? Whatever tattered or out-of-date sheet he had, his earnestness is amusing; James had long since given up studying the outline of Scotland's much indented coastline.

However much Charles might long for the execution in 1741, James was still content to wait. His inherent caution grew more pronounced as he aged – which he had done markedly the last decade – and the thought of precipitating his adored son into disaster was a further brake. Two men tried to take that brake off. The first was John Gordon of Glenbucket who had visited James in 1737 and had informed him that conditions were now favourable for a rising. James was polite on that occasion but did not believe it, nor did he feel attracted by the 'open' support promised. But in 1739, when William MacGregor of Balhaldy came to Rome with a similar message, circumstances had changed. A rising in Scotland might now be backed by France, at war with England. James promptly sent Balhaldy to Paris to meet his agent Lord Sempil so that they could jointly persuade Louis XV to send an expedition to Scotland.

The negotiations that followed were tortuous in the best Jacobite tradition. The French wanted names, Scottish names and English names, names signed in real ink on real paper containing a real promise to help. The Scots, for their part, wanted arms, ammunition and men: then they would sign names. That, at least, was something. The English Jacobites were intent on remaining the shadowy creatures they had always been. The French did not want to back a purely Scottish affair – neither, for that matter, did James. Enthusiasm waned.

In 1743 it was brought alive again by a shift in emphasis on all fronts. In France, Fleury, who had been lukewarm for the venture, died and was replaced by the belligerent Tencin who was a fan of James and an enemy of England. In Rome, James was visited by yet another emissary, John Murray of Broughton, who had become his secretary in Scotland in 1740. Murray was sent to Paris to see how matters really stood. Then in June the French were beaten at Dettingen by the British–Austrian–Hanoverian army. Revenge made Louis XV keen to help the Stuarts. But though everything now looked a simple matter of adding two and two together, it was not. Murray of Broughton saw at once that Sempil and Balhaldy were pushing an expedition on the basis of a large spontaneous rising in England for which no evidence existed. The French, for their part, were trying to promise as little as they could get away with. What Broughton wanted was a little more honesty from everyone, but then he was in no position to get it for he too was exaggerating the support in Scotland. To do him justice, it was virtually impossible to pin the clan leaders down to unconditional support – quite naturally because they knew only too well what they risked. An Association of Jacobite leaders (The Concert) had been formed in 1741, but some of its members would rise only if a French army landed.

Curiously, it was during this time – the early 1740s – that Duncan Forbes, who by no means lived in a fool's paradise, was congratulating himself that with the economy on a firmer basis prosperity was laying the old bogey of rebellion. While the Association was being formed, the Lord President worried only about tea. He blamed the new habit of tea-drinking for a decline in the Excise. People were drinking it instead of ale and if the habit was not destroyed 'it will most certainly destroy us and that very soon'. Forbes thought the solution 'by Act of Parliament to prohibite, under sufficient Penaltys to be recovered with certainty and dispatch, the use of Tea among that Class of Mankind in this Countrey whose Circumstances do not permit them to come at Tea that pays the Duty'. The whole of Scotland was to be covered with informers who would report tea-drinking – cheap Dutch imported tea – among servants. The fine was to be twenty or thirty shillings for the first offence, half to go to the informer. With such matters did the Lord President occupy himself while his country moved towards the rising that was to pain him so much and which he had worked so hard, with genuine conviction and love, to prevent. He had grown tired of lecturing the Government on the dangers of a French-backed invasion and begging them to station permanent Highland regiments in the Highlands: all he could do was try to make everyone more content by making them solvent.

In these circumstances it needed a strong initiative to come from someone to get things moving. It came from Balhaldy, who, in December 1743, after a trip to England where he got verbal support from some

English Jacobites, persuaded Louis XV to let him go to Rome and bring Charles back to head an expedition. James had always said that if Louis XV invited his son with a clear promise of support he would let him go. Now that the moment had come he felt neither the invitation nor the support were unequivocal enough, but it was that or nothing. Balhaldy promised all things to all men. Charles' presence, he assured James, was essential, his arrival eagerly awaited. Marshal Saxe, who was sweeping all before him, would head the French force. What more did James want? James did not know: if what Balhaldy said was true, nothing. It was a question of trust, and with so much at stake he did not trust anyone. With his eyes too near his vast correspondence James was incapable of opportunism. He knew – his letters told him – that there were too many loose ends. In an agony of indecision he took every available piece of advice, all of it conflicting. Finally, with many misgivings, he gave his consent to Charles setting out. His son, who all this time had been waiting in the wings, was as joyful as James had been so many years before. He was less of a pawn than people realised. From the first stirrings of activity he had been in the know, closely consulted at every turn by his father and willing for once to listen and take in what was said to him. His opinion had carried little weight, but it was not an uninformed opinion. Charles knew most of the men involved, he had met and talked to them, and James' often voiced doubts had given him a broader outlook than he might otherwise have had. But he was obedient: he went because his father sent him. There was no question of him leading the enterprise. In fact, his dependence on James was the first clear result to emerge from this venture. It was to be at least eighteen months later before the enterprise became his and not James'.

PART II

The Campaign 1744-1746

CHAPTER FOUR

Lesson in Patience

Once the decision had been taken by James to trust in Balhaldy's message, speed was vital. As yet – it was hoped – nobody in England knew what was planned. While the French massed ships and transports on the northern coast, Charles must get out of Italy and to Paris as quickly and secretly as possible. Rome, as usual, swarmed with spies so a plot was worked out to give Charles the best possible start. It was on a bigger scale than James' own escape in 1715 from Bar-le-Duc, and was a good deal more successful. On the evening of 8th January Charles sat down as usual to play cards. Murray, watching him, wrote later that anyone who knew him as intimately as his father, brother and tutors could have told at once that he was agitated – not because he dropped cards or made silly mistakes but because, on the contrary, he played with great concentration, something he seldom did. His greatest difficulty was 'to curb his extraordinary joy' and the way to do it, he thought, was to be painstaking and solemn. In these circumstances there could be no touching parting from his father. When the time came to set off on the proposed hunting expedition to Albano that was to be his alibi, Charles took his leave affectionately but quite casually. James could hardly control his emotion as he watched his son mount one of the two black horses – specially chosen to blend with the night – and ride off with Henry and their attendants and servants. Nobody thought anything of such a departure at such a time, nor that Charles rode instead of travelling in a carriage. There was nothing out of the ordinary about the procedure. When the party was safely outside Rome and on their way into the hills, Sheridan nobly pretended to let his horse slip and precipitated himself into a ditch. During the commotion Charles removed his wig, slipped on a mask that covered his face to his eyes, covered his clothes with a plain dark cloak and rode off with one attendant and two servants.

So far so good. Nobody suspected anything. When the party arrived at Albano a messenger was there to say Charles had had a slight accident and was staying at Frascati till he recovered. Henry, who was not in the secret, sent a solicitous message. A reply was sent back. It was eleven days before the ruse was discovered and by that time Charles was well on his way. He had picked up passports and post-horses and made for Genoa. From there he went to Savona and was delayed for several days by contrary winds before he could sail for Antibes. He eventually arrived in Paris on 10th February. It had been a journey of great length and difficulty but Charles had enjoyed every arduous minute. The minute he arrived he sat down and wrote to his father – an event so astonishing that it deserves special mention. Either Charles wrote with a fluency and enthusiasm never before seen because at last he had something to write about and no tutor to do it for him, or else absence had already made the heart grow fonder.

'I thank God,' he wrote, 'I arrived here Saturday last after being a little fatigued but now I am perfectly recovered and ready to go as far again were it necessary but that is not the case for I have nothing but the approaching campaign to undergo which will be a great pleasure to me who have desired to see and understand Military Matters as they best become my situation ... Mr Graham has been very careful of me and has done everything with great affection ... Both he and the two servants have suffered by my impatience to arrive at the end of my journey.'

It was, as James noted, a new Charles. Never before had he shown the least interest in anybody's feelings except his own and to write not only straight away but express solicitude for his companions was totally new. Even more indicative of a great change was the anxiety he revealed to hear from James. On 29th February he wrote an ecstatic appreciation of his father's letter and by 6th March he was falling over himself to be grateful and dutiful: '... the little difficulties and small dangers I may have run are nothing when for the service and glory of a Father which is so tender and Kind for me ...'

Charles, in fact, had been thrown in at the deep end and was suffering from too sudden and complete an independence – something he had always thought he wanted but now found not as much to his taste as he had imagined. Paris in itself was a bewildering experience, and though Charles had not exactly come from a tiny village to a metropolis, it seemed to him that he had. The population of Paris was not so much greater than that of Rome but there the resemblance ended. In size and scope it was bigger, more urbanised and sophisticated than Rome had ever been. Though a young man of considerable grace, to whom manners and social accomplishments came easily, Charles recognised at once that a code obtained in Paris that did not run in Rome. He had to learn what was done and what was not done in a society that watched for every mistake. It was a game he was perfectly equipped to play but it took time to learn the rules. Used to an unquestioned ascendancy in such matters, Charles did not like being pupil. Nor did he like being unsure of his position. He had assumed that once in Paris he would be taken to Versailles and welcomed to the bosom of Louis XV where he would remain until he began his campaign. No such thing happened and Charles began to feel more and more like a guest not quite sure either of his status or even his welcome. He must have had some kind of meeting with the King, for he wrote to James that his reception had been everything he expected, but other observers in Paris and at Versailles record no such meeting. In spite of Charles' alleged contentment, the sharp-eyed court barometers were busily recording that Charles had been rather ignored. Since England and France had not yet officially declared war no one expected Charles to be sitting on Louis' right hand all the time, but there were subtle ways of showing how he rated and these were generally reckoned to be missing.

News of Charles' arrival in Paris was no secret in London. On 16th February Horace Walpole reported that though the King was confined to his bed with rheumatism, he had sent a message 'to both Houses to acquaint us that he had certain information of the young Pretender being in France and of the designed invasion from thence, in concert with the disaffected here'. The state of the Navy was to be inquired into at once and all the troops were sent for 'in the greatest haste'.

There were naturally a great many new people to meet, both French and English or Scottish. Charles had always enjoyed meeting new people and prided himself on the ease and speed with which he made friends. He was not in the least shy or reserved but came straight out to meet any advances. The trouble was, too many new people made advances and all of them said things behind the backs of the others. Charles had met Balhaldy already but not Sempil. He knew Murray of Broughton but not George Kelly or O'Brien, two Irish Jacobites who had for long been faithful adherents of the cause. Sempil and Balhaldy told him one thing and Broughton another. Who was he to believe, if either? His father had long been distressed by the 'continual jarrings' that went on among his followers but he had been unable to give Charles any guidance. He must get to know them all and make up his own mind. Charles tried hard but could come to no conclusion except that it was not safe to trust anyone at all. What he wanted was an old friend he could have confidence in and he wrote to James asking for Sheridan to be sent to him – a singular compliment but also, in addition, a sign that Charles was fed up having to do all his own correspondence and make his own arrangements.

There was only one arrangement that he wanted made and that was the date for embarkation. At first, he wrote 'all gose well', but by the beginning of March he was beginning to wonder. Were the French in earnest? Sempil and Balhaldy assured him that they were, but then whose ear did they have? The King's? Charles had not been long in France before he discovered that there were kings and kings: not all were like his father. Louis XV might have clapped his hands for joy when Charles was born but if so it was no guarantee of his sustained interest. Until he was thirty-three – that is, until Fleury's death in 1743 – Louis could not be said to have ruled for himself. He was lazy, except where pleasure was concerned, and irresolute. At the time when Charles arrived in France the government of the country, at a time of crisis, had gone to pieces. The King had no intention of taking over from the dead Fleury but it had not yet been settled who would. Intrigue at court reached new heights and nobody – least of all Sempil and Balhaldy – knew quite who was who. There was Cardinal Tencin, who might gain the ascendancy Fleury had had and was the Jacobites' greatest supporter, but there were also d'Argenson and Amelot and numerous others. Charles could not cope. All he could do was sit tight and wait for his orders. But it did not agree with him. The impatience and anxiety he felt began to turn into anger that he should be kept hanging about.

In fact, Louis XV had decided to send an expedition and, while Charles tried to sort out all the personalities, his very best general, the Comte de Saxe, was on his way to Gravelines where Charles himself was summoned during the first week in March. A French fleet of fifteen ships and five frigates was already at sea when Charles joined Marshal Saxe and went with him to Dunkirk. Here seven thousand men were embarked but no sooner were they all on board than a violent gale blew up. Many of the transport ships were damaged and the soldiers drowned. Meanwhile the two rival fleets had collided and the French fleet got the worst of the engagement. To James, at home, it was the old story of storms and missed chances. To Charles, watching from the shore, it was all frustrating and incomprehensible. So a storm had interfered, so it was now over, so why didn't Saxe get on with the job? Saxe, amused rather than angry by Charles' arrogant demands to set off at once, said he had to wait for new orders. Orders given for one day and one set of circumstances did not necessarily hold good for another. The position was different. England was aware of what before had been secret. His master might not want to continue.

It was, for Charles, a necessary lesson in patience. Writing to his father on 13th March he managed to take a cheerful view. Looking on the bright side, he said he was glad about the storm because if it hadn't happened they would have put to sea and been captured by the British fleet. Nevertheless, he was at a loss. He complained that he hadn't had any instructions from James lately, nor had Sheridan arrived. With every day that he waited on the northern coast his dissatisfaction grew. Saxe had gone. D'Argenson advised him to go into the country and have a holiday while things got sorted out, but Charles did not want to go and was indignant at the suggestion. His letters to his father became irritable – why hasn't he written? Then when a letter arrives by one post and not the other that annoys him. He wishes he had a 'sipher' to write in, but wryly confesses 'at present really I could say nothing'. He wants his father to know that 'you may be sure no disappointment will slacken my duty'. He can think of nothing else in those grey days, waiting: 'whether I am free from company or diversions its all alike to me for I can think of nothing ... but your service which is my duty.'

All this time, since the failure of the projected invasion at the beginning of March, Charles had been living at Gravelines under the name of Chevalier Douglas. War had now been declared between France and England and his presence had been officially objected to, but he had neither been asked to leave France nor openly championed. In London, the Opposition had brought in a bill 'to make it treason to correspond with the young Pretenders'. The Lords added a clause making the penalty forfeiture of estates and it was carried by 285 to 106 votes after what Horace Walpole called 'the best debate I ever heard'. Charles hated the kind of existence that was now his lot. The French insisted he should remain incognito which meant living quietly and keeping himself to himself. Never with many resources of his own, Charles found the enforced seclusion hard to endure, however much he might swear he didn't care. Only rarely was his position amusing: '... everybody is wondering where the Prince is, some put him in one place and some in another but nobody knows where he is really and sometimes he is told news of himself to his face which is very diverting.' But not diverting enough. What was to be done? He had moved to Paris in April but he could not hang around there for ever.

There were others who saw the problem but knew no better than Charles what solution there could be. James expressed his fury that Charles should be treated so shabbily but his fury was a feeble thing. 'Your situation,' he wrote, 'in all respects pierces my heart but there is no remedy but patience and courage.' Charles should perhaps come home to Rome and wait till he was sent for again. This attitude more than anything prepared Charles for a break with his father. James' resignation was something he could not understand. He himself had no awe for Louis and his ministers but rather a growing contempt. His father seemed to think the favour was all on one side, France's side. Didn't he realise that France *needed* the Jacobites? Charles fumed at his own impotence. He wanted nothing to do with those who counselled no action without French sanction. Gradually he built up around him a collection of followers known for their zeal rather than their wisdom. Among these hotheads Sheridan, who had finally arrived, proved the point that the old can be as rash as the young. Sempil complained he had a bad influence on Charles, leading him into ridiculous schemes when he ought to have known better. But then Earl Marischal, a wise and cautious old Jacobite, told James that Sempil and Balhaldy were doing the leading astray. He apparently did not agree with the opinion of Lady Sandwich who had written to James how impressed she was by Sempil's 'sagacity, penetration and integrity' which he employed in the cause with 'so much Vigilance and prudence that I cannot make a better wish, than all who have the honour to be imployed in you Majestyes affaires may be indowed with such qualities as he possesses'. Charles, for his part, was quite sure he saw through everyone and even boasted to James that while everyone thought he was taken in, he was actually doing the taking in.

Throughout 1744 Charles continued to write to his father that he was living quietly, doing his own shopping, keeping his tastes simple. The picture was none too accurate. Charles ran up considerable debts during this period which don't look like the debts of a man living the life of a hermit. The opera lured him from his hiding-place wearing a mask, and he saw more of the social life of the capital than he cared to admit. Yet at the same time it was true that he never for one moment lost sight of his real objective, and that he thought he was engaged in a battle of cunning that he was winning hands down. Part of the cunning was to let his father think he was being a good boy minding his own business. To this end, he took care during the spring of 1745 to stay with various gentlemen on their estates and give every appearance of simply passing the time. It made James quite nostalgic to hear that Charles had been to the Fitzjames country-house which he remembered very well from his own youth. He approved, too, of Charles' friendship with the Duc de Bouillon, his cousin, of whom he wrote 'the more I am acquainted with him the more I like him for he has the best Hart in the world'. He liked, too, the young Prince de Turenne who is 'a very preety yong man in every way'. There was not a single mention of any preety yong ladies. Another 'very preety yong man' was a certain Mr Cary or Kary for whom Charles got a commission in the French Army, apparently on the grounds of his preetiness alone. He wrote, in January 1745, 'I am going two or three days to my contry howse, where I will be at full liberty to have the spleen. It is now to months I have not handeled a gun because of the bad weather and cold ... As soon as I am arrived at Fitzjames I intend to begin again to shute but not whin it rens. You see by this that according as one advanses in years one gets reason.' Very witty – much too jolly to come from the pen of Charles if he really thought the future gloomy. What had induced this spirit of light abandon was the beginnings of a friendship with one Antoine Walsh and his friends.

Charles had not discovered this influential man on his own, nor had he been led to him by any of the accredited Jacobite agents like Sempil. Lord Clare, commander of one of those famous Irish Regiments in the King of France's service because they were unable to serve their own King James, was the person who put Charles into touch with this band of Franco-Irish shipowners. Lord Clare's motives were of the purest. His whole life had been dedicated to the service of the Jacobite cause and, knowing that Charles was not content to remain idle while France deliberated, he could think of nothing more useful than providing him with the means to carry out any project he might have in mind. This may suggest Walsh was a desperado who would do anything for the money, but this was not so. Walsh was a complex character. His Jacobite sympathies were genuine enough – 'My zeal for your cause has no limits and I am prepared to undertake anything where the service of your Royal Highness is concerned' – but so were his trading instincts on which his fortunes were founded. A former officer in the French Navy, Walsh was born at St Malo in 1703, the son of an Irish shipbuilder, Philip Walsh, who had had the distinction of commanding the ship that brought James II to France after the Battle of the Boyne. It was he who had begun the slave-trading that Antoine was to carry on to such purpose. He also built ships for the French Navy so that by the time Antoine was born he was already a wealthy man. He had, in all, five sons to carry on the family business, of whom Antoine was the third and most successful.

The Walsh family were not the only ones to make money in this repugnant way. The slave-trading attracted other Irish families who had settled in France with James II, among whom were the Hegartys, the Ruttledges and the Butlers. Daniel Hegarty was an even more zealous Jacobite than Walsh in that he was more active. He was one of the founders of the masonic lodges that were scattered round France with the avowed purpose of restoring the Stuarts. Richard Butler was a naturalised Frenchman, although he had been born in Ireland. He was a powerful contact because he had been admitted to the French nobility in 1740. Married to

Walsh's sister, he was not however engaged in the slave-trade. Another valuable member of this set was Sir Walter Ruttledge, a banker and shipowner, who had actually been born at St Germain-en-Laye. He too was a naturalised Frenchman and had further improved his status by marrying the daughter of a rich landowner. All these men were extremely wealthy, all of them had connections with the French Navy, all of them had at their command men and ships. It was to them that Charles was introduced at the end of 1744 and to them that he addressed his by then general plea for help. It was in character that after decades of letter-writing to his many friends and agents James had never sought to make use of this group who longed to serve him, whereas Charles was instantly attracted to them. The attraction was due to the fact that Charles was now going to attempt something James emphatically disapproved of: a rising in Scotland commanded by himself with a small band of men.

No accounts of the meetings between Charles and Walsh and his friends have survived but in later correspondence it is clear that they all got along very well. Walsh and company were snobs. They were proud of their Irish origin, proud of their Royal friendship. They were excited by Charles' presence and honoured that he should want to use them. It was, in a way, something worthwhile to spend their money on. They were more than willing to accord Charles the deference and respect which he had missed since he left Rome, and he responded openly to their admiration. As for Charles, he liked the fact that they were businessmen, hard-headed, dealing in facts. It was a perfect partnership, as perhaps Lord Clare knew it would be. While James still droned on to the effect that 'there is no remedy for certain things which must go as they can, for I fear neither you nor I can get a remedy to them', Charles was already deep in plans for just such a remedy. He told his father nothing without actually lying to him, but this was for reasons of secrecy as much as anything. James, though his views on a Scottish rising had been heard by Charles a hundred times, had gone so far as to say that Charles must in general decide for himself, because he was now old and weak and a long way off. Charles intended to. He was going to play the whole thing very close indeed. The circle he trusted was a tight one and consisted, apart from Walsh and his friends, only of those who were to go with him, and were with him at the time in Paris.

James and many other respectable Jacobites worried excessively about the company Charles was keeping. Indeed, James back in Rome received several letters of complaint that Charles did not have 'suitable' companions and was being led astray. The complaints did not refer to Walsh and company, but to the actual members of Charles' household. Sempil –

definitely out in the cold, together with all other accredited agents whatever Charles might say – raged furiously about a 'spirit of giddiness', that included even Sheridan whom he listed, slightly ludicrously, as 'the boldest adventurer I ever yet knew or heard of'. Charles was furious and maintained Sempil was 'using me as a child'. All Sempil's allegations were untrue, especially the ones about Charles keeping things to himself: 'It is very extraordinary Sempil and Balhaldy complaining I would not see them, which is not so, for I have on several occasions said to them over and over again that they were always wellcum wherever I was.' By the end of March Charles was joined by Strickland, about whom James had the gravest doubts. He wrote two long letters to Charles when Strickland was en route warning him to be very careful, in which he made mysterious references to Strickland being 'an ill man' and told Charles he 'owed it to his character' to keep away from him. But Strickland was given the warmest welcome by Charles, who was sure James had got Strickland all wrong. He was tired of his father's warnings and wrote, somewhat selfrighteously, 'I am very young and it is very hard for me to foresee many things for which all I aim at is not to do harm not being able to do good.' Conversely, James was glad Charles had made a friend of John O'Sullivan, though nobody else was. John William O'Sullivan was another Irish-born Jacobite who was more French than Irish. Intended for the priesthood, he had been educated first in Paris, then Rome, before becoming tutor to Marshal Maillebois' son. Charles was impressed by the fact that O'Sullivan could claim to be a soldier since Maillebois had taken him on a campaign to Corsica in 1739 where the responsibility of organising the campaign had become his.

Surrounded now by people who approved of any attempt, however desperate, Charles had no restraining influence on him. James rapidly began to count for very little, though he wrote copious letters still. He was, ironically, pleased with Charles keeping him up to date just when in fact he was being most kept in the dark: he thought 'very kindly of you, your having been at so much pains to inform me of what you are doing'. Charles had served his apprenticeship and now had his own designs to get on with. He paid only lip-service to the official efforts made by Sempil and Balhaldy to get the French to mount another invasion and meanwhile busied himself with his clandestine arrangements. In fact, there is a good deal of doubt about just how much Charles was hoodwinking the French and how much the French were hoodwinking him. Charles thought he was equipping an expedition to go to Scotland unknown to the French or his father. He firmly believed it would come as a great shock to Louis XV to hear he had sailed. But Charles had under-estimated the duplicity of which the French authorities were capable and what he thought he did against their wishes he may actually have done almost under their orders, serving their purposes to the letter by creating a diversion from the war in Flanders without them having either to take the responsibility or to spend a penny or lose a man. The evidence for this rests on the details of how Walsh and his friends set the expedition up. To begin with, they needed suitable ships. These they could charter from the Navy when not in use. Each charter was granted for an express purpose and therefore the Minister of the Navy, Maurepas, must have known who was hiring ships and for what. Even supposing Walsh lied and said the ships were for privateering, there remained the other point that the ships were to carry men, and ammunition and arms. Walsh raised a company of cadets of the French Navy for the purpose, and the supplies for them were raised on the express authority of the Ministry of War. How could Charles imagine Maurepas did not know what was going on? And if Maurepas did the King did, and if the King did not stop it it was because he did not want to.

The initiation of the scheme however was Charles': it was simply that the French could have scotched it if they had wanted to, and he never realised it. He wrote to his father confidently: 'If your Majesty was in this country I flatter myself you would be surprised to see with your own eyes how I blind several and impose upon them at the same time they think they do it to me. If I was not able to do this things would go at a fine rate ...' If only he had listed who he thought he was kidding we might have been convinced. But what is important is that Charles *thought* he was in absolute control, *thought* he knew precisely what he was doing.

Back in Rome, Henry was full of admiration and envy. He too had been trying to get himself on a campaign – with the Spaniards – but with no more luck than Charles. It was no fun at home, with James only interested in what was happening to Charles and growing increasingly deaf. Henry wrote regularly to his brother, with great affection, sometimes as often as twice a week. In February 1745 he sighed: 'I am realy quite tiered of this Idle Life' – so tired his spelling was as bizarre as Charles'. He longed to join his elder brother who he imagined at the centre of events and excitement. He had little to write about: 'Last Tuesday night I went to a concert ... that ended with a little dancing and what with the fewness of ladys and what with the want of my dear brother the Country dances went very ill ... We are all in the Spleen here as well as you, liveing of (I am affraid) chimerical hopes and expectations.' Charles was offended that Henry should think them so chimerical when he thought them sound, however frustrated he felt. But then Henry knew nothing of Walsh and company. All he had to go on was the steady flow of letters from Charles full of no real news, only trivialities. Half of every letter consisted of 'nothing to report' and the other of moans about Sempil or Charles' state of health. Henry could not help feeling cynical when Charles fretted about his mail being 'pillaged by five people Masked in Provence' and then the said mail consisting of news like 'I am mightily troubled with a fluctione on my gums'. Henry despaired and a dreadful boredom overwhelmed him.

But Charles in fact remained optimistic. During this period of waiting and preparation he had kept closely in touch with the current state of the war in Europe upon the course of which so much depended. Knowledge of, if not a complete grasp of, current affairs was one of Charles' strong points. He was able in letters to his father to show that he knew what was going on and did not for one minute think his expedition was all that mattered. Nobody needed to point out to him that whether France was defeated or victorious there was still no guarantee that he would benefit. If successful in her struggle, she would not need to create a diversion, if defeated she would not have the means. He was not in the least grateful for the measure of acknowledgment Louis had given him, though in London it seemed highly significant that 'The Pretender's son is owned in France as Prince of Wales – the princes of the blood have been to visit him in form'. Charles, who was slowly coming to believe that a diversion was all France was interested in, could see that the prolonging of the struggle was in his best interests with neither side gaining a complete ascendancy. That was what was happening in the early spring of 1745.

Then on 11th May the battle of Fontenoy was fought and the English beaten. Marshal Saxe inflicted the defeat on a combined British–Austrian–Dutch army, but it was thought of in France as Britain's defeat. As a prelude to Charles' expedition it is interesting for the light it threw on both the British army and the Duke of Cumberland, the commander and third son of George II. John Munro wrote: 'The British behaved well; we the Highlanders were told by his Royal Highness that we did our duty well. I cannot fail telling you that the Duke shewed as much real courage and temper as ever Caesar or Hannibal did. By two of the Clock we all retreated ... but the Duke made so friendly and favourable a speech to us that if we had been ordered to attack their lines afresh I dare say our poor fellows would have done it.' Charles envied the Duke the opportunity of proving his valour and though he was glad of the defeat of a Hanoverian he grieved for the defeat of his 'people'. He was sad that his Mr Cary – 'a very preety yong man' as he reminded James – had been killed in action. What the effect of Fontenoy would be he wisely did not try to forecast: 'it is not esy to forsee if it will prove good or bad for our affairs.' What it was easy to see was that England had not only suffered what looked at the time like an important defeat but that with Saxe moving relentlessly on, the country would have to be emptied of troops to fight in Flanders. Now, if ever, was surely the time to strike.

Charles had plenty of reports of the state the country was in – for the past year agents and correspondents had been urging that advantage should be taken of the absence of both King and troops. Horace Walpole who had written with confidence in March 1744 when the Saxe invasion had been attempted 'the spirit of the nation has appeared extraordinarily in our favour', was now much more worried. Like others in Parliament, he did not approve of the denuding of the country of troops to fight what he thought of as Hanover's war. He described the battle of Fontenoy as 'without palliating, it is certainly a heavy stroke. We never lost near so many officers ... it is almost the first battle of consequence that we ever lost.' But other people were not so worried, which worried Horace even more: '... the King minded it so little, that being set out for Hanover, and blown back into Harwich Roads since the news came, he could not be persuaded to return but sailed yesterday with the fair wind.' The Prince of Wales acted equally casually by going to the theatre the night the news came. With a printed list of 7,300 either killed, wounded or missing, Walpole was outraged. London, he reported, seethed in this normally dull time of year – Parliament gone down and most people of consequence off to their country houses – with rumours of the remainder of the army cut to pieces and an invasion imminent. The plot was thought to be a final defeat in Flanders, then on to boats and over to England. Walpole wrote: '... our army in Flanders is running away, and dropping to pieces by detachments taken prisoners every day; while the King is at Hanover, the Regency at their country seats, not five thousand men in the island, and not above fourteen or fifteen ships at home! Allelujah!'

Charles, in France, had now decided that his expedition must get off as soon as possible since there was no denying the vulnerability of England. What enraged him was that in these altered circumstances France should not come right out and mount a proper campaign and he waited as long as he thought possible to give them the chance to do this. D'Argenson, the Minister of War at the time, later wrote that France missed the best opportunity she ever had in the spring and summer of 1745, but apparently his opinion was not shared by Louis XV and his other advisers. What held Louis back were the same two things that had always held him back – firstly, the knowledge that however strong his military position might look he was already straining his resources to the utmost, and a campaign in the British Isles was a luxury he could not afford without a guarantee of success. This guarantee was the second point that there had always been: who exactly would support Charles, especially in England? For years France had been trying to get signed promises from English Jacobites. They had never been forthcoming. Sempil had never been able to produce any. Charles had never even tried. And now, by Act of Parliament passed by a large majority, correspondence with either Charles or Henry had not only been made treasonable but involved the forfeiture of estates. Did that look like a welcome for Charles? Louis did not think so. James and Sempil might talk constantly of friends in England who had committed themselves and worry about the correspondence falling into the wrong hands, but Charles himself was no more taken in than Louis. What he hoped to do was persuade the English Jacobites to support him when he arrived, which he firmly believed they would do. With a confidence which inspired everyone except the head-counting French, Charles thought they would not be able to resist his cause.

There remained the Scots. Here, there was more to go on. Murray of Broughton had been back to Scotland and said later that he sent Charles a letter telling him not, after all, to come unless he brought a substantial force. Charles never got the letter. As far as he was concerned, he had a definite invitation to which at least eight chieftains had put their names, two without conditions. Duncan Forbes, the Lord President, might write in July that Scotland was in a state of 'profound calm' while London was tense, but Charles was told that in fact discontent was rife. He believed this. Whatever else he was, Charles was ultimately honest and did what he did with conviction. Though he kept his father in the dark up to a month before, he did not in the end try to pretend that his venture was anything it was not. In a well-known letter he confessed, 'I have, above six months ago, been invited by our friends to go to Scotland and to carry what money and arms I could conveniently get ... Our *friends*, *without exactly saying it directly*, have spoke in such a manner that I plainly saw that if the winter and spring passed over without some attempt they would rise themselves ...'

Charles was wrong. He had been deceived, but most willingly deceived, into believing this was the case. Scotland would never have risen of itself. Duncan Forbes was a far more reliable and well-informed observer than Murray of Broughton and he could see that Scotland was at last settling down. The Union was still hated – it still basically is – but the feelings of hate and anger would never have erupted into open rebellion. But Charles could question Broughton and be truthfully told that the Scots loathed the English, disliked the Hanoverian King and resented union with them bitterly. He chose to interpret this as support for himself and saw his expedition as that of a deliverer's, come to free his people. There is no doubt about this mission he thought he had. Over and over again in his letters he talks passionately of freeing his people, using the same emotive words each time. He writes, too, of dying on the job. Constantly he refers to his own death – 'I have taken a firm resolution to conquer or die', 'if I did not succeed I would perish as Curtis did to save my country and make it happy', 'the worst that can happen to me iff France dos not succor me is to dye at the head of such Brave people'. And yet the very cheerfulness with which he talks about it surely shows that Charles did not really for one minute imagine that he was either going to fail or die. He wanted to risk himself against great odds, the greater the better. It was not that he did not think of the consequences but that at the worst he thought them as acceptable to others as to himself: glory or death. That there might be something in between, a degree of suffering that would be his responsibility, was never envisaged by him. That had been his father's problem. He was determined that the attempt should be made.

During the time that Charles was making his final preparations he stayed at Navarre, at the house of his much admired friend and relation, the Duc de Bouillon. He did not intend to go entirely unprepared but had for some time been trying to buy swords and collect together guns and ammunition. To get the money for these he had pawned his jewels and borrowed from Waters, James' bankers in Paris. Meanwhile, Ruttledge had chartered a big old ship called *L'Elizabeth*, originally captured from the English early in the century. She was a sixty-four-gun ship and was to carry the company of sixty cadets and officers that Walsh had raised, and paid for. The other ship, that was to carry the Prince, was smaller, a light frigate called *Le Du Teillay*, of forty-four guns. Between them these two ships would carry the twenty field-pieces, fifteen hundred muskets, and eleven thousand broadswords which was the sum total of Charles' endeavours.

His last few days at the end of June were exciting ones. Either of two things might happen that would change everything: Louis XV might decide to back him, or to stop him. When he reckoned he would be safely on board, Charles arranged for several letters to be delivered – to his father, to Louis XV and to the Spanish court. To his father he confessed the truth, asked for his blessing, and advised him to start moving to Avignon to be at hand for his restoration; to Louis he sent a reminder that he had been invited by him to come and go on a campaign which had not yet taken place and that he hoped he would be backed to the hilt; to the Spanish court he addressed a straight plea for help. That done, Charles was ready. He ordered those who were to go with him to assemble at Nantes. He himself gave out that he was going to visit the monastery at La Trappe, and then disguising himself as an abbé (Walsh's idea) left for Nantes. The little town was full of strangers all in some kind of disguise, all with orders not to recognise each other so that they were constantly obliged to look the other way. Aeneas Macdonald described how during their residence there 'they lodged in different parts of the town, and if they accidentally met in the street or elsewhere they took not the least notice of each other, nor seemed to be in any way acquainted, if there was any person near enough to observe them'. On 20th June Charles set off in a fishing boat down the Loire and on the 21st boarded the *Du Teillay* at St Nazaire. 'Before she set sail all her lights were put out, except that for the compass, which still was so close confined that not the least ray could emit. This caution was observed every night, through the whole voyage.'

CHAPTER FIVE

Voyage to Scotland

Charles' voyage is sometimes spoken of with such awe that one imagines him actually setting off in little better than a rowing boat with a couple of friends, but not only were the *Elizabeth* and *Du Teillay* substantial ocean-going vessels, they carried, at least at the outset, more than is often realised. Puny though the expedition was in terms of conquering a nation, it was not quite so puny, looked at from St Nazaire, as to invite open ridicule.

The wonder was not that Charles took so few companions with him but that he managed to scrape together so many. Nobody could have gone with him who was not either mad, desperate or in it for some strange reason of self-interest. Not a single companion went with Charles' confidence and conviction. Those who were confident lacked conviction, and those with conviction were far from confident. Why, then, did anyone go at all, taken that all of them lacked Charles' passionate belief in the enterprise? There were twelve men in Charles' party, three of whom might have been omitted from the accepted lists because they were servants. Sir Thomas Sheridan went because he had no choice. He had been with his pupil now for twenty years and was used to being dragged everywhere with him. Sempil might call him the boldest adventurer ever but the facts were that Sheridan had had one stroke, suffered from asthma and was an old man. Far from being Charles' evil genius, he went because it never occurred to him that he could get out of it. Whatever influence he had over the Prince does not come out in his letters. On the contrary he seems to have been a little afraid of Charles. So Sheridan went because it was his duty and he had no option. His equal in age and infirmity was the Duke of Atholl, William Murray, an attainted exile since the '15. Atholl certainly went because he wanted to, but it was in the spirit of a noble last gesture in the tradition his life had been lived in. He wanted to see Scotland again before he died, and his family estates that had passed to his Government-supporting brother. Gout permitting, he hoped to help rally his clan.

In a different category were George Kelly and Francis Strickland. Both were tried Jacobites, but they also went as boon companions of the Prince. Strickland in particular was in it for the adventure, wherever it might lead. They knew perfectly well that James, still the titular King, disapproved of them and that their hopes rested on staying in the good books of the rising star, to whom they intended to stick very close indeed. Also in it for whatever it might bring them, and with fewer credentials to produce that might convince genuine Jacobites, were two military gentlemen of whom Charles was very proud. He would naturally have liked to take a general or marshal of note with him, but failing that he was pleased that Sir John Macdonald and John O'Sullivan were with him. Macdonald had served in the Spanish cavalry, though he was a naturalised Frenchman, and never stopped talking about his experience. O'Sullivan had an equal tendency to boast of his limited experience in Corsica. Charles was impressed by both, and in particular by their enthusiasm. Both were opportunists, especially Macdonald, and distrusted by the Scots.

This leaves six men. First, there was Aeneas Macdonald, the banker. Aeneas was a man of sense and discretion who would not lightly undertake any mad exploit, but he had been intending to go to Scotland in any case and a little persuasion made him see the trip as combining business with, if not pleasure, heroic duty. He was an important addition to the party because of his powerful contacts in Scotland. Abbé Butler, of the family of the Duke of Ormonde, was another man of value. He went as Chaplain to Charles. Then there were the servants. Duncan Buchanan was Aeneas Macdonald's clerk, and had already made several journeys with messages. Donald Cameron, a one-time servant to old Lochiel, was a valuable addition because he could act as pilot once they got to the Scottish coast. Michele Vezzosi was an Italian who had been in James' service for years and had helped Lord Nithsdale get out of the Tower, and had been specially sent by James to Charles. Lastly there was Walsh himself.

Charles' relationship with all these people varied, as did theirs with him. Between Atholl and Charles there was an old-fashioned romantic gallantry: they both talked the same idealistic language and just the sight of Charles could reduce Atholl to tears where the sight of Atholl brought a lump to Charles' throat. They almost strangled each other with sentiment. To Kelly and Strickland Charles was the outside chance they were betting on. They were familar with him, boosting his opinion of himself, intent on accelerating his own inclination to be bold. They had everything to gain and little to lose. While he had little respect for them, Charles liked them and their ideas because they agreed with his own. From them he got a degree of friendship tinged on their part with the right amount of deference, and that was a mixture he liked. With John Macdonald and O'Sullivan he had a more complicated rôle to play. They knew more than he did about war, so he respected them but he slightly resented their superiority and wanted it dispensed with as soon as possible. They could, to a certain extent, influence him. He liked to talk to them about tactics and they were always ready to oblige. Towards Aeneas Macdonald Charles displayed a degree of caution. He wanted Aeneas on his side, and he knew it would be men like Aeneas that he would need to convince. He felt his way carefully.

They were, therefore, a far from homogeneous group of men; nor did they impress contemporaries any more favourably than they do us. According to the Chevalier de Johnstone Charles could have taken any officer in France instead of the worthless bunch he did. Charles did not care. It was basically unimportant whom he took with him because his real supporters were out there waiting for him. This was merely a group of fellow-travellers he was giving a lift to and, as far as he was concerned, he was in spirit keeping his promise to go on his own if necessary. If anyone had asked him what a handful of men like that could do he would have said nothing. The point was, the men he needed were already on the other side of the water. Furthermore, he was sure that he only had to sail for France to 'throw off the maske or have an eternal shame on them'. He never doubted that, the glove thrown down, they would pick it up.

On 2nd July Charles and his party were all safely on board the *Du Teillay* and were joined by the *Elizabeth*. He wrote to his father that '... 700 men aboard, as also a company of 60 volunteers, all good men, whom I shall probably get to land with me ... which though few will make a show, they having a pretty uniform. I keep this open ... so that I may add a note to it, if being sea-sick does not hinder.' His prophecy was correct, but he managed to add the promised note: 'I am, thank God, in perfect good health, but have been a little sea-sick and expect to be more so; but it does not keep me much a-bed, for I find the more I struggle against it the better.' In spite of Charles' cheerfulness when he wrote this, disaster had already struck – this time not a storm but a chance encounter with a British ship on her way to join a squadron in the Bay of Biscay. Not knowing the circumstances, Captain Day of the *Elizabeth* thought the *Lion* might just be the first of a fleet of warships and that battle would have to be given. Charles was all for it, Walsh against involving the *Du Teillay*. It was Charles' first experience of real warfare and he found his position as spectator intolerable. As the guns of the *Lion* hammered the *Elizabeth* he tried to persuade Walsh to go to her aid. Walsh not only refused but threatened to have Charles taken down to his cabin and locked in. It was a humiliating hour for Charles: the first decision of importance had been taken and it had not been his. Any visions he had had of seizing command and driving all before him vanished. Immediately he had to depend on Walsh for an even greater decision: to go on or not. It was Walsh's ship, Walsh's sailors, Walsh's seamanship that was taking them. Charles could ask, but not command. To his pleasure – but not without him noticing his own position – Walsh decided to carry on.

Charles had never, of course, been to Scotland but he had examined, as best he could from the maps at his disposal, all the different routes attempted invasions had taken. One plan had never been used. The Duke of Berwick had once proposed sailing round the west coast of (friendly) Ireland and approaching the north-west coast of Scotland. That way an expedition would avoid running the gauntlet of the well-patrolled English coast. In the event, after the sea battle on the 9th, a mist came down which, though a blessing as far as safety went, made it hard for Walsh to keep rigidly on course. On the 15th there was a violent storm, but then fine weather until the 20th, when they had to ride another gale. Charles endured it all stoically, but the general atmosphere on board was gloomy. No one doubted that the men on the *Lion* would have given the alarm and pursuit seemed only a matter of time. On 23rd July, with the return of fine weather, Charles had his first sight of Scotland, land of Jacobite myth and legend. More by good luck than by good management, it proved to be the west coast. The rocky islands of the Outer Hebrides were like nothing he had ever seen before. The rain and wind had temporarily stopped but on a cold, grey evening the black rocks are more like the humps of some prehistoric monster than a place of welcome. Captain Durbé piloted the ship into Barra where Aeneas Macdonald landed for a few hours only to return with the frightening news that his brother-in-law had been arrested and the whole plot perhaps discovered. What should they do?

The answer came clear and strong from the majority: go back to France while there was time. Charles disagreed, quite sensibly arguing that nothing had in essence changed. One man's brother-in-law being arrested was neither here nor there. Walsh agreed with Charles and it was the strength of *his* resolve that prevented an immediate return. As everyone was well aware by now, the ship was Walsh's and Captain Durbé under his orders. So on the 24th an anchorage was sought while followers could be contacted. A mysterious ship – never identified – scared them and the Prince and his immediate entourage were hastily dumped on the west side of Eriskay while the *Du Teillay* stayed near by at a safe anchorage, ready to play hide-and-seek.

Eriskay, even on a brilliant summer's day, is not a lush place. As an introduction to Scotland it would take a very acquired taste to appreciate. Four miles long and two miles broad it was, and is, entirely Catholic, inhabited by fishermen evicted from South Uist, a place 'where never was heard the screech of English – beautiful Gaelic we always used'. On a night that O'Sullivan described as blowing hard with cruel rain, Eriskay was a desolate place to find oneself after a long sea voyage, a place where even in summer 'fierce squalls from the north shake every gable, hard hailstones which would cut the top off one's ears, men so chilled with cold they cannot look outside, huddled indoors at the edge of the ashes'. Struggling up from the beach of white sand where he had jumped from the boat, Charles and his companions found only a hut to shelter in. It was a dwelling such as he had never seen before, a mere shelter from the rain and wind and not too efficient even for that. There were no windows, only a hole in the roof above the smoky fire in the middle of the room. As such, it was a typical Highland dwelling: 'their cottages are in general miserable habitations; they are built of round stones without any cement thatched with sods ... they are generally though not always divided by a wicket partition into two apartments, in the larger of which the family reside ... the other apartment, to which you enter by the same door, is reserved for cattle and poultry, when these do not choose to mess and lodge with the family.' The thick smoke was due to the peat nearly always being wet 'for want of convenience'. The Highlanders liked the smoke for they said it kept them warm. Angus Macdonald, mine host, was none too pleased to see this strange party who spoke French and English but no beautiful Gaelic. But he was hospitable in so far as he could be. There was no food, but they caught flounders and cooked them on the fire and then ate the half-raw, smoke-tasting, fire-blackened offering. He offered them one bed and the floor. Naturally he was curious to know who they were, particularly Charles who annoyed him by first examining the bed to see if it was dry and then by rushing to the door and coughing every five minutes. Charles had no luck with his famous charm. He could not talk to Angus, and Eriskay fishermen were not susceptible to flashing smiles and gracious nods. Angus stared quite openly at Charles, who had let his beard grow and looked rather odd in his, by now, very grubby abbé's outfit. The innate majesty that others later swore they saw through layers of grime was not in evidence that evening.

It was the beginning of a new way of living for Charles and he took to it straight away. He was in good physical condition, strong, with excellent general health. All the hunting and riding he had done had made him tough and capable of enduring long, tiring journeys. The last eighteen months had seen him become, perhaps, a little soft, but at the various country-houses he had visited he had tried to keep himself in trim. But nevertheless, in both Albano and France he had always at the end of every night gone back to a comfortable lodging where his every need was catered for. There he could take off his dirty wet clothes, have a hot bath and eat substantial meals in a warm room. From now on, except for brief breaks, all that disappeared. Lying down to sleep on wet ground in wet clothes with very little in his belly became the general rule. Charles not only never complained, he actually relished the hardship, particularly since he shared it with the ordinary Highlander. It became an obsession with him to identify himself with them so that no one could ever accuse him of asking others to do what he refused to do himself. But the point was he liked doing it. Charles was one of Nature's Boy Scouts, at his best when he was one of the lads roughing it. What would have depressed his father exhilarated him. He never fussed about the absence of home comforts and seemed to feel no ill effects at all. This reaction of his to what the rest of his band regarded with distaste and aversion naturally made him popular with the Highland clansmen. Yet genuine though Charles' enjoyment was, this behaviour had its own pitfalls. Charles, from the moment he landed in Scotland, was in danger of cultivating the clansmen to the exclusion of the gentlemen. There, he made a big mistake. The Highland clansmen lived lives of such grinding poverty and were so securely at the disposal of their chiefs that Charles would have had them whether he was popular or not. They had no choice. Furthermore, they had very little to lose, except their lives. The gentlemen, on the other hand, not only had a choice – a choice involving many others apart from themselves – they had much to lose. They had estates, houses, possessions, names: things harder to give up in many cases than a life. They had generations of accumulation behind them which they had inherited and which they wanted their sons to inherit. Charles, concentrating so hard on the ordinary men and having a natural affinity for the details of their daily life, completely failed (at least temporarily) to take the same care with these much more important adherents. They would come to the standard because it was their duty. That was enough.

Charles found out very quickly that it was far from being enough. Waking up on sodden Eriskay on the morning of 24th July, he was visited by Alexander Macdonald of Boisdale. Boisdale came from South Uist, separated from Eriskay by a thin strip of rock-strewn water. Charles prepared himself for the meeting with some complacency – he was looking forward to receiving the homage of the men, loyal to his family for so long, whom he had come to deliver. The Macdonalds were particularly vital to Charles, for they were one of the largest clans and traditionally supporters of his cause. There were nineteen principal clans, each chieftain known by the place he came from. It was therefore a great blow when Boisdale came over to Eriskay and declined to join the Prince – or it ought to have been. Charles, however, was determined to ignore this refusal. There were bigger fish to catch. He turned a deaf ear to Boisdale's anguished entreaties to go back to France and instead dispatched a message to Sir Alexander Macdonald of Sleat, the head of the whole clan, believing – rightly – that if he gave the lead all the rest would follow. Unfortunately, Charles had mistaken his man. Boisdale would at least visit the Prince and try to dissuade him: Sir Alexander would not even do that. Murray of Broughton may have reported the general aversion that existed to the Hanoverians, but in the case of many of the chieftains it had been commuted to either tolerance or cooperation in their own interests. Boisdale did not like the Government but he had benefited from thirty years' peace. If an army had landed with Charles he might have risked everything he had gained but to back a scruffy man with no following was suicide. Sir Alexander would not dream of going to see Charles. Unequivocally, he was for the Government. The same attitude was taken by the head of the Macleods. That these two men were so resolute came as a shock to Charles, who had not realised the headway made by Duncan Forbes, the Lord President of Scotland. Every bit as much a lover of his people as Charles professed to be, Forbes had made it his life's work to bring peace to his country through the acknowledgment of a government that was a fact. He had toured the Highlands regularly to keep restless chieftains loyal and had tried to bring both industry and justice to the most lawless regions. It was a measure of his success that Macdonald and Macleod remembered hard facts and refused to be swayed by romantic appeal. They lost no time in confirming the stand they were prepared to take, but wrote to Forbes that they had done their duty 'for the best'. Charles was up against more than he knew. Macleod swore that 'not one man of consequence benorth the Grampians will give any sort of assistance to this mad rebellious attempt'.

Charles was not discouraged, though everyone else was. He had this blind faith that he could convince 'men of consequence' that he was worth following whatever evidence there was to the contrary. It was a faith based on no kind of statistics but on emotion and principle. Charles was rigid when it came to Right and Duty. He had never had to learn that Right and Duty could be tempered with Sense and Responsibility. Again, Walsh's agreement was essential to Charles' plan to go to the mainland and contact other chieftains: if Walsh had decreed they must sail for home

Charles would have had no option. Walsh, impressed by Charles' determination and optimism, and being of the same nature himself, did agree. Boisdale returned home again, the bedraggled party weighed anchor and sailed for the mainland where they landed at Borradale, at the head of Loch nan Uamh.

Nobody on board was happy, except Charles, who was impatient with their misery. Obstacles, as far as he was concerned, were made to be overcome. The sail from Eriskay across to the mainland was a rough one and Charles was never a good sailor, but the sight it brought him of the 'real' Scotland was a reward in itself. Creeping up the loch as far as she could get, the *Du Teillay* was soon enveloped by a different kind of landscape from the barren islands. Even in the dark, edging their way along, the giant mountains could be felt as well as seen and the scale of the Kingdom he had come to reclaim made itself felt. Captain Burt, an English observer a little earlier in the century, had found the scenery dreadful: 'But of all the views, I think the most horrid is, to look at the hills from east to west, or vice versa, for then the eye penetrates far among them, and sees more particularly their stupendous bulk, frightful irregularity, and horrid gloom, made yet more sombrous by the shades and faint reflections they communicate one to another.' Charles never mentioned what he thought but since his spirits were high he can have felt none of Burt's depression. At four o'clock Charles got into a boat with three or four others and landed. They crept to the house of another Macdonald and told him that they were smugglers, until they felt sure of their safety, when they revealed to this Macdonald of Borradale their real identity. His amazement was matched only by his horror.

For two weeks the *Du Teillay* remained at anchor either around the inlets of Borradale or at sea not far off. While Walsh methodically went about seeing to it that casks were filled with fresh water, supplies unloaded under cover of darkness, repairs made where the damage the storms had done made it necessary, Charles struggled to set up his cause. Time was short. The *Du Teillay* could not hang about for ever. She was too valuable to sacrifice to the first British man-of-war that flushed her out. Charles knew that the ship was his lifeline: once she had gone it really was glory or death. Before she went back, therefore, he had to make sure that there was something to stay for, and this he set about doing. One by one he was visited either on the ship or near by on land by 'men of consequence; some of more consequence than others. When each came, their coming in itself a courageous act and testament of sincerity, he saw for himself the circumstances of Charles' visit. A handful of men, mostly old, a puny stack of arms and equipment. These were inescapable facts, which spoke loudly to the visitors. But Charles spoke to them too, and while the vague magnetism that everyone talks about did its work, so also must his words. It was not enough to look a Stuart, to be a fine figure of a man and so forth. The Macdonalds of all the neighbouring regions who came were not going to be seduced by a pretty face. Charles had to make sense.

All the contemporary accounts agree that those who came to visit Charles spoke with him 'for hours'. Without descending to verbatim conversations they make it plain that a great deal of discussion and arguing went on, on both sides. Charles undoubtedly used as his main plank the assurance that France was behind him and that French forces would be on their way. He was not asking them to rise on their own – though in fact he was – but as part of a greater design. His visitors must have asked for proof: he had none to give except his presence. Would he have risked coming if he thought France would not back him? Nobody knew Charles, nobody knew that was just precisely what he would do. He did not seem wild or mad, but patient and calm. They were swayed not by anything so fey as charm but rather by the very opposite: Charles seemed solid. They watched each other, none wanting to be first to commit himself, none wanting to be alone. Meanwhile Charles maintained his air of confidence and continued to summon the most important chieftains. Macdonald and Macleod continued to ignore him, but Lochiel came. Lochiel was Charles' greatest conquest, without whom he would have been on his way home.

If there was one clan in Scotland more important to Charles than the Macdonalds it was the Camerons, of whom Donald Cameron of Lochiel was the head. Their seat was at Lochaber, where they had been since their arrival in Scotland with the younger son of the Danish royal family hundreds of years before. Their name meant 'crooked nose' but there was nothing crooked about their loyalty. The clan had already suffered for the Stuarts. John Cameron, Donald's father, had come out in the '15 and lived in France ever since. He had had twelve daughters before Donald was born and through their marriages had enhanced his political importance. Donald himself was accomplished, refined, courteous and yet brave and daring. He never took any oaths to the Government but was permitted to remain in peace. He was a moderate, a calming influence among hotheads, and it was said of him 'he loved his King well but loved his country better'. Duncan Forbes, though he knew Lochiel was no friend of the Government and had not been detached from the Stuart cause like Macdonald and Macleod, depended on his good sense. In fact, Lochiel had given Murray of Broughton an assurance of support in 1740, and again in 1743, but when France withdrew her aid he had withdrawn his support. Less violently prejudiced than many other chieftains, Lochiel was determined to do nothing rash. He had his father's fate as a constant reminder of what could happen before him, and his people to think of. The condition of these people was much as it had always been – poor. Despite the valiant efforts of Duncan Forbes, too little had been done to reform the Highlands. They were left to rot as far as the central Government was concerned. What Lochiel had to weigh up was whether peace in itself was worth preserving – any kind of peace – when the clansmen suffered so horribly during war. Macdonald and Macleod thought it was. Lochiel decided he agreed: peace was better than another failure.

Once he had decided to have nothing to do with a prince who had come without an army, Lochiel sent his brother Archibald to tell Charles to go back to France in everyone's interests. Charles sent, in reply, a messenger to Lochiel asking him to come in person. Reluctantly, Lochiel decided that he owed it to Charles to give him a straight no to his face, so he set off for Borradale. He called on the way on another brother who advised him not to continue for 'if this Prince once sets eyes upon you he will make you do whatever he pleases'. Scorning such nonsense, Lochiel continued. His interview with Charles was private, in contrast to others which had been in semi-public. They remained closeted together for a whole afternoon. Those outside remained uneasy. Macdonald of Clanranald had already declared for Charles but the rest wanted a stronger indication of success before following suit. After a final refusal, Charles is reputed to have said to Lochiel, 'Very well, stay at home and read in your newspaper of your Prince's fortunes.' This piece of contempt is supposed to have spurred Lochiel to action but it seems highly unlikely. Such a piece of arrogance would have been much more likely to turn him the other way. What Charles did was to convince Lochiel that there was a chance. He raised his clan because he saw there was a chance, and what can possibly have made him think there was except a belief that France was behind Charles? Charles had no other card to produce. It was all promises, promises, but the promises were made. Lochiel returned home dejected but committed, acting not in anger or defiance but after long, deep thought.

Later, and before, many were to say that Charles was a puppet in the hands of Sheridan or O'Sullivan or whoever was about him at the time. Only Lord Lovat was shrewd enough to observe: 'If he succeeds, the whole merit will be his own; and if his mad Enterprize bring misfortunes upon him, he has only himself to blame.' At this crucial stage, however, nobody mentions anybody else at all except to say they were for giving up the enterprise – 'the Prince was single in his resolution of landing' – and in all that followed. This says something for Charles' fluency, coherence and powers of reasoning rather than for anything so nauseating as his famed charm. He was not a feeble, pathetic creature for Lochiel and the others to take pity on: nobody goes to war for pity. Nor, even in an age of witchcraft, had he any supernatural powers to bewitch them. Charles, at that time, was strong and he did a strong man's job. Lochiel was convinced by his arguments, not his physique. The most difficult job any leader can have is to rally support in the first place when nobody wants to give it. Though he deluded them, Charles did a magnificent job – for himself. The credit, or the blame, was all his. Nobody else helped him.

Duncan Forbes, also a man of great charm, could not believe his work was being undone. At the very time Lochiel was agreeing to rise, he was writing: 'In a state of profound tranquility we have been alarmed with advise ... of intended invasions ... These informations ... I must confess have not hitherto gain'd my belief ... So far as I can learn there is not the least apparatus for his reception, even among the few highlanders who are suspected to be in his interest.' He proposed to go north at once 'to the end that, though my fighting days are over, I may give some countenance to the friends of the government, and prevent the seduction of the unwary, if there should be any truth in what is reported'.

Charles was now in a hurry to get the *Du Teillay* back to France, not simply because he wanted to be left irrevocably on his own, but also so that she could carry the good news of the support he had gained back there and get help sent out. He parted from Walsh, to whom he owed so much, with a grand gesture of the kind that was to become so typical. He handed him a letter that said:

Chevalier Walsh, notwithstanding all I said to you verbally, I cannot let you leave without giving you a testimonial in writing of the satisfaction which your services have afforded me. I have begged the King, my father, to give you a mark of it, which I would do myself at once if I had it in my power. Thus you may rely that if ever I reach the throne to which my birth calls me, you will have occasion to be as pleased with me as I am with you, and I could not say more – your good friend – Charles P.

With this flowery epistle, Walsh said goodbye and set off for home, feeling a pang or two at the sight of Charles on shore, still with such a small gathering.

There was now a great deal of work to be done, which Charles set about while Sheridan and Co. were still feeling sick at the sight of the disappearing *Du Teillay*. It had been agreed with Lochiel that the standard should be raised on 19th August. The place chosen was Glenfinnan, some thirty miles away, because it was a convenient meeting place of several glens. Charles had to get himself, and stores and such Macdonalds of Clanranald who had already joined, to Glenfinnan. He also had to organise the arrival there of as many people as he could manage, and he dictated to Sheridan numerous letters summoning them. The tone of these letters was a little high-handed, full of the usual stuff about winning or perishing in the attempt, but Charles had the sense to couch his actual order in gracious language. As though inviting them to a ball he said he 'shou'd be very glad to see you on that occasion. If time does not allow it, I still depend on your joining me with all convenient speed' – that is, if they could not manage the 19th. While Clanranald's men marched by the shore to Glenfinnan, Charles went by boat with the baggage to Kinlochmoidart and from there by boat and on foot to the same place. At Kinlochmoidart, where he remained a week, he had an encouraging piece of news. A detachment of Guise's regiment, on their way to Fort William, had been taken prisoner by some of Keppoch's Macdonalds on 14th August. The day after some other Macdonalds attacked and captured two companies of the Royal Scots, also on their way to Fort William, at Spean Bridge. The latter incident was of immense publicity value for, regardless of the fact that there had been no straight battle but rather a misunderstanding as to the numbers of Macdonalds actually about, it was the first outbreak of hostilities. Forbes understood exactly the effect it would have and wrote gloomily: 'I am afraid [this success] will elevate too much and be the occasion of further folly. Two companies of the Royals made prisoners sounds pretty well and will surely pass for a notable achievement.'

It did. Nobody took into account that these Scots were 'lads picked up last season ... with nothing Royal but the name'. The Keppoch Macdonalds were cock-a-hoop and Charles delighted. What particularly pleased him was the opportunity it gave him to show the world how he would treat prisoners: with solicitude and respect. They were to be given the chance of joining his cause now that the error of their ways had been pointed out to them, but if they refused they were still to be regarded as guests, to be fed and sheltered as well as his own men. It was a ridiculously exaggerated notion of chivalry and quite impractical. Whatever good impression it made on the prisoners – a useless thing in itself – this was more than outweighed by the resentment it roused in the Highlanders. As Maxwell of Kirkconnell, one of Charles' officers, wrote, 'none of them would take parly, they were a great charge to us, being oblidged to escort them and to set them every night into houses whereas our men lay out in

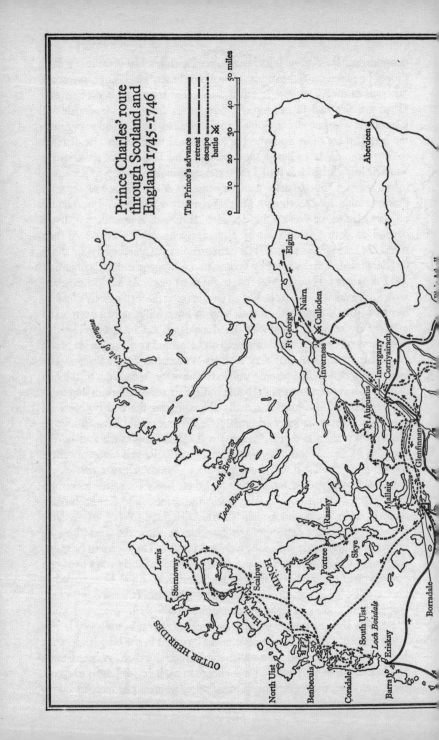

Prince Charles' route
through Scotland and
England 1745-1746

The Prince's advance
retreat
escape
battle ✕

0 10 20 30 40 50 miles

Kyle of Tongue

OUTER HEBRIDES

Lewis

Stornoway

Scalpay

MINCH

Harris

North Uist

Benbecula

Coradale

South Uist

Loch Boisdale

Barra

Eriskay

Portree

Skye

Raasay

Loch Broom

Loch Ewe

Mallaig

Glenfinnan

Borradale

Ft Augustus

Invergarry

Corriyairach

Inverness

Ft George

Nairn

✕ Culloden

Elgin

Aberdeen

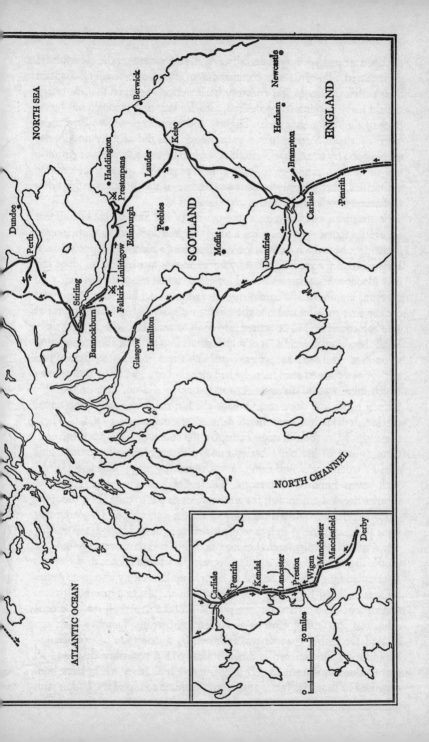

NORTH SEA

NORTH CHANNEL

ATLANTIC OCEAN

SCOTLAND

ENGLAND

Dundee

Perth

Stirling

Bannockburn

Glasgow

Hamilton

Falkirk

Linlithgow

Edinburgh

Haddington

Prestonpans

Lauder

Peebles

Berwick

Kelso

Hexham

Newcastle

Brampton

Carlisle

Penrith

Moffat

Dumfries

Carlisle

Penrith

Kendal

Lancaster

Preston

Wigan

Manchester

Macclesfield

Derby

50 miles

0

the open air and yet very cheerfully'. As the days went on the cheerfulness disappeared. Towards the commander of the Guise soldiers, Captain Sweetenham, Charles was courtesy itself. Always anxious that his image should leave nothing to be desired, Charles saw that there should be no trace of the conquering hero. Dignity and graciousness were his watchwords. Captain Sweetenham was impressed and did actually do Charles a little good by taking back with him – when he was released on a promise not to take up arms again – glowing reports that quite depressed the authorities, plus a highly inaccurate estimate of the numbers in his army that seemed to confirm their worst suspicions.

Sweetenham was a witness at the raising of the Standard at Glenfinnan on 19th August – an occasion Charles looked forward to with intense excitement but which, at first, looked like being a hideous disappointment. He arrived at the meeting place by boat and was met by one hundred and fifty Macdonalds, whereas he had expected to find the place seething with cheering hundreds. His confidence seemed to desert him temporarily and for the first time he had not the heart to display himself smiling and at ease before anyone, so he retired into a hut to wait. He waited a long time. While he waited, he had a lot of unpleasant things to think about, crowding in on him. The stark facts were that Walsh had gone home, France had not yet had time to send help, he had already begun an insurrection from which there was no going back, and if Lochiel did not turn up with his Camerons he was done for. Outside the hut there was an uneasy quiet: the Macdonalds had even more depressing calculations to make. Then, romantically, as though stage-managed, the sound of bagpipes was heard. Coming out of his hut Charles stood with everyone else straining his eyes to where the sound came from. At last, over the hill came Lochiel with seven hundred Camerons. The relief was enormous. Instantly, Charles decided not to wait for any more clans but to cash in on the spirit of elation that now seized his army of almost a thousand. The ceremony went ahead as planned and, though as stirring as he had hoped it would be, it was not without its farcical moments. When it came to actually holding up the flag the Duke of Atholl, who was the natural choice to do it, was so crippled by gout that he had to be held up himself by two men. James III was declared King and loud cheers split the air. In a quavering voice that cannot have carried far, the poor old Duke of Atholl read the proclamation appointing Charles as Regent, written by James as long ago as 23rd December 1743. It was followed by a manifesto of excruciating boredom which the men endured stoically as a necessary drag and all part of the momentous day. If they listened at all, they might have been surprised to hear that James at no time promised to repeal the Union with

England that many of them thought the object of the exercise. All he promised was to call 'a free parliament' which would help him 'repair the breaches caused by so long an usurpation'. His other important promise in this document of great length, that must have taken all of half an hour to read, was to protect his Protestant subjects as well as his Catholic. After the Duke had finished there was more cheering and the excitement had hardly had time to die down before it surged up again with the arrival of three hundred more Macdonalds.

That night Charles tasted success for the first time and felt justified already in what he had done. He walked around among the Highlanders, flushed and happy, speaking to those who understood his English and trying hard to pick up Gaelic words to communicate with those who did not. The men lay on the ground, the pibroch whined, there was bustle and activity everywhere as men renewed acquaintances. Even those forced to turn out because their chieftain insisted in the cruellest of ways were temporarily reassured. Twelve hundred men can look a great army to those used to passing weeks without seeing more than their own immediate family. Charles himself inspired them with hope. He had cast off his abbé's disguise and appeared resplendent in full Highland dress such as few Highlanders had ever seen. Their own dress was not so splendid: 'With them a small part of the plaid, which is not so large as the former, is set in folds and girt round the waist, to make of it a short petticoat that reaches half way down the thigh, and the rest is brought over the shoulders, and then fastened before, below the neck, often with a fork, and sometimes with a bodkin or sharpened piece of stick, so that they make pretty neatly the appearance of the poor women in London when they bring their gowns over their heads to shelter them from the rain.' Only gentlemen wore the 'trowze' – breeches and stockings all in one piece. It seemed to them that Charles was the perfect leader – so strong, so dignified and yet so approachable, so concerned for their welfare, so eager to involve himself with them. And Charles, with little idea how reluctant many of them had been to come and for what widely differing reasons they thought they fought, felt everything was as it should be.

Back in his hut that night Charles was far from being deluded enough to imagine his Kingdom was already regained. Already, the mechanics of leading an army of the sort he found himself with were beginning to present themselves. He had eyes. He saw there were no 'pretty uniforms', no rows of splendid chargers, nor gleaming stands of armies and flashing swords. The men gathered round him that night were lucky to have a weapon of any kind. Their chieftains had tried to see that every man had at least a knife or axe but beyond that it was a case of grab what you can.

Those who had firearms of any sort often had no ammunition of any kind, or if ammunition was available it did not fit their gun. Nor, as far as Charles could see, were the men equipped to face the rigours of a campaign. There were enormous variations in their dress, but the majority looked half naked and ill-shod. Those who had horses had animals that resembled pit ponies. The only really decent horse in Glenfinnan was the charger captured from the Captain of the Royal Scots which had been presented to Charles himself. The behaviour of the men was not that of a disciplined army, and their organisation was non-existent. Drill was something they had never heard of. They were tough and brave and loyal, and that was all.

Whatever the state of his army Charles loved them – every Highlander that joined had a personal guarantee of Royal love. But love was not going to feed them. Charles had by this time seen something of the country in which he was in. There were no fields of waving corn, no fat cows grazing, no fruit weighing down bushes or trees. There seemed to be nothing. How the people existed was a puzzle, but it was a puzzle he had to find the key to quickly. He would not move an army through a country already barren and let it steal from the people he had come to deliver from their unhappiness. He was anxious that by his impeccable conduct he should gain more and more adherents, not alienate the population by pillaging and plundering. But how was he to get food when in the first place there was so little to be got and in the second he could not spare what money he had to pay for it?

CHAPTER SIX

The First Victory

Charles now had in his company men who knew every inch of the country through which he was passing. Lochiel, Macdonald of Keppoch, Macdonald of Clanranald – they were all intimately acquainted with every hill and bog and stream. Where the knowledge of one ended that of the other began. They could tell Charles the layout of the existing Government fortifications, of how three forts – Fort William, Fort Augustus and Fort George – stretched in a line joined by a road from the south-west to the north-east of Scotland following the natural geographical split in the Highlands. Fort William was the nearest. It could be taken, and would give the Macdonalds and Camerons great pleasure to take since it had been built there with the express purpose of controlling them. But there were other men in Charles' party, the men who had come with him, who were more contemptuous of the rabble so far gathered. They urged marching south to join up with more clans and adherents of better quality. As yet, no council had been set up. Charles was eager to set one up but he did not yet know the full quota he had to choose from, so he delayed.

One factor Charles had always felt very much in his favour and which he had stressed time and time again was the element of surprise, coupled with the scarcity of Government troops in the country. Nearly all these were in Sir John Cope's force, and in the whole of England there was not a full regiment. At Glenfinnan, when he had been in Scotland over three weeks, he had to try to calculate how much that element still held good. We know what the Government knew, but it is much more interesting to calculate what Charles thought they knew, and what he thought they thought he knew. He knew, by Glenfinnan, that his presence in Scotland was now known: with an army of over one thousand it could hardly be otherwise. Two days after the raising of the Standard he heard of the proclamation issued for his capture with a reward of thirty thousand pounds (the Hanoverians were economising: James might have said with some pride that they had thought he was worth more in 1716). The element of total surprise therefore no longer operated, but he still reckoned on being able to move towards Cope quicker than the Government could recall troops from Flanders, and that left him with only one body of men to deal with: Sir John Cope and his army. Now Charles' exact knowledge of Cope's forces was no more correct than Cope's knowledge of his, but from what Lochiel and the Macdonalds could tell him of the pattern of troop movements he knew that force could not be vast. What he hoped to do was to challenge Cope before reinforcements were sent to him and defeat him the way that a handful of Macdonalds had defeated the Royal Scots. He was keen to give battle and be on the offensive. What he wanted to avoid was being holed up in this remote corner of the Highlands with his back to the sea. Therefore, as in a game of chess, he must move rapidly forward, hoping to be joined by more clans before clashing with Cope. He had no intention, nevertheless, of trying to give Cope the slip and make for Edinburgh: that would have been pointless. Then he would have enemies behind *and* ahead. As Murray of Broughton wrote, 'nothing on earth was further from his thoughts than marching South before a battle … all were of the same mind with himself, all wishd with uncommon ardour to come to an Engagement'. So Charles left Glenfinnan to hunt Cope, making towards Fort Augustus, the crucial central link in the chain towards which he estimated Cope would march. He thought Cope would also be hunting for him. In this he was right – everyone on the Government side realised the importance of 'crushing this insurrection in the beginning' now that 'this horse play' had begun.

On the march towards Fort Augustus Charles was brought to appreciate the difficulties that were to confront him every time his army moved. These were difficulties all commanders had to face – difficulties of transport and terrain. He was determined to cling on to the arms he had brought from France, which included twenty field-pieces, plus all the ammunition. Any chieftain looking at these objects could have told Charles not to waste his time: he was not about to operate in a theatre of war like Flanders. There would be no setting up of cannon on flat fields if they could help it – this would be guerrilla warfare, quick sorties suited to mountainous country with hand-to-hand fighting. But Charles set great store by his equipment, which helped him to feel a proper soldier. Unfortunately, he could not prevail upon his army to see it his way. They were not common labourers. It was beneath their dignity to carry such cumbersome stuff and they refused to do it. In no position to bring out a whip and make them, Charles had to accept their refusal and leave half his precious war-toys behind. It taught him a little, at least, about the character of his army. Scruffy and poor they might look but they were as obstinate as an Emperor when it came to what they thought they should and should not do. This attitude, though, had nothing to do with genuine laziness for Burt had noted that though the ordinary Highlander was renowned for indolence, 'I had occasion to employ great numbers of them and gave them good wages, the solicitations of others for employment were very earnest and would hardly admit of a denial: they are as willing as other people to mend their way of living ... they work as well as others.'

In England, the progress of the Jacobite army was speculated about with great anxiety. Dr Waugh, the Whig Chancellor of the border city of Carlisle, wrote: 'if an invasion should be attempted in England before these people are dispersed ... or if ... these Rebels should ... gain an advantage over General Cope ... we have strong reasons to fear all Scotland would soon be in an uproar and we not in a very pleasant situation.' He went on to say he had faith in everyone's loyalty to the King and Government but even to himself such optimism sounded hollow. What worried him most – as it did all astute observers the length and breadth of the country – was what the French were going to do. 'Surely if the Pretender trusts to a Rebellion at home only, it is as mad a piece of work as ever was set about, which has made us fear something more.' With every report of Charles' advance – and there were many – Dr Waugh's worry grew. No preparations had been made for defence – no militia raised, not even Lord Lieutenants named. He waited in a very troubled state of mind to see which way Charles would go.

All the way to Invergarry Charles marched on foot with the men, leading all the way. This was no empty show, to be done at the start of every day and then dropped whenever everyone had been sufficiently impressed. It was all Charles' own idea and was not necessarily approved of by the Highlanders. They were amazed, and flattered, and yet not quite comfortable – they liked their chieftains to enjoy their privileges. It was also galling to discover how fast Charles could walk: 'he walked 16 miles in boots and one of the heels happening to come off, the Highlanders said they were unco' glad to hear it for they hoped the want of the heel would make him march at more leisure.' Those long days walking around Albano were paying dividends. At Invergarry, Charles had a decision of importance to make, the first, it could be said, as a general: he had to decide which way Cope would come. The answer seemed obvious: over the Corrieyairach Pass. Therefore, if an engagement was sought, this pass was vital. Ignoring advice to gather more clans from the north first, Charles wheeled south and marched his army up into the pass. If he thought the road rough he should have seen it as Burt had: 'The roads on these moors are now as smooth as Constitution Hill' compared to days when 'I had been obliged to quit my horse, it being too dangerous or impracticable to ride and even hazardous to pass on foot'. He intended to catch Cope there whether he was marching direct to Fort Augustus over the Corrieyairach Pass or first to Inverness and then down the road joining Fort George to Fort Augustus. Once in the pass, Charles did not just stand and wait but, with the bulk of his army on the Corrieyairach road, he also set about planning an ambush for Cope on the other. Unfortunately, this plot was betrayed and Cope, by forced marches, was able to march to Inverness before the ambush could be effectively prepared. Charles now had no choice but to march south. Far from being delighted that Cope had evaded him and left open the way to Edinburgh, he was furious. He did not want to go south. The only alternative – chasing Cope up the road he had taken – was equally abhorrent. Cope would reach Fort George and Inverness first and turn on them from a position of strength. A worried Charles had the greatest difficulty persuading the disappointed clansmen to go south at all. If from the London and Edinburgh ends it looked as though Charles had cleverly given a cowardly Cope the slip, from the clansmen's point of view Cope had pulled a fast one. It was with considerable gloom that the march south began.

Though he did not appreciate it, Charles had gained a great psychological victory. In England the news was not that Cope had escaped a trap, but that Charles had given him the slip and there was a good deal of consternation. Well-informed correspondents of the day thought it very significant. Horace Walpole wrote: 'The confusion I have found, and the danger we are in, prevent my talking of anything else. The young Pretender, at the head of three thousand men, has got a march on General Cope.'

Charles' gloom soon lifted. It was typical of him that he could find a silver lining in almost any cloud, a habit more realistic people found very annoying. On the way down to Perth he was heartened by the addition of more men, particularly Lord Nairne and Macpherson of Cluny. Cluny was a most important convert since he commanded a disciplined force of some three hundred Macphersons. He joined, though the circumstances in which he did so have always remained unclear. He had certainly set out to raise his clan not for Charles but for the Government. Charles would have had it that he was made to see where his duty lay – another blow to Duncan Forbes who had been sure that Cluny, like Lochiel, would stand fast. His grief at the desertion of both was far greater than his pleasure at Sir Alexander Macdonald and Norman Macleod standing firm. Charles was also cheered by the evidence along the route that Cope's army had endured acts of sabotage and that virtually no recruits had joined him. They might not join Charles either, but he felt the pressure of sympathy on his side. At Blair Atholl, where Lord Nairne joined, Charles had his first experience of a Scottish country-house on a vast scale, which he found edifying. Up to then the houses he had seen were modest affairs and he had begun to think civilisation totally lacking. At Blair Castle, the seat of the Duke of Atholl, he realised his mistake. He had seen nothing as magnificent in his life. Situated in the wide Strath of Garry, the white castle is approached by an avenue of lime trees through which its castellations and turrets can be seen. All around this ancestral home of the Murrays is a path of overwhelming lavishness – trees, shrubs and rolling lawns stretching for miles. If for Charles it was an inspiring moment – for it proved the quality of the men who followed him – for William Murray it was one of great emotion. His brother James, a Government supporter, had fled leaving the castle to his rebel elder brother. William entertained Charles with pride and dignity and little else for brother James had taken everything eatable with him. Charles couldn't have cared less. It was enough to sit in the great hall and feel his dreams had substance. The next morning he reviewed his men in front of the castle and received a shock: a good number were missing. Some officers were sent to round them up and Charles had to face the unpleasant truth that half his army regarded their adherence as purely casual. It was a timely reminder not to let Blair Castle carry him away.

Meanwhile, his brother Henry had at last set out to France on his way to join Charles. James did not approve, writing '... you will easily believe that the Duke could not think of remaining here – he followed his own inclination – he had run any risk to go and joyn his Brother'. He had wanted to go straight to Scotland but James wrote: 'I could not on any account allow of, for the real and solid good of my family, and the cause, as well as the Prince's personal security and interest in his present undertaking, require that he should not cross the seas as yet.' Poor Henry. While Charles was having all the fun he followed in his trail, doomed to the frustrations his elder brother had already endured. His first stop was to be Avignon where to support himself 'he has pawned here his jewels for his brother's service'.

From Blair to Perth there were other houses to visit though none so palatial. At Lude Charles 'was very cheerful, and took his share in several dances, such as minuets, Highland reels etc. The first reel the prince called for was "This is no my ain house" and a Strathspey minuet.' The gliding motion of the Strathspey was perfectly suited to his elegant form and he danced with such grace that the camp was awash with sentiment.

There was doubtless not a dry eye in the house. His progress uninterrupted, Charles was having a good time. There was dinner at Lord Nairne's house the next day, and then a triumphant entry into Perth, the first city he had seen. Charles rose to the occasion. Wearing a superb tartan outfit, trimmed with gold, and for once mounted instead of walking, he entered Perth where his father was proclaimed King at the Cross. There was no resistance from either magistrates or principal inhabitants.

Perth was another watershed. So far, as Charles was fully aware, his army consisted of ill-armed clansmen and few gentlemen. He did not make the mistake of numbering Lochiel or the other chieftains among the rabble but the fact was that he was short of men of influence. At Perth, the balance was slightly redressed. He was joined here by the Duke of Perth, Lord George Murray, Lord Ogilvy, Lord Strathallan, Laurence Oliphant of Gask and others of less note but nevertheless some standing. Of all of them the arrival of Lord George Murray was of the most importance and significance.

Charles never came anywhere near realising just how lucky he was to gain Lord George's support. Lord George was symbolic of a type of Jacobite Charles had not come across before. He was a Jacobite through principle, the principle of the divine right of Kings, who had proved his loyalty on more than one occasion but then had come to terms with the *status quo* when it seemed unalterable. He had built up, since the acceptance of a pardon granted by the King in 1725, an estate of value and at the time of the '45 had succeeded in providing a livelihood in good conditions for large numbers of his clansmen. Duncan Forbes had used every inducement to keep Lord George loyal, and he had in fact obeyed Cope's summons to present himself at Crieff, though he did not follow this through and engage his men. Instead, Lord George went home and wrestled with his conscience. It was a conscience of the most exacting kind. A stern, unbending figure, Lord George had the highest moral standards. There would be no romantic appeal for him about Charles – quite the reverse. Nor would he be shamed into joining – Lord George was not acquainted with the feeling. As a very young man he had been out in the '15 and again in the '19 and afterwards, while he was abroad, James had been very kind to him, paying his debts on more than one occasion and generally doing as much as he could for him. Returning on a secret mission to see his dying father in 1724 Lord George, at the age of thirty-one, had been given permission to apply for a pardon by James. Asking for any kind of pardon went against the grain. He was a fighting man who had barely had a chance to fight and to doom himself to the life of a farmer following far-off battles on a map was not attractive. But the lure of Scotland and the weight of family responsibilities had made up Lord George's mind. Now, twenty years later, he gave up all he had gained and left a pregnant wife he dearly loved and children he adored to follow Charles. Why?

Characteristically, Lord George, once he had made his mind up, sat down and wrote a letter to leave behind for his children, feeling that they had a right to know why he was imperilling their inheritance. He gave his reasons for joining the Standard as, firstly, that the setting aside of the true Royal line was an unjust act that he felt bound to put right; secondly, that the present Government allowed widespread corruption and bribery; and thirdly, that Scotland was unfairly incurring debts due to the war in Europe. But however cogently he tried to marshal his arguments they were not convincing enough and he knew it. From the moment his decision was made Lord George was filled with a terrible sense of doom. He felt drawn in a nightmarish way towards a course of action his common sense told him would be disastrous. He told himself duty called him, but scorned his own assurance. He would never have admitted that he could not resist the challenge presented to him, but there was that element in his decision. His feelings of guilt as he rode off to join Charles were heavy, and of all the adherents he knew the least joy. He had a compulsion to join which he felt incapable of disobeying, even though he knew the chances of total victory were small, and only total victory was of any use. Charles might gaily say he only had his life to lose and nobody had more, but Lord George had much more: everything he had built up in twenty years for his family and the lives of all his men. Death would be a relief compared to the agony of surviving defeat.

Knowing nothing of the grim spirit Lord George brought with him, Charles noted only his military experience and prestige and was delighted to welcome a recruit of such calibre. Equally pleasing, though more expected, was the loyalty of James Drummond, Duke of Perth. Born in 1713, James had been educated at the Scots College of Douay until he came into his estate at twenty-one. His entire family, especially his mother, were violently Jacobite and there was no question of not joining any Stuart attempt. The Duke was a highly talented man, a lover of literature, with a taste for horse-racing rather than soldiering. His health had never been good since his lungs were bruised as a child, but he was very determined and what he lacked in physical strength he made up for with stamina. Joining Charles had not been easy. Since his support was expected, a close watch was kept on him and an attempt made to imprison him in his own castle which he only evaded by a trick. Charles respected the Duke not only for himself but for the sacrifices his family had made and its distinguished history. In fact, he valued him more than Lord George: having no qualms was always an asset in Charles' eyes, for he regarded anything less than total loyalty with suspicion whereas his father looked on it with understanding and compassion.

The date was now 4th September. Charles had been in Scotland six weeks and though his progress was judged remarkable he had achieved nothing solid. No battle had been fought, no test passed – and, when it came down to it, only victories could guarantee his success. But at Perth, within striking distance of Stirling and Edinburgh, a clash could not be far off. Meanwhile, in Cumberland the first steps, feeble though they were, had been taken on 5th September for the defence of the county in case of attack. Orders were sent by the Lord Lieutenant (who was in York) to Thomas Simpson, Clerk of the Peace, at Penrith 'To put the Laws into execution against Papists, Reputed Papists, Non-Jurors'. The 'whole militia' of the county was to be put into readiness, which sounded impressive until the muster roll revealed the state of its arms: 'no sword, bad gun, no bayonet' or 'bad sword, no gun, no bayonet'.

Cope would not stay for ever in Inverness, and Charles could not expect to walk into Edinburgh without encountering hostility. Charles tried, therefore, to put his army in order. Now that he at last had a choice, he must make appointments. Three had already been made. O'Sullivan had been made Quartermaster, Sir John Macdonald Master of the Horse and Murray of Broughton Secretary. He now made Lord George Murray and the Duke of Perth Lieutenant-Generals of his army. To them he handed over the unenviable task of organising the ill-assorted crowd who followed him, while he himself wrote to his father and to France and tried to finance the daily needs of his men.

His letters were long and full, describing in detail everything that had happened so far without exaggeration. They are buoyant in tone, optimistic, and yet surprisingly cautious. Charles did not over-estimate his achievement, merely dwelt on all the promising signs. His chief worry was money, but even the lack of this essential commodity did not depress him unduly. At Perth, he had exactly one guinea left out of the money he had brought with him, but his army was paid two weeks in advance, the front rank getting one shilling a day. Confident though he was that fresh supplies would turn up, he could not depend on personal contributions from rich supporters, declared or secret, nor on more arriving from France. What he decided to do was tap the available public money which, as rightful King, it could be argued his father was entitled to. Collectors were appointed to gather public money from Perth, Dundee and other towns in the neighbourhood. This money was the excise money levied by the Crown, not a lump sum demanded as a contribution. It brought in considerable amounts and meant that the Jacobites could boast they did not rob from the countryside they passed through. Only the excisemen knew why they could afford to be quite so well behaved.

Charles and his army stayed at Perth a week. At the end of that time he held what was in fact his first real council, though no council had as yet been officially appointed. The council decided to leave Cope to his own devices and try to seize Edinburgh. Charles himself had by now decided this was the best course. He had money in his pocket and more expectation of success with men like his Lieutenant-Generals in command. If he could take Edinburgh before Cope got back then it would be he who had the advantage. So out they marched, an improved army in every way. Lord George Murray had already achieved miracles. Knowing perfectly well that the Highlanders would desert to look for food at regular intervals he arranged for small knapsacks to be made containing a peck of meal for each man. He also tried to see that arms were more evenly distributed and the men taught how to use them. In particular he emphasised that after firing a shot the Highlanders really must break their habit of throwing their rifles away. He tried to introduce regular drilling habits, and the organisation of smaller units than clans so that authority should be efficiently delegated. It was all uphill work, but suited Lord George's personality admirably. The army was watched all the way by those eager to report to various masters in England. Mr Goldie of the Whig town of Dumfries admitted: 'We are uncertain as to the real strength and designs of the Highlanders. Our best accounts say, they have 2,000 fine fellows and desperate, who are well-armed; and upwards of 1,000 more, who are very indifferent, and by us termed Waliedragles.' It was the Waliedragles Lord George struggled so hard to do something about.

From Perth they marched to Stirling where there was a very strong castle. Looking at it, Charles can have felt no surprise that Scotland was divided into Highlands and Lowlands, for at Stirling the great plain explains all. He longed to take the castle, sitting so indomitable on top of its hill, high above the whole wide, flat area. To possess such a sentinel would be enviable. But he resisted the temptation – and the shots fired at him – and went instead to dine with Sir Hugh Paterson at Bannockburn. From there it was a straight run through Falkirk to Linlithgow and Edinburgh. So far, all was unity. Charles still held the respect of everyone. There had been no serious arguments to mar what was becoming a triumphal march. Beneath the surface, however, the rifts were there: Lord George was already irritated by O'Sullivan; half the army were already regarding the taking of the capital and the defeat of Cope as their sole objective; the Irish were already accused in private of forming a ruling clique. Charles was oblivious to these rumblings of internal dissension, and had not himself crossed anyone's path.

Charles had now covered a good many miles and was in a better position to judge what kind of 'home' he had. Captain Burt before him had noted the absence of carts and the small numbers of cattle and sheep. The sheep were a breed he could never have seen before, their wool so coarse 'that they seemed to be clothed with hair'. He had seen the rivers jumping with huge salmon and the seals that pursued them into the lochs. He had seen the hard life the common people led, particularly the women: 'women with their coats tucked up, stamping in tubs, upon linen by way of washing; and this not only in summer but in the hardest frosty weather, when their legs and feet are almost literally as red as blood with the cold; and often two of these wenches stamp in one tub, supporting themselves by their arms thrown over each others shoulders'. He had passed the houses they lived in, most just miserable huts and even the better sort built of rubble: 'stones of different shapes and sizes; and many of them, being pebbles, are almost round, which, in laying them, leave large gaps.' The land he travelled through was not enclosed but every scrap of grass was preciously guarded. A man would stand all day holding the halter of a cow or horse to see that it did not eat more than its share. Few he saw on the road wore shoes, and when they did – perhaps on Sunday on the way to church – they walked as awkwardly 'as a cat shod with walnut-shells'. The shoes when worn would be the famous brogues which bore no resemblance to the heavy leather shoes that they are today. They were 'a sort of pumps without heels which keep them little more from the wet and dirt than if they had none but they serve to defend their feet from the gravel and stones'. The distinctive holes were deliberately made to let the water out. The hardiness of the people was daily witnessed. Even when there were bridges, which was rare enough, they were not used if there was the smallest toll. 'I have seen women with heavy loads, at a distance from the bridge ... wade over large stones which are made slippery by the sulphur, almost up to the middle, at the hazard of their lives being desirous to save or unable to pay, one single bodle.' It was clearly not a land that flowed with milk and honey.

On 15th September Charles occupied Linlithgow, recently hurriedly vacated by Government troops, a good morale-booster. The next day, they reached the three-mile stone from Edinburgh and had to decide how their offensive should be conducted. As a starter, Charles sent a summons to the magistrates demanding the surrender of the city. A deputation arrived to ask for more time which – taking it as a sign of weakness –

Charles refused, though receiving the party with great courtesy and honouring their safe conduct. He then had to consider what strategy he was going to adopt. Storming the place was hardly feasible since he did not have the equipment to overcome any serious resistance; besieging it was, in view of Cope's approach, too lengthy. Therefore all that was left was an attempt at surprise. The city, well known to most of Charles' army and certainly to his officers, had four main gates manned by guards which were regularly changed. The gates had to be opened at some point to let carriages in and out unless the city imposed a siege on itself, which seemed unlikely. Showing considerable initiative, the Jacobites split themselves into small groups, each concentrating on a gate, hoping to take advantage of any opportunity that presented itself. They also hoped for support from within since it was well known that the recently elected Provost was a sympathiser and the populace more interested in a quiet life than supporting the Government come what may. In the event, Lochiel and a band of Camerons rushed the Netherbow gate when, as anticipated, it was opened to let a carriage in. It was early morning in broad daylight. The regular troops retreated to the Castle and Edinburgh was taken – excepting this important building – with hardly a blow struck.

The city Charles entered that momentous day – when it seemed that at last a Stuart had come into his own again – was no Rome or Paris. But it was the capital of Scotland, and its appearance, on first acquaintance, was nevertheless imposing enough. 'When I first came into the high-street of that city,' wrote Burt, 'I thought I had not seen anything of the kind more magnificent: the extreme height of the houses which are, for the most part, built of stone and well-sashed; the breadth and length of the street, and (it being dry weather) a cleaness made by the high winds, I was extremely pleased to find everything look so unlike the descriptions of that town which had been given me by some of my countrymen.' Later, Burt had some fellow-feeling with these countrymen. Finding his way through the narrow alleys of the city became a daily torture – the filth, it seemed, was much worse than any he had ever known. The city was built on a rock for protection but the rock was too small to take enough houses. To cope with demand the buildings were ten or twelve storeys high with no gardens or yards. This overcrowding was the cause of the 'extreme nastiness'. Towering above the city was the Castle, an impregnable-looking fortress, and the crown steeple of St Giles, the church which since the Reformation had been the focal point of the city. The High Street, which had excited Burt's admiration, that Royal Mile which someone else described as 'the fairest and goodliest street', was the home of the merchants and tradesmen who lived above the Netherbow Gate.

Below, on the Canongate approach to Holyroodhouse, lived the nobility – when they were in town – in houses with walled gardens. These gardens were planned with 'such elegance, and cultivated with such diligence, that they might easily challenge comparison with the gardens of warmer climates'. But in spite of such horticultural splendour, Edinburgh was little more than a market-town – overcrowded, busy, but in essence not so different from the countryside around it. Women stood knee-deep in filth washing their clothes at the Cross, cattle crowded the streets leading to the market, and there were few signs anywhere of opulence. The cold was usually intense. Burt remarked there was 'nine months winter and three months bad weather'. The peat fires, even in frost and snow, were so small they could be covered with both hands.

Charles entered the city, so unlike any other he had known, at noon on 17th September after a bad night during which he had slept only two hours. His march, with the rest of the army, took a roundabout way to avoid the guns of the Castle, entering the King's Park surrounding Holyroodhouse from the south side. Once in the park, he was surrounded by people, Whigs and Jacobites alike, who had come to stare at him. With the Duke of Perth on one side and the recently joined Lord Elcho on the other, he made his way slowly through the throng. There was an unusually large proportion of women in the crowd, all wearing the plaid: 'it is made of silk or fine worsted, chequered with various colours, two breadths wide, and three yards in length; it is brought over the head, and may hide or discover the face according to the wearer's fancy or occasion; it reaches to the waist behind; one corner falls as low as the ankle on one side; and the other part, in folds, hangs down from the opposite arm.' Many of them were pretty, but in a robust way since they were used both to walking and a hardy climate. Children, with little idea of what was going on, thronged the streets too. Burt had made them sound very unattractive: 'Their wretched food makes them look pot-bellied; they are seldom washed; and many of them have their hair clipped, all but a lock that hangs down over the forehead ... the boys have nothing but a coarse kind of vest, buttoned down the back, as if they were idiots ... the girls have a piece of blanket wrapped round their shoulders ... But what seems to me the worst of all is, they are overrun with the itch.'

He gave them all a chance to see him properly, frequently stopping and once getting off his horse. Among the spectators was a Mr Home, a violent anti-Jacobite who had done his best to prevent the authorities giving in to Charles and was furious that the city had been taken over so easily. Grudgingly, he had to admit that physically at least Charles was impressive. He saw a man of five feet ten measure himself against the

Prince and find he was smaller. He noted Charles' healthy complexion, strong build, regular features and his graceful deportment. His dress, in a city not famed for its fashion, excited great interest. He wore a blue velvet bonnet decorated with gold lace, a white satin cockade, a tartan short coat, red velvet breeches, a blue sash, a pair of military boots and a silver-hilted broadsword. While setting no store by it, Home admitted a spontaneous cheer went up from the crowd inspired by the splendour of Charles' appearance. He looked every inch a Prince and the citizens of Edinburgh were not used to Royal visitations.

Charles' response to this enthusiasm was variously reported. Home maintained he was languid and looked melancholy. Certainly, he was not giving the crowd any dazzling smiles or treating them to quips. But what Home overlooked was Charles' mental state. Far from being sad, he was immensely happy, but he was also acutely aware of the new dimension he was moving into. Always capable of giving a studied performance, he wanted to convey his sense of responsibility and not have anyone thinking him silly or conceited. He had decided to go for dignity and modesty, hence his grave face and carefully controlled gestures. Moreover, he knew that this was only the beginning and that it would not do to start congratulating himself yet. It was ironic that at this moment – a moment one would have thought made for Charles to let his exhibitionist tendencies have full scope - he should in fact have felt irritation that he had to put up with it. He wanted to get on, to achieve the concrete things that had so far eluded him. There was so much to be done and no time at all for parading himself.

Once in the ancient palace of his ancestors, Charles made one brief appearance on the balcony where he smiled and waved and then went inside. No amount of cheering brought him out again. James was proclaimed King at the Cross by the heralds (under duress from the Highlanders) and a manifesto read while Murray of Broughton's beautiful wife handed round white cockades. A drum was beat for volunteers to join and inspired by the spirit of the thing several did. Meanwhile, Sir John Cope was landing his troops at Dunbar. Told that Cope had landed Charles remarked, 'Is he, by God?' A battle was now expected daily and Charles' first job was to prepare for it. To those who suggested a celebration ball he was curt: the dancing could come afterwards.

The first headache was weapons. Every man must be used in the approaching battle and every man must have a weapon that was of more use than a farm implement. Not that the dirk, which they all had, was to be despised. It was a formidable weapon: 'The blade is straight, and generally above a foot long; the back near [one eighth of] an inch thick; the point goes off like a tuck, and the handle is something like that of a sickle ... in a close encounter, there is no defence against it.' Nor was the 'skeen-ochle' to be forgotten – a knife concealed in the sleeve near the armpit. Since no arms had arrived from France, the only thing to do was commandeer them. Accordingly, a proclamation was issued demanding the surrender of firearms. This brought in 1,200 muskets and some powder: not enough but better than nothing. Charles would have liked to use the cannon captured in the city – he had an obsession about cannons – but he had no artillerymen and in any case, as it had been patiently explained to him already, heavy cannon were useless on this kind of terrain and with these kind of troops. Charles was anxious to move out of Edinburgh and towards Cope as soon as possible, so on the 19th the bulk of the army moved out to Duddingstone and set up camp there. He took up quarters in the village near by. A council of war was now held and to Charles' pleasure there was a unanimous decision to move forward to meet Cope. He announced he would charge personally at the head of the front line. This met horrified opposition. If anything happened to him, the chieftains said, 'defeat or victory was the same to them'. They threatened to go home unless he agreed to a safer position and Charles was forced to comply. Once that question had been settled, there was the tricky one of deciding which clan should have the place of honour on the right. That was left to Lord George Murray to settle as best he could (he decided on turns).

Charles, waiting with his army at Duddingstone, was in high spirits and displayed none of the tension he had revealed in Edinburgh.

It was as though he thought courage and spirit alone would conquer. Lord George, looking hard at the two and a half thousand men, decided that was all they had to offer anyway. He did not know that Cope felt much the same way about his troops, mostly new recruits as untried in battle as the Highlanders and a good deal less willing. Lord George, though he knew Cope's numbers were about the same, thought they would at least be disciplined and well armed. He listened to Charles' speech on the morning of the 20th with misgivings. Everything, Charles said, had been arranged and agreed upon and all now depended on their order and conduct. He wanted them to win not for his own or his father's sake but so that they might be delivered from their present slavery. As he finished, he drew his sword and shouted, 'Gentlemen, I have flung away the scabbard; with God's help I will make you a free and happy people!' The response was dramatic – 'all the Bonnets were in the Air and such a Cry, yt it wou'd be wherewithal to frighten any enemy'. Charles raised his arm and they were off – at tremendous speed, moving in columns of three, literally on the rampage to meet the enemy.

The mass emotion had time to cool. Rather to Charles' disappointment Cope did not come thundering up the road to meet them. Scouts reported that he was taking his time and seemed to be making for Falside Hill. Instantly, Lord George was on the alert, for he knew that if there was one disadvantage that would be fatal to a Highlander it was being attacked from above. They liked such a position themselves when their first charge would carry so much more weight. Without consulting Charles or Perth, his co-commander, he tore off to reach the top of the Hill himself. Once gained, he saw the Government army on the plain of Prestonpans below, but his satisfaction at towering over them was spoiled by the discovery that the ground sloping towards the enemy was useless for an attack. It was more likely they would all fall flat on their faces than overcome Cope.

Cope, below, waited. It was now nearly dark and Charles, quite under-standably, feared that Cope, who seemed reluctant to engage, might try to slip through to Edinburgh, so he ordered some Athollmen to guard the road. Now Athollmen were Lord George's men. When he heard of Charles' order he was furious: no Athollmen were to be sent anywhere without his permission. When he drew near to the Prince, Lord George asked 'in a very high tone what was become of the Athol Brigade; the Prince told him, upon wch Ld George threw his gun on the Ground in a great passion and swore God he'd never draw his sword for the cause if the Bregade was not brought back'. Charles was stunned. He was the commander-in-chief, he had given a sensible order and now here was an inferior officer having hysterics because he had dared to. It did not make sense. But Charles did not make a similar scene. He said nothing, but then turned aside and cancelled his previous order. It was a stupid thing to do and a great mistake. If there was anything Lord George despised it was weakness. Charles ought, at this point, to have been resolute. He ought to have said his order stood but in future he would consult Lord George. In a very short time Lochiel had made the latter ashamed of himself and he asked that the order should stand. But the damage was done: Charles had seen that he was not general of his own forces, and Lord George had seen that Charles was afraid of him. Neither was prepared to excuse the other.

This ugly incident had to be forgotten by both parties if they were to concentrate on the coming battle. Both Charles and Lord George seemed to think the only way to do so was to keep apart, and this inevitably led to Lord George continuing to take a free hand. He did what he thought necessary without asking Charles' blessing. In one respect he was right so to use his initiative – what did Charles know that he did not? But on the other hand, by not even paying lip-service to Charles' generalship, he made it easy for O'Sullivan to encourage Charles' resentment. Charles himself could not understand Lord George's attitude. He wanted only to be successful, which was what Lord George wanted too. He had gone out of his way to be courteous at all times and defer to informed opinion. Why should there be friction? Charles could not appreciate, since he was not worried himself, that anxiety caused his Lieutenant to fuss over details.

Lord George had decided the hilltop was useless: the attack must be made from the east. Accordingly, he began moving the army, sending an ADC to Charles telling him what he was doing and asking him to follow. O'Sullivan was aghast. It was not only a case of how dare a Lieutenant-General give a General orders, but how dare Lord George make such a move in broad daylight. He had, however, made it, and Charles was not disposed to challenge him. Obediently, he followed. When darkness fell there was a council of war where Charles listened carefully to Lord George who announced he had a plan. He proposed continuing the march east and falling on the enemy's flank. Lord George maintained he, or men with him, knew 'every part thereabouts' and this local knowledge would be on their side. They could move swiftly, at daybreak, and fall on the enemy before he knew what had happened. Nobody had any alternative suggestion so it was accepted. Charles was particularly anxious that Lord George should have his approval. They settled down amicably for the night, Charles and Lord George 'great at Cup and Can' together.

They lay, that night, on the prickly ground where pease had just been cut, wrapped in their plaids. It was dry but cold. Beyond them lay cornfields, 'plain and level without bush or tree', the ground covered with a thick stubble that rustled with any movement. In Cope's camp a constant watch was kept though nobody expected any move before dawn. There were 200 dragoons and 300 infantry on guard duty and three large fires were lit on the front line. Someone who did not sleep was Robert Anderson, son of a local laird. He lay awake wondering if he should tell Lord George he knew a better way to approach the enemy, better even than those who claimed to know 'every part thereabouts'. Finally, he told a friend who persuaded him to brave the awfulness of rousing Lord George. Anderson told Lord George of the secret track he knew that he had discovered snipe-shooting. Instead of going round the bog they could go through it and approach from an angle Cope would never suspect. At four in the morning the army began marching along this track. They moved not quite so secretly as they had hoped, for some of Cope's dragoons heard a movement and gave the alarm. The Government lines were fully formed by the time the second Highland line came through the bog, though they had still to turn. In that sense, it was more of a fair fight than it sometimes sounds.

It was only a little after dawn when the Highland front line attacked, Lord George ordering the left wing to advance without synchronising with the right. But once the left had begun to swoop down, the rest followed. They ran with fury and eagerness, whooping and screaming, enough to make the young recruits on the other side turn pale before anything had happened to them. To his anguish Lord George saw that, as usual, the Highlanders were throwing away their firearms after one shot and resorting to their much preferred claymores. Cope lost the fight through the cowardice of his troops, not any fault of his command. It was simply no good 'begging them to keep up their Fire and keep their Ranks and they would easily beat the Rebels', nor shouting (as one officer did), 'What do you mean, Gentlemen, by reining back your Horses? Advance upto your Ground; have you anything to fear? We shall cut them to Pieces in a moment.' It was patently untrue. Encouraged to think they were to deal with a few peasants, the soldiers were stunned by what looked like the professionalism of the enemy: 'to my astonishment every Front Man covered his Followers, there was no man to be seen in the Open ... in short, tho their Motion was very quick it was uniform and orderly.' Only the officers distinguished themselves, riding up and down yelling, 'For shame, Gentlemen, don't let us be beat by such a Set of Banditti.' But they were. The rout was complete, and an exodus in full swing within ten minutes.

Charles, who genuinely longed to be in the front line, was mortified to find that though he was with the first of the second line, the battle – or, as General Wightman said, 'I say scuffle, for battle it was not' – was over before he arrived. Johnstone, who was with him, wrote: 'we saw no other enemy on the field of battle than those who were lying on the ground killed and wounded though we were not more than fifty paces behind our first line, running as fast as we could to overtake them and near enough never to lose sight of them.' It was not as Charles had envisaged it, nor were the scenes he was now surrounded with. For the first time he saw the difference between the siege at Gaeta and proper war. The Highlanders were men possessed. Not for them the distance a gun gives, but the close, hand-to-hand horror of swords severing heads and dirks plunged into necks to be twisted about and pulled out covered with blood ready to use again. The area round him 'presented a spectacle of horror, being covered with heads, legs and arms and mutilated bodies'.

No neat lines of dead soldiers, flat on their backs in serried ranks, pretty pink stains on their fronts. This was butchery, which not even the animals escaped. Though it drove Lord George wild with the stupidity of it, the Highlanders believed the horses fought as well as the men and attacked them too, thereby disposing of valuable assets. He and the Duke of Perth rode round once the outcome of the battle was certain trying to prevent such savagery, but to little purpose. With disbelieving eyes Charles saw the Highlanders move on from slaughter to plunder, ripping clothing and belongings off bodies they had just killed. It pained him deeply and was quite alien to his ludicrous notions of chivalry.

That night, Charles slept at Pinkie House after a day that had etched itself on his mind more than any other. Maxwell of Kirkconnell commented on the fact that he was not elated by his victory. On the contrary, one of his first acts was to issue express orders that there were to be no public celebrations 'for he was far from rejoicing att the death of any of his father's subjects, tho never so much his Enemys ...' Maxwell maintained he had 'a livelier sense of other people's misfortunes than his own good fortune'. He refused – when some crass people tried it – to be congratulated on the killed, and was in absolute agreement with Lord George that the wounded of both sides must be cared for. Since there were not enough surgeons available to undertake this, Charles sent a messenger to Edinburgh to bring more. He was shocked that his Highlanders would not bury the dead among the enemy, and that the local country folk would not either. He wrote to his father: 'Those who should bury the dead are run away, as if it were no business of theirs. My Highlanders think it beneath them to do it, and the country folk are fled away. However, I am determined to try if I can get people for money to undertake it, for I cannot bear the thought of suffering Englishmen to rot above the ground. I am in great difficulty how I shall dispose of my wounded prisoners ... Come what will, I am resolved not to let the poor wounded men lye in the streets, and if I can do no better, I will make a hospital of the palace and leave it to them.' His Highlanders did not share his concern. Moving among them, Charles grew used to the one topic of conversation: boasts of their own strength. Young boys of fourteen or fifteen were brought to him to tell of how they had killed a dozen men. Each tale was better than the last. It gave Charles a lot to think about on his way back to Edinburgh the next day: only now was he becoming intimately acquainted with the kind of army he commanded.

CHAPTER SEVEN
Edinburgh

————————◆◆◆◆◆————— ◆◆◆◆◆————————

Naturally, Charles' re-entry into Edinburgh differed from his previous one since he had now proved himself in battle. The week before the citizens of Edinburgh who were not Jacobites had developed squints from gazing so long at the weather vanes which would indicate the wind needed to bring Cope's ships in. Now there was no point hoping. Cope had been defeated, London was a long way off. Instead of being tolerated Charles must be given cooperation. Though he understood this, Charles for his part was determined not to act the conqueror. Everything was to carry on as usual. Since it was a Sunday, this meant church services. He was particularly anxious that all denominations should feel free to worship as they chose, and only laughed, rather admiringly, when it was reported that one minister had wished him death and a crown of glory, leaving King George to have the earthly crown. It made a change from those who leapt on the bandwagon and became Jacobites overnight. Duncan Forbes marked the new enthusiasm for Charles, the victor, and analysed it astutely: 'All Jacobites, how prudent soever, became mad; all doubtful people became Jacobites; and all bankrupts became heros and talked of nothing but hereditary rights and victories; and what was more grievous to men of gallantry, and if you will believe me, much more mischievous to the public, all the fine ladies, except one or two, became passionately fond of the young Adventurer and used all their arts and industry for him in the most intemperate manner.' It was all true, but none of it was Charles' fault. Cynicism was a quality totally lacking in Charles, but he was not entirely naïve. He knew all the world loves a winner, but he honestly believed that since all Britons were his subjects he did not have to separate the ever-loyal from the newly-loyal. He would accept their change of heart, and believe in it, and everyone would start with a clean sheet.

The news of Cope's defeat had shocked London. Walpole had to confess: 'We are sadly convinced that they are not such raw ragmuffins as they were represented.' He joked, rather feebly, to his friend in Florence that 'your two or three Irish priests ... will have set out to take possession of abbey-lands here'.

Charles, in the name of his father, was now the government in Scotland. He was conscious that his rule had begun and that he must put into effect the intentions expressed in his proclamations. He also knew that the basis of his rule, as long as he held only Scotland, was shaky. He must strike at England while he was strong. It was Charles' personal conviction that the army should be given only the shortest breathing-space possible and then, leaving a detachment behind, pursue Cope and encounter Wade at Newcastle. His opinion was violently opposed by his commanders, especially Lord George, who came near to wishing that the battle had not seemed so easily won since it had given Charles an exalted idea of the strength of his own force. Lord George knew perfectly well that the victory had been incredibly lucky, hanging not so much on the valour of the Highlanders – which he did not for one minute doubt – but on a combination of luck and cowardice on the part of the other side. This could not be expected again. He could not say to Charles that Prestonpans was a fluke, but he knew it was, proud though he might be at the outcome. Furthermore, Charles knew nothing of Highland battle customs. He did not know that half his army would promptly disappear, only to turn up again (with luck) after their loot had been deposited back home and the harvest gathered in. For good measure, Lord George threw into the argument the fact that many more would now flock to the Standard and by marching immediately he would deprive himself of this much-needed boost.

The decision to stay in Edinburgh for the meantime was taken at the first meeting of the newly-constituted official council. This consisted of the Duke of Perth, Lord George Murray, Lord Elcho, Lord Ogilvy, Lord Pitsligo, Lord Nairne, Lord Lewis Gordon; Lochiel, Keppoch, Clanranald, Glencoe, Lochgarry, Ardshiel; Sheridan, O'Sullivan, Glenbucket and Murray of Broughton. The strongest voice from the beginning was Lord George's and what he said was usually echoed by the Highland chieftains. The Duke of Perth was more independent. O'Sullivan, Sheridan and Broughton all tended to go in for whispering in Charles' ear without ever coming out into the open. Charles did his best to be neutral, and to listen to all sides. He went to great lengths to have it understood that his was just another vote and not a casting one at that – rather to his own undoing. The council met every day at Holyrood to consider not just major decisions of policy but day-to-day details of organisation. They were not always all present, especially when business was dull, but

Charles was always there, listening carefully and trying hard to master whatever it was that was going on.

His attendance was fitted into a busy day, for not only did he sit at all council meetings, he supervised the drafting of proclamations and the sending of messages, and visited his army every day at Duddingstone. A girl of a Whig family who had watched him review his troops described how she had been overcome with admiration.

O lass such a fine show as I saw on Wednesday last. I went to the camp at Duddingstone and saw ye Prince review his men. He was sitting in his tent when I came first to ye field. The Ladies made a circle round ye Tent and after we had Gaz'd our fill at him he came out of the Tent with a Grace and majesty that is unexpressible. He saluted all ye Circle with an air of Grandeur and affability capable of charming ye most obstinate Whig and mounting his horse which was in ye middle of ye circle he rode off to view ye men. As ye circle was narrow and ye Horse very gentle we were all extremely near to him when he mounted and in all my life I never saw so noble nor so Graceful an appearance as His Highness made, he was in great spirits and very cheerful … indeed in all his appearance he seems to be cut out for enchanting his beholders and carrying People to consent to their own slavery in spite of themselves. I don't believe Caesar was more engagingly form'd nor more dangerous to ye liberties of his country than this Chap may be if he sets about it.

Charles' one idea, as Lord George noted, seemed to be to go out and fight Cope with about as much idea of Caesar-type generalship as the writer of the letter herself.

In the evenings he was present at the balls that force of popular demand made necessary. The fact that he obviously did not enjoy them very much caused a lot of comment. Lord Elcho wrote: 'At night came a Gt. many Ladies of Fashion to kiss his hand but his behaviour to them was very cool.' Elcho's explanation differed from Charles' own: 'He had not been much used to Women's company and was always embarassed when he was with them,' said Elcho, but tackled on the subject Charles said, 'It is very true I like danceing and am very glad to see the Ladys and yu divert yr selfs but I have now another Air to dance [and] until that be be finished I'll dance no other.' It was the kind of pompous, self-righteous and yet endearing remark that was becoming Charles' stock-in-trade. Since, when he came out with this kind of thing, his sincerity was obvious nobody ever seems to have laughed or even groaned. On the contrary, it impressed anyone who heard, and they tended to rush off and repeat it with admiration. Yet Elcho had a point. Charles was not comfortable in women's company, even though his manners were exquisite and they swooned at the sight of him. At twenty-five his name had never been linked even in the most tentative way with any woman. At his court his detachment drove women frantic and added to his attractions immeasurably. As Forbes had said, the entire female population of Scotland was at his feet without him giving them the slightest encouragement. If he had tried, he could not have been cleverer, but it was simply a case of finding none of them in the least attractive. He said, with what we would think irresistible innuendo, 'I had rather be with one of my brave Highlanders.'

Once the decision to remain in Edinburgh had been taken, there was a great deal of work to do. Charles was not averse to doing it. He considered of prime importance the establishment of fresh contact with France, telling Louis of his success and the possibility of greater success if help was sent immediately – though Charles more than half hoped it was already on its way. He asked Lord Elcho to go as his ambassador, but Elcho declined the honour, without giving any reasons. Since he had been in Paris in 1744, Elcho probably understood only too well that to go to France on official business for Charles would be to become embroiled in the rivalries and jealousies that existed among the Jacobite agents there and his task would be impossible, carrying altogether too much responsibility. Besides, he did not want to miss the chance of some action. He was proud of the lifeguard troop he had raised – the only smart regiment in Charles' army – and intended to enlarge his experience beyond the few days' soldiery which was so far all he had had. Instead, Charles sent Kelly, on 26th September, five days after the battle. It was a poor choice. Kelly was as Irish as his name and too prone to exaggerating Charles' success to the extent of making it sound as though he had no need of the help for which he asked.

In fact, help already had been sent before Kelly reached Versailles. The minute the news of Glenfinnan came – the minute, that is, that Charles had anything that could be called an army – arms and money had been sent to Scotland under the orders of Maurepas. Walsh, returning on 23rd August, had more than done his bit, driving straight to Versailles to urge backing on a grand scale for Charles. It was due to his efforts that four small ships sailed at the end of September for north-east Scotland carrying volunteers as well as arms. The day *before* the news of Prestonpans came, Louis had ordered Lord John Drummond to take his Royal Scots regiment to Scotland. This amounted to 'a thousand men full of zeal and desire of shedding the last drop of their blood'. It looked as though Charles' conviction that Louis would support him if he made the first move had been justified, but it was illusory. Help came in dribs and drabs in spite of the sensation caused by the taking of Edinburgh and defeat of Cope.

There was no plan for the large-scale invasion Charles counted on. Louis was still making his mind up. He was, however, cunning enough to send an accredited representative to Charles to keep him happy. This was Monsieur du Boyer, Marquis d'Eguilles, who arrived at Holyrood on 14th October by way of one of the four small ships. He was ecstatically received by Charles, who displayed him triumphantly as evidence that he had been truthful in assuring everyone of French help. For the moment, it assuaged the doubts of those like Lord George who had begun to wonder.

In the middle of all this excitement Charles found time to write, in his own hand, to his father, on a note of great optimism and yet at the same time showing an unexpected restraint and appreciation of his position that ought to have pleased James.

Sir.

I have atlaste had the Comfort of receiving Letters from you, the lettest of which is of ye 7th Sept. N.S. I am Confounded and penetratd with so much goodness and tenderness Yr. Majesty expresses to me in all yr. Letters. It is grife to me that my keeping Strickland has given you one Moments Concern but shall send him away in all hest. I hope yr. Majesty is persuaded that this fault or any others I may have committed is not want of ye. Respect and submition which you will always find in me. I remark your Letter to ye. K. of Fr. in which you do me more honour than I deserve. I wish to god I may find my Brother Landed in England by the time I enter it which will be in about ten days having then with me near 8.000 men and 300 hors at. lest which as matters stand I shall have one desive stroke fort, but iff ye French land perhaps none. I cannot Enlarge on this subject as in many others for want of time becase of such a multiplicity of things which aurly occors for ye. cervice of ye. Affair Adam has sent me a Gentleman (who brought me yr. Letters) to stay with me for to give notice of anything that I may want, which as he says will be don immediatly accordingly I am sending off immediatly three or four expresses all to the same purpose so that sum one may arrive, what is sed is very short, pressing to have succor in all heste, by a landing in England for that as matters stand I must either conquer or perish in a little while. Thank god I am in a perfect good health but longing much for ye. Happy Day of meeting. In ye. menetime I remain Laying myself at yr. Majestys Feet moste humbly asking Blessing

Your Moste ditiful son
Charles P

P.S. The ship being just redy to go of I have only time to enclose here (-) of ye. account of ye. Battle which I in a hurry writ some days ago.

Edingbourgh ye. 7th Otobre O.S.

It is impossible for me to give you a distinct jurnal of my procedings becase of my being so much hurrid with busines, which allows me no time; but notwithstanding I cannot let slip this occasion of giving a short accoun of ye. Battle of Gladsmure [Prestonpans] fought on ye. 21 Septembre which was one of ye. moste surprising actions that ever was; wee gained a complete victory over General Cope who commanded 3,000 fut and to Regiments of ye. Best Dragones in ye. Island, he being advantagiosly posted, with also Baterys of cannon and Morters wee having neither hors or Artillery with us and being to attack them in their post and obliged to pas before their noses in defile and Bog. Only our first line had occasion to engage, for actually in five minutes ye. field was clired of ye. enemy (—) ye fut killed wounded or taken prisoners and of ye. horse only to hundred eskaped like rabets one by one, on our side wee only losed a hundred men between killed and wounded and ye. army afterwards had a fine (—).

France was not the only place Charles sent messages to. Undeterred by their obvious hostility, he sent dispatches to Macleod and Sir Alexander Macdonald, sweetly informing them that far from taking offence that they had not yet joined him he quite understood that it was only caution had held them back due to the private way he had arrived. Now that he had gone public and beaten Cope he eagerly awaited their deferred arrival. He also sent letters to the Earls of Sutherland and Cromarty, Lords Reay and Fortrose and the chief of the Grants asking them to raise companies. He was nothing if not sanguine. The arrival of Lord Ogilvy, with six hundred men, and of Lord Pitsligo and Gordon of Glenbucket – both old, but valuable additions – had done little to assuage Charles' rising discontent. Why did not more come? What was holding back the rest of Scotland? Since he could never see it might be lack of interest in his cause, he had to conclude it was fear. Perhaps he still had not proved himself enough.

The precariousness of his position was daily underlined by the existence of the Castle, still held by Colonel Guest for the Government. On 29th September, after a round of fire in no particular direction, Charles decided this state of affairs could not go on. His newly established authority was being undermined. Accordingly, he ordered a blockade. Guest replied that unless the blockade was lifted he would bombard the city and slaughter the citizens. After several lengthy exchanges, Guest did indeed begin a cannonade and Charles was obliged to lift the blockade for humanitarian reasons. The Castle remained, a reminder that he was far from master even in this one city.

As well as the challenge presented by the Castle, Charles also had to deal with scores of other lesser issues. He was now professed governor of a capital and discovered within a few days that this amounted to an administrative nightmare. If, in the army, he lacked a general of experience and standing – for not even Lord George could be called that – he lacked also a minister who knew anything about government. Murray of Broughton was the only public servant of any use, but he knew nothing of the running of a city. Neither did Charles. His way of dealing with problems was to issue a proclamation, drafted and written by Sheridan. These proclamations with which he attempted to rule Edinburgh for six weeks were wordy, extravagant affairs full of endless vindications for whatever order was being put forward. Charles attempted, through them, to prove what a good chap he was. He worried about the ordinary people being plundered and issued a proclamation on 23rd September ordering death to be inflicted on any soldier or person connected with his army who should be guilty of taking 'from the good people of Edinburgh' any of their goods. He worried, too, about the harm done to commerce by the removal of all notes and money to the Castle by the directors of the two banks, and issued a proclamation inviting them to resume business under his protection. They refused, but did give him money on application in exchange for his own notes. It was no way to govern, but it was the best he could manage. He could not, with his campaign barely begun, devote himself to supplying an entire new government to Edinburgh. Yet his lack of success rankled. On 10th October he could not resist expressing his irritation that his motives were misunderstood and cooperation denied him. They were all distinctly lacking in gratitude and appreciation and ought to be ashamed of themselves.

I, with my own money, hired a small vessel, ill provided with money arms or friends; I arrived in Scotland, attended by seven persons, I publish the King, my father's declarations, and proclaim his title, with pardon in one hand and in the other liberty of conscience; and the most solemn promises to grant whatever a free parliament shall propose for the happiness of the people ... Why, then, is so much pains taken to spirit up the minds of the people against this my undertaking?

The reason is obvious; it is, lest the real sense of the nations present sufferings should blot out the remembrance of past misfortunes, and of the outcries formerly raised against the royal family. Whatever miscarriages might have given occasion to them, they have been more than atoned for since.

With their appeals to 'listen only to the naked truth' and their alternately arrogant and hysterical tone, many thought Charles should have confined himself to short edicts and much more manoeuvring behind the scenes. Lord George was disturbed by the legal content of the proclamations. It seemed to him Charles was proving as guilty as Oliver Cromwell had been: if Parliament could not act without the King, the King ought not to set himself above Parliament. That, in his opinion, was what Charles attempted when he seemed to hold out a promise to set aside the Act of Union. He accused Charles of acting in an arbitrary and unconstitutional fashion, and Sheridan of encouraging him. The job of writing most of the proclamations did seem to have gone to Sheridan's head, but then he was far removed from James' restraining influence and not prepared to exert such an influence himself. Yet nobody could have been clearer on more occasions about his intentions that James himself, and Charles was only acting for him. In March 1741 James wrote: 'We have been now more than 50 years out of our country, we have been bred and lived in the school of adversity ... Long experience teaches us how little we can depend on the friendship of foreign powers ... But should it happen that any foreign power contributed to place me on the throne it must be visible to all thinking men that I can neither hope to keep it, nor enjoy peace and happiness upon it but by gaining the love and affection of my subjects. I am far from approving the mistakes of former reigns ... I am fully resolved to make the law ye rule of my government and absolutely disclaim any pretensions to a dispensing power.'

Faced with the fact that occupation of the capital and victory on the battlefield had not filled his pockets, Charles had to devote a large proportion of his time and energies to doing this. He employed the means used already but on a larger scale. He assessed the burghs of Scotland in sums relating to excise duties and ordered the contributions to be paid to Holyroodhouse. He made Edinburgh cough up equipment to the tune of £15,000, and from Glasgow he demanded £15,000 in cash – but on receipt of a prompt £5,500, let the rest hang fire. Every tax collector in the land was hounded to produce his books so that Charles could see how and where his money came from. Requisitioning from the wealthy went on continually – this way horses and food were obtained. Without wanting to, Charles was using a means it pained him to acknowledge to obtain an end he held sacred. During his stay in Edinburgh he achieved nothing which would be remembered for all his grand promises. There was no anarchy – though real government was in abeyance – but neither was there order. Everything was done on a day-to-day basis which did nobody any good.

Charles was restless. According to O'Sullivan he 'never thought of any pleasures and was as retired as a man of sixty'. It did not agree with him, and increasingly it seemed to him that until his father's government was put on a national basis – until, in fact, London was taken – nothing could be achieved. He wanted to march south before winter came, even without a large French force and more clansmen. Edinburgh was good for neither him nor the army. Accordingly, on 30th October, Charles brought up again at the council the proposed march into England. It was no good waiting any longer – it could always be argued more recruits were coming. Meanwhile, their own army lost its spirit and the enemy's gained in size. He wanted to march towards Newcastle where the elderly Wade camped with not many more troops than he had himself. Lord George disagreed. Wade, for one thing, was a highly experienced soldier, not to be scorned. For another, however much Charles ignored the fact, his own army was still neither strong nor well armed. The march would be long and exhausting and they would arrive in a strange country at a disadvantage. Better to avoid battle. Better, also, to march to Carlisle on the other side of the border where there were as yet no troops. Wade would then have to chase them. Furthermore, the north-west of England was traditionally Jacobite and was near to Wales, also friendly. What Lord George seems to have overlooked, or not known, was that Cumberland was not Lancashire: 'the north-west' could not be lumped together like that. In fact, the Lowther family held most influence in Cumberland and they were very definitely on the side of the Hanoverians. Butler had described this county as 'the poorest and most disloyal county in the whole of England'. But, with perhaps a slight edge to his voice, Lord George suggested it would give the Prince's English friends a chance to join forces. Charles, who had been as firm in his belief that adherents in England would indeed support him as he had that France would, could only agree. The arguments seemed strong. But he was not happy agreeing and this was the second instance of going against his own instinct. He wanted to march south after Prestonpans, but stayed; he wanted to attack Wade at Newcastle, but attacked Carlisle. He was developing the bad habit of agreeing openly with a plan of action which ran contrary to his own instincts, either because he was being overborne or for the sake of a quiet life, and then, when things went wrong, saying he had always really been against it. It was a dangerous procedure. Majority rule became the order of the day, to the detriment of the enterprise. So firmly was Charles establishing this precedent in his eagerness to be fair that he would not be able to break it when he wanted to.

The composition of the Highland army when it marched out of Edinburgh on 1st November was very different from when it had marched in. For a start, it was no longer almost entirely Highland but contained several Lowland gentlemen of standing who led regiments of their men which corresponded more closely with Charles' idea of an army. One such was Lord Ogilvy, eldest son of the Earl of Airlie who had joined Charles on 3rd October with a regiment of six hundred men raised from his father's estates around Forfar. Red-headed and thought very handsome, particularly by the French among whom he had spent some years, Ogilvy brought with him his newly married wife. She was incredibly beautiful and he did not dare leave her behind. He was certainly a man of quality of the kind Charles craved, and his men were a well turned out bunch. Another such man was the Earl of Kilmarnock, William Boyd, who joined on 18th October. Outstandingly handsome, tall, slender and well-bred, Kilmarnock had led a dissolute youth but left it behind him when he married Anne Livingstone, a zealous Jacobite. It was she who begged her husband to forget his previous Government connections and join the Standard. Kilmarnock was influenced not only by his wife's entreaties but by Colonel Gardiner's predictions, before Prestonpans, that Charles would win. He was hard up and wanted to be on the winning side. The curious thing was that Charles did not naturally gravitate towards the company of these, and others less well known, Lowland gentlemen. Many were near his age, but he seems to have kept his distance, and where one would have thought he would have found friends he made none. He continued to keep close company only with the associates that had been with him from the beginning or, in a detached way, with the clans among whom he moved freely and regularly. This had a doubly unfortunate effect. Not only did it mildly offend the gentlemen in question who wondered at their lack of popularity, but it prevented Charles from discovering the talent there was among his own officers. His reason for continuing to prefer the clansmen was that he felt these were the men who must be kept loyal, whereas the gentlemen he considered needed no morale-boosting. In this he was making a big mistake.

The army was also bigger, though not nearly as big as Charles had hoped. He had fought with around two and a half thousand men at Prestonpans; he now marched with around five. Many of the Highlanders still had not returned and many more that he had expected after a victory (Charles expected everybody) had not come in. Still, he now had something for Sir John Macdonald, Master of the Horse, to do; for as well as Lord Elcho's one hundred and twenty horse-guards, Kilmarnock brought some horse grenadiers, and Lord Balmerino forty more. Lord Pitsligo had a hundred and twenty mounted men and there were eighty hussars commanded by one Baggot, an Irishman newly arrived from France. These combined made two fairly respectable troops of cavalry. Elcho's were the most impressive since they all wore blue uniforms. They were given the job of leading the army into towns as, impressed by show himself, Charles reckoned others would be. The infantry consisted of thirteen regiments, six of the clans proper. None of them had any uniform except Highland garb – not smart kilts or trews but the much stained brief skirts of tartan, bonnets and plaids. In addition, there were now a few carriages with ladies like Lady Kilmarnock and Lady Ogilvy in them, as well as a carriage for Charles should he care to use it.

Lord George and the Duke of Perth had managed to organise the army into some kind of shape. In each regiment there were companies and each company had two captains, two lieutenants and two ensigns. The captain got half-a-crown a day, the lieutenant two shillings, and the ensign one-and-six. The front line of each regiment got one shilling, and the rest sixpence. All the front lines had a musket and broadsword and a pair of pistols and a target and a dirk. The rest did not necessarily have anything but a dirk. Charles had been unable to supply the arms demanded by his Lieutenant-Generals.

Before Charles marched, he was well acquainted with the situation on the enemy's side. A parliament had met on 17th October and George II had asked for immediate assistance to put down the rebellion. The Habeas Corpus Act was suspended for six months. Two days later the King's son William, Duke of Cumberland, who had been winning his spurs in Flanders, arrived back to take charge of the infantry and cavalry that shortly followed him. To Charles, in Edinburgh, it looked as though the enemy was at last bringing up its big guns and he must move fast. He had news of the extravagant demonstrations of loyalty up and down England on 30th October, the King's birthday, and of the raising of companies by private gentlemen to support him. Yet it was all on the surface. The general organisation of the Government's forces was confused and inadequate, and those in exposed areas like Carlisle were in a state of total panic, knowing perfectly well that they were being more or less left to defend themselves. Charles knew nothing of this. The unpreparedness of the enemy no longer entered his calculations. What he was banking on was his appeal to the ordinary folk and the swelling of his army as he marched south. Edinburgh seemed to have taught him nothing: few 'ordinary people' had joined. Yet others thought he had gained many supporters. Sir Andrew Mitchell wrote, furiously, 'I need not describe to you the Effects the surrender of Edinburgh and the progress the Rebels made, had upon this country. I wish I cou'd say that they were confined to the lower sort of people; but I must fairly own, that their betters were as much touched as they. The reflections were national ...' Charles could have told him it was mostly show. Those who came were brought by their masters. Who were the masters to bring them to him in England? Charles in one sense deluded himself but in another did not. Since the failure of the 1744 enterprise 'our friends in England' had earned nothing but his scorn. He had never expected them to come forward *unless he was victorious*. Now, he had made the first move; now he expected them to act as the Highland chieftains had done. But more than that, he expected a tide of popular feeling to sweep along with him. Where he got that idea is to be found in his upbringing: he had always been told that the Hanoverians were oppressors and that the people suffered, and he believed it. Nothing he had seen in Scotland convinced him that it was not true. He could see no evidence of prosperity or contentment. Once in England, support would come to the deliverer. Furthermore, once he moved south France would find it easier to fulfil the particulars of the Treaty of Fontainebleau in which Louis had at last promised help. He expected Henry to command the expedition on a grand scale that he was still sure Louis meant to mount, and indeed Henry was already in Paris waiting. He had given up with significant eagerness the daily more secluded and religious life he had been leading, and was impatient to go to war. By going into England and marching rapidly south Charles hoped to meet him.

Duncan Forbes watched, from farther north, the departure of the Jacobite army, and a great weariness overtook him. In a letter he wrote soon afterwards he confessed, 'I am mortally tired with writeing a letter to the Marquis of ane immoderate length, and in a hand so like Arabick that I doubt your help will be wanted to decipher it.' He reflected bitterly on the value to Charles of his recent successes. He had done all he could, with little help from the Government, and though Lovat assured him his efforts had quartered the numbers Charles had expected to march south with him, it was no consolation.

CHAPTER EIGHT

March Into England . . .

The route Charles took into England was a two-part one. To make it look as though he was going to Newcastle one column went via Peebles and Moffat while the main body went by Lauder and Kelso. Although successful, this ruse was thought of in London as a sign of weakness, Walpole writing, 'By their marching westward to avoid Wade it is evident that they are not strong enough to fight him.'

The Prince went with the main body, marching on foot at the head with the clans, as he had done coming down from the Highlands. On 8th November he crossed the Esk and was in England. Dr Waugh, the Chancellor of the diocese of Carlisle, who had been writing confidently two months before, 'I have no fears of his coming into Cumberland', and 'I am clear, that unless it were a few poor papists, and few we have, he would hardly get a man in the country to join him, and he has no invitations from hence I most sincerely believe', was now not so sure. In spite of his assertions that 'every method that could be contrived for saving this little city, the castle, and stores had been endeavoured', Carlisle's defence was in a poor state. But Charles did not know that. He had nobody in his army with inside information on Carlisle, as he had had on the Scottish fortresses. As far as he knew, Carlisle Castle was as impregnable as Edinburgh. It was, after all, a border town with a long history of sieges, and could therefore be assumed to be used to the kind of attack it now faced and capable of dealing with it. Charles did not know that the wall was crumbling in places, that the cannon would not work, that the place was manned by a few invalids and the local militia, and that Captain Durand, sent up by the Government to take charge, was at his wits' end. Sir George Fleming, the Bishop of Carlisle and lifelong Whig, had written on 14th September that the state of the guns was awful. They were not nailed up but 'by the carelessness of those whose business it was to take care of yᵐ, Boys had been suffered to play there, who had taken off yᵉ leather caps from yᵉ Touch Holes placed there to preserve from wett, and put the wood plugs into the sth holes, and this was all'.

November 9th was Martinmas Saturday in Carlisle. The country people thronged the town and the roads leading into it. In the middle of them, towards the end of the afternoon, appeared a party of fifty or sixty of Charles' cavalry. They were stared at with interest but aroused neither fear nor enthusiasm, except in the Castle where Captain Durand raged at the impossibility of firing on them while so many locals were about. With great coolness the men 'supposed to be officers' reconnoitred the whole town in perfect safety and then returned to the main body of the army. Up in the Cathedral tower the excited clergy kept a constant watch through a large spy-glass. The town was in total darkness that night except for one low candle in each window next to the street. The following morning there was a thick fog and the Castle fired blindly into it, hoping to stop the assault they expected. Some groups of Jacobites did appear and fire back but there was no serious engagement. Then, 'about three o'clock that afternoon, one Robinson, a countryman, who said he was compelled to come, brought in a letter directed to the Mayor from the young Pretender, setting forth that he was come to claim his father's rights, and was sorry to find the Mayor preparing to resist him; that if he was quietly admitted he promised protection to all; if not, he must use the means God had put in his hands, and could not be answerable for the consequences that must attend the town entering by force; desired him to consider this and return an answer in two hours.' No answer was sent. Instead, the messenger was detained and the Castle began firing again. An urgent entreaty was sent to Wade at Newcastle to come to their aid quickly and the town settled down to wait.

Charles was undaunted. He realised that Wade would obviously come to the city's aid and that if he could stop him coming he could yet take it. So he marched out to Brampton, a village on the way to Newcastle about ten miles from Carlisle, to meet Wade. Wade did not appear. A council of war was held, at which Lord George proposed some of the army should stay and wait for Wade while the rest returned to besiege Carlisle. To his dismay, Charles heard several chieftains propose that the entire army should go back to Scotland and agreed hastily with Lord George. So, on the 13th, seven regiments went back to Carlisle while Charles stayed at Brampton. He drafted a letter from Brampton to Barrymore, one of his supposedly firmer English supporters.

This is to acquaint you with the success we have had since our arrival in Scotland, and how far we are advanced without repulse. We are now a numerous army, and are laying siege to Carlisle this day, which we are sure cannot hold out long. After this we intend to take our routs straight to London, and if things answer to our expectations we design to be in Cheshire before the 24th inst. Then I hope you and all my friends in that county will be ready to join us. For now is the time or never.

Adieu. Charles P.R.

The letter was, unfortunately, delivered to Barrymore's son who was a Hanoverian, and it never reached him.

While Charles busied himself, Lord George turned to the besieging of Carlisle with a certain relish: it was a job after his own heart requiring a good deal of organisation and planning. As ever, his hopes of success were low, but he enjoyed displaying his ingenuity. Some tall fir trees were cut down to make scaling ladders, and on the 14th 'at day break the Rebels were perceived throwing up a small entrenchment about three hundred yards from the citadell'. This put the inhabitants in a panic, but Captain Durand assured them 'it was nothing but a poor paltry ditch, that did not deserve the name of entrenchment'. It looked convincing enough nevertheless, and had cost the Duke of Perth a good deal of sweat. Since, as usual, the Highlanders would not do manual work, he had taken his coat off himself and leapt into the ditch to shovel the earth out as an example. All this work was, however, getting the Jacobites nowhere. Everything, as they were well aware, hung on the state of arms and provisions in the Castle and the arrival of Wade.

Meanwhile, the local population had made no move either way, to Charles' intense disappointment. The only welcome he received was from Mrs Warwick of Warwick Hall. She was a daughter of Thomas Howard of Corby Castle, of a family Stuart to the core. She invited Charles to dinner on 13th November. 'She received him in the "Oak Parlour" and entertained him with such a shew of genuine affection and loyalty, that the young Prince, touched by the contrast it afforded with the cold backwardness of those from whom he probably had received invitations and promises of support, observed that these were the first christian people he had met with since he passed the border.' The Squire was not there and had no intention of allying himself with his wife's impetuous action. Nobody joined Charles, which depressed him. Nobody cheered, or even jeered. Their attitude was that of George Williamson, the curate at Arthuret Church, who during this period kept a diary in which seeing Charles rated the same number of words and the same importance as killing a hare or attending a funeral. The curate could watch bonnets with white cockades flash past through the hedges and suffer neither curiosity nor agitation. He thought the whole thing a military manoeuvre that was nothing to do with him. He stayed at home and minded his own business as did anyone else with any sense. On 14th November he had an additional reason for keeping indoors for that night it snowed and was stormy. At five in the morning Lord George was writing to his brother that Charles would have to sanction a change of plan. He wanted fifty men from each regiment in Brampton to come and take their turn with the siege. At a council held on receipt of this suggestion, it was decided not to comply with it. The reason why was not given: probably Charles did not want his force further depleted if it was to face Wade.

Lord George was livid. Everything seemed to him to be in a mess. He sat down and wrote as follows to Charles, whom he now regarded with the utmost contempt.

Sir,

I cannot but observe how little my advice, as a general officer, has any weight with your Royal Highness ever since I had the honour of a commission from your hands. I therefore take leave to give up my commission. But as I ever had a firm attachment to the Royal Family, and in particular to the King my master, I shall go on as a volunteer, and design to be this night in the trenches as such, with any others that will please to follow me, though I own I think there are full few on this post already. Your Royal Highness will please order whom you think fit to command on this post and other parts of the blockade. I have the honour to be, Sir, your Royal Highness's most faithful and humble servant,

George Murray

It was a slap in the face and Charles' reaction was understandable. Every line carried an insult. What rankled most was the unfairness of the allegation that Lord George had not had his own way when it was because of Lord George that Cope had not been followed, because of Lord George that they had marched to Carlisle and not Newcastle, because of Lord George that they had not gone in search of Wade. Charles was incensed. It seemed to him that all along the line he had followed Lord George's advice. He hated, too, the distinction made between his father and himself, as though they were not of one mind, and the pious way Lord George talked about going in the trenches. Unfortunately, when the letter was shown to the Council, nobody had any sympathy for Charles. They were not interested in the rights and wrongs of the case, but thought only of the practical implications. Lord George could not be done without – he must be begged to resume his commission. Charles was indignant and most reluctant to do this but he was left with no alternative for it was made quite plain that if Lord George was not reinstated half the army would go home.

In the middle of this explosive situation when the whole enterprise seemed endangered by a clash of personalities, Carlisle surrendered, to Lord George's amazement. Their surrender had only a little to do with the success of the siege. What had decided the inhabitants to open the gates was a letter just received from Wade telling them that he was leaving them to their own devices and hoped to meet the rebels himself in Lancashire. Pandemonium broke out, in spite of poor Captain Durand's attempts to make them stand firm. Crippled with gout he tried to rally them 'but a General Confusion ensued, numbers went over the walls, others forced their way out of the gates'. It was now only a matter of terms. Charles was not going to make the same mistake twice: city *and* castle must be surrendered. Such pressure was brought to bear on him that Durand had to agree. City and castle were duly surrendered. Two weeks later, such was the disgust felt about this surrender in London, that at the christening of George II's new grandson the centrepiece of the table was 'the citadel of Carlisle in sugar ... and the company beseiged it with sugar plums'. In Florence, Horace Mann thought it worth translating 'the Taking of Carlisle' into Italian.

Lord George, delighted though he was at this event, now had further cause for imagining he was slighted, for the surrender terms were arranged by the Duke of Perth and Murray of Broughton. He was not consulted. But now Carlisle was taken, and knowing how indispensable the rest of the army regarded Lord George, Charles was prepared to swallow hard and ask him to take back his commission. The Duke of Perth, with a sense of proportion and maturity totally lacking in Lord George, helped him further by resigning his own command and leaving the way open for Lord George's total supremacy. Only the pleasure of marching into Carlisle could overcome Charles' annoyance. In victory, bygones were allowed to become bygones but the nastiness of the episode remained.

Carlisle was Charles' first taste of England. He entered the city on the 17th and stayed there at Mr Highmore's house in the main street, until the 21st. It was no Holyrood Palace, but it was a large, spacious house with a garden behind. Charles paid twenty guineas rent for it to the owner even though 'he furnished nothing – not so much a coal or candle'; neither did it affect his appetite, for we are also informed that, 'besides this liberal payment, he had every day two dishes of meat at dinner and as many at supper for himself and his wife at the Prince's charges'. Charles was anxious that his army should behave itself now that it was in – for them – a foreign country. There had already, while at Brampton, been some shooting of sheep, and small-scale plundering which the chieftains had with difficulty stopped. It was apparently a widespread belief that the

Highlanders ate children and it needed this to be disproved before every-body relaxed. The daughter of the Bishop of Carlisle had given birth the day after the surrender, and just as the baby was about to be baptised some Highlanders appeared. Terror spread among the family's servants, and one of them ran out to beg that the baby and lady should be spared any alarm or they would both die. Captain Macdonald asked how long it was since the baby was born and when told only an hour ago he took off his cockade and said, 'Let her be christened with this cockade in her cap; it will be a protection now and after if any of our stragglers come this way; we will wait the ceremony in silence.' As a public-relations exercise, it could hardly have been bettered and had Charles' touch. Dr Waugh lost a large map of England and some wine but nothing more, even though he vacated his house the day Charles entered. Gradually, those who had fled in terror among the ordinary folk began to return when they heard nothing dreadful had happened. Charles turned to the same problem as had faced him in Edinburgh: administering the city he had taken. It was – being a very much smaller city – a much smaller problem which encouraged him to approach it more sensibly. He appointed a Governor of the Castle, Captain John Hamilton, and put in the garrison a hundred men. He also appointed a Governor of the Town, one Sir John Arbuthnot. No people of consequence came forward to assist him: they were all Whig to a man.

Charles was not so naïve as to imagine that the taking of Carlisle was so much a credit to him as a discredit to the inhabitants and there was about their surrender a puzzle which led him to expect support. He could now see for himself the poor state of the defences, but nevertheless the Castle could have been held much longer. Why was it not? It did not escape his notice that the invalids under Captain Durand were veteran soldiers who would have done what they were told. The same did not apply to the militia who, when they surrendered, were as ill-armed as many of his own army. He felt – rightly – that the militia must be held responsible for the surrender. He assumed they had been sympathetic to his cause and would now join him, having already secretly helped him by refusing to fight. Not a man came forward. The truth was that the men of the militia, hastily called together, were angry at being called at all. The last thing they wanted to do was fight. Anyone could have Carlisle so long as they got back to their farms. This was what Charles could not understand. In an area traditionally loyal to his family he had expected support. He was devastated by the total lack of it. There was no one to explain to him that since 1715 there had been thirty years of growing prosperity for this corner of England, a gift too precious to overthrow for sentimental reasons of loyalty. Loyalty to what? Charles and his father had remained alive in the Highlands through constant contact with men who came from there. They had represented a future that offered them rewards they did not enjoy under the Hanoverians. But in Cumberland no fires had been kept alight and Charles could not kindle any.

There were no balls at Carlisle. A strategic victory of importance had been gained but there was no time to be lost: the Government net must surely be closing. Not only was there Wade, snowed up in Newcastle, to contend with but the veterans of Flanders under Cumberland. Charles saw it as a race for London, where at least he had evidence of support, and a union with the French and the southern English with whom his father had so long been in correspondence. Leaving the garrison behind him, Charles marched out of Carlisle on the morning of 22nd November in full Highland kit. The curate at Arthuret noted: 'Domi-Funeral from poorhouse. Highland Army sd to be marched for Penrith and Kendal except about 200.' That was all the interest he could rouse – not even enough to put the event before the funeral. The people they left behind seemed, according to Kirkconnell, 'generally disaffected, but all expressed their sense of the great civility and amity with which they had been treated'. It was small comfort.

The army, with Charles always at its head, made excellent progress in spite of bad conditions. The good weather with which they had been blessed in Scotland – 'they have been from their first rising highly favoured with glorious weather – the season even in this month of September is more mild and comforting than it has been in June for the last half century' – had deserted them at Carlisle. Snow and ice lay thickly on the ground, and since the tents provided at Edinburgh had been left on the road from Moffat to Carlisle – an act of criminal carelessness – it was imperative that each night should find them in a village of some size so that quarters could be provided. The going was hard, through unknown country, and many deserted. All along the route over the fells people rode or walked from miles about to stare at them. Invited to join the army they declined and said they didn't know how to use guns. The fact was, the army did not inspire confidence. Elcho and his smart dragoons (getting less smart every mile) were one thing, but the 'Waliedragles' were another. They were desperate-looking characters, bearded, wearing tattered rags and given to a good deal of wild shouting. Who wanted to join them? Certainly not the cautious, dour Cumbrians.

After Penrith, the first stop, there was Shap Fell to face before Kendal was reached. At night, each officer had to billet his men as best he could.

This took so much time that when it was finished the night was often half over. There was not a minute to hold councils – everyone was much too intent on housing and feeding the men. Charles, though he kept contact with the men through marching with them, rarely saw his officers. Sheridan, O'Sullivan, Murray and Macdonald alone enjoyed his company. Strickland, whose bad influence James had worried about so much, was no longer around. He had taken ill at Carlisle and stayed there, near to where he had been born.

An unusual melancholy began to settle on Charles which was not caused by the dreadful conditions under which they were marching. He was always cheerful about physical hardship. Though his deprivation was nothing like as severe as that of his officers or men, he was never upset by the lack of bathing facilities or opportunities for changing clothes, advising Gib, his Keeper of the Household Book, to 'do as he did, never strip at all'. As they passed out of Westmorland and into Lancashire he had looked eagerly for signs, at last, of support, but none came. At Lancaster, a Government spy relished Charles' discomfiture: 'I happened to sup with the Duke of Athol ... What I observed from their discourse was that they designed to push for London with all speed, but did not themselves know the route ... their chief is about 5' 11" high, pretty strong and well built, has a brown complexion, full cheeks and thickish lips that stand out a little. He looks more of the Polish than the Scotch breed, for he is nothing like the King they call his grandfather. He looks very much dejected ... His guards were in a horrible pother at Lancaster in the night thinking they had lost him, but he was only gone for a little walk in the garden.' Even after walking all day Charles was always restless, and when the others dropped with exhaustion needed to roam about. There were no social rounds on the march. For the ladies it was agonising. All day they bumped and jolted in their coaches, often getting out at the difficult parts and trudging with the army up the hills. Charles was never anywhere near them, and their husbands were much too occupied to care.

Every day, scouts rode ahead, fanning out in all directions to a distance of many miles to try to see what the enemy was up to. Lord George had wanted to establish a thorough network of spies but Charles had said they could not afford to. The Government could. They kept close tabs on the Jacobites, reporting back every little incident that occurred and constantly re-assessing their numbers. This way, both sides had a good idea which way the armies were heading, though both tried to trick the other. As the Jacobites left Preston behind the big question became would they, after Manchester, go on to Liverpool and Wales, or would they continue south for London? Not even the Jacobites themselves knew. At Preston a council of war was held, and they halted there a day to hold it.

Since Carlisle, the Highlanders had been no happier than Charles, but they were willing to follow him, if their chieftains did. The chieftains were not nearly so keen. No fresh recruits had joined, except at Preston when Mr Townley, two other gentlemen, and a few 'common folk' had come in. Nobody had welcomed them – except now at Preston where bells were rung. Where were Charles' English friends? Charles said they still lay ahead. Preston was a beginning, small but significant. They must press on to London by the quickest route possible. Lord George for once backed him but suggested he should take a column to Liverpool and join up with them all later, but everyone considered this much too dangerous. It was agreed the whole army should press on to Manchester.

Charles was very tense. Lancashire, next to London itself, was the area he hoped most from. What happened at Manchester was going to be crucial. As if realising this, a sergeant enlisted at Preston called Dickson, together with his mistress and a drummer, went on ahead of the army and spent the day drumming up recruits. His daring aroused fury on the part of the Government supporters, but also rallied to him Stuart followers and by the time the army entered Manchester he had one hundred and eighty recruits to present to Charles. Treating Manchester as important, the Prince rode into the town wearing a light tartan plaid belted with a blue sash, a grey wig and a blue velvet bonnet. The whole of the next day, after the standard proclamation had been read, drumming for recruits went on. A few young men from local respectable families joined, but mostly the recruits were 'rough fellows'. In all, they amounted to about two hundred. They were joined with the Preston recruits and called, rather grandly, The Manchester Regiment. Charles had to pretend to be pleased, but it was a struggle. He had looked for a spontaneous rising and the arrival of a strong contingent from Wales. Not enough were inspired, as John Daniel was, by the sight of him: 'The brave prince marching on foot at their head like a Cyrus or a Trojan hero ... struck with this charming sight and seeming invitation "Leave your nets and follow me" I felt a paternal ardor pervade my veins.' Nobody could pretend that the rabble picked up in Manchester amounted to anything worth having. Again, the whispering began: why should they go further since they received no encouragement? Kirkconnell wrote: 'I have been well informed a retreat was talked of – Ld. George Murray sd they might take a further trial and go the length of Derby.'

The next stop, en route for Derby, was Macclesfield. Here, news came from the scouts that the Government force under the Duke of Cumberland was at Lichfield, determined to engage Charles before he got any nearer London. A council of war was held, where it was determined, apparently unanimously, to get past the Duke. Lord George led a feint similar to the one used from Edinburgh, while the rest of the army went straight ahead. Misled, Cumberland fell back, and Lord George joined up with the main body. On the evening of 4th December Charles entered Derby and heard the next day that not only was Cumberland near but Wade had at last struggled to Wetherby and the militia awaited him at Finchley. Battle was inevitable, with one of the three. What was feared was that Wade and Cumberland would effectively corner them and fall upon them. Wade was known to have about three thousand men; Cumberland, more exactly, to have 2,200 horse and 8,250 foot. Their own army was now reduced to not much over four thousand.

Derby, the town he now entered, was not far from the centre of England, described seventeen years later as 'a rich and populous Town, delightfully situated on the Brink of the River DAREWENT, which is lately made navigable into the Trent'. Its population was around the six thousand mark which for the times made it a sizeable town and not the village it would now be rated. In sympathy, Derby was thought to be Jacobite. Hostile demonstrations had taken place there on the accession of the Elector of Hanover, though later, in the '15, Derby had hardly figured. Nevertheless, Butler, in his report to Louis XV in 1744, had reported that the town and county would be favourable to the cause. His forecast was optimistic: on 28th September 1745 a meeting was held at the George Inn 'to consider of such measures as are fit to be taken for the support of the Royal Person and Government of His Majesty King George, and our happy constitution in Church and State, at a time when Rebellion is carrying on in favour of a Popish Pretender'. It was largely attended, and 'a considerable sum' was promised by 'the greatest appearance of Gentlemen ever seen here, who having entered into an Association, cheerfully signed the same'. The formation of the Derbyshire Blues for the defence of the town looked like a spirited resistance, but on the approach of the rebels the army melted away and no battle was offered.

Charles' army began to enter, peacefully, at 11 o'clock on the morning of 4th December and throughout the day the cavalry clattered in, followed by the clansmen. These aroused astonishment and derision. 'Most of their main body are a parcel of shabby, lousy, pitiful looking fellows, mixed up with old men and boys; dressed in dirty plaids, and as dirty shirts, without breeches and wore their stockings made of plaid, not much above half-way up their legs, and some without shoes or next to none, and numbers of them so fatigued with their long march that they commanded our pity rather than our fear.' Another observer wrote: 'the Hole of men and Cannon near the Poorest That Ever Was Seen to pass through a Countrey, Men Women and children Did not Amount to 8,000 to the Utmost and scarce 2,000 fit to face a good Army, poorly armed for Genneral part; Sum shoes, sum nighter shoe or stocken.' What the spies missed, or chose not to report, was the high morale of this rabble (which contrasted so sharply with the depression of their commanders). Hardly were the men settled in Derby than many reached for a pen and wrote enthusiastically of their situation and prospects. One Alexander Blair wrote: 'The 3rd we came to Ashbourne, and on the 4th arrived here in Derby. At every town we were received with ringing of Bells, and at Night we have Bone fires and Illuminations ... our whole Army is in top spirits and we trust in God to make a good Account of them [the enemy].' Peter Ouchterlony wrote to his wife Jeanie equally jubilant: 'Wee arrived here last night amidst the acclamations of the people, and public rejoicings which wee have had in severall places.' Other writers talk of being in 'the greatest spirits' and welcome both the challenge of Wade and Cumberland and the nearness of London.

Charles felt more cheerful. He wanted a battle. The Highlanders, out in the streets of Derby sharpening their dirks and swords, wanted one too. Only the officers recoiled from the idea, particularly Lord George. A battle now would mean a massacre, for which he was not prepared to accept the responsibility. No man of any sense would wilfully take on such numbers. He regarded Charles as someone indulged enough: he had been given enough rope and was now going to hang himself and everyone else with him. Lord George could not allow it. He decided the only sensible thing to do was to retreat while there was still time, withdraw to Scotland and think again when they got there. Anything else was sheer madness. Charles must be told. The snag was, how? Lord George did not want to request the summoning of a council. If he did, it would give rise to speculation and he wanted to avoid that. The retreat must be made quietly and calmly and without the men knowing for as long as possible. The daily council meetings had lapsed since the march in England began.

Lord George decided to tackle Charles on his own. On the morning of 5th December he left his quarters and walked round to Exeter House in Full Street where Charles was lodged. He practically collided with Charles, who had just put on his bonnet and was going out. Abruptly, Lord George stopped on the steps, grasped Charles by the shoulder and

snapped, 'It is high time to think about what we are to do.' Charles stared
and said, 'What do you mean? I thought it was resolved to march on?'
Curtly, Lord George disillusioned him. The decision to march on had
always been a temporary one. The news that had come in that morning
had changed everything. A council must be called at once including
commanders of battalions and squadrons as well as regular councillors.
Hustling Charles back into the house, Lord George set about herding
together as many people as could be obtained at such short notice.

They all sat in the long first-floor drawing-room, 'wainscotted with
ancient oak, very dark and handsome', overlooking the garden on that
cold winter's morning, many more asleep than awake. Outside, the shouts
and yells of the Highlanders could be heard as they argued the coming
battle. Inside, it was quiet. Charles spoke first. He tried to make what he
had to say as matter of fact as possible, beginning by a reference to the
next day's march towards London. He paused. Nobody spoke. Encouraged, he continued to act as though he was giving a briefing and went on to
describe what he thought the order of the march should be and who should
lead. He paused again. Still no objections. Then, as though he had deliberately let the silence continue to get the maximum possible effect, Lord
George spoke. He said, very clearly, that perhaps they ought first to
discuss whether it was 'prudent to advance further' at all. Charles turned
to the others, speechless. Suddenly, everyone began to talk at once, now
that Lord George had opened the floodgates that had penned up all their
fears. An advance, they said, would be most dangerous because there had
been no English rising – far from it – and no French landing that they
knew of. How could they continue without support – support Charles
had promised would be forthcoming. They were a long way from home,
among enemies, their numbers thinning daily with desertions and illness,
what chance did they stand now?

Lord George let them rant on, each repeating more or less what the
others had said. Only when they had all finished did he take charge. He
was a fluent speaker, who never attempted a speech without mastering
all his facts beforehand. In manner, he was straightforward, solid, sometimes ponderous, whatever the dramatic nature of his content. He began by
saying nobody wished to see a Restoration as much as he, nor was anyone
more willing to do his best toward that end. But, he said, if they marched
on there never would be a Restoration. Cumberland would tear them to
pieces; if they escaped this fate, Wade would fall upon them; if they
escaped, or beat, Wade, then the militia at Finchley was still to be reckoned
with. Even supposing all the enemy was beaten, they would arrive in the
capital bedraggled and exhausted and cut a poor figure. What was needed

was a safe and quick retreat while this was still a matter of choice. A safe and honourable retreat was often preferable to victory, for the one is the effect of skill and the other of mere chance. Modestly, he said he did not profess to much skill but he guaranteed that he could get the army safely back to Carlisle. Once there, there might be news of a French landing. He ended by saying that if anyone had better advice he would willingly follow it.

Charles was not the kind of person who could effectively argue with a man like Lord George Murray. In fact, Lord George's argument was full of holes and taken point by point could at least have been contested. He had on his side, it was true, two inescapable truths that Charles could not get away from – the lack of English support so far and the presence of an enemy army vastly superior in numbers. But nevertheless Charles could have made a case for advancing – indeed, he badly wanted to be as ruthlessly logical as Lord George. The trouble was that his response to Lord George's speech was so emotional that he was incapable of speaking coherently at all. Elcho says he swore and abused his officers, that swords were drawn and voices raised in passion. So far from being persuasive, Charles could only fly into a rage at what he considered a betrayal. He made some attempt to put forward the view that to retreat would be as dangerous as to advance but could not keep his temper enough to convince anyone. He hated Lord George's attitude so deeply that he could hardly bear to be in the same room. The basic difference between them was now revealed for all to see – if ever they had been in any doubt. Charles was a gambler, Lord George was not. Charles was an optimist, Lord George a pessimist. With Lord George at hand, Charles would not have sailed in the first place – it was not sensible. Charles relied on intuition, which Lord George regarded with contempt. He *felt* it was right to go on. Lord George did not go in for feelings. Reason was all that was on his side.

It was at this point that Charles ought to have made his decision: he ought to have walked out, appealed to the men and marched on, leaving Lord George and the rest of his council to follow or go home. The consequences of such a step are irrelevant: as far as Charles and his whole future was concerned it was essential. He did not take it. From that point on he disintegrated as a man. Not to have the courage of his conviction was fatal. It showed he was no leader. Instead, he said – as he had said before – that he would abide by the majority decision, and when this was unanimously in favour of retreat he had no alternative. As usual, he said he still thought he was right but he would do what they wanted. In the state he was in, he could not resist saying that this was the last council he would ever hold and in future he would be beholden only to his father.

He dismissed them, all agreeing before they left that no one should be told of what had been decided.

Charles, left to himself, passed from despair to resentment. It seemed to him that the whole enterprise was in jeopardy through a lack of faith. What could he do to restore this faith? He needed to produce some evidence that marching on London was worthwhile, that large numbers would rise once they were farther south. He needed to prove that France, once he was in the capital, would act. This was exactly what he could not do. In spite of James' anxious twittering in the Stuart papers about 'the English correspondence' Charles had no names to cite in his support. He could not even convey the current mood in London to the chieftains because he did not know it. Horace Walpole might be writing 'there never was so melancholy town … Nobody but has some fear for themselves, for their money, or for their friends in the army … I still fear the rebels beyond my reason' – but Charles could not use it. He sat and fretted at the non-appearance of men he had been sure would rise if he gave them the chance. Where was James Barry, Earl of Barrymore; the Duke of Beaufort, of whom, back in March, the ever watchful Horace had written 'a most determind and unwavering Jacobite'; Sir John Hynde Cotton; Sir Watkin Williams Wynn – all men who lived in the surrounding counties of Cheshire, Shropshire and Denbigh. Messages had been sent to them but none had been sent back. Charles – always ready to provide excuses – believed that they had not had time to join him. Even to himself he had to admit it was a poor argument: he had been marching south since he left Edinburgh on 30th October and they could not be ignorant of that. He turned, therefore, to another excuse – these men needed him either to win a battle or to take London, and then, like Prestonpans and Edinburgh, the magic would work. If he retreated, they would never rise. No matter which words Lord George wrapped it up in, retreat would look like defeat. At all costs they must never turn back, no matter what he had agreed to. He could only cling to the belief that the English Jacobites were waiting their moment and it had not yet come. That moment had always been elusive. In October, when Charles' fortunes had been at their height, a Mr Moor could write to Balhaldy in Paris that Watkin Williams 'ordered me to assure you, as many of *the King's friends in England* as possible could, would *join the Prince* when *he* gave them an opportunity'. What had happened to him?

It seemed to Charles that he had made a great mistake holding a council. He should have dealt with Lord George himself and seen all the officers separately. Lord George should never have been given an opportunity to sway the others. Naturally, Charles did not keep all these turbulent thoughts to himself – he used Sheridan, O'Sullivan and Broughton, the old gang, as confidants. Although they had voted with the majority they were now prepared to go back on what they had said. Encouraged, Charles decided to try interviewing other members of the council, but they were not as craven. He could not get them – embarrassed though they were – publicly to support him. Dejected, he had to give up. He spent a wretched night, uninterested in preparations for the retreat. The whole thing was unbearable and he could see no sense in it. It was little comfort to know that the men would share his horror. He was tormented by the significance the world would put on his retreat – and rightly so. Again and again he came back to that glorious death as the worst that could happen. What was an ignoble life beside that? How could anyone care to live with the shame?

Lord George could, for one. As Charles' spirits sank to the very depths, he was almost cheerful for the first time. While around him the town seethed with rumours, he sat down to plan the most difficult task ever entrusted to him. He knew, as well as Charles, the reaction of the men: it would be violent. Retreat must be concealed from them as long as possible. Since none of them knew the country and none had maps it would be possible to delude them into thinking they were advancing for a good long time, although he planned to take exactly the same route back and re-occupy exactly the same quarters to save time. Once the news broke, they would rage, therefore it was important to keep them tightly together, moving rapidly, with no time to think. As a morale-booster he had never needed Charles more to march on foot and keep the men happy. But Charles had given all that up. Bitterly, he intended to hold Lord George to his promise to see the army safely back. He could get on with it. He himself would ride and have nothing to do with it: let Lord George take the odium. It was understandable, but childish. Charles never understood what *agreeing* meant, never entered into the spirit as well as holding to the letter of anything unpleasant he had agreed to.

CHAPTER NINE

... And Back to Scotland

December 6th was a Friday, Black Friday. Lord George was up early organising the evacuation of the town. The men were in high spirits, sure that this was the day of another Prestonpans. There was no difficulty getting them moving. A circuitous route was taken out of the town and it was not until the men were well on the way back that they began to recognise places they had passed before and to register their anger. Then the officers rode up and down keeping them going. Charles was nowhere to be seen. Explanations were avoided – the men were told to keep marching. Their mood was predictable – the whole army was affected by an air of gloom. The first night was spent at Ashburne and already the difference in the Highlanders' behaviour had made itself felt. A party of them visited Okeover, ransacked the cellars and took away the horses, terrifying the inhabitants, one of whom wrote later: 'We have had a dreadful time ye last week; upon Tuesday night we had five lay with us, and upon Friday night as they returned from Derby four lay with us and about Seven a clock came six Horsemen and said they wanted Armour and plunder'd ye House and Stables and Barns and ye church ... upon Saturday morning after they was gone came Three Ruffians and said they wanted money ... they kill'd none of us but threatened us much.'

It was the same story all the way back. The men wanted their revenge somehow, and in addition were provoked by the locals who now, instead of just staring, came out of their houses and threw things at them. Keeping discipline in such circumstances was almost impossible – it was only the extreme speed of the retreat that prevented a mutiny. Back they went, at the double, through Leek and Macclesfield, Manchester and Wigan. They were booed and hissed and jeered at and no one saw any of Lord George's honeyed words like 'honourable' in their retreat. At night, they could not always do anything so simple as re-occupy their previous quarters for the inhabitants now had the courage to deny them entry. They had to buy food at even more exorbitant prices than on the way down or get nothing. As Horace Walpole wrote, jubilant, 'we dread them no longer' – and once dread was removed they were treated by the populace with contempt.

Charles kept out of the way because he could not bear to acknowledge the truth of the retreat, but he was wise to do so. He behaved in a disgraceful fashion but saved his own image in front of his men. They somehow did not associate him with this disgrace because they did not see him, so that later he could emerge apparently untainted. He relished Lord George's difficulties, doubtless seized with a desire to say 'I told you so'. It took him at least three days to readjust to what had happened, and once he had he immediately moved on to wanting a battle even on retreat. He longed for Cumberland or Wade to chase him so that he could turn and fight and defeat them and the whole retreat would then look like a clever trick. While Lord George hurried on, Charles was all for taking his time: nobody must be able to say he was running before the enemy. At Preston, he forced a halt and began agitating for a stand to be made and Cumberland fought. The men needed a halt but Lord George was determined it should be as short as possible: one day. Charles announced, defiantly, that 'he was resolved to retire no further till he met them and then march to London, be the consequences what they would'. The Duke of Perth was dispatched to Scotland to bring up reinforcements. Lord George did not interfere. Perth would be back before long, he was sure, and Charles would move on because those nearest him would want to save their own skins. Reluctantly, Charles was persuaded to move on by O'Sullivan. They moved to Lancaster. Here, to Lord George's consternation, another halt was called. Cumberland was reported to be very close behind. Charles was the only one pleased: he sent an officer to reconnoitre the surrounding countryside to see if there was a suitable battlefield and when he returned he made O'Sullivan and Lord George both go to inspect the pitch. Tired and angry Lord George dismissed it as useless. As they left the town, Charles still protesting, he said, 'As Your Royal Highness is always for battles be the circumstances what they may. I now offer you one three hours from this time with the army of Wade which is only about three miles behind us.' Charles did not reply.

Without knowing that Wade had been outmarched and that he was pursued by only a swift body of cavalry, Lord George faced the long haul up Shap Fell. Knowing the problem ahead, he had asked for light two-wheeled ammunition carts to replace the four-wheeled heavier variety, but none had been forthcoming. The supplying of them should have been O'Sullivan's job, but O'Sullivan was too busy keeping Charles' spirits up. Lord George knew Charles had a phobia about his equipment and that if any was lost there would be hell to pay, so he prepared to do his best. As they left Kendal and faced Shap the rain fell heavily. The carts stuck, streams swelled to rivers and could not be crossed, and the entire army spent most of the day up to their middles in water. By nightfall they were nowhere near a village. Lord George luckily remembered there was a farm a mile or so off the road, and here the rear of the army camped in the 'barns, byres and stables'. It was fortunate that they were used to wet and cold, and had many times wrapped themselves in their plaids and slept on the hillsides. 'The wet, they say, keeps them warm by thickening the stuff, and keeping the wind from penetrating ... they have been accustomed from their infancy to be often wet, and to take the water like spaniels.' Showing a good deal of enterprise Lord George borrowed some farm carts and transferred the heavier stuff to these. The men had cheered up and faced the inevitable. They worked with a will, without complaining, and he was proud of them. It rankled all the more to have a message sent back from Charles 'not to leave, upon any account, the least thing, not so much as a cannon ball; for he would rather return himself than there should be anything left'. Lord George was determined that he would do just that. He 'got the men to carry to Shap a good many cannon balls ... I gave sixpence the piece for the doing it, by which means I got above two hundred carried'. The money came out of his own pocket. He knew he was making this mammoth effort to carry goods that were in many cases of doubtful value: some of the powder in the barrels was wet and useless; two casks marked 'ammunition' turned out to contain stale biscuit. When, after a gruelling day, they arrived at Shap village it was to find Charles and the advance party had eaten everything in sight. Ever provident, Lord George had bought cheese at the farm where they had spent the previous night. This they cut into rounds and toasted on the points of their claymores and put between hunks of stale bread.

The worst was now over, in terms of physical hardship. Ahead lay the plain of the Eden with Carlisle two days' march. But the pursuers were catching up, and naturally they caught up with Lord George and the baggage first. Hardly had they started to move out of Shap village before horsemen were spotted silhouetted against the sky. Without any bidding, half the Glengarry regiment deserted the precious carts they were lugging along and ran up the hill yelling battle-cries. The horsemen promptly disappeared. A careful watch was kept all day but though horsemen occasionally reappeared no attack was made. By nightfall they were at Clifton, near Penrith. Lord George sent a message to Charles asking for reinforcements as attack was imminent and without them he and the baggage train would be cut to pieces. Charles replied, as he had done once before, that none could be spared. All speed must be made to Carlisle. Lord George decided to ignore the message and take his own reinforcements. It was as well he did – that night there was a skirmish with Cumberland's cavalry and thanks to Cluny Macpherson and the narrowness of the roads they were effectively dealt with. Next morning, the victors entered Penrith revitalised. They had bought valuable time by beating off the pursuers. Charles was pleased with them and said so. Lord George said he and his men would follow later as 'some of them have need for refreshment'. He always knew how to drive a point home in a way Charles found unbearably self-righteous.

Carlisle awaited a second visit without the trepidation that had attended the first. Hamilton, the Governor appointed by Charles, had held the Castle in spite of a plot by some townsmen to recapture it. There were frequent fights between locals and the garrison but the violence that continually threatened did not break out into anything serious. Sir John Arbuthnot made a good job of governing the town and actually made friends with the few inhabitants of standing who had not fled. Once the news of the retreat came, measures were taken to prepare for the returning army – prices were fixed on all commodities, supplies laid in, the post stopped and so forth. On 2nd December there had been a bit of excitement – 'our strangers today fired the cannons and rejoiced they say upon the landing of 10,000 French in Scotland' – but since then nothing but apprehension that the army would be defeated before it got back to Carlisle.

The curate at Arthuret recorded that on the evening of 18th December it was stormy and that on the 19th 'the whole Hgd Army came into Carlisle. An Account of a skirmish beyond Penrith.' On the 20th he stayed at home all day because 'the whole of ye Hgd army (except 700 to be left in Carlisle) passed by here'. Between the two entries was a drama almost equal to Derby. Lord George had assumed Carlisle would be evacuated – the Castle blown up, walls knocked down, gates smashed in, then a quick hop into Scotland. He had been as good as his word and brought the army safely to the border city, a distance of two hundred and forty miles, with only forty men lost: now they were almost home. Surely Charles did not intend to sacrifice them all in the defence of a city they had themselves discovered virtually defenceless? In fact, Charles did not intend any such thing – he had something much more suicidal in mind. He was about to make one of the few independent decisions he had ever made in the course of the campaign, with the merit of being perhaps the only truly senseless one. His plan was to leave a small garrison in

Carlisle to defend the city and hold it for him to return to when he had joined up with reinforcements in Scotland. Lord George was stunned. What possible justification could Charles have? Kirkconnell says his aim was to 'facilitate his entry into the kingdom' again. If that was the aim, Charles had no need of Carlisle: he had the whole border to choose from. He knew how close Cumberland was, he knew how long it would take him to get to Scotland and return, he knew how easy Carlisle was to take. He was depending on the bravery of the men he left behind and in doing so placed upon them a monstrous and unfair burden. The truth was, his pride would not allow him to leave England without something to show for it. Carlisle, his one English victory, was important for prestige reasons and nothing else.

Charles received support for his scheme only from O'Sullivan, who saw nothing wrong with it. His main idea seems to have been to have somewhere safe to run if they found it impossible to get back into Scotland either through unfordable rivers or some military manœuvre on Cumberland's part. He asserted that it was 'better to sacrifice a party than the whole' which rather made nonsense of his later statement that 'Cumberland could not take the castle'. The delicate question of who was to be of 'the party' was more easily resolved than one would have imagined. Lord George, while stating it was certain death, offered to remain. Charles would not let him. Not only did Lord George's spirit of self-sacrifice grate on his nerves but he could not afford to lose a key man. But when Mr Townley, Colonel of the Manchester Regiment, volunteered, Charles accepted his offer. He was appointed Governor of the City. Hamilton expressed himself willing to remain at his post as Governor of the Castle which, since he knew its condition, was heroism of the first order. The bulk of the Manchester Regiment stayed too – more because they feared going into Scotland than anything else. They had joined an army marching south, not north. To this number was added two hundred and seventy Highlanders, four French officers and a few privates of Lally's regiment. Only the French were reasonably happy, knowing that as prisoners they could not be executed. While Lord George waited with the rest of the army on the north side of Stanwix bridge that spanned the Eden, Charles had the volunteers drawn up to receive his farewell words. 'He thanked them for what they had done and suffered in his cause, and cheered them with assurances of his speedy return with augmented forces to relieve them before the enemy could reduce the place. He then bade them adieu ...'

Charles set off in better spirits than he had been in since Derby. At Carlisle he had received dispatches of a very optimistic nature from Lord John Drummond and Lord Strathallan about the forces they had collected.

Lord John had actually set sail from France in mid-November in a twenty-six-gun frigate, accompanied by two others and five Dunkirk privateers, but one was captured off Deal and another two wrecked. Nevertheless, the news he had set out with, and now communicated to Charles a month later, was more than sufficient to justify Charles' raised spirits. Maurepas had expressed the feeling then prevalent in France when he wrote (on 10th December), 'Here we are at last on the eve of a mighty event. We have completed at Dunkirk and neighbouring ports all the necessary preparations for the embarkation of twelve thousand men commanded by the Duc de Richlieu. I have taken very great care over my part in all this; if all goes well with what lies to others to do, the disembarkation [in England] could take place before this month is out.' The news of Derby changed all that, but Charles, as he prepared to re-enter Scotland, did not know it. He was buoyant because the French at last seemed to be behind him: too late. It even looked as though a retreat might not have been disastrous since Lord John told him that Louis was particularly anxious that he should avoid decisive action till help he was sending arrived.

According to the English calendar, 20th December was Charles' birthday. He had never spent one in a more bizarre fashion. Once out of Carlisle the problem was how to cross the Esk, which was in full flood and stated by several Carlisle correspondents to be impossible for the rebels to pass. They had not reckoned with the strength and courage of this army they despised as a rabble. There was hardly a man in it who had not crossed more uncrossable rivers than these writers had had hot dinners. Lord George cherished the memory: 'We were a hundred men abreast, and it was a very fine shew: the water was big, and took most of the men breast high. When I was near cross the river, I believe there were two thousand men in the water at once.' They went into the rushing, freezing torrent in long lines, holding each other's coats at the neck, forming a solid, moving barrier against the tremendous pressure of the current. When one part of the line lost its footing the other held theirs and pulled the rest to safety. The women went in the same as the men, half dead with fright, and their screams rose above the noise of the water. A few were swept away, but not more than six or seven. Once on the other side, they lit fires – a long struggle with wet wood – and then the pipers played and everyone danced round to get dry, and to celebrate both their return to Scotland and Charles' twenty-fifth birthday. He was among them again, cheering them and chatting to them and telling them how well they had done. Lord George had a cold, and could think only of the hot oatmeal bath he was going to take the minute it could be arranged.

In England, there were sighs of relief all round. While nobody doubted there would be more trouble – 'they are mostly got safe back to Scotland, and may do much mischief before any army of the King's can now over-take them. They will be able, I fear, soon to join their companions, and God only knows what will be the consequences' – they felt for the moment happier now that 'the rebels have dribbled back to Scotland' – which, as John Forbes in London commented acidly in a letter to his father, 'to the generality here is the same as Norway'. They also believed they would not come back into England again and nobody minded a war as far away as Scotland. 'Into England I scarce believe the Highlanders will be drawn again: to have come as far as Derby – to have found no rising in their favour, and to find themselves not strong enough to fight either army will make lasting impressions!' Still nobody was taking any chances. On 20th December, the day Charles went back to Scotland, the House of Commons divided 190 to 44 in favour of 'all the troops we can get' in spite of the remonstrances of 'Pitt and that clan' against the use of foreign troops. There was a general feeling that backs were no longer to the wall, that they had been incredibly lucky, but that they had still better watch out, particularly if a French invasion materialised.

Charles had hardly expected the situation in Scotland to have remained the same, but he was dismayed as he marched to Glasgow via Annan and Dumfries to discover from news that came to him of the extent of the changes. For a start, Edinburgh was retaken. Only a few days after Charles had marched out, Lieutenant-General Roger Handasyde had marched up from Berwick and retaken it without any trouble. Farther north, Lord Loudon, commanding the forces raised by the indefatigable efforts of Duncan Forbes, held Inverness and stiffened resistance there to the rebels. Forbes, who himself had never stopped trying to rally support for the Government, thought Loudon worth his weight in gold. At sea, the Navy under Rear-Admiral Byng were doing a magnificent job gradually tightening a cordon that French ships of any size found difficult to break. Forbes might fret that the Government still hadn't done any-thing, but the fact was that the opposition to Charles in Scotland was in a much better state to defend itself than it had been in November. Charles could not come back and take over where he had left off and his temper suffered as he began to realise this. It was not improved by his reception along the route he took to Glasgow. The whole of the south-west of Scotland was solidly Presbyterian and anti-Charles as much for economic as religious reasons. On his way down, Dumfries had already been forced to pay a contribution as punishment for not sending men to join the Prince's army and now it awaited, like its big sister Glasgow, the arrival of his returning army with great fear. There were no attempts to cheer Charles. Those who did turn out to watch him stood sullen and silent. Charles ordered them to pay a fine of £2,000 and to give a thousand pairs of shoes. Only £1,100 was raised so he took two hostages as security for the rest. The whole experience upset him deeply. Even in England there had not been such open hatred.

Worse awaited him at Glasgow, where he arrived on 26th December to meet up with Lord George Murray and the rest of the army who had arrived the day before by a different route. It was a very different town then to what it is today, arousing more admiration than Edinburgh in visitors: 'Glasgow is, to outward appearance, the prettiest and most uniform town that I ever saw; and I believe there is nothing like it in Britain. It has a spacious "carrifour", where stands the cross; and going round it, you have, by turns the view of four streets that in regular angles proceed from thence. The houses of these streets are faced with Ashler stone, they are well sashed, all of one model, and piazzas run through them on either side, which give a good air to the buildings.'

Glasgow's attitude to Charles had been clearly expressed in a letter from the Provost as early as September when Charles had sent a demand for contributions. He wrote: 'We were yesterday very uneasie about our mob, from whom we are in more danger than from the Highlanders army; and their madness was such there was great fear of their falling upon the Commissioners that were sent to treat with us about our contributions ... I'le make half a dozen drunk Tradesmen putt us in greater fear by raising our common people than as many expresses from the enemy would.' When Charles upped his demand to £15,000 the Provost wrote 'We are all mad at the proposal' but the threat on the part of loyal citizens to 'go to arms as we can' was not kept. The Provost explained: 'You would have thought we were determind to make a stand at all events and in consequence of it, I and many others were sent out, to bring intelligence of the enemy and to desire the country to come in with what arms they had. I did not return till eleven this morning, and then found all over.' Charles had moved on to Edinburgh, satisfied with a proportion of the money demanded.

Now, in December, Glasgow trembled again. It was in the middle of a boom that looked like having no end and no one wanted their prosperity interfered with. Charles had nothing whatsoever to offer them. Since the Union with England its population had doubled and its trade multiplied beyond all expectations. The city was determined to keep its wealth intact. On Christmas Day, a messenger came into the city to say that

Charles was at Hamilton enjoying a day's hunting and demanded clothes and money 'under pain of military execution'. The next day, when Charles himself entered, no resistance was offered to him: the spirit that had been there in September had apparently now disappeared. Only the Provost showed any courage, staunchly refusing to name those people who had subscribed against Charles in the autumn. While he waited for the magistrates to furnish twelve thousand shirts, six thousand coats, six thousand pairs of stockings and brogues, Charles settled into a house in the Trongate where he lived in some state. The anger that he had felt since Dumfries at the coldness of his reception provoked him into a display of grandeur. He was out both to show how successful he was being and that he couldn't care less what his detractors thought of him. He put into this performance all his enthusiasm and energy. Every day he dressed with great care, dined in public, went to balls and made himself affable to everyone. The citizens of Edinburgh were never given such a treat. The citizens of Glasgow hardly appreciated it – they were determined to remain aloof. A few Jacobite ladies like Clementina Walkinshaw, niece of the Sir Hugh Paterson of Bannockburn with whom Charles had already stayed, waited on him at table, but the rest satisfied themselves with a look and then made a point of saying they did not know what all the fuss was about since he wasn't even handsome.

On 30th December Charles took the unprecedented step of reviewing his entire army on Glasgow Green. Not all of them were present, many slipping off home with their new clothes. Some of the Irish officers had suggested that as this was bound to happen the new equipment should be withheld until they were ready to march, but for once Lord George and Charles were in agreement (on humanitarian matters they usually were). Many of the Highlanders had marched without shoes through the snow and frost for weeks. Their clothes, little better than rags in the first place, had disintegrated, leaving them exposed to the wind and rain. 'If good usuage would not keep them nothing would,' said Lord George, 'and those who were determined to go home would not be kept for so small matters.' So the numbers that stood to be inspected were sadly depleted – they were easily outnumbered by the crowd who had come to watch. Maxwell of Kirkconnell said Charles did it 'to let the world see with what a handful of men he had penetrated so far into England, and returned almost without any loss'.

The loss was greater than he knew. Shortly after Charles disbanded his men to await orders to march, he received news of the taking of Carlisle by the Duke of Cumberland with all its gory details. Two men had escaped over the wall to bring him the sad story. The garrison he left behind had more than done its duty, moving Horace Walpole to comment acidly, 'The Duke has taken Carlisle, but was long enough before it to prove how basely or cowardly it was yielded to the rebels.' The Duke was annoyed to find that it did take him so long to reduce what he termed on first inspection 'an old hencoop'. Hamilton had done his best to fortify the castle, strengthening the ramparts at their weakest places with sand-bags and earth works, but he knew that he could not protect himself from heavy cannon. The Duke arrived outside Carlisle on 21st December. From then until the 30th when the heavy cannon arrived from White-haven, Hamilton bombarded the troops with everything he had to stop them setting up batteries. Finally, he hung out the white flag before the big guns could be brought into play: he had done his best, there was no need for senseless slaughter. Charles heard all this with pride, and no apparent guilt. What distressed him most was his counterpart's ungentle-manly behaviour. The Duke had sent a message back to Hamilton: 'All the terms his R. Highness will or can grant to the rebel garrison of Carlisle, are, that they shall not be put to the sword, but reserved for the King's pleasure.' Their fate was a foregone conclusion.

There was no point in crying over spilt milk. Charles had now to decide what he was going to do. His original intention had been to head back to England as soon as possible when he had been joined by Lord John Drummond and Lord Strathallan with the fresh forces they had managed to raise. These were centred at Perth, the other side of Scotland. It annoyed Charles that this new army had not already joined up with him as he had expected, but they, for their part, had not known where to join him. He now decided not to march straight back to England, nor to try to retake Edinburgh, but to lay siege to Stirling Castle. It seemed to him that if he took Stirling Castle he could dominate Scotland and move on from there in a position of strength. If he could then, with his new forces, take Edinburgh Castle too his march into England for the second time would take on a new aspect. He therefore sent orders to Perth that the new forces were to join up at Stirling. On 4th January the army marched out of Glasgow in two columns to meet them there.

Charles had taken this decision either on his own or in consultation with O'Sullivan, Sheridan and Murray of Broughton. There had been no council. Once, a mere few weeks before, he would have been careful to find out the decision of the majority, anxious to hear everyone's opinion, eager to respect those with superior knowledge. Now, he apparently did not care. He was keeping his threat to take orders from none but his father. Lord George obeyed the order to march towards Stirling, but with a bad grace. At Carlisle, he had stood aside while Charles made up his own mind. At Glasgow, he had done it again. He was not prepared to let this state of affairs continue, because the decisions Charles was making were stupid ones. No council would have agreed to leave a garrison at Carlisle; no council would have agreed to lay siege to Stirling Castle. All the way from Derby Lord George had been struggling with his conscience: was he going to carry out bad orders simply because Charles was his Prince, or was he going to see the issue as a greater one and depose Charles for his own good? Lord George could never mutiny – it was not his way. Nor could he desert. All he could do was go through legal channels to force Charles to do what he thought should be done. So, on 6th January, three days after they had left Glasgow, Lord George drew up an official Memorial requesting another council meeting at which an executive committee would be appointed to take major decisions jointly. Like all Lord George's missives, it was couched in strong language – he could never resist the temptation to be sanctimonious, to drag up old issues and point out how right he had been. He could never forget the past and make suggestions for the future without references to previous mistakes.

It is proposed that His Royal Highness shou'd from time to time call a Council of War to consist of all those who command Battalions or Squadrons; but as severals of those may be on partys, and often absent, a Committee should be chosen by those Commanders, to consist of five or seven, and that all Operations for the carrying on the War shou'd be agreed on, by the Majority of those in His Royal Highness presence, and once that a Measure is taken, it is not to be changed except by the advice of those, or most of them, who were present when it was agreed on.

That upon any sudden Emergency such as in a Battle, Skirmish, or in a Siege, a Discretionary power must be allowed to those who command. This is the Method of all Armys, and where so many Gentlemen of Fortune, not only venture their own and their Familys All, But if any Misfortune happen are sure of ending their lives on a Scaffold should they escape in the field, if this plan is not followed the most Dismal Consequence cannot but ensue.

Had not a Council determined the Retreat from Derby, what a Catastrophy must have followed in two or three Days! Had a Council of War been held the Army came to Lancaster, a Day (which at that time was so precious) had not been lost. Had a Council of War been consulted as to the leaving a Garrison at Carlisle it would never have been agreed to, the place not being tenable, and so many brave men wou'd not have been sacrifized, besides the reputation of his Royal Highness Arms.

It is to be considered that this Army is an Army of Volunteers, and not Mercenarys, many of them being resolved not to continue in the Army, were affairs once settled.   GEORGE MURRAY.

Charles was, at the time of receiving this document, in bed with a cold and fever at the house of his old host Sir Hugh Paterson of Bannockburn. It was the first time his constitution had shown any signs of cracking under the strain of repeated soakings and exposure to intense cold. He was impatient with his own weakness at such a time but could do nothing except rest and hope he would recover quickly. It was not exactly a good time to be presented with Lord George's ultimatum and Charles reacted predictably. His rage at what he thought of as insolence and insubordination drove him to get out of bed and write a reply straight away. Into this reply went all the frustration he had been feeling up to now. Lord George, he said, wanted to dictate to him: he would not be dictated to. He would take advice – he had always been pleased to take it, he maintained – but he would not have his authority usurped. He agreed his army consisted of volunteers but far from giving them the right to decide their own fate it ought to make them behave with 'better manners'. He would not call a council, he would not appoint a committee. Lord George could like it or lump it. It was the first positive stand Charles had taken as far as his relationship with his commander went. The change that had come over him was a sign of the new recklessness that was appearing. He had always been reckless in the sense that he took unjustified chances but never, in his own eyes, to the detriment of his cause. If he could foresee the consequences might be fatal, he always gave in. When he stood firm it was because he could see no such thing. At Bannockburn he saw quite clearly that his reply might make Lord George resign. That would be as fatal as it would always have been – but this time he did not care. Derby stuck in his throat. He regretted being browbeaten. He had hated the retreat, and his progress through South-West Scotland: they were Lord George's fault. If Lord George was now going to start again, he could go. From now on, he was going to do what he wanted. Charles' actual words were as strong as Lord George's own:

When I came into Scotland I knew well enough what I was to expect from my Ennemies, but I little foresaw what I meet with from my Friends. I came vested with all the Authority the King cou'd give me, one chief part of which is the Command of his Armies, and now I am required to give this up to fifteen or sixteen Persons, who may afterward depute five or seven of their own number to exercise it, for fear if they were six or eight that I might myself pretend to ye casting vote. By the majority of these all things are to be determined, and nothing left to me but the honour of being present at their debates. This I am told is the method of all Armies and this I flatly deny, nor do I believe it to be the Method of any one Army in the World. I am often hit in the teeth that this is an Army of Volunteers, and consequently very different from one composed of Mercenarys. What one wou'd naturally expect from an Army whose chief Officers consist of Gentlemen of rank and fortune, and who came into it meerly upon Motives of Duty and Honour, is more zeal, more resolution and more good manners than in those that fight meerly for pay: but it can be no Army at all where there is no General, or which is the same thing no Obedience or deference paid to him. Every one knew before he engaged in the cause, what he was to expect in case it miscarried, and should have staid at home if he could not face Death in any shape: but can I myself hope for better usage? at least I am the only Person upon whose head a Price has been already set, and therefore I cannot indeed threaten at every other Word to throw down my Arms and make my Peace with the Government. I think I shew every day that I do not pretend to act without taking advice, and yours oftener than any body's else, which I shall still continue to do, and you know that upon more occasions than one, I have given up my own opinion to that of others. I staid indeed a day at Lancaster without calling a Council, yet y^{r}self proposed to stay another but I wonder much to see myself reproached with the loss of Carlile. Was there a possibility to carrying off the Cannon and baggage, or was there time to destroy them? and wou'd not the doing it have been a greater dishonour to our Arms? After all did not you y^{r}self instead of proposing to abandon it, offer to stay with the Athol Brigade to defend it?

I have insensibly made this answer much longer than I intended, and might yet add much more, but I choose to cut it short, and shall only tell you that my Authority may be taken from me by violence, but I shall never resign it like an Idiot.

Lord George was shaken, but he neither resigned nor tried to snatch the command himself. He was much too good a soldier to really do either. Instead, he resolved to continue to do his best but to take the first opportunity to make Charles see the error of his ways. That moment, he was well aware, would only come when Charles needed something. With new forces joining him, this was not the moment. The duel would have to be postponed. What pained Lord George most about the delay was not that he thought Charles would imagine he was the victor but that Charles might think he wanted this duel at all. What Lord George wanted was to serve under a strong, able commander who knew what he was doing. He did not either want or relish the unpleasant task of taking responsibility upon himself.

CHAPTER TEN

Falkirk and Retreat

Charles spent ten days at Bannockburn, recovering from his influenza and from the attack on his self-esteem. Lord George was encamped with the bulk of the army nine miles away at Falkirk, enduring the same kind of awful conditions that had plagued them all winter. At Sir Hugh Paterson's house Charles enjoyed every comfort and seems for once not to have been in any hurry to join his men. Part of his contentment during such a crucial phase of the campaign – for Government forces were massing under a newly-appointed general, Hawley – was due to his hostess and nurse, Clementina Walkinshaw, whose acquaintance he had already made during his unhappy stay in Glasgow. Not only had Charles never had mistresses, he had never had female friends. But now he found in her a sympathetic companion at a time when sympathy was what he most craved. He discovered in fact for the first time the delights of feminine company and it thawed in him the shyness and reserve he had always felt towards them. The way to his heart was very definitely through his mind and not any appeal to his sex. That might come later, but not, as with most men his age, first. If Clementina had been a seductive beauty Charles would have remained as frigid as he had always been with women. It was her very plainness that made him feel safe and relaxed.

Clementina was the youngest of the ten daughters of the third marriage of John Walkinshaw of Barrowfield. Her father was very active in the Stuart cause and had been envoy to Vienna. He died in 1731 and Clementina and her sisters were taken under the wing of an uncle, Sir Hugh Paterson. She was named after Charles' mother Clementina Sobieski, and was about a year older than Charles. Selected by Sir Hugh to come to Bannockburn and be his hostess during Charles' stay, Clementina was delighted. At twenty-six she had had no attachments. Life in Scotland was dull and Charles' campaign had provided her with the first bit of excitement that had ever come her way. She was wholly and willingly prejudiced in Charles' favour, quite prepared to agree with every single word he said.

Elcho maintained she 'forthwith became his mistress' but how he could know when he was miles away is difficult to see. The chances of it happening are remote. Apart from his 'flu, Charles had other things to think about, and seduction is unlikely to have been one of them. He seems, nevertheless, to have exacted a promise from her that if he should ever need her she would come to him. It was the kind of romantic gesture Charles loved to make and suggests more a promise of attachment than an existing one. What despoiled twenty-six-year-old virgin would have been content with that?

While Charles was telling the story of his life to a rapt Clementina, events were rapidly moving towards a confrontation between his troops and the Government's. Towards the end of December the Hanoverian forces had begun to move north, from Newcastle to Edinburgh, until by the second week in January their twelve battalions assembled there. These were no raw recruits, like Cope's troops, but veterans, many of them fresh from Flanders. They were commanded by Hawley, a grim and vicious general who ruled through terror. The first thing Hawley always did was set up a gallows when he struck camp. That way, your men knew you were more terrible than the enemy. He was not too thrilled with his men, veterans or not, but that did not worry him because he had the greatest contempt for those in the Jacobite army – 'they are the most despicable enemy that are'. All his men need do was to forget the 'Lyes and Accounts which are told of them' and 'fire by ranks diagonaly to the centre'. Hawley looked forward to an easy victory. Together with General Huske, he intended to march west and challenge the Jacobites first.

Lord George was aware that the challenge was coming and raged at the energy, time and materials that were going into the siege of Stirling Castle. Charles' determination to subdue it had reached a new level of obstinacy when he heard that Lord John Drummond had brought with him two sixteen-pound guns, two twelve-pounders and two eight-pounders. He loved big guns. The problems of transporting them were swept aside. With great difficulty they were brought from Perth and the job begun. Unfortunately, the operation was put in the hands of a newly arrived French engineer, Mirabel de Gordon, a fool of the first order to whom Charles paid great deference. Lord George could hardly bear to hear about it. Not even the arrival of the reinforcements, who 'looked mighty well and were very hearty', could compensate for such idiocy. While Charles was messing about at Stirling, Huske and Hawley advanced and took the initiative. Lord George decided to take matters into his own hands. Ordering Elcho and Pitsligo to join him, Lord George marched to Linlithgow towards the advancing army in the hope of sabotaging their progress. He surrounded the town but when his scouts brought him news of the whole Government army being almost upon them he decided it was too late for any delaying action and returned to Falkirk.

Charles, fully recovered and cheered by his new troops, received the news that the enemy was almost upon them with pleasure. On the morning of 15th January he ordered the Highlanders to draw up on Plean Muir, two miles south-east of Bannockburn. This they did, but since no Hawley appeared they were disbanded. Next day, they met again, only to disperse. On the 17th, they arrived again and Charles actually called a council of war, to Lord George's relief and surprise. He wasted no time in recriminations for once but suggested to Charles that they should make for a hill to the south-west of the town. This was agreed. To fool the enemy, Charles left his standard flying on Plean Muir and Lord John Drummond galloped off with a small force to act as a decoy. The only jarring note in this new unanimity was Charles' refusal to call off the siege of Stirling Castle: a thousand men were left there, to Lord George's horror. Charles wanted it both ways. As usual, his confidence and faith in the invincibility of his army pushed him into gestures he could not afford.

The movement of the Jacobite troops went more smoothly than they had a right to expect. Organisation was at a minimum, but somehow the men were capable of moving where they should quickly and quietly. Their mobility never ceased to amaze. Hawley, for his part, had occupied Falkirk and felt he had deserved a treat. Accordingly, he descended on Lady Kilmarnock at Callender House and made himself very much at home. He was having a splendid dinner in front of a roaring fire when news came that the Highland army had suddenly emerged on the offensive. Irritated, he sent orders back that the men could put on their equipment but otherwise there was no cause for alarm. The Highland army continued its advance. When they were almost upon them, urgent messages were again sent to Hawley and this time he arrived, without his hat, cursing and raging because his meal had been interrupted. Panic stations took over.

It was only the second battle the Highland army had fought and it was very different from Prestonpans. The ground was different, the enemy was different, the weather was different. Instead of a bog, there was a hill with a moorland plateau above; instead of a fine autumn morning, it was a stormy winter's evening with a strong wind blowing and rain threatening; instead of untested soldiers led by a man worried out of his mind, there were battalions of experienced troops led by a man who had no doubts or fears at all. Yet, in essence, the battle was the same: the Highlanders had only courage and manœuvrability on their side. Their numbers were greater but no better trained or disciplined, and hardly better armed. The chances were still heavily against their winning without luck and the mistakes of the enemy on their side, and Charles was every bit as irresponsible to engage in battle when and where he did as he had been at Prestonpans.

Lord George had this time chosen to fight on foot. His aim was to keep as close a contact as possible with the men in order to restrain their attack until he ordered it. By dint of repeated orders and strict discipline he got the men to advance in line without one part getting ahead of the other as they had done at Prestonpans. Charles was in the rear of the second line with Lord John Drummond and his troops who had rejoined after their feint. Grimly, Lord George held the long line but his insistence on a uniform advance made Charles impatient. He sent O'Sullivan to organise it better. Naturally, this led to squabbles with Lord George, who knew exactly what he was doing. Before their argument had time to reach serious proportions, the rain began and Lord George had the gratification to find that he had successfully got it behind his men and facing the enemy because of the carefulness with which he had placed his advance. The advance of the Hanoverians up the hill was a disaster. They came on at a run 'quite out of breath with the fatigue', into the teeth of the wind and rain. With them came three regiments of cavalry, in whom Hawley placed such confidence. Lord George, shouting all the time, made the front line hold its fire until the horses were ten yards away. Then they fired. Eighty went down at once. Still yelling, Lord George ordered the men to stand firm and reload but as usual an irresistible temptation to run after the retreating enemy overtook half the line and throwing down their firearms they rushed in pursuit. Chaos took over, to Lord George's rage. It was the precise moment when defeat could overtake them as he well knew: it only needed another charge and, with broken ranks, the enemy would be in the heart of them and the tables turned. The fact that this did not come was irrelevant: it meant victory came because the other side made mistakes and that was dangerous. Lord George knew the men on the other side had fought at Fontenoy: he expected them to rally, and if they rallied all was lost.

No rally came. Some regiments fought bravely, but the majority ran. Once he realised the body of the enemy were on the run, Lord George was driven to even greater despair: they must be followed in an orderly fashion and dealt with. No final victory could be obtained while the pursuit consisted merely of groups of Highlanders running wild. Now, if ever, was Charles' opportunity to show his generalship. In the rear of the second line he was in a position to see the men held ranks and advanced relentlessly in formation to replace the broken front line. No orders came.

Some of the Jacobite army thought they had been defeated and went back to Stirling; the rest followed Lord George, who made all haste to Falkirk and a further encounter. It was only when Falkirk was reached and found evacuated that victory was certain. The time it had taken to follow Hawley had been to his advantage for it gave him the chance to salvage the bulk of his men.

The battle had lasted twenty minutes. The Jacobites lost fifty men, Hawley at least four hundred, among them some of his best officers. He wrote to Cumberland: 'Sir, My heart is broke. I can't say We are quite beat today But our Left is beat and their Left is beat. We had enough to beat them for we had Two Thousand Men more than they. But suche scandalous Cowardice I never saw before. The whole second Line of Foot ran away without firing a shot. Three Squadrons did well. The others as usual ...' Hawley set about mending his broken heart by hanging as many soldiers as he could find gallows for: 'Thirty one of Hamiltons dragoons are to be hanged for deserting to the rebels and thirty two of the foot to be shot for cowardice.'

In London, there was universal consternation where lately there had been growing complacency. Horace Walpole, who on the very day of the battle had been chortling 'What a despicable affair is a rebellion upon the defensive!', changed his tune to 'with many other glories, the English courage seems gone too!' No one could pretend, this time, that it had not been a true test. A Mr Corse, writing to Duncan Forbes, expressed the general feeling of admiration and hoped 'I wish they may have a good Historian; for that about 4,500 men should come from the remotest parts of Scotland, penetrate into the heart of England, fight battles, and lay siege to Castles, seems pretty odd and must contain things worthy of our Curiosity.' If this rabble could defeat crack regiments of the line, what would happen next? Nobody knew, least of all the victors. Crouched in the tents recently and so conveniently vacated by Hawley's troops, Charles and his officers took stock while outside the men ignored the lashing rain and looted Falkirk. Lord George, ever one for gloomy post-mortems, began straight away to point out what a mess had been made. There was no excuse for not totally annihilating Hawley's foot except their own incompetence. With difficulty, he was persuaded to consider instead what should be done now. Lord George had no hesitation: Hawley should be pursued even though he now had a head start. But 'others' (not named in any of the narratives) were for continuing the siege of Stirling Castle and then proceeding. M. Mirabel assured Charles it would fall within the next ten days. Never liking to leave a job unfinished, Charles decided to wait. Lord George remained at Falkirk and he went back to

Bannockburn which was fast becoming a home from home. While there, he also waited to hear not only from the French but also – amazingly – the English. Charles, whatever he thought of them, could never give anyone up. His father was more realistic (and because of it always less successful). Writing at this time to Henry he remarks: 'I don't see how it is possible for our friends in England to order what you therein propose to them for how can they, without arms, without regular troops, without, enfin, any support, pretend to rise in arms and much less to sieze any seaport while the government have so many regular troops in the island and at present even a considerable body of men near London. I have often blamed the indolence and timidity of our friends in England; but in the present moment, I own I think they would act imprudently and even rashly not to ly quiet still.' Charles saw no problem, accepted no excuses.

It took ten days for the full realisation of how wrong was the decision to continue at Stirling to come through to Charles. M. Mirabel made a laughing-stock of him. Having spent all this time building a battery for the precious guns – watched from inside the Castle by Blakeney who knew he could blow it to pieces whenever he chose – he opened fire on 29th January. Blakeney let them have a go, and then decided the sport had gone on long enough. In half an hour he had wiped out the battery and Stirling was as impregnable as ever. Charles found it hard to accept and even harder to go back on what he had decided. One of the first things he had done after Falkirk had been to dictate a letter to Sheridan to send to Louis XV reporting his victory: 'This victory removes my difficulties for the present but your Majesty will recognise that the contest will be very unequal if I do not receive much more help soon. The troops and officers commanded by Lord John Drummond which have been sent me have distinguished themselves and it is plain to see from this what a greater number might achieve. If the invasion which I have been expecting for so long now takes place, all will soon be over; otherwise each day will see me forced to risk my life and all my hopes with an enemy who will soon have all the resources he needs.' He wished, when all hopes of capturing Stirling Castle vanished, that he had made his position sound more desperate.

At Falkirk, Lord George and the army were not in good spirits. How good a victory Falkirk was could be measured by the lowness of general morale. They were stuck in the mud and rain, uncertain of their future, still bickering over what should have happened in the battle. There had been more than the usual number of desertions, many due to the accidental shooting of Angus Macdonell, Glengarry's son. Charles had not been to visit them, no councils had been held. In the middle of this depression

O'Sullivan arrived to say that Charles now agreed to follow Hawley. Lord George decided the moment had come for a showdown more complete than any at Derby. This time, it would all be done as a joint thing and in writing. An address was drawn up and signed by all the chiefs present stating that an advance was impossible. The men were in no condition to fight. A second retreat must be made, this time to the mountains beyond. There, they could carry out guerrilla-style warfare during the remainder of the winter and mass their forces in the spring for another campaign. They would not follow him to certain defeat. A messenger went with the letter to Bannockburn at once. Over the letter was a note to John Hay of Restalrig, one of the Prince's aides-de-camp, saying: 'Take the most prudent method to lay this before his Royal Highness without loss of time. We are sensible it will be very unpleasant but in the name of God what can we do?'

Poor John Hay did not manage to deliver the letter that night in spite of his instructions. A hurried meeting took place between O'Sullivan, Broughton and himself. Nobody dared wake Charles to give him such news. Instead, they decided an attempt must be made to dissuade Lord George and the chiefs from this step before Charles knew of it. Broughton was elected to ride off in the middle of the night to Falkirk to do the persuading. He returned unsuccessful in the early hours of the morning. Hay was left with no alternative. He presented the letter to Charles, who read it and immediately had a kind of fit – 'He struck his head against the wall until he staggered and exclaimed most violently against Lord George' whose fault he was sure it was. His words were 'Good God! Have I lived to see this?' It took him a long time to calm down sufficiently to consider an answer, but eventually he summoned Sheridan and dictated one:

Bannockburn, Jan. ye 30th.

GENTLEMEN, – I have received y^rs of last night and am extremely surprised at the contents of it, wch I little expected from you at this time. Is it possible that a Victory and a Defeat shou'd produce the same effects, and that the Conquerors should flie from an engagement, whilst the conquer'd are seeking it? Shou'd we make the retreat you propose, how much more will that raise the spirits of our Ennemys and sink those of our own People? Can we imagin, that where we go the Ennemy will not follow, and at last oblige us to a Battel which we now decline? Can we hope to defend ourselves at Perth, or keep our Men together there, better than we do here? We must therefore continue our flight to the Mountains, and soon find our selves in a worse condition than we were in at Glenfinnen. What Opinion will the French and Spaniards then have of us, or what encouragement will it be to the former to make the descent for which they have been so long preparing, or the latter send us any more succours? I am persuaded that if the Descent be not made before this piece of news reaches them, they will lay aside all thoughts of it, cast all the blame upon us, and say it is in vain to send succours to those who dare not stay to receive them. Will they send us any more Artillery to be lost or nail'd up? But what will become of our Lowland friends? Shall we persuade them to retire with us to the Mountains? Or shall we abandon them to the fury of our Merciless Ennemies? What an Encouragement will this be to them or others to rise in our favour, shou'd we, as you seem to hope, ever think our selves in a condition to pay them a second visit? But besides what urges us to this precipitate resolution is as I apprehend the daily threats of the Ennemy to come and attack us; and if they should do it within two or three days our retreat will become impracticable. For my own Part I must say that it is with the greatest reluctance that I can bring my self to consent to such a step, but having told you my thoughts upon it, I am too sensible of what you have already ventured and done for me, not to yield to y^r unanimous resolution if you persist in it. However I must insist on the Conditions wch Sr Thomas Sheridan the Bearer of this, has my orders to propose to you. I desire you wou'd talk the matter over with him and give entire credit to what he shall say to you in my name.

Your assured friend.

[Endorsed] – 30 Jan. 1746.

The chiefs were adamant. Lord George refused to be the scapegoat so Keppoch and Cluny were sent to reason with Charles. They had never seen him in such a despotic mood, but they held fast and said they spoke for all and could not have their minds changed. Charles dismissed them, but then wrote another letter to the chiefs.

I doubt not but you have been informed by Cluny and Keppoch of what passed last night and heard great complaints of my Despotick temper, I therefore think it necessary to explain my self more fully to you. I cant see nothing but ruin and destruction to us all in case we shoud think of a retreat. Wherever we go the Ennemy will follow, and if we now appear afraid of them their spirits will rise and those of our men sink very low. I cannot conceive but we can be as well and much more safely quarter'd in and about Falkirk than here. We have already tried it for several days together, and tho' the men were order'd to be every day on the field of Battle early you know it was always near noon before they cou'd be assembled. Had the Ennemy come upon us early in ye morning, what wou'd have become of us? and shall we again wilfully put our selves in ye same risk? Believe me ye nearer we come to the Forth the greater the Desertion will prove. But this is not the worst of it. I have reason to apprehend that when we are once here it will be proposed to cross the Forth it self, in wch case we shall be utterly undon and lose all the fruits of ye success providence has hitherto granted us. Stirling will be retaken in fewer days than we have spent in taking it, and prove a second

Carlile for it will be impossible to carry off our Cannon, etc. In fine why we shoud be so much afraid now of an Ennemy that we attacked and beat a fortnight ago when they were much more numerous I cannot conceive. Has the loss of so many officers and men killed and wounded and the shame of their flight still hanging upon them made them more formidable ? I woud have you consider all this and represent it accordingly, but shew my letter to no mortal. After all this I know I have an Army y^t cannot command any further than the chief Officers please, and therefore if you are all resolved upon it I must yield; but I take God to witness that it is with the greatest reluctance, and that I wash my hands of the fatal consequences wch I foresee but cannot help.

When it brought no reaction his anger dulled to a sullen acceptance of his position. Yet again, he bowed to the inevitable but pointed out that he did not agree. He wrote to them saying that as they wished it, the retreat northwards would begin but that he washed his hands of the consequences. They would never convert him to their opinion.

The retreat began on 1st February. On 30th January the Duke of Cumberland had arrived in Edinburgh to take over the command of the army. He was presented with the Freedom of the City in a gold box and at a kind of levée he held one lady wore a bush inscribed with the words 'Britain's Hero William Duke of Cumberland'. The next day he left to seek Charles, with a gesture worthy of his romantic cousin: 'Shall we not have one song?' he asked, as he prepared to gallop off, and then broke into:

> Will ye play me fair ?
> Highland laddie, Highland laddie

The retreat from Falkirk could not have been more different from the retreat from Derby. It was as chaotic as Derby had been orderly, as panic-stricken as Derby had been calm. From the moment it began everything went wrong, and the tone was set for the hard weeks to follow.

It had been agreed that the army would meet early in the morning near St Ninians, when Lord George would organise the order of marching. The meeting never took place. For some unknown reason, bands of men began marching west before it was light and by nine o'clock, the appointed rendezvous time, many were miles away. 'Never was a retreat resembled so much a flight, for their was no where 1,000 together, and the whole army passed the river in small bodies and in great confusion, leaving carts and cannon upon the road behind them.' It put Lord George into a raging temper for if there was anything he could not stand it was inefficiency. Then, as he neared St Ninians, already furious at the breakdown of his plans, there was a loud explosion. Galloping on, Lord George found the church had been accidentally blown up. It had been used as a powder store and during the evacuation some powder had spilt and been ignited. The mess seemed completed.

Lord George had to wait two days, till the evening of 2nd February, before he could demand an explanation. By then, the army had reached Crieff, and a council of war was called. Lord George threw aside any pretence at politeness or deference to Charles. He took charge at once: 'Ld Geo. would suffer no body to speak but those he named and us'd to perscribe to one, to give his opinions and his raisons to another, to give his oppinions without any raisons; if the Prince offered to speak, he'd treaten to go off, and told the Prince he must not speak until every man had given his opinion. Ld. Louis Gordon asked him if he was mad and if the Prince was not master to speak when he thought fit; the Ld George said not and yt the Prince ought not to speak until every man had given his opinion.' Charles, faced with such dictatorship by a subordinate, came out of it rather well. Asked by Lord George to name names, to say who was responsible for the disgraceful disorderliness of the last forty-eight hours, Charles replied with great dignity that since he was commander-in-chief of the army the responsibility must be his. Lord George could have no comeback to this. The council moved on to discuss what should be done next. 'After a great deal of wrangling and altercation it was determind that the horse and low country regiments should march towards Inverness, along the coast, while the Prince and the Clans took the Highland road thither.'

At Blair, which the Prince reached two days later, he and his division halted a few days. Sir Thomas Sheridan spent some of the time writing a letter to his friends at Versailles, the same friends he had assured after Falkirk 'We are indeed like the old man who said "I am feeling very well, thank God, but I am going to die soon".' The spirit of his letter conveyed the same feeling of approaching doom. 'You will no doubt be surprised,' he wrote, 'that a fortnight after a victory of the kind I had the honour to tell you about in my last letter, we are now retreating.' He went over the reasons for it, and then exclaimed passionately, 'For the love of God, what do you think? Doesn't France give a damn what happens to us?' They were in great need of everything, especially money. Charles did not himself put pen to paper, nor had he done since Prestonpans. He wrote through Sheridan to France, but his poor father had to do without. Charles' feelings, however, were no doubt adequately expressed by his old tutor. The lack of substantial aid from France was a continuing sore, its arrival the only medicine that could rejuvenate his cause. He continued, in the face of overwhelming evidence to the contrary, to have faith in Louis; he continued to look on the bright side. But his cheerfulness began to take on a note of hysteria and his daily performance in front of others became more strained. Captain Warren wrote of him at this time: 'they could not but admire his spirit, heart and conduct, he has taught them how to bear the inconveniences [of] adversity, or a misstep commonly drawn on by looking forwards providing for the time to come, and taking lesson by what [is] past; and all this with such prudence, dignity, caution and dexterity, that really show him to born a General.' What this smiling optimism had to do with generalship it is difficult to see, but Warren does convey a picture of Charles being philosophical that is almost ludicrous.

It was lucky Lord George was not there to see him radiating good fellowship: he was slogging through the snow on the eastern road to Inverness. As usual, he had undertaken the worst task, and as usual executed it with grim determination and skill. The officers with him had their own worries and did not always relish his minute day-by-day instructions. The farther they went, the heavier the snow fell, and by comparison Derby to Carlisle seemed a picnic. In addition, they were not just retreating: the whole object of the exercise was to keep the coast road open for the arrival of the French and supplies, so wherever they went Lord George tried to leave a garrison – however pathetically small – of men. The attitude of the locals in these villages and towns was ambiguous. They were not openly hostile but neither did they cooperate. They were scared and worried about possible reprisals from Cumberland and were taking no chances. Food was a constant problem. High prices had to be paid, prices which could not be afforded. Thinking ahead – though the current situation was bad enough – Lord George busied himself with plans to collect meal and have it sent into the mountains to provide food during the hiding period he envisaged would soon follow.

Charles had no intention of hiding. He had entered Inverness on 18th February, and far from thinking of going up into the hills he could only watch in hypnotised fashion the approach of Cumberland. He seemed to be taking a long time coming. Pressed by Lord George, Charles was forced to outline his objectives at what was now a critical pre-battle time. His main aim was still to keep the road open to the east coast where a French landing might be expected; secondly, to try to disperse the army collected by Duncan Forbes, and now commanded by the dogged Lord Loudon, to the north – Cumberland's army was enough, they had no room for another enemy; thirdly, Charles suggested laying siege to Forts William and Augustus. This last idea was probably more the chiefs' than his for most of them had lived for years under the shadow of these forts and longed to destroy them. Pursuing all these different goals meant scattering his forces over a wide area, but Charles considered it might be more of an advantage than a disadvantage. He had no money to pay his men and no food to give them. These expeditions would keep them busy and therefore more contented as well as being, if successful, of great value. Cumberland came on so slowly he was sure there would be plenty of warning before they needed to reassemble.

March was a backs-to-the-wall month, full of ups and downs. Charles spent most of it at Elgin where he was very ill. 'H.R.H. was very Ill at this time with a spotted favor, but it was kept so secret ... The Prince happily recovered and got up the ninth or tenth day, against the doctors advise, being still in the favor, and said yt peoples were sick only when they thought themselves so.' Were people also only beaten when they thought themselves so? Charles might have conquered his 'favor' by mind over matter but he could not improve his material situation. 'Mony was the word, there was none to give them. The French ambassador kept buckle and tongue together and sustained the regular troops so-so, but the Prince had hardly wherewithal to pay the officers.' In these circumstances, it was unbearable to have news brought towards the end of the month of the loss of a French treasure ship. This was the *Prince Charles* commanded by a Captain Talbot. Loaded with gold, he reached the latitude of Aberdeen on 24th March but was scared off by a British squadron. He raced north, was followed, and made a crash landing in the Kyle of Tongue. Knowing full well how vital his consignment was, Talbot fought heroically to save it. Abandoning his ship, he and what was left of his crew set out carrying as many boxes of gold as they could. They marched in darkness, through wild and rough country they did not know. Their first encounter was, luckily, with the Laird of Melness who 'seemed very much for us but told us that we were in enemy country, that there were troops about, and that we were far from Inverness, fifty Scotch miles distant. We bought from him two horses to carry the money and he gave us his son to guide us ... and so we resumed the march along frightful roads.' It was an impossible escape. Near Ben Loyal, Talbot and his men surrendered, utterly exhausted, with the one satisfaction that just before their capture they had managed to throw twelve thousand pounds in English guineas into the heather.

'This last misfortune,' wrote Maxwell of Kirkconnell, 'soon took air ... and disheartened the army.' It also disheartened Charles. Surmounting such a loss was the hardest test yet that he had had to pass. None of the other bits of good news were sufficient to dispel the gloom cast over his men. Fort Augustus had been taken, Lord George had harried Cumberland in Perthshire to great effect and the Duke of Perth had completely dispersed Lord Loudon's army. There was a lot to rejoice about. Kirkconnell wrote that this, in his opinion, was 'the finest part of the Prince's expedition. The vulgar may be dazzled with victory but in the eyes of a connoisseur ...' He gave Charles the credit – 'the Prince, as it were, in the centre, whence he directed all these operations' – but in fact necessity, not military skill, had dictated the various expeditions and the individual courage and cunning of his officers was more responsible for their success than any overseeing on Charles' part. Instead of working tirelessly to organise things, as Kirkconnell's tribute suggests, Charles spent most of his time, when he had recovered from his illness, hunting, shooting and fishing. Since the minute he himself had recovered his Secretary, Murray of Broughton, fell ill, there was in fact no central clearing house for orders at all. No attempt was made to foresee that, as Cumberland would have to cross the Spey, that would be the time to launch a full-scale attack with everything they had. The Duke of Perth needed to be strongly reinforced to dispute Cumberland's passage. Instead, depleted by losses sustained during the campaign against Loudon, he had to stand by and watch this marvellous opportunity slip by. Cumberland, who had expected to be challenged at this point, crossed on 12th April, unable to believe his luck. He had not been enjoying his campaign: 'The Duke complains extremely of the *loyal* Scotch; says he can get no intelligence, and reckons himself more in an enemy's country than when he was warring with the French in Flanders. They profess the big professions wherever he comes, but before he is out of sight of any town, beat up for volunteers for rebels.' As Kirkconnell said, without seeming to attach the responsibility to Charles, 'more mistakes were committed the two or three last days than formerly in as many months'. There had never in Charles' army been the organisation and efficiency needed as a base for any sustained campaign. This weakness, when his treasure chest was empty and his men hungry, now began to tell.

Charles' reaction to the news that Cumberland was safely across the Spey was instant: a battle must be fought. He sent immediate expresses to all his men to come at once. By that time, when he had travelled the length and breadth of Scotland, he ought to have had a more realistic appreciation of the time it would take for them to arrive. On a map, none were more than a hard day and night's march away, but the nature of the country made progress slow. There was nothing to prevent him waiting for every single man to arrive: Cumberland, whose entire progress had been leisurely, was not immediately threatening him. But Charles could not wait. He was obsessed by the idea of a final battle to be fought on his and not Cumberland's terms. He could not bear the thought of waiting to be attacked – he must do the attacking. Nor was his desire really the product of despair for in spite of the condition of his men he still thought that their bravery could, and would, achieve miracles. He was not fatalistic, wanting to hurry to his doom, but, as ever, optimistic. He believed in his men, and he believed they wanted to fight. He interpreted his responsibility towards them as *demanding* a battle. In this he could not have been more different from his father who, at the end of the 1715 campaign, avoided such an onslaught when defeat seemed inevitable. 'To offer battle,' James had said, 'would be to expose brave men for no reason, since the enemy is twice as strong as we are, and I wish to preserve them for a more fitting occasion.' He could have done with his father's advice contained in a letter not even written until (unknown to James) Culloden was over: '… but if you really cannot maintain yourself in Scotland do not for God's sake drive things too far; but think of your own safety on which so much depends … so that you should really have no temptation to pursue rash or desperate measures at this time … In fine, my dear child, never separate prudence and courage.'

Charles chose to fight at Culloden, not blindly, but reckoning luck and courage greater than numbers. Battles were fickle things, in which the better and stronger side did not always win. Unfortunately, in the calculations he made, he left out one important factor that was different from Prestonpans and Falkirk: the other side were now commanded by the Duke of Cumberland. Cumberland, Charles' cousin, was no Cope or Hawley. He took no risks, made no mistakes, and had time and resources on his side. While Charles was right to think the Government troops, vastly superior in numbers and equipment, could still be defeated as they had been before, he was wrong to miscalculate Cumberland's importance. He did not know his cousin, and the little he did know did not dispose him to be impressed. Cumberland would have beaten Charles anywhere, simply by the ruthlessness of his system.

It was a pity there was no one in Charles' camp to tell him about his cousin. William was no mere brute, all brawn and no brain. On the contrary, he had been a bright boy (unlike Charles) and had applied himself diligently to his studies, especially Latin which he had begun to learn at a very early age. Military matters had always interested him, and, like many a princeling, he had had his own miniature battalion of boy soldiers which were exercised by him in the courtyard of St James. He had a natural gift for languages, but was also interested in chemistry and a laboratory was provided for him at Richmond. His military career began early. In 1740, when he was twenty, he was appointed to command the

Coldstream Guards; in 1742 he was transferred to the First Guards, and in April went with his father, George II, to Hanover. He was present at the battle of Dettingen where, says Wolfe, 'he behaved as bravely as a man could do.' He was wounded in the leg but bore his wound bravely. Already, he had earned himself a reputation for strictness and his distaste for amateur soldiering was well known. It was his ambition to root out all that hindered the British army from working well. In April 1745 he had been made Captain General of all His Majesty's forces on land, and at Fontenoy distinguished himself by being everywhere at once.

As a soldier, Cumberland was impressive. He worked hard and knew what he wanted. As a man, he was unpleasant, with no time for the knights-of-old chivalry Charles set so much store by. The people of Carlisle, who had joyfully welcomed him as their deliverer, soon learnt their lesson: without manners or finesse, Cumberland took what he wanted and treated them with contempt. Though a womaniser since his early teens, his behaviour towards women was hardly gallant – Mr Wardale of Carlisle wrote to Dr Waugh after Cumberland's stay: 'He's represented as a mightly uncomplaisant getn. by the ladies, and I am afraid the evil report will spread further than them.' But whatever the ladies thought, he was popular with his own soldiers, for he was the kind of hard man they could not only fear but respect. He wasted no time currying favour with theatrical gestures, but set about preparing his army to beat the rebels. Prestonpans and Falkirk should have been Government victories but there had been bungling. Cumberland neither under- nor over-estimated his opponents. All he was interested in were facts, and the facts were that he had drilled his men mercilessly, seen to it that they were supplied with adequate arms and ammunition and above all had restored their shattered morale. Take nine thousand men, train them, equip them, provision them and lead them out against half that number and the result ought to be obvious. Cumberland was there to see that it was. Of all this, Charles really had no inkling. He had little idea of what was happening on the other side.

CHAPTER ELEVEN

Culloden

Early on Tuesday morning, 15th April 1746, the Jacobite army took up a position on the moor above Culloden House to await the expected attack. As usual, Lord George, who thought this the final insanity, had quarrelled with O'Sullivan about the choice of ground. He himself had found a better place, near Dalcross Castle, but O'Sullivan had rejected it as unsuitable. Lord George's contempt was strongly expressed: 'Not one single souldier but would have been against such a ffeld had their advice been askt? A plain moor where regular troups had ... full use of their cannon so as to annoy the Highlanders prodigiously before they could possibly make an attack.' No attack came that day. The men stood, hungry and cold, exposed to the full force of the east wind, until well into the afternoon when Charles dismissed them with their day's ration of one biscuit each. He then held a council of war. It was at this council that the suggestion was made to attack Cumberland in his camp at Nairn by night. Nobody seems quite certain who proposed it in the first place, but the important thing was that everyone unanimously agreed. The plan had a genius about it, a daring originality, that was reminiscent of other inspired moves like the path through the bog at Prestonpans. A new enthusiasm ran through the council and it was resolved to march off towards Nairn at eight that evening. Lord George expressed himself 'very sensible of the danger should it miscarry' but raised no objections.

At seven o'clock that evening, when it was time to begin to get into marching order, it was found that half the starving men had gone off to try to find more food. 'When the officers who were sent on horseback to bring them back came up with them, they could by no persuasion be induced to return again, giving for answer they were starving; and said to their officers that they might shoot them if they pleased, but they could not go back till they got meat.' Charles was not as disconcerted as his officers. He thought of the battle ahead as a kind of treat or tonic –

'His Royal Highness said that whenever the march began the men would be hearty, and those that had gone off would return and follow.' Few agreed with him, and wished, in the light of this situation, to lay aside the plan, but Charles was adamant. If Lord George had wanted to, he could at that moment have prevented it, but he chose not to. It was decided to go with what men were available.

The secret had been well kept. The first column moved off under the guidance of a party of Mackintoshes, whose country it was, in good order. Their progress, however, was slow because they had to go in single file through the boggy parts and they moved only two miles an hour. This caused Lord George great anxiety, for he knew that if they could not get to Cumberland's camp before dawn the whole plan would become an unmitigated disaster. It also caused Charles concern for a different reason – the second column could not even keep up this slow pace and he sent messages asking Lord George not to speed up but slow down. Half-way there, as though realising the army was going to arrive in sections, Charles sent another message that astounded Lord George: the first to arrive were to attack straight away without waiting for the others. This was the deciding point: already, seeing that many of the men could not keep up and had collapsed – 'by faintness for want of food for it could not have been weariness in a six mile march' – Lord George had come to a decision. The plan had failed. They must give up. They were a mile short of the place where they had intended to cross the Nairn and the sky was lightening. If they crossed, now a straggling first line separated by a considerable distance from the second, they would have to march the last two miles in sight of the enemy. It would, Lord George said, 'be perfect madness'. A drum could be heard beating in Cumberland's camp; Lord George gave the order to turn back.

For Charles, it was a traumatic moment. Told by John Hay, whom he had sent with his message, that 'unless he came to the front and ordered his Lordship to go on nothing would be done', Charles had ridden on only to meet his own men coming back. 'Where the devil are the men a-going?' he demanded, and when he was told that they were Perth's men, ordered by him to return, he shouted, 'Where is the Duke? Call him here. I am betrayed! What need have I to give orders when my orders are disobeyed?' It took time to find Perth. When he appeared, Charles said, 'What do you mean by ordering the men to turn about?' The Duke said Lord George had turned back three-quarters of an hour before and he was following. 'Good God!' cried Charles. 'What can be the matter? What does this mean?' He begged Perth to call them back but Perth, who saw what a state of excitement Charles was in, took him aside, together with Lochiel, and explained the situation. If it had been Lord George, Charles might have been incensed enough not to listen and to challenge the decision made. But Perth and Lochiel were a different matter. Confused and shaken, but with no alternative, Charles was obliged to be convinced. The rest of the army turned back too, by a different, more direct route, to Culloden.

The men were totally exhausted. It was only the toughest that were still left, though in a land where 'The moment a child is born ... it is immerged in cold water, be the season of the year never so rigorous', there were no weaklings in the first place. On the way back, many joined those who had already fallen by the wayside and slept where they fell in the mud. Some did not collapse but deliberately used what strength they had left to make off into the woods and hide – those same woods Burt had described as 'a most romantic wood, whereof one part consists of great heights and hollows; and the brush-wood at the foot of the trees, with the springs that issue out of the sides of the hills, invite the woodcocks, which, in the season, are generally there in great numbers, and render it the best spot for cock-shooting that ever I knew'. Those who managed it back to Culloden pulled their plaids about them and slept where they could, mostly on the wet ground without any kind of shelter. It was six o'clock in the morning and 'everybody seemed to think of nothing but sleep'. Charles was last back. He had decided to go to Inverness to get some meal there to give to the men, but Perth had persuaded him to send someone else and he rode into Culloden House behind the rest. Like the men, he was worn out, but the French ambassador, d'Eguilles, insisted on an interview. Charles granted it. 'In vain I represented to him that he was still without half his army; that the great part of those who had returned had no longer their targets ... that they were all worn out with fatigue ...' But Charles was inflexible. D'Eguilles wrote bitterly that 'he could not bring himself to decline battle even for a single day'. Even after this interview, there were others who wanted to see Charles before he slept. Keppoch and Lochiel came out strongly against fighting and the arguments raged backwards and forwards. Finally, still determined, Charles lay down in his boots to sleep. They would all sleep for twenty-four hours, have a meal and then fight.

He slept one hour, when Cumberland's guns and the arrival of one of his own patrols shattered him into consciousness. Cumberland was no gentleman. Fair play and consideration for the enemy meant nothing to him. Discovering what had happened and knowing the state the Jacobites would be in, he had quite rightly decided to attack. The confusion in the Jacobite camp was predictable. Men who were in a coma-like sleep leapt up and staggered about not knowing what was going on. Others could not be wakened even if it was the Day of Judgment (as for many of them it was). Charles rushed about trying to do weeks of work in minutes, but it was pointless to try to issue new orders or plan strategy: he and his officers would be lucky to get the army upright and facing the right way. Once in motion, Charles rode about shouting cheering words that had never sounded more hollow – 'Here they are comeing, my lades, we'l soon be with them. They don't forget Glads-mur nor Falkirk, and yu have the same Armes and swords, let me see yours … I'll answer this will cut of some heads and arms today. Go on my lads, the day will be ours, and we'll want for nothing after.' Only O'Sullivan was lost in admiration at Charles' spirit: it was noticeable that the men were much too tired and bewildered to make any response.

Charles gave the impression that Cumberland was nearer than he was. If he had stayed calm and listened properly to the reports his scouts brought in he would have realised there was more than enough time to do one of several constructive things. But he was anxious to see his men formed in battle order as soon as possible and refused Lord George's request to look at the battleground in more detail. Lord George was still arguing about it with O'Sullivan. The main bone of contention was the wall which ran round the grounds of Culloden Park. O'Sullivan saw it as a protection for the right flank, Lord George as a hindrance. Charles wasn't interested – it didn't matter what the ground was like, the important thing was to encourage the men to fight like lions. Everything was as ready as it could be by eleven o'clock. Behind the Jacobites were the hills denuded of leaves, brown and bare on this cold wet Monday morning. Below them was the long drop to the sea. Where they stood was a plateau, with a slight dip in it to one side. For a good mile to either side there was open, flat moorland with little shelter except the odd tree or boulder. Charles was in the rear of the centre of the second line with a good view of the battlefield. The opening shots were fired by the four-gun battery in the Jacobite rear, aiming at the rear of the enemy front line where they thought Cumberland was positioned. One round only 'nearly missed' the Duke, and another 'took off two men exactly before him'. Cumberland's artillery then opened fire, two minutes later, also aiming for the rival commander. They had the same kind of near miss – Charles' face was splattered with blood and his groom decapitated.

The battle being now begun, the whole fury of the enemy's artillery seemed to be directed against us in the rear; as if they had noticed where the Prince was. By the first cannon shot his servant scarcely thirty yards behind him was killed; which made some about the Prince desire that he would be pleased to retire a little off; but this he refused to do, till seeing the imminent danger from the number of balls that fell about him, he was by the earnest entreaties of his friends forced to retire a little off attended only by Lord Balmerino's corps. Frequent looks and turns the Prince made, to see how his men behaved ...

In his new position, Charles no longer had a good view of what was happening. While below Cumberland's cannon continued for half an hour, creating appalling casualties on the Jacobites, Charles saw none of it. He waited for the enemy to attack and his own men to tear them to pieces in personal combat. The attack never came. The cannonade was proving much too effective to bother attacking at all. It was the first time the Highlanders had been exposed to wave after wave of accurate firing and they could not possibly endure it. They screamed for the order to charge, but Charles, who had no idea what was happening, wanted the enemy to come nearer first. Lord George sent a message to Charles begging that the order should be given. It duly was, but the messenger was killed en route. Lord George charged in the end, but the delay had been fatal – there were huge gaps in what had been tightly packed ranks of men. Nevertheless, the attack, when it came, was stupendous – Charles could not say there was any lack of effort, any diminution of the spirit at Prestonpans and Falkirk: 'They came up very boldly and fast, all in a cloud together, sword in hand.'

It did no good. There was no cowardice on the enemy side this time, even though men 'like Wildcats ... came down in Swarms upon our left Wing' and 'began to cut and Hack in their natural way without ceremony'. The front line enemy regiments stood firm till this frightening mob were thirty yards away and then fired 'with a complete running Fire that Dropt them down as they came on'. Still they did not give up. Clambering over their own dead men, 'making a dreadful huzza and even crying "Run, ye dogs!" they broke in between the grenadiers ... However, such as survived possessed themselves of the cannon and attacked the regiments sword in hand; but to their astonishment they found an obstinate resistance ...' Lord George himself was no less brave. During the charge he was thrown from his horse and lost his sword, but he grabbed another and forced his way through his own men to bring up reinforcements. Finding Lord Lewis Gordon's last battalion and the Royal Scots, he led them back into the fray. But the right wing was irretrievably broken. On the left, there had been no charge. The men here had been hard-hit by the fire of the battery opposite, and feared to charge across the swampy ground immediately in front. Furthermore, they could see what had happened to the right wing and also that Cumberland's cavalry was outflanking them. They turned and fled, all except a brave few.

The field was now the scene of terrible slaughter in which men were dying deliberately and heroically. Macdonald of Keppoch, in anguish at the desertion of his men, shouted 'O my God, has it come to this, that the children of my tribe have forsaken me!', then rushed to his death. The Duke of Perth, trying desperately to stop the rout, was wounded in the shoulder. Macdonald of Scotus fought to his death, killing half a dozen of the enemy before he went. Lord Strathallan, with defeat inevitable, rode straight into the enemy fire and was killed. Charles could not understand what was happening. Frantically, he rode about trying to stop the men from running away but they paid no attention. He had never seen his Highlanders run before, never, in a way, understood that they were mortal. The sight completely unnerved him.

seeing this, runs to Shea yt commanded fitz James' squadron and tells him 'yu see all is going to pot. Yu can be of no great succor, so before a general deroute wch will be soon, sieze upon the Prince and take him off.' The Prince was at this time rallying the right, his horse is shot in the shoulder, and kicks and capers, he's obliged to change horses ... The Prince won't retire not withstanding all yt can be told him ... Sullivan ... runs to the Prince and tells him he has no time to loose yt he'l be surrounded immediately if he does not retire ... 'Well' says the Prince, 'they won't take me alive.'

They didn't, but then they hardly took any alive. Quarter was given to few except officers recognisably French through their uniform. Lords Kilmarnock and Balmerino were lucky not to be shot on the spot. The moor was covered with blood 'and our men, what with killing the enemy, dabbling their feet in the blood, and splashing it about one another, looked like so many butchers'. The officers seemed neither able nor willing to stop the slaughter, 'since the time was now come to pay off the score, our people were all glad to clear the reckoning and heartily determind to give them receipt in full'. The cavalry were the worst, trampling over the wounded and shooting everyone in sight. Cumberland imposed no restraint – the outcome of the battle gave him a deep personal satisfaction and he saw no reason why his men should not get theirs. It still amazed him that the Jacobites had had nothing up their sleeve, for the one thing he had expected of them, which had made him very uneasy, was some measure of improvisation. There had been none. It had all been straightforward and might had told. More than half his men had never needed to fire a shot: there had been no waste. He could retire to occupy Inverness with every cause for congratulation.

Charles, meanwhile, was galloping along the road to the Ford of Faillie over the Nairn. He was in a terrible state, shaken and distressed, and was already inventing theories to explain what had happened. It seemed to him that he had been betrayed, that half his army had not fought because they were persuaded not to. The real explanation was totally unpalatable. The fact that he himself had been persuaded to flee, while behind him brave officers tried to recover the retreat, and that he had not died on the field as he had sworn he longed for the opportunity to do, did not seem to cause him any remorse at that point. He could only have ridden to his death if he had thought it was the end and as far as Charles was concerned it was never the end. At the ford, he stopped and saw behind him a number of officers naturally following him, their leader. A quick meeting was held between Charles and his immediate entourage – Sheridan, O'Sullivan, John Hay – and it was decided that they should press on into Fraser country while the rest were sent to Ruthven where orders would be given to them. Who was to give them was never mentioned. Charles continued his flight to Gorthlick, some twenty miles from the battlefield, where he spent the night at Simon Fraser's house. Those others who escaped made for Ruthven, to await his pleasure. No rendezvous, in the event of a defeat, had ever been arranged. All they could do was hide there in terror and wait for Charles to act. It never occurred to them that they were not going to rally to make a new stand. After three days during which they expected at any minute to be found and killed, a message arrived from Charles to them: it told them simply to disperse and each to look after himself.

Lord George was overcome with disgust. He listened to the men howling and wailing as they were turned loose, and a bitterness so complete it obliterated all other feeling took control of him. He sat down and wrote to Charles a letter that roared with feeling. The image of him doing so, spending an hour in the middle of great danger when every minute counted, composing this letter, sums up his character neatly. He absolutely had to write it. Before he thought of his own safety it was essential for his peace of mind that Charles should be told exactly whose fault all this was. To do so, in the terms he did, went against every code of eighteenth-century behaviour imaginable. Lord George was not taking defeat like a man, not letting bygones be bygones; he was crying fiercely over spilt milk, hitting a man when he was down. He had been saving it up for a long time, and it came out fluent and coherent, marred as usual by that self-righteous streak in his nature which he could never subdue. To have told Charles to his face would have been far more satisfactory, but in fact the written word, in Lord George's hands, was far more potent, far more wounding. It stung, it bit, it rankled and was all the more effective for not being distorted as a red face and shouting would have been.

May it please your Royal Highness, – As no person in these kingdomes ventured more franckly in the cause than myself and as I had more at stake than almost all the others put together, so to be sure I cannot but be very deeply affected with our late loss and present situation, but I declare that were your R.H. person in safety, the loss of the cause and the misfortunate and unhappy situation of my countrymen is the only thing that grieves me, for I thank God, I have resolution to bear my own and family's ruine without a grudge.

Sᵣ, you will I hope upon this occasion pardon me if I mention a few truths which all the Gentlemen of our army seem convinced of.

It was highly wrong to have set up the royal standard without having positive assurance from his most Christian majesty that he would assist you with all his force, and as your royal family lost the crown of these realms upon the account of France, The world did and had reason to expect that France would seize the first favourable opportunity to restore your August family.

I must also acquaint your R.H. that we were all fully convinced that Mr. O'Sulivan whom your R.H. trusted with the most essential things with regard to your operations was exceedingly unfit for it and committed gross blunders on every occasion of moment: He whose business it was, did not so much as visit the ground where we were to be drawn up in line of Battle, and it was a fatal error yesterday to allow the enemy those walls upon their left which made it impossible for us to break them, and they with their front fire and flanking us when we went upon the attack destroyed us without any possibility of our breaking them, and our Atholl men have lost a full half of their officers and men. I wish Mr. O'Sulivan had never got any other charge in the Army than the care of the bagage which I have been told he had been brought up to and understood. I never saw him in time of Action neither at Gladsmuir, Falkirk nor in the last, and his orders were vastly confused.

The want of provisions was another misfortune which had the most fatal consequence. Mr. Hay whom Y.R.H. trusted with the principal direction of ordering provisions of late and without whose orders a boll of meal or forthing of monie was not to be delivered, has served Y.R.H. egregiously ill, when I spoke to him, he told me, the thing is ordered, it will be got etc. but he neglected his duty to such a degree that our ruin might probably been prevented had he done his duty: in short the three last days which were so critical our army was starved. This was the reason our night march was rendered abortive when we possibly might have surprised and defeat the enemy at Nairn, but for want of provisions a third of the army scattered to Inverness he and the others who marched had not spirits to make it so quick as was necessary being really faint for want of provisions.

The next day, which was the fatal day, if we had got plenty of provisions, we might have crossed the water of Nairn and drawn up so advantageously that we would have obliged the enemy to come to us, for they were resolved to fight at all hazards, at prodigious disadvantage, and probably we would in that case have done by them as they unhappily have done by us.

In short Mr. O'Sulivan and Mr. Hay had rendered themselves oddous to all our army and had disgusted them to such a degree that they had bred a mutiny in all ranks that had the battle come on they were to have represented their grievance to Y.R.H. for a remedy. For my own part I never had any particular discussion with either of them, but I ever thought them uncapable and unfit to serve in the stations they were placed in.

Y.R.H. knows I always told I had no design to continue in the army: I would of late when I came last from Atholl have resigned my commission, but all my friends told me it might be of prejudice to the cause at such a critical time. I hope your R.H. will now accept my demission. What commands you have for me in any other situation please honour me with them. I am with great zeal,

Sʳ, Your R.H. most dutifull and humble servant,

GEORGE MURRAY.

Ruthven, 17th April 1746.

Charles, from the moment that letter caught up with him, hated Lord George. He was determined never to forgive, for of course he thought Lord George would eventually repent and ask for forgiveness. He did not deign to reply, but in a general letter to the chiefs a few days afterwards – a letter which was meant to be a formal leave-taking before he left for France – the influence of Lord George's letter to him is felt.

For the Chiefs –

When I came into this country, it was my only view to do all in my power for your good and safety. This I will always do as long as life is in me. But alas! I see with grief I can at present do little for you on this side the water, for the only thing that can now be done is to defend yourselves till the French assist you, if not to be able to make better terms. To effectuate this, the only way is to assemble in a body as soon as possible, and then to take measures for the best which you who know the country are only judges of. This make me be of little use here; whereas, by my going into France instantly, however dangerous it may be I will certainly engage the French court either to assist us effectually and powerfully, or at least to procure you such terms as you would not obtain otherwise. My presence there, I flatter myself, will have more effect to bring this sooner to a determination than anybody else, for several reasons; one of which I will mention here; viz. it is thought to be a politick, though a false one, of the French court, not to restore our master, but to keep a continual Civil War in this country, which renders the English government less powerful, and of consequence themselves more. This is absolutely destroyed by my leaving the country, which nothing else but this will persuade them that this play cannot last, and if not remedied the Elector will soon be as despotic as the French King which, I should think, will persuade them to strike the great stroke which is always in their power, however averse they may have been to it for the time past. Before leaving off I must recommend to you, that all things should be decided by a council of all your chiefs, or, in any of your absence, the next commander of your several corps with the assistance of the Duke of Perth and Lord George Murray, who, I am persuaded, will stick by you to the very last. My departure should be kept as long private and concealed as possible on one pretext or another which you will fall open. May the Almighty bless and direct you

Charles P.

It was a letter of staggering conceit, condescending, patronising and utterly lacking in any appreciation of either what had happened or was now happening. The tone, which suggests the chiefs brought the whole thing on themselves and Charles was only trying to help them out, was hurtful. But the man who wrote it was already in the grip of a giant illusion which he maintained to the end of his life. Charles had, within a week of Culloden, when he wrote this letter, become the Wronged One. Nothing was his fault: he alone had tried to do his best and had been let down. He had already detached himself from those who followed him and now, though he felt pity for them, he no longer felt involved. He was distant, fatherly, full of friendly advice – an attitude which bore no relation to that of the Prince they had known. Luckily, though the letter was left to John Hay to give to young Sheridan (Sir Thomas' nephew) for delivery, there is no record of any of the chiefs either receiving or hearing about it. It was just as well. However perplexed Charles' message to disperse had left them, they could at least preserve the opinion they had had of him without too much lying to themselves. The letter would have made that impossible.

By the time he wrote the letter, Charles was on the west coast of Scotland, convinced that he was about to be taken off by a French ship. He had ridden by night and day across Scotland, passed from one hand to another like a red hot coal. Everyone had wanted rid of him. With astonishing speed, those in whose hands he found himself passed him on to others, more out of anxiety for themselves than for him. But he did not, at the end of that first week, get away to France. Instead, he spent five months as a hunted man, living from hand to mouth, before he was so lucky. For him, those months became a kind of testing time in which he sank to depths of depression hitherto unknown to him and yet at the same time enjoyed himself as he was never to again. He was physically and psychologically battered, but emerged essentially unchanged, so that all the suffering did not seem to have made him a finer man, only a more experienced one.

In Rome, James had not yet heard of his son's defeat at Culloden. Charles had never had greater need of his father's sensible, restraining influence and yet communication between them had never been worse. He had written only after his victories – after Prestonpans and Falkirk – and James had little idea of the true situation.

By the time he knew what had happened on 16th April Charles was somewhere hiding in the hills and beyond reach of letters. His anxiety rose to a new pitch and he became demented by fears for his son's safety. His fears, though not realised, were for once fully justified.

PART III
The Escape 1746

James Francis Edward Stuart, The Old Pretender, Charles' father
Contemporary portrait by Belle
(National Portrait Gallery)

Clementina Sobieska, Charles' mother
Contemporary portrait attributed to Trevisani
(Scottish National Portrait Gallery)

Charles Edward Stuart as a child   Contemporary miniature
(Reproduced by kind permission of the Revd J. G. Antrobus)
Charles Edward and Henry Stuart as boys   Contemporary miniature
(Reproduced by kind permission of The Duke of Buccleuch, PC, KT)

Dear Papa

I am glad you find the good weather
at Albano so favorable to your health
tho it hinders me so much longer from
the happiness of seeing you Whesher
absent or present I hope you will allways
continue your love to me My brother
is very well and so it is Dear Papa

your most Butifull Son

June the 10.th   Charles P.
         1729

Letters from Charles to his father
(Reproduced by gracious permission of Her Majesty The Queen)

Edinburgh y.e 4.th 8obre, O.S.
                                    1745

I is impossible for me to give you
a distinct gurnal of my proseidings
because of my being so much hurrid
with business which allows me
no time; but notwithstanding
I cannot Let slip this occasion
of giving a short accoun of y.e
Battle of Gladsmure fought on

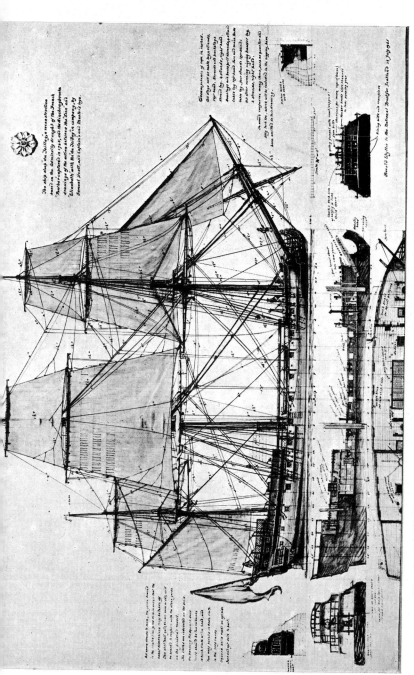

The ship that took Charles to Scotland   Scale drawing of the *Du Teillay*   (*The National Trust for Scotland*)

Lord George Murray
Contemporary painting
(Reproduced by kind permission of The Duke of Atholl)

The Duke of Cumberland
Painted *c.* 1758 after Reynolds
(National Portrait Gallery)

An Incident in the Rebellion of 1745
Culloden painted by P. D. Morier
(Reproduced by gracious permission of Her Majesty The Queen)

Donald Cameron of Lochiel
Painted by George Chalmers in
1762 fourteen years after
'Gentle' Lochiel's death

*(Reproduced by kind permission of
D. H. Cameron of Lochiel)*

The Lord President
Duncan Forbes
Portrait attributed to
Jeremiah Davison

*(Scottish National Portrait
Gallery)*

Flora Macdonald
Contemporary portrait by Allen Ramsay
(Ashmolean Museum, Oxford)

Charles Edward Stuart in 1745
Miniature painted in oils on
   copper
*(Reproduced by kind permission of
The Earl of Wemyss and
March, KT, LLD)*

Clementina Walkinshaw,
Charles' mistress
Miniature
*(Reproduced by kind permission
of The Duke of Atholl)*

Louise of Stolberg, Charles' wife
(Stonyhurst College)

Louise of Stolberg and her lover
Alfieri
Portraits by Fabre

(The Mansell Collection)

Charlotte, Duchess of Albany, daughter of Charles and Clementina Walkinshaw
Chalk drawing by Gavin Hamilton

(Reproduced by kind permission of The Lord Primrose)

Henry Stuart, Cardinal York, Charles' brother
Portrait by Batoni
(National Portrait Gallery)

Charles Edward Stuart, The Young Pretender
Painted by H. D. Hamilton *c.* 1785
(National Portrait Gallery)

CHAPTER TWELVE

On the Islands

It is maddening, but true, that the sight of an aristocrat, never mind a prince, in tatters enduring hardship for which he has not been created, moves ordinary people to depths of compassion they could never feel for one of their own kind. Charles traded on this emotional reaction, not entirely unintentionally. He had a habit of moving his bloodstained feet or waving his dirty calloused hand that somehow made people feel that it was all their fault. Their pity knew no bounds. Many a poor Highlander who had fought at Culloden, who was wounded, tired and hungry, was turned brutally away by people frightened out of their normal humanity, while Charles was taken in, if reluctantly, at whatever risk. He remained princely at all times, ever ready with a noble line, ever issuing invitations to the St James's Palace he had never seen. Nobody ever laughed in his face.

The first few days after Culloden were all action. Few decisions were made by Charles, except to head for the west coast rather than the east. He took only four days to reach it, and went from Invergarry onwards on foot. At a time when all over Scotland men without Charles' advantages of guides and protectors were performing feats of amazing physical endurance, it seems slightly ludicrous to marvel at his particular stamina. But, though it may not be worth much, Charles at least proved tough. Cumberland, covering the same number of miles under the same conditions, would never have lasted five minutes. It became a point of pride with Charles never to complain, never to rest. In a way, it was all he had left. There was nothing else he could take pride in. The miles he covered and the exhaustion it reduced him to were all a relief: physical exertion wiped out unpleasant thoughts. With him were Ned Burke, a Highlander who acted as guide, Allan Macdonald, a priest, and O'Sullivan. It was O'Sullivan who all the time worked on Charles to make him go back to France at once. All the gruelling miles from Invergarry to Borradale he kept up a constant propaganda so that Charles, who might have come round to wanting to go back and try again, would not think of such a thing. It is one of the few times one really feels Charles was under anyone's influence. It could only have happened because he was more than willing to be so.

Once the party had arrived in Borradale, their problems were far from over. They were hunted men in an occupied country and made contact with people at the risk of instant betrayal. There was no chain of loving Scots ready to suffer death for their Prince: those Scots had been at Culloden. They were now among a population who awaited reprisals from the Hanoverians and there were many among them who had no romantic notions of loyalty. Self-preservation was their motto. In these circumstances, for Charles to involve anyone at all was an act of cruelty. He might escape: the ordinary man or woman could not hope to do so. At first he may not have realised what helping him would mean but later, as the Government net tightened, he could have been in no doubt. To save his own skin he brought death or imprisonment to those he had been so fond of saying he would die for. But then, under stress, perhaps all fine moral standards go overboard.

There were no French ships conveniently hanging about Borradale at the time, so Charles decided to go back to the islands where he had landed, hoping to find one there. He actually seemed to imagine that Sir Alexander Macdonald and Macleod would shelter and help him in spite of their very clear refusal before. He sent for one Donald Macleod, who he hoped would take a message for him. Donald met him in the wood. The meeting was typical of many to follow. Standing before him, Charles said, 'You see, Donald, I am in distress. I therefore throw myself into your bosom; do with me what you like. I hear you are an honest man and fit to be trusted.' It was all there, in that little melodramatic speech: the charming understatement of his condition, the total trust, the implied flattery, the giving of responsibility. Donald was touched, as they were all to be. The formula hardly ever failed. But he also had his head screwed on the right way and was taking no messages to well-known Government supporters. Charles would have to think of something else, then he would be pleased to serve him. Charles had to think quickly: news had just come that a detachment of Cumberland's force was near. All he could think of was to get off the mainland, so Donald was entrusted with the job of finding a boat. He found it, and seven boatmen, and four pecks of oatmeal and a pot to cook it in – but having done all this he advised Charles to wait a day for a storm was approaching. Charles refused. He got in the boat with O'Sullivan, Allan Macdonald, Ned Burke and O'Neil (who had joined up with him again), and ordered Donald to set sail. Hardly had they lost sight of land before the storm broke. Cowering in the bottom of the boat while the rain lashed, thunder roared and the waves threatened to engulf them at any minute, Charles told Donald to turn back. Donald took a grim pleasure in telling him it was impossible – their only hope was to go with the wind.

In the morning, they found themselves off Benbecula, the middle island of the Outer Hebrides, and anchored at Rossinish. For Charles, it was a moment of realisation. Benbecula is the most desolate place on earth, a flat, barren island, treeless, intersected at every point by arms of the sea that make it resemble a jig-saw. There was nowhere to hide, no forests, no hills, no rocks, no houses, only dreary wastes of sea-washed peat and the company of birds. The storm still had not died out, so they camped for two days in a deserted hut, glad of Donald's oatmeal. Though such a sojourn in such a place might be expected to utterly demoralise anyone, it had the reverse effect on Charles. He had begun to cheer up. It was as if he had been through the valley of the shadow, and come out again. The eternal optimist in him took over and he was ready to make the best of it. He was visited by old Clanranald and advised to go to Stornoway to get a ship. They set sail, but another storm blew them to Scalpa, and from here the faithful Donald went on alone to Stornoway. When he had hired a boat to take them to the Orkneys, he sent back for Charles, but another storm blew him to Lewis and he had to walk the rest of the way to Stornoway. It was a very dark rainy night. By the time Charles, O'Neil and O'Sullivan had arrived outside Stornoway they were soaked to the skin and shivering with cold. Macleod, waiting for them, had bad news: the men of Stornoway, realising who Charles was, refused to let him have a boat. They wished him no harm but they would not help him in any way and furthermore they wanted him off the island as quickly as possible.

It was Charles' first introduction to hostility since Culloden and it roused him to fury. He expected everyone to be like Donald Macleod – loyal, brave, ready to put him before themselves. The humiliation of being turned out hit him hard and all the way back to Scalpa he seethed. Spending four days on an uninhabited island on the way there did not improve his temper, nor did the news from Scalpa, when they got there, that Donald Campbell, who had been his host there, was now imprisoned for his hospitality. A man-of-war sighted them and they made all speed to escape. This time the inevitable storm was welcome for it enabled them to reach Benbecula. They had come full circle.

Clearly, a French ship was not going to be easy to contact, and, clearly, they could not go on running in circles to avoid capture. The first essential was to find some safe place to hide while messages were sent to get help. It occurred to Charles that in leaving the mainland he might have done a very silly thing, for at least there there were plenty of hiding-places and two routes for French ships to arrive, west and east coast. Poor Donald was sent to the mainland to contact as many of the faithful as he could, and to bring back money if he could find Murray of Broughton. Charles meanwhile walked to Coradale on South Uist, a walk more gruelling than any map could ever show. It was almost a month after Culloden by this time – 14th May – and underneath his cheerfulness a feeling of panic grew. 'The Prince,' said O'Sullivan with a good deal of fellow feeling, 'began to be very low, tho' he did what he could not to appear so and never complained.'

Coradale provided Charles with a curious interlude. It is a good place to hide, one of the few on the Outer Hebrides. Behind the little cove is a mountain range two and a half thousand feet high, in front of it the sea, across it the hills of both Skye and the mainland can be seen. Charles camped here from 14th May to 5th June, in a forester's hut. The weather, which until now had been atrocious, was suddenly good. The sun shone, the sea was calm, there were birds to shoot and fish to catch, and even agreeable company for as well as O'Sullivan and O'Neil Charles had had, since Benbecula, a new companion sent to him by Clanranald. (The Clanranald Macdonalds were the chief family of these outer islands and many of the younger members had fought for Charles, though the Macdonalds of Sleat, Sir Alexander and Lady Margaret, preserved an outward façade of loyalty to the Government.)

This companion was one Neil Maceachain, a young schoolmaster of about Charles' age, a lively fellow with whom Charles had many agreeable conversations. He observed the Prince closely and saw how his moments of melancholy alternated with a boisterousness he could not suppress and which Neil felt was more truly him: ' ... at other times he was so hearty and merry, that he danced for a whole hour together, having no other musick but some highland reel which he whistled away as he tripped along.' He also provided some insight into Charles' character:

It happened one day as he was walking along the coast with Neil and the rest of the gentlemen being an excessive hot day they spied a number of young whales approaching near the shore and observing them to make straight for the rock whereon they sat down, he sent immediately for his fusee, and as they came within his reach he fired at them; and being informed some time before that Neil was an incomparable good swimmer, he ordered him to strip and haul the whale ashore, which he swore he had shot dead. Neil, in obedience to his orders, and to humour him, began to strip very slowly till he saw the whale, which had received no hurt, out of sight.

Around 3rd June there was even a party to liven things up. Boisdale and some other local Jacobites visited Charles in his hide-out. Boisdale actually arrived after the main party was over:

> Boystile came next day, and was received by the Prince with open arms, and found some of the gentlemen of the country who came to see him the day before of whose number was Hugh Macdonald, of Balisher from North Wist, who was ready to sacrifice his life and fortune for the prince's safety (I say) Boystile at his arrival found all these lying in their bed, very much disordered by the foregoing night's carouse, while his royal highness was the only one who was able to take care of the rest, in heaping them with plaids, and at the same time merrily sung the 'De Profundis' for the rest of their souls.

There was no doubt that Charles had a stomach of iron. Never fussy at the best of times, he ate anything that came his way while those with him turned up their noses. Nothing affected his appetite and he could drink any of them – as on this occasion – under the table, his early taste for liquor, of which James had so disapproved, standing him in good stead. Neil admired this capacity unreservedly: 'and he had always a good appetite and could eat any meat that came his way, as well as those accustomed to it from their infancy. He took care to warm his stomach every morning with a hearty bumper of brandy, of which he always drank a vast deal; for he was seen to drink a whole bottle of a day without being in the least concerned.'

It was lucky that Lady Clanranald had supplied him not only with shirts, shoes and stockings but plenty of brandy, for Charles was fast approaching the stage when he not only liked but needed it. Since it seemed to do him no harm whatsoever, nobody thought of restraining him. Even if they had done, they probably would not have dared. For all the apparent camaraderie, Charles was always the Prince and never more so than when he was supposedly living simply. He was charming and friendly but liked things done for him and was quick to assume a masterful tone when it suited him.

Charles, as at other times in his life, never lacked faith. He remained firmly convinced, even at his lowest moments, that he would be helped. It never entered his head that he might have to manage on his own: all this was merely an interval while his friends arranged something. His astounding faith was not misplaced. All the time Charles hid, there was no lack of activity to rescue him and transport him to a safe place. This would have been achieved much more quickly if it had not been for the need for absolute secrecy, which meant information as to his where-abouts was kept to a very restricting minimum. Furthermore, there was the complication of getting this information to the people who needed it. All messages went by hand, all messengers took days to reach their destination. Only the last man in the chain ever knew where Charles was the night he left him: not the night after. It was precisely because they knew how quickly Charles would be betrayed, because they had no con-fidence at all in the local population, that his friends dared not make communication smoother.

It was French efforts to rescue Charles that suffered most, which was all the more tragic because they were the only ones really in a position to help him – his friends on the mainland, for all their willingness, were having quite enough trouble saving their own skins. France had far from abandoned Charles, even if she had not lived up to his expectations. She had no intention of leaving him to his fate. Far from it: plans to rescue him *in the event* of defeat were being made two months before Culloden, by Walsh. Writing to Maurepas in March he said, astutely, 'But the Prince's fortunes could so decline that he would have no alternative to seeking refuge in the hills, and this could make him think of returning to France.' Walsh went on to suggest the fitting of two privateers to sail at once for the west coast of Scotland. This was done. On 30th April the two ships were at anchor in Loch nan Uamh, ready and waiting to take Charles off. There they learnt of his defeat at Culloden and how timely their arrival was, but try though they might they could not contact him. No one knew where he was (on Scalpa en route for Stornoway). News of the ship spread through the area and Jacobites flocked to take advantage of this gift from heaven. Among them were some who had heard, without being sure, that Charles had gone to the Hebrides. Plans were made to send a message to him but, before it could be sent, Captain Noel in the *Greyhound* battered the two French ships mercilessly, leaving them with just enough strength to limp home, loaded to the gunwales with the fugitives of Culloden. Before they arrived, France had news of Culloden. On 13th May rumours of defeat circulated, on 18th May they were con-firmed. Walsh, without waiting to see what had happened to the two ships already dispatched, urged others should be sent from some neutral country under cover of commerce. Maurepas and the King did not agree. Smaller ships should be sent, they said. Accordingly, at the beginning of June as Charles basked in the Coradale sun, the first of them searched Lochs Broom, Ewe and nan Uamh.

He felt sure French ships would be hunting for him and spent hours looking out to sea. All he saw were the vigilant British men-at-war, drawing ever nearer. But it was troops moving towards his hiding-place from the interior of South Uist that finally forced Charles to leave Coradale. On 6th June he was on the run again, back to Benbecula, where he and O'Neil hid for three days before Donald and O'Sullivan picked them up in a boat. A storm prevented them going back to Coradale and they had to spend the night cowering behind a rock in an anchorage on the coast. The enemy was very near and not even Coradale was reckoned to be safe.

The weather had broken again and with it his luck. Charles and his companions made for Loch Boisdale at the top of South Uist, hoping that Macdonald of Boisdale would help them. Unfortunately, he had already been taken prisoner. All they could do was hang about the hills, thinking frantically what they could do. They seemed back to square one with a vengeance. 'We were never a day or night without rain, the Prince was in a terrible condition, his legs and thy's cut all over from the bryers; the mitches or flys wch are terrible in yt. country devoured him and made him scratch those scars wch made him appear as if he was cover'd with ulsers.' Burt had already noted what a pest these flies were, bearing out this description: 'there are great swarms of little flies which the natives call "malhoulakins" ... These are so very small that separately they are but just perceptible and that is all; and being of a blackish colour, when a number of them settle upon the skin, they make it look as if it was dirty; there they soon bore with their little augers into the pores, and change the face from black to red.' Charles' iron stomach had also begun to show signs of wear and tear. O'Sullivan says: 'he took a looseness which turned to a bloody flux.' Somehow they managed to get some treacle which apparently cured it. But they could not go on hiding like this, constantly almost caught by the redcoats. Once, their precious single tent almost betrayed them, but luckily they took it down first thing every morning. They decided to split up. Charles would go north with O'Neil and Neil Maceachain while O'Sullivan and Donald Macleod and Ned Burke were left to take their chance. O'Sullivan says Charles told him: 'My project is to make the best of my way to Lacy Clanranalds, get myself drest there in womens cloaths and if yu can bring me the boat to go off imedatly to Lady Margeurittes to the Isle of Sky.'

There is no doubt that if, at this desperate time, the help of Flora Macdonald had not been given, Charles would have been caught. It was only by moving from Loch Boisdale when he did that he escaped capture and he would never have got off the island at all without her cooperation.

Knowing that behind him he left a trail of captured helpers, it is all the more amazing that the chivalrous Charles should have gone along with O'Neil's suggestion to use a woman to escape. O'Neil had met and been impressed by Flora when visiting Clanranald. She struck him as intelligent – which she was – and sensible, a creditable product of the classical learning found so surprisingly in Skye at that time, where Latin was taught for half-a-crown a quarter, and English and writing for a shilling. He knew she was uniquely positioned to travel between islands, for she had a home on South Uist but her mother, who had married again, now lived in Skye. She was therefore well known in both islands, with a good alibi for travelling between them. In these difficult times it was also useful that her stepfather commanded a company of militia in South Uist and so could provide her with a pass. All this had occurred to O'Neil, but he still had to present his scheme to Flora. Although she had expressed a desire to help Charles, this might be going too far. All he could do was ask. So he and Charles and Neil walked all the way to Ormaclett in the north of South Uist. When they got there, at midnight, O'Neil went ahead to Flora's home and, risking alarming her by his late knocking-up, told her his plan and her part in it.

Flora was every bit as sensible as Donald Macleod had been. Her first reaction was that it was a fantastic, dangerous scheme which she wanted nothing to do with. O'Neil was persuasive, but not sufficiently so. Flora continued to say no. It was to her credit that she never at any time rebuked O'Neil for asking her. There was now only one card O'Neil had to play – Charles himself. Asked if she would like to meet him, Flora replied 'that as she had not that happyness before, she did not look for it now, but that a sight of him would make her happy tho he was on a hill and she on another'. It was arranged forthwith. If he had been specially made-up and cued for the part Charles could not have done better. Flora was appalled as he stood before her, filthy, ragged, covered in sores and yet dignified. She was not a romantic girl, any more than Clementina Walkinshaw had been, but she was exactly the type to whom Charles appealed. If there was one thing calculated to appeal to a woman who prided herself on her own honesty, decency and virtue, it was the sight of someone else struggling to maintain those standards in spite of their circumstances. She said she would help.

Her assistance was a morale-booster for Charles at a vital time, but did not prevent his growing anxiety displaying itself in attacks of nerves. While Flora made all the necessary arrangements, he hid in the open with his two friends. When Neil brought the message to meet Flora, they had to trust some local boatmen to take them by sea because all the fords on land were guarded by soldiers. They were landed on the farthest tip of the island.

Neil observed an arm of the sea come in betwixt him and the rest of the land, which formed an island; he returned immediately and informed the Prince who started up like a mad man and walked to the end of the island at such a rate as if he had a mind to fly over to the other side, but his career soon stopped; whereupon he fell a scoulding Neil as if it had been his fault and the cursed rascals [meaning the boatmen] who land'd them upon that desert island designedly that he might starve with hunger and cold, in short, there was no pacifying him, till, at last, Neil told him to comfort himself, that he would sweem over to the other side and would bring a boat in half-an-hours time, from that moment he never gave Neil one minute's rest, till, to please him, he began to strip, notwithstanding that it rained most prodigiously.

Luckily, Neil found a way at last of wading across and they reached Rossinish late at night. Here they were able to shelter in the house of one of Clanranald's tenants. Charles was jumpy. He had not, perhaps, the same trust in Flora as he had had in Donald Macleod and feared she would not be at the meeting-place with the passes. But she was. Calmly and quietly she had seen to everything and was waiting for him. They had 'dinner' together in a hut with Lady Clanranald and her daughter. His spirits quite restored, Charles was full of life and entertained them all. The next night he put on his female clothes, rather reluctantly and self-consciously, and together with Flora and Neil he got into a boat rowed by four trustworthy men, each one risking his life with no name to protect him. O'Neil was left behind. According to Neil, he resented this not only because he wanted to stay with Charles but because he fancied Flora. Charles begged her to take him, but she was adamant: she had passports for only three people – herself, one male and one female servant. Neil knew the islands and could act as a guide so he must go. She would stand no soft-hearted nonsense.

The sea which they crossed to Skye was infested with British ships and the chances of being taken by them were high. Flora and the boatmen were well acquainted with stories about the character of Captain Ferguson, the most feared of them all. A Lowland Scot, he carried out a system of persecution worse than any Cumberland had devised. Flora and all those involved knew that though they might get Charles safely away, they would then have to go back to their homes, where searching questions would await them. There was not a hope, situated as they were, of evading, at the best, interrogation. It was lucky that there was no touch of Lord George Murray about Flora Macdonald or Charles would have had a miserable passage being told what was risked for him. As it was, he did not have the imagination to suffer on their behalf.

The passage was, in any case, miserable enough. They left Benbecula on a fine evening, but once out in the open sea a strong wind blew up. Even in a large steamer, that stretch of water feels dangerous, but Charles had by this time withstood so many beatings from the sea that he believed himself invincible. He sang songs and was full of soothing words – a hero because he did not really understand how near disaster they were. Arriving, after a terrible night, off the north-west coast of Skye they were fired on by the militia and had to creep in very slowly. Charles found it all exhilarating. They landed near the house of Sir Alexander Macdonald who was helping Cumberland at Fort Augustus. It was a delicate situation. Would his wife, known to be Jacobite at heart, risk helping Charles, proving what he had maintained all along – that really they wanted to support him? Flora was given the job of finding out. When she got to the Macdonald house it was to find an officer of the militia there who questioned her very carefully. She answered sensibly and he was satisfied. Lady Margaret Macdonald was in a panic but determined to help Charles, in spite of her husband's and the Government's wrath. She arranged for him to go to the house of her factor, Macdonald of Kingsburgh.

A new chain had begun. Charles took it all for granted, seeming above worry and quite happy to trust himself to others. It was this child-like trust they found so appealing. The only times Charles ever felt near despair were most noticeably when he was both not on the move and not being looked after. Other people always gave him confidence. His position in Skye was in fact as perilous as it could be, but he walked to Kingsburgh's house without a qualm. It was an embarrassing experience. His long strides were not suited to a skirt and he did not enjoy masquerading as a woman – he felt he looked a fool, which he did, and that hurt his dignity. At Kingsburgh's house there was a treat in store – good wholesome food and a real bed to sleep in. It was also balm to his injured soul to find himself treated with such awed respect and he enjoyed being gracious and bestowing smiles. The Kingsburghs found it hard to smile back, worried to death about the consequences of their hospitality. One's sympathy for them lessens slightly when one hears Mrs Macdonald wanting locks of Charles' hair: it puts her courage on a different level from Flora's. Not, of course, that Charles minded. On the contrary, such a piece of silliness seems to have gratified him and he was pleased to lay his head in Flora's lap and have some hair cut off. Kingsburgh himself was hardly any better, for he kept and cherished Charles' worn-out shoes.

Charles left the next morning, changing his clothes for Highland ones in a wood near by. It had been decided for him – which was the way he liked it – that the best plan would be to go to the tiny island of Raasay to throw himself on the protection of the laird there. Unfortunately, the laird himself was a fugitive, but since Raasay was clear of troops the plan was kept to. Those thinking for Charles could only think one step at a time so they could hardly be blamed for making mistakes. Charles was lucky that though Raasay proved a mistake – it was too small to offer any cover – he got off again. During his stay with the Macleods on Raasay Charles had some interesting conversations, particularly with Malcolm, which reveal his train of thought at the time. He observed that his way of life at the moment was certainly a hard one, but that he would rather live it for ten years than be captured because he dreaded they would secretly poison or assassinate him. He also heard, for the first time, of the atrocities committed after Culloden, which were a great shock to him. 'Surely that man who calls himself the duke, and pretends to be so great a general, cannot be guilty of such cruelties. I cannot believe it.' Malcolm could not get him to believe it, no matter how convincing he was. It was vital to Charles that he should preserve the idea that he had done no harm even if he had done no good: he could not go on believing that innocent civilians had been butchered as part of a reprisal campaign against him. This idea of being ordained to do some final good was beginning to obsess him – he could not live with the thought that no great destiny awaited him. 'Do you not think, Malcolm,' he said on one occasion, 'that God Almighty has made this person of mine for doing some good yet? When I was in Italy, and dining at the King's table, very often the sweat would have been coming through my coat with the heat of the climate, and now that I am in a cold country, where the climate is more trying, and exposed to different kinds of fatigues, I really find I agree equally with both.' It was either pathetic or impressive depending on which way one looks at it, but it shows that Charles at least turned over in his head the purpose of his existence as he walked along in the wind and rain.

The Macleods took him to the south-west of Skye where some new protectors, the Mackinnons, took him to the mainland. Charles arrived at Mallaig on 7th July, two and a half months after he had departed so hopefully for the islands. During the three days he then spent in the open he had plenty of time to reflect on how utterly useless those weeks had been. He had not got away to France, he had not come anywhere near it. Behind him he had left a trail of captured helpers, bringing suffering to countless families. Nor, now that he had returned to the mainland, was the position as it had been when he left, for in ten weeks Cumberland had turned Scotland into a country of occupation. The whole of the Highlands had been systematically settled with soldiers, soldiers who hated their posting, soldiers who were barely restrained from taking their resentment out on the civilian population. Charles was now in touch with people who could swear the truth of what Malcolm Macleod had told him on Skye. They could tell him of the wholesale burnings – the homes of Lochiel, Glengarry, Kinlochmoidart, Keppoch, Cluny, Glengyle and other lairds had all been rased to the ground. They could tell him of the shootings of women and children, the driving away of the cattle, the destruction of the crops. From the moment he landed at Mallaig he saw with his own eyes the evidence and could be in no doubt what he had brought to Scotland. It never for one moment made him think that enough was enough: all it did was harden his resolution to get back to France and start again.

The immediate problem was, as ever, to find someone to trust, someone who knew the country and the hiding-places. Soldiers, stationed at the head of every glen, fired on them as they tried to find shelter, and for the Mackinnons the problem was agonising. It was all very well for Charles to say that he trusted them, but who were *they* to trust? They were in Clanranald's country, so they tried the old chief. He refused to help. Charles was astounded: it was one of the few direct refusals he had ever had. What he could not understand was that it came from the head of a family who had joined his cause right at the start. Worse was to come. In desperation, the Mackinnons started off to take Charles to Macdonald of Morar's country. Morar's house had been burnt to the ground and he was hiding in a cave, but he seemed willing to help. When he realised, however, that the Mackinnons wanted to pass Charles on to him, his willingness vanished. Disgusted – disgusted, not compassionate – Charles set off for Borradale to try the Macdonalds there. To the enormous relief of the Mackinnons, Borradale took the burden firmly on his shoulders even though he too hid in a cave near his burnt-down house. The Mackinnons left Charles to his care. They were both captured soon after.

Borradale had not shirked to accept what he chose, and Charles regarded, as his responsibility but others might think of as an imposition. The countryside crawled with redcoats, so Charles would have to be moved out of the tight ring they formed up into the more inaccessible mountains. At the same time, he must be moved in one direction: towards the area where there might be a French ship. Such travelling was impossible during the day, but Glenaladale, the local Macdonald chief, undertook to get Charles through the chain at night. They moved very slowly, using information supplied by tenants to evade traps, always watching the fires burning on the hilltops where the sentinels passed and repassed. It took patience and stamina. The heather provided an invaluable surface for travelling over for 'it is more difficult to find a Highlander among the heather, except newly tracked, than a hare in her form'. The going was rough and would have been impossible without intimate local knowledge. Charles kept up with his guides, but had several falls and narrow escapes. They had to abandon the plan to look for a French ship and strike instead into the safer interior.

This running from cave to cave, sleeping fitfully during the day, alternately devoured by midges or soaked with rain, came to a temporary end on 24th July when Charles came into the hands of the Glenmoriston men. These eight men had been in the rising and were now banded together as outlaws to keep out of the way of capture. They were basically robbers, very rough characters, not perhaps originally attracted to Charles' cause by principle so much as expediency. But whatever their background Charles was lucky to be taken in by them. They took an oath to him – 'That their backs should be to God and their faces to the devil; that all the curses the Scriptures did pronounce might come upon them if they did not stand firm to the Prince in the greatest dangers' – but refused his offer of a like oath to them. They gave him, in both the caves they took him to, the first dry bed he had had for weeks and the first hot food. Their devotion to him seems to have been absolute. Because he did not like it, they gave up swearing when he was about, and if they did not join in his prayers, which he amazed them by saying every day, they did not jeer. Together they hunted and caught birds, keeping very close to the cave, and they admired his skill. At night they sat and talked and they listened respectfully to his stories of his good friends, the King and the Dauphin of France. He was one of them and yet set apart, which was how they all liked it. Wearing a coat of dark cloth; a tartan vest, plaid and trousers; a saffron-coloured shirt; a scarf knotted round his neck; a dreadful wig and bonnet and a pair of brogues tied together with string – he was indistinguishable from them to look at. It was, for Charles, a relief to be in their company. They were men already outside the law, not peaceful farmers he had precipitated from their homes. He need suffer no pangs of conscience on their behalf. The rest was much needed, though Charles had stood up to his ordeal better than the sneers of Horace Walpole implied: 'he is concealed in Scotland and devoured with distempers: I really wonder how an Italian constitution can have supported such rigours!'

CHAPTER THIRTEEN

Hide and Seek

This interlude did not last long. At the end of the week news came that the militia were only four miles away. Regretfully, the cave was abandoned, and the small band of men moved north again retreating into the mountains. Charles was more than ever anxious to make contact with the French ships he was sure must be at Poolewe, and sent messengers to contact them. After two days the messengers returned: a French ship had indeed been but it had gone again leaving two officers who had gone off carrying dispatches to Charles. The game of hide-and-seek was on: Charles immediately began searching for the officers who were searching for him, with the redcoats and militia playing piggy-in-the-middle. It seemed more than likely that both parties would miss each other and that this last in a long series of attempts to rescue Charles would fail as the others had done. That it did not was due entirely to the persistence and courage of individual Frenchmen. Left in the care of the Scots, Charles would without any doubt have been captured.

By the middle of June, when the second attempt to find Charles had failed, Maurepas was writing: 'It seems certain that the Stuart Prince is in one or other of the small islands of the north of Scotland. But he is so well concealed from his enemies and from those who would help him, that both seek him with the same lack of success.' At the beginning of July, a French ship almost had him. Instead it found, at the third attempt, O'Sullivan and O'Neil who had both so recently been with Charles. If Charles had not crossed to Skye he would have left for France at this moment. Everything possible was done to find him, O'Neil going off to Skye to search for him and in the end not getting picked up by the ship at the rendezvous arranged. She sailed for France via Norway with only O'Sullivan on board. The decision to sail on and not hang about trying to contact Charles, who they knew was very near, was made on the grounds that the chance of continuing to escape capture by the ever-vigilant British Navy was slim. If they were caught, no one would carry back the vital information France needed to know: that Charles had left the Hebrides and his pursuers were much stronger than had been thought.

It took the enemy ten days to discover that Charles had escaped the net. Then they picked up the trail and the captures and punishments began. Flora Macdonald was taken, Kingsburgh was taken, Malcolm Macleod was taken, all the boatmen were taken and brutally dealt with, the Mackinnons were taken. It was now known Charles was back on the mainland. On 13th July five hundred redcoats and the Highlanders of the Munro and Mackay Independent Companies marched westward to cordon off all the hill tracks and passes from Loch Hourn to Glenfinnan. It was in these circumstances, with every day counting, that a fourth attempt was made even before O'Sullivan's ship had returned.

The *Bien Trouvé* was a little ship which had already had a go at rescuing Charles. She carried the same company of volunteers who had been on the ill-fated *Elizabeth*. The minute they left France trouble began – one man-of-war chased them for six hours. They hit Scotland at Cape Wrath, which could hardly have been more useless, and then moved on to Loch Broom and Loch Ewe, where they learnt definitely, as de Dupont, one of their officers, wrote, that 'the Prince himself was in hiding, but no one knew where. It was even rumoured that he had embarked for France but they did not believe this to be so. After all he had said to them when his fortunes were at their peak they could not think that he would abandon them now to their grim, menacing fate.' Obviously, no breath of the Prince's letter to the chiefs had ever reached them. To keep the ship safe, it was agreed she should stand out to sea while volunteers continued the land search and then come back. When she came back 'we had nothing to tell ... All of us were beginning to fall quite sick, this due to the poor food, the unending Vigilance and our exposure to the winds; for we had only found one wretched hovel and that had been ruined by the weather.' They decided to move to Lochaber, but to let two of their officers go overland to search for Charles. They were all worried and depressed for the locals they came into contact with told them a minister had informed the Duke of Cumberland of their whereabouts.

The ship made for the open sea, to shake off pursuit, but was continually followed. On 22nd July the end came: 'Six times we had tacked about when, to our dismay, a sixteen gun snow named the "Tyral" came in to block our way ... we were obliged to surrender. The stormy weather gave us no chance to run ashore.' On board a prison-ship they suffered the usual fate of those taken: 'Throughout we slept on the hard deck, hourly victims to the impertinence of the merest cabin boy. Foul water was our only drink. Salt beef and biscuit, disgusting to eat in the severest famine, all we had for food. These beastly conditions brought us to a very low ebb.' The only thing that kept them going was the thought of the two officers and three cadets they had put ashore and even that did not make them very hopeful.

They should have had more faith. One officer and two cadets had been captured, but another officer and a cadet were still at large. The officer, de Lancize, and his companion had struck off into country they did not know, whose language they barely spoke, without maps or guides other than general directions given to them about how to find Lochiel's country, where they believed Charles would be. While they struck deeper into the country, they tried to keep contact with their ship by sending letters with messengers they had to hope were trustworthy. They finally got to Lochiel, but it did not seem to do them much good. They were not at all sure Lochiel was Lochiel and told him only vague tales of their mission. Lochiel, for his part, was not at all sure they were French officers: they might be Government spies. It was up to Charles, to whom he was now giving shelter, to decide whether he wanted to risk meeting them. He did. On 21st August at Achnacarry, in a wood, Charles and de Lancize at last met.

It was a strange meeting for both sides. De Lancize had not expected Charles to be dressed to kill – he had personal experience of what months in the open in the Highlands did to one's appearance – but he was not quite prepared to believe this rough creature was the Prince who had been his inspiration. He wore 'an old black Kilt, a plaid, philabeg and waistcoat, a dirty shirt and a long red beard'. Charles, who had hoped for help more substantial than two scruffy men, was not impressed either. There was a good deal of careful scrutinising, a lot of suspicious glances. To complicate matters Charles started off pretending to be simply a Captain Drummond in touch with Charles, and de Lancize pretended simply to have dispatches with no mention of an escape plan. But the two days they talked together seems to have convinced them of each other's sincerity. There was only one problem: no ship. De Lancize had lost touch with his ship, which anyway had been captured, and could only swear to Charles that another would soon be here to find him. Charles and the French had made contact, but what good was it going to do them?

In France, Versailles was in mourning for the death of the young Dauphine and, though interest in Charles still ran high, everyone was getting more than a little annoyed that his rescue was proving such a difficult, time-consuming business. Maurepas wrote crossly: 'It seems that, if he is still alive, he is unwilling to let anyone know where he is hiding. So far, all the trouble we have taken to find him and give him the means of leaving the north are futile.' He made Charles sound like a rather naughty, wayward boy. The extent of the problem still had not penetrated, but with the return of the ship carrying O'Sullivan a new slant was cast on it. O'Sullivan wrote the minute he got to Bergen, stressing the great danger Charles was in and the scale of the hunt after him. Meanwhile, another expedition was being planned: two frigates would sail to the west coast, two to the east, and they would all mount a massive search for Charles at the same time. A Captain Warren was the senior officer, a man who had already fought in Charles' army and successfully made his way back to France afterwards. The day Warren went on board his ship and prepared to sail with two and not four frigates – 'half a loaf is better than no bread' – O'Sullivan arrived in Paris. There is no record that he met Warren, but he certainly made straight for the authorities behind the new expedition and told them who would know how to get in touch with Charles. Warren had time, before he left, to be sent the news and the fact that he picked up the trail much quicker than any other French expedition seems too much of a coincidence.

Once Warren had gone in high spirits – 'Tis the height of my ambition and I shall always look upon it as the happiest action of my life, and I have great confidence that Providence has this blessing in store for me' – O'Sullivan did not let up in his efforts on Charles' behalf. He haunted King and court, the spectre at the feast, till they were heartily sick of him – 'Sullivan never misses the hours of the Minister's audience and has every night almost an hour's conversation with him ... Two or three days after, Sullivan has an audience from the French King, who enters into all that the Prince had done from the beginning to the latter end and what had happened to him since the battle of Culloden. The King seems to be really touched of what the Prince had done and suffered and shows all the good will imaginable, not only to do what can be done to save the Prince's personne, but to re-establish the King.' O'Sullivan was not alone in urging yet another expedition – a sixth – for Henry had never ceased his efforts on Charles' behalf. The next plan was to take O'Sullivan back to Scotland – 'I am extremely satisfied with the conduct of O'Sullivan,' Henry wrote. 'He will certainly never come back to France without the Prince.'

But Warren had not yet failed. Charles waited for him confidently, without knowing for whom he waited, or where or when he would appear. The British Government waited for him too, informing all men-of-war in north-west Scottish waters to be more than ever on the alert.

Through fog and mist, frequently sighted and followed, they made their way to Loch Boisdale. Here they found a pilot to take them across the Minch and into Loch nan Uamh. No sooner were they in than a gale blew up, which was an unexpected piece of luck since it kept other ships out. Warren got down to trying to contact Charles. Unfortunately, his information was obtained through a man nobody knew was a spy, so although they were duly put in touch with Glenaladale, who immediately set off to bring Charles, the Government were also informed at the same time. Another race had begun: could Charles be on board and away before the army arrived to arrest him? And could Warren safely stay till he did arrive? As a precaution, should he be obliged to run for it, Warren began inquiring for a pilot to take him round the north coast so that he could wait for Charles on the other side. He hoped it would not be necessary.

Glenaladale hoped so too, but his hopes seemed to be dashed when, coming into Lochiel's country, he found Charles had gone, and he 'could get no person that could give any certain account whereabouts his royal highness might be'. He did not know Charles had been almost surprised by a party of redcoats and had once more been on the run, sleeping in the rain under whatever rock he could find. By the time Glenaladale was looking for him he had moved to Ben Alder, in quite another direction, and here he was hiding in 'Cluny's Cage' together with quite a crowd of fugitive Jacobites including Lochiel himself. Glenaladale could never find them, nor anyone else who did not know where to look. 'It was,' said Cluny, 'situated in the face of a very rough, high and rocky mountain called Letternilichk, still a part of Benalder, full of great stones and crevices, and some scattered wood interspersed. The habitation, called the Cage, in the face of that mountain, was within a small thick bush of wood. There were first some rows of trees laid down, in order to level a floor for the habitation; and as the place was steep this raised the lower side to an equal height with the other, and these trees, in the way of joists and planks, were levelled with earth and gravel. There were betwixt the trees growing naturally on their own roots, some stakes fixed in the earth, which, with the trees, were interwoven with ropes, made of heath and birch twigs up to the top of the Cage, it being of a round or oval shape; and the whole thatched and covered with fog.' How could anyone find Charles there?

But someone did. An old woman told the disconsolate Glenaladale where Cluny was hiding and Cluny sent his son to bring Charles. The son confidently set off to where Charles had last been, and contacted a tenant there who he was sure would find him. The tenant could not, but by pure chance met Cluny himself, on the way back to his cage after an expedition, and all was well. Charles got the message on 13th September, only nine days after the ship had arrived. It almost came too late for Charles was beginning to think Lochiel's plan of making for the east coast the best after all. Relieved, the party set out for Loch nan Uamh, travelling with great caution, moving only at night. On 19th September, 'about six in the evening, after sitting to supper, a message came from "Le Conti" upon which Colonel Warren and the Captain of the Frigate got up in a great hurry, got on their best clothes, ordered us on board our Vessell with our chests ...' Charles was safely on board. All that remained was to get him back to France. There went with him about a hundred Highlanders who had come from all parts of Scotland when they heard there was a ship, but he left many more behind. The ships could only carry so many, but there were some, like Cluny, who did not want exile at any price. Once a reluctant convert to Charles' cause, Cluny had come to admire his prince. 'In deliberations he found him ready, and his opinions generally best; in their execution firm, and in secrecy impenetrable; his humanity and consideration showed itself in strong light, even to his enemies ... In application and fatigues none could exceed him.' In spite of this tribute, Cluny felt more attached to his country than to Charles. To him Charles wrote: 'Thanks to God I am arrived safely aboard the vessell, which is a verry clever one, and has another alonst with her as good, the first is of 36 guns and the second 32.' To the men who were not to come with him he made a pretty speech that showed how little effect the months after Culloden had had on his ego. 'My lads, be in good spirits, it shall not be long before I shall be with you, and shall endeavour to make up for the loss you have suffered. I have left money for your subsistence that are officers and have also left money to provide meal for all the private men.' Who could not sympathise with John of Borradale's bitter comment that he left them in a worse state than he found them? What could the puny amounts of money and meal he talked so grandly about do to feed the hundreds who now starved, homeless, with the winter about to come? His words made a mockery of their suffering – suffering that had still far from ended.

On board *L'Heureux* Charles slipped out of Loch nan Uamh early on the morning of 20th September. They made a safe passage across the dreaded Minch because the British men-of-war had been called to the east coast. The voyage proved uneventful and much shorter than the return of any other expedition. On 29th September the Prince disembarked at Roscoff, near Morlaix, in Brittany. Warren immediately wrote to James in Rome: 'I have the happiness to advise your Majesty of my wished for success in meeting His Royal Highness the Prince on the continent of Scotland and bringing him safe back to France, ... tis scarce to be imagined what a crowd of dangers he has run thro' by sea and land, but Providence has been visibly in special care and will doubtless in time complete his Wishes ... I congratulate your Majesty on this happy event, and think this is the happiest day of my life to see our great Hero delivered so miraculously from his enemys.'

Charles was now to know what it was to be treated like 'a great Hero', while in Scotland and England men died, as he had sworn he longed to, because he had failed them.

CHAPTER FOURTEEN
Prisoners and Martyrs

The real tragedy of Charles' five months in the heather was that it did not strip him of his illusions. He came to Scotland with them, he left with them intact. Seeing with his own eyes and hearing with his own ears that the entire population was very far from regarding him as its saviour had done him no good at all. He clung obstinately to the belief that he was a Deliverer in the face of all the evidence. When, in France, his thoughts turned to those who languished in gaol or were hanged for his cause, he was moved by their loyalty. He remained unmoved by the plight of those who had never been loyal, only coerced, and yet he must have known that a large part of his army had marched under duress. It was an element he ignored at the time and consigned to oblivion afterwards.

A great many of the three thousand prisoners taken during and after the rising were brought south to be tried, to Carlisle, York and London where dependable Whig juries could be guaranteed. Horace Mann thought the fact that there were trials at all highly commendable: '... nor can I understand what they mean by severity when in all other countries hundreds of them would have been hung up as soon as taken.' Brought with the prisoners were the witnesses of importance, but it was also the custom to parade batches of prisoners in front of the locals and see who could offer evidence against them. It is in these bits of evidence, reported by Baron Clarke, one of the judges, in his notebook, that the 'loyalty' Charles depended on can be seen for what it was in so many cases – not so far removed from that of the men in the apocryphal story told in later days of the Highland recruiting officer who announced 'The volunteers are ready; they are all lying bound hand and foot in the barn.' There was the case of sixteen-year-old John Coppoch about whom one witness testified: 'Sunday morn. saw the Pipers at his father's door – asking for this lad and said they would have him – they broke in and I went with them and they searched the House and in a loft I saw 'em pull him out in his shirt with a blanket about him. Saw him afterward – beating with men following with drawn swords and when he had done he put out his hand and said Dick, farewell.' Then there was Thomas Warrington, aged fourteen, about whom a woman testified: 'Boy lived with her at Manchester and was afraid of ye Rebels and said before he would go would beg his bread' – but they took him. They also took one John Ballantine, in whose defence a witness stated: 'Prisoner was my servant in Harvest 1745 and about Midnight 3 rebels came to my house and because I would not let them in they ask'd for the Prisoner and took him out of bed – bid him rise and go with them or they would kill him and drew a sword at his breast. He cried and took on much – didn't allow him any time to dress scarce. Made him take his pipes with him, about 8 days after he came back for his violin – and four men arm'd came with him to guard him from deserting him.' Could Charles be proud to have these in his army? Could he really pretend he was a Deliverer to the poor fiddler?

But for every one who had such a tale of woe to tell, there were a dozen who either suffered in silence or were proud to attest their sincerity. Baron Clarke himself was touched by the case of little John Thoris 'a little deformed boy' who was acquitted 'by favour of ye King's Counsel, though he bravely stayed loyal to his master'. The judge recorded the following anecdote in his notebook without comment: 'The Pretender ask'd this boy what use he could be of – to which he answer'd "Sir, tho' my body is small my Heart is as big as any Man's you have."' Words after Charles' own heart, and in them poor Thoris captured the feeling that led so many to the noose: Charles' most fervent supporters were all heart and no head. They died, when they died, still inspired after months in prison-ships or gaols, and the words in which they expressed their devotion are instructive. Charles thought he had been followed because he was the son of the rightful King come to restore peace and justice, but though Lord George Murray may have acted on such a principle, the rank and file did not. Hear Robert Lyon, executed at Carlisle in October, who followed Charles not just for religious reasons but because he was 'a Prince adorn'd with every quality that could attract the hearts of a wise people or make a nation happy'. Hear Thomas Syddal, executed on Kennington Common, who had never even seen Charles but was 'well assured of his excellent wisdom, justice and humanity' and who was 'too great and good to stoop to a falsity'. Hear David Morgan, no ruffian but a barrister by profession, who said of Charles: 'His character exceeds anything I could have imagined or conceived. An attempt to describe him would seem gross flattery.' They were all quite happy to die. Since their speeches were made on the scaffold they cannot help but redress the balance slightly in Charles' favour. What clearly emerges is that his behaviour earned him a devotion his cause never would have done. He was thought to be a good man. Stories were told of his care for the wounded, his good manners at all times, his policy of clemency even when to be merciful was directly against his own interests. He was an old-fashioned knight in a brutal age and they loved him for it, ignoring entirely that his charm might in itself be a weakness that caused the brutality of others to fall upon them.

Charles probably never heard of the words spoken by those who died for him in comparative obscurity at Carlisle, nor could he follow their trials. It was left to Bishop Fleming to record that when they were hung, drawn and quartered on Harraby Hill 'the crowd is said to have been v. gt. upon the occasion but many returned home with full resolution to see no more of y^t Kind it was so shocking'. Others were not so shocked, but remained relatively unmoved, like the curate at Arthuret who reported on 18th October: 'Ale brought Home, posted to Netherby, stay'd supper, paid 2 subscriptions, 9 executed at Carlisle.' But reports of the trials of the principal prisoners had certainly drifted over to France and he was able when he got there to follow the fate of those men who had so recently been in his army and were now scapegoats for his cause. On 23rd July, when Charles' own safety was still in doubt, bills for high treason had been issued against the Earls of Kilmarnock and Cromarty and Lord Balmerino. The trials of these rebel lords began on 30th July, while Charles sheltered in Glenmoriston. Horace Walpole called it 'the greatest and most melancholy scene I ever yet saw! ... this sight at once feasted one's eyes and engaged all one's passions ... their behaviour melted me!' Nobody expected the death penalty though 'the Duke, who has not so much of Caesar after a victory, as in gaining it, is for the utmost severity'. But the supreme penalty was announced and though Cromarty was reprieved, the other two were executed on 18th August. Balmerino wrote a letter to James which Charles was to see:

> Sir – You may remember that in the year 1716, when your Majesty was in Scotland, I left a company of foot purely with a design to serve your Majesty, and had I not made my escape then I should certainly have been shot for a deserter. ... Sir, when his Royal Highness the Prince your son came to Edinburgh, as it was my bounden and indispensable duty, I joyn'd him for which I am tomorrow to lose my head on the scaffold whereat I am so far from being dismayed that it gives me great satisfaction and peace of mind that I die in so righteous a cause ...

He went to the block firmly shouting 'God Save King James!' though Kilmarnock proclaimed King George and professed himself repentant. Their deaths were watched 'in amazing numbers, even upon masts of ships in the river', and many heard Balmerino call Charles 'so sweet a Prince that flesh and blood could not resist following him'. There remained only the deaths of Lord Lovat and Charles Radcliffe among those of note, and these did not follow until December. But Balmerino became the martyr whose words everyone repeated and Charles was left to ponder.

Once Charles was in Paris, there arrived every day refugees from Hanoverian wrath with pitiful tales to tell him of how their companions fared. The final number of men, women and children taken was 3,470. Of these, only 120 were executed and 684 simply disappeared, their fate unrecorded. The rest either died in prison, escaped, were banished, pardoned or – the greatest number – transported. A large number was released or exchanged. It was all quite arbitrary, the lotting of prisoners for trial or transportation being the common rule. Alexander Stewart recorded how: 'About two o'clock in the afternoon a rascall of the name of Gray ... with his hatful of tickets presented the hat to me, being the first man on the right of all the twentie that was to draw together. I asked Gray what I was going to do with that, and he told me that it was to draw for our lives, which accordingly I did and got number fourteen. So he desired me to look and be sure. I told him it was no great matter whether I was shure or not.' They were told to sign a petition to ask King George for mercy and when Stewart refused his name was put there all the same. In the end, he was taken to the county gaol to await transportation.

The gaols, however dreadful, were preferable to the prison-ships that sailed south for London while Charles hid. Disease and hunger increased the suffering of the poor Highlanders crammed head to toe on the decks. A letter to Bishop Forbes described how 'you'd have laughed to have seen them lying between decks like fish in a pond and everyone had a twig in his hand, to defend himself from the attacks of his neighbours lice'. When they were crawling with lice and too weak to move, 'they'd take a rope and tye about the poor sicks west, then they would hawll them up by their tackle and plunge them into the sea, as they said to drown the vermin; but they took specell care to drown both together. Then they'd hawll them up upon deck and ty a stone about on the leggs and overboard with them.'

Not all the prisoners so treated died. Some were lucky enough to escape when they got to London and get themselves a passage to the Low Countries or to France. Many arrived in Paris with their harrowing stories and Charles could no longer believe it was all exaggeration.

Charles never saw a single man hanged on his behalf. He never saw what a Jacobite's body looked like cut into quarters with the heart and bowels taken out. He never saw his men lying more dead than alive on the transports, never saw the inside of a single stinking gaol. It was a pity. The horror of battle had been an eye-opener to him, how much more so would the horror of failure. All he had seen were burned houses and lands, and to one who lacked imagination that was not enough. It was not that he did not believe stories of atrocities, but that he failed to estimate their cumulative effect. The depression that had come down on his father after the '15 – when he wrote 'Our Poor Scots have fled to the hills; it is a death by slow fire for them; God knows how they will exist or what conditions they will obtain in the end' – was never his. His reaction was one of rage and a desire for revenge. He failed completely to understand that revenge was a luxury that those who had endured the harshness of Hanover reprisals could not afford. What had happened was too much: revenge was not what they wanted – it was oblivion. The policy of Cumberland to exterminate the spirit of rebellion was more than successful – rebellion needs energy and strength and both were drained from the Highlands. Charles thought it was his duty to return to Scotland as soon as possible. In fact, it was his duty to stay away for ever. If his welcome had been doubtful in 1745, how much more so would it be ever after.

The laws which were enacted to complete Cumberland's work were not yet on the statute books when Charles returned to France so he could, theoretically, be forgiven for thinking that when the soldiers were withdrawn everything would return to normal. He had experienced himself the effect of the military occupation but never appreciated how well-organised it was. By the time he left Scotland, it was divided into four distinct military districts, under the Earl of Albemarle who had taken over from Cumberland, and whose headquarters were in Edinburgh. Each division had patrols of soldiers who went out hunting for fugitives, covering their area systematically. A chain of outposts was established throughout all divisions, and some old forts reoccupied. There was a permanent garrison at Stirling. The civilian population, even the anti-Jacobites, hated this military rule but there was nothing they could do about it. It had to be endured, the innocent suffering as well as the guilty. The ingratitude of the Government to its supporters broke Duncan Forbes' heart, though bitterness could never make him, or any other Whig, a Jacobite. 'Here I have been for above nine months playing the Knight Errant,' he wrote, 'at least acting with a perfect heart' – and those in London would not even cough up the puny expenses he was obliged to claim.

Charles never stopped to take any kind of consensus of opinion among the survivors of his campaign as to what should be done. Clearly, he must get back to Scotland as soon as possible with a large French force. Only then could he justify his leaving at all: he had not given up or run away or left the sinking ship or anything else unpleasant like that – he had gone to get help. With him were some of his officers and clan chiefs who would appear to have agreed with him. Men like Lord Ogilvy took positions in the French army till they should be called to the standard again. Men like Lochiel stayed at his side and encouraged him to beseech French assistance. Some old cronies like Strickland were dead, or recalled to Rome like Sheridan, but Kelly and O'Sullivan were still around doing the same ego-boosting service they had always done. But cooler, more influential heads were lacking. The Duke of Perth had died on board a ship bound for Holland, and Lord George Murray was in exile, suffering tortures for the fate he had consigned his family and people to. Charles would not have seen him even if he had come to Paris, not after his letter. There was no one, therefore, except his father to say that enough was enough, and for a long time now Charles had not listened to his father.

It seemed, in September 1746, that the blame for what had happened was France's. Charles would accept no responsibility. His passion in life became a determination to make France admit that blame and redress it. Neither his vigour, enthusiasm or singlemindedness had been affected by either his own or other men's sufferings. He wanted back in the ring as soon as possible. Far from fading away, his ambition reached a new crescendo during the next two years and revealed a man more complex than anyone had thought. The real history of Charles the man began after 1745.

Charles' hour of glory might be over, but no one then knew it, least of all himself. If anything, it seemed still to come. In spite of Culloden and its aftermath, he returned to France with an aura that burned brightly in the eyes of the rest of Europe. Amazingly, men concentrated not on what he had *not* achieved but on what he had, which is surely a rare experience for a loser. Given a proper army, proper weapons, proper support – there was no knowing what he might yet achieve. To contemporaries, his adventures seemed as extraordinary as they do to us, and they could not have enough of them. All Paris wanted to see him, all Europe was excited by him. It was felt he had made a great beginning, and where would he end?

PART IV

The Challenge 1746-1766

CHAPTER FIFTEEN

A Hero

Charles came back in October 1746 to a complex political situation of which he knew nothing. Time had not stood still during the sixteen months he had been away. Unknown to him, the power of France had been challenged: far more important than the battle of Prestonpans in 1745 had been the battles of Hohenfriedberg and Soor when Brandenberg-Prussia became overnight a threat to France. In the Netherlands, Marshal Saxe continued to win battles but at enormous cost, a cost which was beginning to cripple France. The war against England at sea and in the colonies was not going well. On all fronts, including the position financially at home, Louis XV was having a bad time. In these circumstances, there had never been less chance of Charles getting backing for another expedition. As far as Louis was concerned, he had, in providing a valuable diversion, served his purpose. It was to be hoped he realised that and knew his place.

But Charles did not know his place. As far as he was concerned, he had earned the right to a major campaign. He expected Louis to be ashamed and guilty about letting him down. Nothing he could see made him appreciate the delicacy of his situation. There were certainly no signs of approaching austerity or of France taking a back seat: Versailles and Paris seemed exactly the same as when he had left. In fact, Charles during his previous short eighteen-months' stay in France had not even begun to understand the subtleties of the internal administration of this great country he had been taught to revere. He had never begun to fathom the intricacies of where power lay. Henry, who had by now been at much closer quarters with the situation for some time, knew much more. He knew, as Charles did not, that since the death of Fleury in 1743 the government of the country had become increasingly chaotic. Instead of a new order emerging, all order was disappearing. Louis XV was absolute, but his indolence showed up the weakness of a system depending in essence on decisive, prompt action. Each minister did what he liked in his department and hung on to his own position like grim death. The ones who got on with it without bothering him were Louis' favourites. Anyone who wanted to achieve anything had first of all to get the ear of a minister who might, if it was also in his own interests, attempt to get the ear of Louis. It was a process Charles had always regarded with loathing. Now, when it was more necessary than ever that he should take advantage of it, he was even more impatient with it.

There was also a new factor to be reckoned with since he had been away, and here Charles had a perfect opportunity that he threw away. Far more important than any minister's influence was the new influence of the King's mistress, Madame de Pompadour, presented at court in 1745. Jeanne Poisson was almost the exact age of Charles. She was the daughter of a supplier of food to the armies and was therefore very far from being an aristocrat. Charles, who was foolish enough to share the attitude of those in court circles who were snobbish about this, overlooked the fact that the new Marquise was a clever, well-informed woman who could have done him a great deal of good. She was probably the only one who could. Foreign affairs were her particular passion and ambassadors who had more sense than Charles were never away from her door. Charles preferred to take tea with the Queen, who had been a great friend of his mother, and had no influence whatsoever. It was typical not only of his notion of chivalry – which he never would sacrifice to expediency – but of his stubborn refusal to play the system as it was. There ought to be no need to lower himself to backstairs intrigue: everything should be above board and in the open. What he wanted was man-to-man confrontations with Louis. These were precisely what he was not going to get from a king who spent his whole life assiduously avoiding them.

Charles could hardly bear to do all the weighing-up that his arrival on this scene called for. Furthermore, it was not the only kind of homework that had to be done. James' letters caught up with him with a vengeance and caused him as much irritation as sorting out the affairs of the court. According to James, some of their own people had been spending their time making trouble. They had not confined their machinations to the French but were intent on splitting James and his two sons and setting all of them at each other's throats. Charles had heard all this before, but there was a new urgency about his father's admonition to show 'on all occasions your affection and deference for me and your love for your Brother, with a just resentment against any who should presume to endeavor to make insinuations to you to our disadvantage'. The only thing that could really wreck all their hopes was falling out among themselves: 'As long as we are all three united the weaknesses of our friends will be of little consequence, and we shall render abortive the malice of our enemies, and get the better of them at last with Gods assistance; But should any disunion get in amongst us, or even the least appearance of it, it would be the ruin of us all.'

All this was enough to make Charles look twice at Henry. They had appeared, at their first meeting, to slip back into the old, easy relationship they had always had, though it had been disconcerting for Henry to find Charles did not even recognise him, and that as he rushed forward to embrace his brother he was met by an upraised dagger in the hand of a Highlander who thought him an assassin. Once this little matter of identification was over, there were enough hugs, tears and back-slappings to satisfy the most suspicious scrutiny. Henry fell over himself to tell his father how their reunion had been ecstatic enough to end all reunions, and all the worry that had given him 'but three hours' of sleep the night before had disappeared. He boasted Charles had time only for him – 'The Prince sees and will scarce see anybody but myself for a few days ... I go every day to dine with him; yesterday I brought him privately to see my house, and I perceive he has as much "gout" for the chace as ever he had.'

But it was all on the surface. Charles had not changed, but Henry had and in a way his older brother was not prepared to accept. Henry had, in short, grown up since he last saw Charles in January 1744. James warned Charles: 'I need say nothing of the Duke, in whom you will find a great alteration in all respects since you saw him and you will see he deserves to be your friend as he is your brother.' It was nicely put – either Charles had to accept Henry as his equal or there would be trouble. But Charles requested exactly the same allegiance and unquestioning obedience as he had always done. Henry was there to work for the common cause and that was all that mattered. He never thought that to Henry other things might matter. Though Henry had to listen *ad nauseam* to Charles' tales of his adventures, Charles had little interest in what had been happening to Henry. It was a pity he ignored the chance to hear such an instructive story.

Henry, after Charles left Rome, had taken refuge, as his mother had done before him, in an increasingly religious life. It was no sudden change for in 1742, just two years before, Dunbar had written of how the seventeen-year-old boy spent his day: 'called at 5.45 – rises at 6 – prays – $\frac{3}{4}$ hr washing, 1 hr prayers, half in closet another half walking in bed chamber. Always aloud. Break for $\frac{1}{4}$ hr. Dresses, goes to mass' – and so on. The entire day was punctuated by prayers. But then, with what looks like totally convincing alacrity, Henry dropped all this to grab a sword and follow his brother. James himself was surprised at how quickly the religious life seemed forgotten. He found himself having to restrain his quiet, studious son from rushing off at once to Scotland. When Henry was at last allowed to leave, first for Avignon and then Paris, it was to find his rôle as a minor character waiting in the wings extremely irksome. He did his best to further Charles' cause and get himself over to join him with an army but even the few interviews he managed to get with Louis proved humiliating experiences. It was heartbreaking work, nagging away, and Henry found it a great strain. James was full of sympathy, reporting to Charles in April 1745, 'The Duke has not been very well of late, which is no wonder, for he has really been so tormented, calumniated and ill used of late that I wonder how he resists it, especially considering his constant and great anxiety for your person and our affairs, and the pains he is at to foreward them as much as in his power, joynd to a natural and commendable impatience to be himself in action, and be of some personal use to you ...' It seemed Henry – who had actually in his childhood been more popular than Charles – was now universally shunned, which James waxed very indignant about, informing Charles that 'the malice of some people may lead them to write to you against the Duke, at a time I may say the fury against him runs so high, higher perhaps than he knows himself, and I own there is some thing so unaccountable and so extraordinary in some peoples behaveour towards him that I cannot but suspect there is more at the bottom and origin than meer extravagance and private views and passions.' Whatever James meant by this rather sinister innuendo, Charles was not going to bother to try to work out. Psychology was never his strong point. All James succeeded in doing was to make Charles suspicious for no reason whatsoever.

Henry was in fact at a crossroads in his life and the next few months after Charles' return would be crucial – as crucial as they were for Charles. If another campaign was to be mounted, Henry wanted to be in the front line with his brother. If not, he would go his own way. He was prepared to wait and see and in the meantime serve his family's interests as best he could. His hopes of Charles' chances were not high, for Henry, in touch with the current political situation much more than Charles, knew that peace was in the air: his brother came back on the very eve of the commencement of peace negotiations with England. This gave an urgency to his efforts that Henry felt nervous about. Did Charles understand how slim his hopes were, how much skill he would need to present his almost hopeless case? Henry thought not. Nor was there anyone among those who surrounded him to tell him, but it was a task Henry sidestepped. He would wait and let Charles discover for himself. He waited with a good deal of sadness for, in spite of his protestations to his father, it was clear that he was never going to be close to Charles again. It was even more tragic for Charles, who was hardly aware of what he was losing. Always short of strong relationships, Charles could not afford to throw away the love and trust and mutual liking which had existed between his younger brother and himself.

All these worries – though Charles would have classed them as irritations rather than worries – were pleasantly obliterated by Charles' official reception ten days after his arrival in France. He had arrived at Morlaix only slightly more presentable than when he had been in hiding – a fact that caused the spiteful Walpole great amusement: 'The Young Pretender is landed in France with thirty Scotch but in such a wretched condition that his Highland Highness had no breeches.' He would have to get some before he met Louis. Those around Charles hardly dared to tell him that the King was not going to receive him publicly. What Charles wanted was a full-dress court presentation at which foreign ambassadors were presented and he was formally addressed as Prince of Wales. Suppers and meetings within the Palace did not count, as everyone knew. He had no inkling that there might be difficulties, and had written with superb confidence on landing to Henry telling him to tell Louis he was here at last and ready and waiting. John Graeme was supposed to do the arranging, but wrote in a postscript to James a week later that 'There was ... at first difficulties as to the King of France seeing the Prince; but at last he consented to it, but not in a publick manner and likewise the Duke might accompany him and that they would be lodged either in or near the castle.' As everyone knew, where one stayed at Versailles or Fontainebleau was as important as actually going, since one's standing with the King was instantly known by one's lodgings. While everyone fretted over protocol Charles went ahead with cleaning himself up. Paris was the place to kit himself out anew and Charles let himself go: it seemed important to him that he should look impressive. He chose a rose-coloured embroidered velvet coat lined with silver tissue, and a waistcoat of rich gold brocade. These he plastered with jewels – diamonds on his breast, in his hat and on his shoes so that 'he glittered all over like a star'. His red beard was shaved off and his moth-eaten wig thrown away. All this tarting up he thoroughly enjoyed, but then at another time he had equally enjoyed discarding his finery and dressing like the Highlanders. All dress appealed to Charles – he was very much the actor who liked to look right before he could feel right.

Thus attired, he set off in a splendid carriage with Lord Lewis Gordon and old Lochiel, preceded by another holding Elcho, Ogilvy and Kelly. According to one account there were ten footmen in livery walking either side of the coaches and pages, almost as resplendent as the occupants, sitting outside them. Whatever the actual details of the procession, it made enough stir to be reported as far afield as Florence as a great event. At Fontainebleau Louis duly received and spoke kindly to Charles. It was the first known time Charles had actually been at court, or met Louis, but it was the kind of occasion he was born to and welcomed. Louis, who never enjoyed meeting new people, was for once genuinely interested in his guest and was able to question him with a degree of fluency and animation normally lacking. With the Queen and her ladies Charles was even more successful – they hung on his words and could not have enough of his company. In short, Charles was a hit. Nobody denied that. But the point was, would it do him any good?

There were many who wondered about this, who watched every movement Charles made and interpreted all the various stages of his welcome expertly. The Duc de Luynes found his popularity at court significant at first. On Saturday 22nd October he recorded: 'Prince Edward and the Duke of York are still here; they dined yesterday with M. de Argenson and supped with M. d'Huescar. Today they dine with M. le Marchal de Noailles and sup with me. Tomorrow they will dine with M. le contrôleur général and sup with Mme de Pompadour.' He was eager to be part of the trend: 'I had suggested to Prince Edward and his brother to either dine or sup with me, and I didn't know till two o'clock yesterday which day would be convenient ... We got together all those who wanted to meet them. We added to this list all those in attendance upon them. In addition we asked all the ministers, but not to sup.' The result was a splendid banquet at which anyone who was anyone was there. Could anyone doubt that Charles' star was once more in the ascendant? The impression he made was good, his love of music standing him once more in good stead. 'Charles plays the harpsichord and violincello; the D. of York loves music more than his brother.' If it was true that, as Horace Walpole maintained, French music at the time was so bad it set the teeth on edge – 'It resembles gooseberry tart as much as it does harmony' – they were probably all the more appreciative. After supper 'the Queen came into Mme de Luynes room for a moment to see Charles and his brother' and later they saw the King privately.

Since this was the first visit they had made to the King, they were shut up with him for half or three quaters of an hour; they also saw the Queen and Dauphin a second time; they were supposed to be incognito. Prince Charles was Baron Renfrew and Henry Count of Albany, but Charles was called Monseigneur Your Royal Highness and the Duke Your Highness.

De Luynes summed up the visit as a success and had some interesting observations to make.

There were a thousand distinctions apart from dinners and suppers. Charles didn't like being incognito; he feels what he is, and though he isn't haughty he has dignity; he is very anxious to please and be approved of. He asked M. de Bouillon and Cardinal Tencin to thank those who had received him and to excuse any shortcomings. He said he was just a highlander and not used to the ways of this country and that besides he didn't know French well and that the inflammation that he had caught in the mountains stopped him understanding as easily as usual. The prince is quite serious, his brother is entirely different; he talks more, laughs easily, he seems lively and loves music passionately; he is much smaller than his brother and his figure isn't so good; they always wear the blue Garter ribbon on their clothes.

The Duke also noted that the King saw Charles on another occasion, which was a special mark of favour. On 24th October he reported: 'Yesterday they dined with M. le Contrôleur Général and supped with Mme de Pompadour, as I have already said. The King came down after the main course.'

But nevertheless de Luynes saw, as did everyone else, that private affability on Louis' part towards Charles did not necessarily mean he would get what he wanted. It was not lost on observers that Louis had been under considerable pressure from some of his ministers not to see Charles at all because of the Breda negotiations where peace with England was being discussed.

If Charles was naïve enough to think this reception meant anything – and he was – he did not make the additional mistake of imagining he could now sit back and wait for something to happen. He knew perfectly well he must cash in quickly on the favour shown him before it evaporated. After he was received by Louis he sat down and wrote him a short letter which displayed a good deal of cunning.

My dear Brother and Cousin

I am taking the liberty of writing to Your Majesty to tell you why I did not talk about my affairs yesterday evening; this was because my brother was there and I did not want to give him any cause for jealousy as I love him dearly. May I dare to beg your Majesty (as caution is one of His great qualities) to have the goodness, at the first opportunity, to allow me to speak with you on business.

Louis, rather surprisingly for a man who liked to avoid all issues, saw Charles again, briefly. Their meeting, though Charles had specifically asked that it should be a business one, was confined again to pleasantries. Three days later Charles composed another missive, saying he had made out a memoir on his affairs which he would pass on to Louis and meanwhile he awaited his orders. None were forthcoming. Louis now felt he had done rather well by his somewhat embarrassing guest and he must now stew in his own juice. When no further meeting was forthcoming, Charles decided to get out of Fontainebleau and go to Paris. It was becoming too frustrating to be near the King and yet unable seriously to engage his attention. Telling his adventures to the Queen soon palled.

Installed at Clichy near Paris, Charles was now in a state of indignation and frustration similar to that he had been reduced to in 1744. This time, however, there was no question of simply setting off with whatever men he could gather together: that lesson, at least, he had learnt. He hated France, but he needed her. At first, he stayed among his own people, refusing invitations from Parisian society, where he could quickly have become all the rage; but, apart from writing a tactful letter of condolence to the King of Spain, his second string as it were, he could think of nothing else to do. He came out of his brief seclusion at the end of October to appear at the Opera, where he was given a standing ovation. Opera-going then became a habit and it was rumoured English ladies of quality came over specially to sit and stare at him. All this Charles lapped up, but it would be unfair to suggest that he was in any way deflected from his main purpose. In his memorial to Louis he had stated very clearly what he wanted: eighteen to twenty thousand men. Nothing else would do. No amount of applause could tempt him to sit back and enjoy his glory. The offer of a pension was contemptuously refused, though a grant of 60,900 livres for the relief of his adherents was accepted and duly distributed. Charles thought of it as guilt money and did not feel that taking it in any way compromised him. But a pension for himself was different – the very name 'pension' enraged him.

James, though full of 'joy and comfort' to hear that his son was safe and well, had anticipated his reception and also his reaction, which worried him extremely. Writing on 3rd November he says, carefully, 'I am afraid you will have little reason to be satisfied with the court of France, and that you will not have less need of courage and fortitude in bearing and suffering in that country than you had in acting in Britain, and let me recommend in the most earnest manner to you patience and prudence; for by contrary conduct you would make things worse and never better.' Charles was as impatient of such advice as he had always been. In any case, he felt he *had* been the soul of patience: he had waited a month, by the time he got his father's letter, and the eighteen thousand men had not come marching up to his door. As for prudence, what about his notes and his memorial? He wrote and told his father that he was taking a firm line and had refused a pension, which sent James into an agony of apprehension. 'I heartily wish you may succeed in your manner of acting towards the court of France,' he replied, 'but I am affrayd you will disgust them quite and that by the way you are taking, not only yourself, but even those who suffer for you and have no other resource but the French, will feel the effects of them …'

The year 1746 ended with Charles determined to continue his policy of browbeating the French into doing what he wanted, though on the surface he continued to keep up appearances, going out from Clichy to see Louis on 15th December as though nothing was the matter. 'Prince Edward, who lives at Clichy near Paris with his brother the Duke of York, has come here today; he is to see the King, the Queen, M. le Dauphin and Mesdames.' It was his own decision to act like this, however much James might blame, as he had always blamed, 'bad influences'. There were among Charles' particular set no strong influences any more. Sheridan, who had, as his old tutor and then his secretary, handled most of his business, was now dead. He had died in Rome in November shortly after James had written to Charles that 'Sir Thomas is here with me, and better in his health than I have seen him these many years'. Kelly was no substitute. There were enough people eager to write to James that Kelly was a thoroughly bad lot, but it was hard even for his detractors to prove he in any way formed Charles' policy. John O'Sullivan was so far from 'influencing' Charles that even James approved of him. He did what Charles told him, working tirelessly in his service but in no way deciding what should be done. The rest were younger men, except for the Highland chiefs who had come with him, and none of them had strong personalities. Lochiel, who one might have expected to have more say in what should be done, was firmly excluded from any consultation. This naturally upset him. While admiring Charles' determination to accept nothing for himself, he wanted him to refuse positions for any of his officers in the French army. Charles thought he should get employment for as many as he could; Lochiel thought they should be kept available for the next campaign and argued that by accepting positions for them he was acknowledging that there would be no campaign. Poor Lochiel, whose conscience tormented him, was reduced to the method that Charles had to use to make his views known to Louis: he wrote a formal letter to James in Rome, so little did he think Charles rated his opinion. In it he said rather bitterly that 'Lord Ogilvy or others might incline to make a figure in France; but my ambition was to serve the crown and serve my country or perish with it. H.R.H. say'd he was doing all he cou'd, but persisted in his resolution to procure me a regiment. If it is obtained I shall accept it out of respect to the Prince; but I hope Yr M. will approve of the resolution I have taken to share in the fate of the people I have undone and if they must be sacrificed to fall along with them. It is the only way I can free myself from the reproach of their blood and show the disinterested zeal with which I have lived and shall dye.'

James was tired and depressed. The elation he had felt when he knew Charles was safe had passed and his temporary rejuvenation was over. He wrote, at the beginning of 1747, 'my health grows so crazy that I am no more able to apply to business as I formerly could and for some weeks past I have scarce been able to read myself the letters I have signed'. He wasn't, he said, lazy or peevish. A great weariness overcame him as he heard how Charles was behaving. He could not understand 'what motives there can be sufficient to authorize a conduct by which, as matters yet appear to me, you venture disgusting the Court of France and wanting one day bread yourself'. In February, he made one last effort to set Charles on the straight and narrow. It was an interesting letter, in which he reviewed Charles' whole development since 1742, the year he rightly took as being the beginning of everything. The key, according to James, was the influence gained over him by 'wicked men' (unnamed) who tried to draw him from his Duty to God and his father. It was all a giant conspiracy, and one gathers James meant a religious one: Charles was to be the tool of Protestant interests. Sheridan and Strickland were the principal agents. Charles had cared only for them, ignoring those in his father's confidence. That could be the only explanation for his rudeness to France. 'It will to be sure have been represented to you that our religion is a great prejudice to our interest but that it may in some measure be remedyed by a certain free way of thinking and acting ...' James ended his summary on a desperate note: 'Enfin, my dear child, I must tell you very plainly that if you don't alter your ways I see you lost in all respects ... When you read this consider that it comes from the most tender and loving of fathers, whose only temporal concern is yours and your brother's welfare and who will wait with impatience your return since by it I shall be able to judge of what I may have to expect for the future, and to take my measures accordingly for your service and my own quiet; for

I have been already too long in hott water on your occasion and that without profit or advantage to any of us.'

With that letter, James relinquished the last of the bonds by which his son had felt bound to him. Charles had always loved his father: his love for him and his brother was the only kind of deep feeling he ever experienced. He had also always respected him, even when he most disobeyed him. On his return to France he had at first been eager to resume the closeness he had missed during his absence, but now he felt his father was utterly removed from any understanding of his position. Charles' way in such a situation was not to explain but to withdraw. He was sure he was right and looked to no one for approval. He now thought he saw that his decision to exclude his father from his plans in 1745 had been the right one, not an aberration to apologise for. James was out in the cold.

It might have given the old man some small comfort to know that before his letter – or rather his ultimatum – reached his son, he had at least left France. He was fed up. There was no sign at all that Louis was going to do anything for him. His restlessness became so acute that he felt he must escape for a time at least and he seems to have thought that his voluntary departure would be a slap in the face for his host. It was foolish thinking: Louis and his ministers could not have been more delighted when Charles trotted off to Avignon. They were sick of having him about, perpetually nagging them, stubbornly refusing to accept the inevitable. They were resentful, too, of his popularity with the Paris mob who had adopted him, for reasons best known to themselves, as their idol. There were sighs of relief all round. The Duc de Luynes noted his departure on 26th January: 'Prince Edward left Paris the night before yesterday; some say that he isn't pleased that so little help has been given to him and that he had retired to Avignon. Others say that the English have asked and been granted that he should leave while the preliminary peace articles are arranged. Still others argue that England is worried about a fleet being armed at Brest.'

No sooner was Charles in Avignon that he wondered why he had come. Instead of curing his frustration, or at least allaying it for a while, it only served to fan his impatience to fever pitch. At least in Paris there had been a feeling of being at the centre of things, when anything could happen. In Avignon, in February, nothing was ever going to happen. Charles probably knew that not only had he made a mistake but that it was going to be difficult to get back gracefully. Henry's letter was therefore a gift from Heaven. It informed Charles that their father was sending his younger brother on 'a project' to Spain to see if he could get any backing there. With somewhat excessive sweetness, Henry commented, 'you know my province is obedience'. Charles was furious: he instantly decided that he had left Paris with that very purpose in mind himself. In fact, 'even in Scotland I formed a project of going myself to the Court of Spain'. He asked Henry 'by all the tyes of brotherly affection' not to even think of going, an impudent request. During the last few months Charles had done nothing but complain, without cause, of his brother's behaviour and had allowed his 'clique', as Henry put it, to tease him unmercifully. Now he threatened Henry with being the reason for 'all our affairs' being destroyed if he went. At his most arrogant he also assured Henry he would be bound to make a rotten job of the mission anyway: 'You will certainly be of more service where you are, and iff my going has no effect, I dare say yourself wou'd have the same fate.' O'Sullivan would be sent to Rome to explain everything to James so there was no question of Henry getting into trouble.

It was ironic that Henry should now find himself courted by Charles, for in spite of the bullying tone that was what his big brother was doing. As early as December 1746 Charles had been writing to James complaining about Henry: '... but I am afraid some people have given him a bad opinion of me for I suppose I must own he does not open his heart to me. I shall always love him, and be united with him. Whatever he does to me, I will always tell him face to face what I think for his good, let him take it well or ill. I know him to be a little lively, not much loving to be contradicted.' Never strong on the humour of a situation, James ignored the irony too and gave way to exasperation. At the same time as Charles pleaded with Henry, James was writing of his distress that the elder should find so much fault with the younger brother. 'You seem to be highly dissatisfied with him ... this is really a riddle to me.' He told Charles, sharply, to remember: 'You are his brother and not his father.' Henry knew that Charles had been complaining about him, and knew too that his father, who was a very fair man, would take his side. There would have been nothing easier than to set off for Spain, pretending either that he must carry out his father's orders or that Charles' letter had come too late. But Henry did neither. There was, in his letter of reply, an air of anxiety to put Charles in his debt – he was almost subservient, falling over himself to assure Charles that he of course quite understood, and was sure his father would, and whatever Charles wanted to do was right: 'I heartily wish you a good journey, attended with all the success and content you can desire.' No brother could have asked for more. Charles never recorded any gratitude he may have felt – he took it as his due. The days when he cared about Henry's feelings had long since passed: his little brother was not prepared to do everything Charles said, to the extent of altering his way of living, and that was that. The only rôle left to him was menial. That Henry, a clever man, should show even signs of accepting it never struck Charles as in the least suspicious. He did not see it for what it was – indicative that Henry wanted no trouble because he had already made up his mind to begin living his own life, on his own terms, in a way Charles would most certainly not approve of. With that in view, going to Spain could not have mattered less.

The trip to Spain did no good whatsoever and was valuable only for the therapeutic effect it had on Charles. Apart from his liking for travelling it also gave him the satisfying feeling that he was actually doing something positive: sitting about was never good for him at any time in his life. He went on horseback with only two companions and a couple of servants, through the Pyrenees via Perpignan to Barcelona. It was a hard journey in winter, through territory as rugged as any he had seen in Scotland or northern Italy, but he enjoyed the trip. At Barcelona he discarded the few companions he had brought with him and put himself in the hands of a Colonel Nagle who had been a resident there for many years. From him he learnt that the best way to proceed was to write to the Chief Minister, Caravajal, enclosing a letter for the King: it was the methods of the French King all over again and Charles had had enough of that. But there was no alternative. He wrote the usual note, asking for an interview in which he could lay his business before the King. Then he went on to Madrid, and waited.

Charles found the waiting irksome, as he found all waiting, but the residents with Jacobite sympathies enjoyed the chance of seeing him. There had never been anything like the number of exiles in Spain as there were in France, but nevertheless there were enough to form a small community. Since 1719, Spain had never backed any Stuart attempt to the extent of mounting a campaign, but James had never halted his correspondence and always counted Spain as an ally. During 1745, Spanish gold had been sent to help Charles. But by the time Charles arrived in Madrid, in March 1747, the Spanish Government knew that France was starting peace negotiations with Britain and that this would force her in turn to call a halt to hostilities. Charles' visit could therefore hardly have been less opportune.

Dealing with Caravajal proved as exhausting as dealing with d'Argenson or Tencin or any of the French ministers. Charles knew perfectly well that the Minister was there to fob him off and he was determined not to be fobbed off. Experience stood him in good stead: the thing to do was to make such a nuisance of himself that Caravajal would be forced to see him for the sake of peace and quiet. With a foot in the door, he could then push hard. Industriously, Charles sat down and wrote another of his inevitable memoirs to be given to Caravajal. It consisted of four points, which was letting the harassed Minister off lightly. Apart from aid in the event of a French-backed campaign, Charles asked specifically for thirty thousand fusils and ten thousand sabres and three ships full of grain. He thought his demands modest – a mere nothing compared to eighteen thousand soldiers. Cautiously, Caravajal said some of these demands could perhaps be met. Encouraged, Charles pressed for a personal interview. Resigned, Caravajal agreed to an appointment. Getting to the meeting place involved a lot of cloak-and-dagger stuff that Charles found very amusing: 'I find all here like the pheasants, that it is enough to hide their heads to cover the rest of the body, as they think.' The interview duly took place, with Caravajal confessing he hadn't actually given the King the letter yet and furthermore he didn't think he ought to and would Charles please go away.

Charles declined. He made it quite plain that he would be quite happy to sit there for ever unless he was presented to the King. Caravajal must have been convinced. At eleven o'clock that night a messenger came to the back door of the house where he was staying to inform him that the King would see him at once, and off Charles went. The court and person of King Ferdinand VI could not compare with that of Louis XV and though he would not in any case have been likely to be intimidated, it gave Charles an even greater air of confidence. He was perfectly polite, giving and receiving his share of royal civilities. He knew that nothing concrete would be promised or even mentioned at such a meeting but he had no intention of allowing the occasion to be turned into a humiliating one. With tremendous aplomb he chatted away making his Royal hosts thoroughly uncomfortable, and when he withdrew he did just that: there was no question of him being thrown out. Nor had he finished. He wanted, he told poor Caravajal, to pay his respects to the Queen Dowager, who had not been present. Really, it would be rude if he didn't. He also wanted on paper whatever measure of assistance Ferdinand could be induced to give. Caravajal said he must leave at once – both requests were impossible. Charles coolly sat down and himself wrote out his requests, for Ferdinand to sign, and then a sweet-as-honey letter to the Queen Dowager:

Mme. My Aunt,

As my main aim in coming to Spain was to pay my respects to the Royal Family, especially to your Majesty, to show how much I appreciate all the King and your Majesty have done for me, you can imagine how mortified I am not to be able to have this honour. But I hope your Majesty will do me the justice of believing that my heart is full of gratitude for the service one who is joined to me by blood has done me. I have the honour to be respectfully –

      Mme. my aunt,
            Your Majesty's very affectionate
              Nephew.

It did no good, of course, but then Charles had not expected it to. The only ones who thought it had were the gossips of Paris, where 'it was heard yesterday (March 30) that M. le duc d'Huescar has spread the news that Prince Edward has left Madrid, heaped with honours and promises by the court, to embark at Bilbao and from there to return to Brest to join up with a fleet being equipped there'. He left the next day, however, in good spirits, feeling that diplomatically he was several points up. His contempt for Ferdinand was expressed in a letter he wrote to James: 'I found ... that he was a weak man just put in motion like clockwork.' This was something Charles was never prepared to say about the equally elusive and vacillating Louis. The court in general he found equally despicable. 'I thought there were not such fools as the French court, but I find it far beyond it.' Charles was never given to reflection, but it did occur to him that, suddenly, there was perhaps something to be said for the French. Perhaps they didn't treat him so badly after all – which his father had been telling him for years. At least he was not hustled about in the ignominious way the Spaniards had done. Appearances were kept up, and were appearances, after all, not worth keeping up? Furthermore, he had friends in high places in France; he had none in Spain. At Versailles, there was hardly a minister who did not know him personally, hardly a member of the court who had not at some time or other paid his respects. At any time, one of them might be in a position to do something for him. Whether he liked it or not, he had better get back quickly.

CHAPTER SIXTEEN
Disgrace and Expulsion

Charles was back in Paris by the middle of April, living incognito at the Maison-Blanche, a house right at the end of Faubourg Saint Marcel on the road to Fontainebleau, which belonged to the Archbishop of Cambrai. His absence had been regretted by one man at least: Lochiel. In fact, Lochiel had been so upset when he went to Avignon that he had written Charles a letter that had only just recently caught up with him. The theme was familiar: Charles was not following the policy Lochiel thought he ought to follow. Accepting anything at all, for others even, was dangerous; leaving Paris was dangerous. Neither would help towards preventing the peace that was openly talked of. Charles must give up thoughts of invading England and be content with Scotland. This Charles was not prepared to do – he had had enough of small expeditions – but he was more than prepared to redouble his efforts to get Louis to back him before it was too late. That was now his whole raison d'être. His chances were small. It was no good Charles humming loudly and turning away every time the peace negotiations were mentioned: they were a fact. James was already considering where it would be best for Charles to go – Avignon, Rome or Switzerland – but as he pointed out 'the question is not where it might be advisable to go, but where you may be allowed to stay'. This attitude threw Charles into a frenzy. What could he do to stop the inevitable?

The truth was, nothing. It was Charles' failure ever to admit this that earned him so much disapproval – which, as de Luynes had observed, was hard on a man anxious to please. There has always been a feeling that Charles ought to have faced up to his fate – it is at this point in his history that curtains are hurriedly drawn. Yet his total commitment to his cause is one of the few really admirable traits in him. He would never give up, no matter how impossible the job seemed – and in 1747 it seemed impossible enough for John Graeme to remark: 'I can compare our situation to nothing better than an immense labyrinth without an ell of thread to conduct us out of it.' Charles did all he could – nagged away at every minister in sight, bombarded Louis with entreaties, kept up a façade of confidence. The news that came from England that spring of the new acts going through Parliament to complete the work after Culloden made haste seem all the more imperative. These prohibited, *inter alia*, the possession of firearms and the wearing of Highland dress – prohibitions to be rigorously enforced. In vain did Duncan Forbes fulminate against them.

To add insult to injury, an oath was devised that any Highlander could be called upon to swear: 'I, AB, do swear and as I shall answer to God at the great day of judgement I have not, nor shall have, in my possession any gun sword pistol or arm whatsoever and never use tartan, plaid or any part of the Highland garb; and if I do so may be cursed in my undertakings, family and property – may I never see my wife and children, father mother or relations – may I be killed in battle as a coward and lie without Christian burial in a strange land far from the graves of my forefathers and Kindred; may all this come across me if I break my oath.' Anything more fiendishly comprehensive it would have been difficult to devise.

There was, as yet, no sense of panic in Charles' behaviour: he continued to act as though another campaign was just round the corner, and even to believe it. There were many in Paris who thought he had good grounds. 'They say that Cardinal Tencin is moving heaven and earth to revive the Pretenders cause and get the ministry to do something for him.' This may have been true but it did no good. Though Charles was supposed to be living incognito, he did not lack encouragement in this attitude. It was at this time that there began to appear in his life a series of intelligent, rich, not unpowerful women who made it their business to fawn upon him and push him farther along the path he had chosen. Why exactly they should choose to do so is difficult to decide. Certainly, they were captivated by Charles – he represented a species not currently in vogue at the time. He was neither cautious, nor sycophantic, nor terrified of Louis XV. They enjoyed egging him on to more outrages – it was all most amusing. Then, too, it was their way of expressing, without danger to themselves, their disapproval of the peace and the policy of Louis and his ministers. They would never be so outspoken themselves, but secretly they gloated. They adopted Charles as a kind of mascot, flattered him, supported him and wondered how far he would go before the fun had to stop. Charles seemed to have no objection. From being a young man who had studiously ignored women, except when occasion called upon him to be chivalrous, and the petticoat rule that went with them, he now seemed taken over by them. It was his own choice. Why it should be was perhaps more due to the kind of woman he now encountered than any real change of heart.

Charles' principal femme fatale was one Marie-Louise, Princesse Jablonowski, who in 1730 had married the Prince de Talmond. This lady was a cousin of the Queen, and it was probably through the Queen that she met Charles. She was in the habit of making up an opera party with the Queen and cannot have failed to see Charles there even before his brief trip to Avignon and Spain. She was about ten years older than him, extremely beautiful, very elegant, and above all intelligent and interested in the arts. Maurepas was sufficiently in awe of her to send her Voltaire's new work *Temple de la Gloire* even though it was the only manuscript and there was no copy. Her position in society was incontestable – there might be seven or eight ranks of nobility in France but Marie-Louise was in the top drawer. She was admired, feared and looked up to in a way Madame de Pompadour, with all her greater influence, never achieved. Once she took Charles under her wing he was made – or unmade.

Her interest was not thought by contemporary observers to be in the least maternal or platonic. On the contrary, it was openly stated that she was Charles' mistress. All the circumstantial evidence would point to this being true. It was Charles' luck to lose his virginity to a woman of maturity and experience who could make up for his twenty-seven years of abstinence. The atmosphere he lived in at the time – with the peace at any minute likely to propel him into catastrophe – heightened the excitement. There was something feverish about his sudden urge to socialise, to have fun, to be seen everywhere splendidly dressed, quite a leader of fashion. Marie-Louise regarded some of his entourage with disdain and he was seen less and less with his old drinking cronies with whom he had spent so many evenings already re-living the immediate past. Whether Charles actually enjoyed his initiation and the period of whirlwind galli-vanting that followed he never recorded, but he certainly imagined him-self to be cocking a snook at Louis with great effect and that was all he cared about. His reasoning was extremely simple: the more he was in the public eye, the more flamboyant his style of living, the more Louis would be reminded of him and his obligations to him.

There was one person in particular in Paris who did not enjoy watching Charles make what he considered a spectacle of himself, and that was his brother Henry. To Henry, it was abhorrent. The more he observed his brother, the more it seemed to him that the Cause was dead. He, as well as Charles, had spent his whole life expecting to see his family restored to the British throne. He had done everything possible. But now, peace with England was about to succeed another failed attempt and there was clearly no future hope worth staking one's life on – one's life, one's career. Henry was ambitious in an unspecific kind of way. As many had noted he had as much if not more fire in his belly than Charles. He was not going to rest content sitting at home as the younger son of a dispossessed monarch, or hanging about foreign courts as the younger brother of an aspiring one. He wanted a place in the world, and, since he was far from being an ascetic, a good one. He knew that whatever he did his father would back him, and so, as Charles tripped farther down the primrose path and the peace negotiations went ahead, Henry decided the time had come to get out. On 17th April he had paid a last visit to Versailles. 'The Duke of York, who is still in Paris incognito under the name of Count of Albany came here yesterday evening,' noted the Duc de Luynes. 'He came especially to see the King and afterwards the Queen.' According to de Luynes, the visit was prompted by no other motive than 'a wish to see the King from time to time', or to say goodbye.

At the end of April, he left for Rome, without telling Charles. D'Argenson says that he invited Charles to dinner and only when he had been sitting there in solitary state for several hours was the news of his brother's departure broken to him by the servants. In any case, Henry certainly never told Charles of his intention. He may not have thought it necessary – James had already written that if they weren't getting on very well he saw no point in Henry staying in Paris and might ask him to come home where 'it would be a comfort to me to have him here were it but for a few months'. Or, more likely, he was afraid of Charles' unjustifiable anger. His big brother was an autocrat where he was concerned – he expected Henry to be obedient and obedience demanded keeping away from Rome. Henry wrote instead one of his too charming letters, begging '10,000 pardons' for leaving without permission. The reason was he just had to see their father and was afraid Charles would not let him. 'As to the motive of my concealing it from you, seek no other reason, but reflect on the tenderness you have for me.'

Charles was furious. Also on the lookout for reasons why nothing was working out right, he swore that Henry's desertion looked as though the Cause was lost. Yet he never suspected worse was to follow, accepting Henry's explanation at its face value. The blow, when it came, came through James and not from Henry himself: in June, Charles learnt that Henry was to become a Cardinal of the Roman Catholic Church. In a letter of beguiling innocence – 'I know not whether you will be surprised, my dearest Carluccio, when I tell you that your brother will be made a Cardinal the first day of next month' – James broke the devastating news.

He defended Henry's action staunchly, speaking of him as being 'as much my son as you, and my paternal care and affection are equally extended to you and to him'. He was not unaware of the implications of Henry's action for the Cause but harked back to a theme he had often used, from his earliest days – what was the point in promising religious toleration to one's subjects if one could not extend it to oneself and one's family? Henry had as much right to be a Roman Catholic cardinal as an Englishman to be a Protestant bishop. He urged Charles: 'Let us look forward, not backward. The resolution is taken and will be executed.' Knowing his son as he did he expected a violent reaction but begged 'for God's sake let not a step ... become a subject of Scandal and eclat ... your silence towards your brother and what you writ to me about him since he left Paris would do you little honour if they were known ... all I request of you hereafter is your personal love and affection for me and your brother.' It was something Charles found hard to give. Nevertheless, he managed to write a short note.

> I have received yrs of ye 13th and 20th June had I got a Dager throw my heart it would not have been more sensible to me than ar ye contents of yr first. My love for my Brother and concern for yr Case being the occasion of it. I hope Your Majesty will forgive me not entering any further on so disagreeable a subject the shock of which I am scarce out of.

The shock Charles found it so hard to get out of was due not so much to fears of the restoration of his family being now irretrievably damaged so much as to amazement and anger at Henry's duplicity. One thing Charles could never forgive was lack of loyalty, and it seemed to him that his brother had betrayed him personally. Perhaps if Henry had retreated into a monastery and become a monk or priest, living a life of exemplary piety and self-denial, then Charles would have been able to accept that, as his father maintained, his brother had to follow his calling. But a cardinal? Charles had lived in Rome for twenty-three years. He knew all about cardinals. He knew the kind of life they led, the richness of their benefices, the splendour of the office. It was utterly unconvincing to describe Henry as saintly when he chose to start at the top without in fact even becoming a priest. Charles saw it for what it was – a gesture of defiance. Henry had abandoned the Cause and gone his own way. The selfishness of it winded Charles for, like all really selfish people, other people's selfishness seemed unbelievable to him.

There were plenty who agreed with him that not only had Henry done a dastardly thing, he had ruined for all time his family's chances. The effect of his action was reckoned by the most gloomy to be worse than Culloden. Many saw it as politically motivated, the whole affair stage-managed by either England or France to get Charles off their back. There was no truth in this, but it gave a sinister depth to the feeling against Henry. D'Argenson spoke of him being 'all Italian, sly, superstitious, miserly, loving his ease and above all jealous and hating his brother' – in spite of the fact that he knew perfectly well how popular Henry was. Sympathy for Charles was much in evidence and, joined to that already felt for him over the approaching peace, a positive tide of feeling in his favour swept Paris. He did not, however, revel in it. On the contrary, he seemed genuinely laid low and announced he wanted to crawl into a hole in a rock and stay there. He was for a time inconsolable, his normal optimism quite deserting him.

It was at this point, when Charles was at an ebb so low that not even the ministrations of Marie-Louise could console him, and when he was plagued by a thousand minor worries such as lack of money, that Lord George Murray chose to visit Paris in the hopes of seeing him. He could hardly have chosen a worse time than July 1747. The subject of betrayal was uppermost in Charles' thoughts thanks to Henry's appointment, and the arrival of a man he had always considered had betrayed him rekindled the old resentment and hatred. These ugly feelings had never in fact either died or been mellowed by time: Lord George's letter after Culloden had sealed his fate. James for one was disgusted by Charles' attitude and showed, in this extract from a letter, how far he was from understanding the hardness his son was capable of:

> If he has been on several occasions of a different opinion from you or other people I don't see what crime there is in that ... and as to what he may have failed against you personally, he has owned his fault to me and begged of me to make his submission to you for him; and I own this last part touched me, for tho' but too many people have failled towards me, yet I scarce ever remember that ever anyone made such an act of submission as he has done. All he seeks is your forgiveness, and to be restored to your favour, which you are, I am sure, incapable of refusing him ...

But Charles was quite capable. The minute Lord George arrived in Paris, he sent a messenger to inform him that he had no intention of seeing him and he would be glad if Lord George would leave Paris as soon as possible. That was at least an improvement on Charles' former orders, given in the spring when he went to Avignon, that if Lord George showed his face the French should be somehow induced to arrest him. Perhaps he had forgotten the clemency he had taken such care to display towards his prisoners during the '45 campaign? In denying a proud man like this ex-Lieutenant-General of his the right to submission and subsequent forgiveness Charles showed he had no conception of the nature of mercy. He had always been fond of behaving like a king, dispensing what he imagined was kingly justice with becoming majesty. Now, he was less than a man, never mind a king. He could at least have accepted Lord George's submission, even if he did not believe in its sincerity – which was probably at the root of his refusal to do so – and told him that though he never wanted to see him again, he was forgiven. But fear was always at the bottom of Charles' displays of weakness and he feared Lord George's righteousness. He wanted near him only those who were prepared at all times to subscribe to his idea of himself. Even a supposedly abject and humble Lord George could never do that. He dutifully did as he was told, returning to exile in Holland where he penned wistful thoughts to Edgar, James' secretary, about 'How happy would you and I be to sit over a bottle in Angus or Perthshire after a Restoration, and talk over old services.'

Charles was not temperamentally suited to staying in the dumps and after a few weeks his customary energy had reasserted itself. He was now convinced that this famous peace, so long mooted, might never take place and that if he could mount a diplomatic rearguard action the French might yet decide to use him to make war instead. He wrote to his father: '... I really do not think a peace so esy at present to be compassed as people are willing to flatter themselves with.' What had given him this idea was a sudden surge of French success – as early as May of that summer a worried Horace Walpole had noted, 'We begin to own now that the French are superior.' On 2nd July the allied English, Austrians and Hanoverians were defeated, under the Duke of Cumberland, by the French under Marshal Saxe at Laffeldt. Charles rushed to congratulate Louis. Surely, he reasoned, if the French were doing so well peace was now unnecessary? But his reasoning was faulty – no last-ditch victory was going to make Louis, frighteningly impoverished by the war, change his mind. All it meant was that he went to the conference table stronger. Charles, however, was all excitement – he must cash in on what he was sure marked a change of direction. What he needed was someone to intercede for him at court, someone the French would approve of. He knew he had no such person of standing in his own entourage. He knew, too, that he would not get very far himself. He therefore fixed, most unfortunately, on the most distinguished Jacobite he could think of who would carry weight: the Lord Marischal. No choice could have been more ludicrous. Apparently blissfully unaware of this, Charles sat down and wrote to him in August, informing him, ingenuously, that his situation was critical and that he needed help: would his lordship please join him with all possible speed, out of regard for his 'bleeding country'? That, with a lavish sprinkling of extravagant compliments, was all.

Charles could not have made a greater mistake or revealed more clearly how little he knew about the state of Jacobitism and his Jacobites. George Keith, Earl Marischal, was a remarkable man whose services to the exiled Stuarts had been great, but he had long ago disassociated himself from anything Charles was likely to do and had acknowledged that he thought the end of the road had come. He had never liked Charles very much, always preferring Henry from when they were children. Out in the '15 and again in the '19, when he commanded part of the expedition that sailed from Spain, he was looked up to by all Jacobites as one of their few able and experienced generals. Charles had been brought up to admire and respect him, and naturally had looked to him for support in 1745. But Marischal not only would not give it – he was almost alone in having the courage to tell Charles he thought he was being irresponsible. He had done it, however, with a good deal of tact and Charles still believed he was a supporter. Marischal had entered the service of Frederick the Great, where he had an outstanding diplomatic success. It had just dawned on Charles that the Prussian ruler now rivalled Louis XV as the most powerful man in Europe, which enhanced Marischal's charms further in his eyes. He was therefore doubly disappointed when, in a skilfully worded letter, the old Jacobite refused to come, pleading ill health. Where could he turn now?

There was only Kelly, George Kelly, his secretary, whose trustworthiness and ability Charles had himself had some doubts about. But Kelly was at least keen and absolutely devoted to Charles personally. The biggest snag was that by no stretch of the imagination could Kelly be said to have any influence at the French court – far from it. They despised him, as they despised anyone without titles or other claims to prestige. It was in spite of, rather than because of, Kelly's efforts that another gesture was made by Louis in the autumn of 1747 – a regiment was given to Lochiel (who did not want one) and a fixed allowance granted for the use of the Scottish exiles which Charles was to be in charge of distributing. Another attempt was made to get Charles to accept a pension for himself. How he existed was a mystery that intrigued many, including de Luynes, who noted 'he is still living in M. le Prince de Rohan's house at Saint-Ouen, from where he often goes to Paris. At the moment he takes nothing from France but he certainly lives in style.' He had now had a year kicking his heels and it was thought his attitude might have changed. But Charles still would not accept – though James told him flatly that he couldn't go on supporting him for ever – unless he could be allowed to pretend publicly that he wasn't getting any money from the French. Louis was not quite as philanthropic as that – half the point of Charles accepting a pension from him was that he should be seen to accept, especially if this was before the official peace negotiations began.

These were opened at Aix-la-Chapelle in March 1748. If there was one clause that was going to be quite straightforward – perhaps the only one – that was the exclusion of Charles from French dominions. All Paris turned towards him with the greatest curiosity to see what he would do. What he did delighted them with its flamboyance: he had a medal struck with the inscription 'Carolus Walliae Princeps' on one side and on the other 'Amor et Spes Britanniae'. The engraver had naturally been terrified to carry out his orders and had insisted on seeking permission from the King. Amazingly – or perhaps very cleverly – Louis gave no objections, but the place (Paris) and name of the engraver (Roettier) were left out. If Louis did not care, many others did. They particularly disliked the 'Amor et Spes Britanniae' phrase with the accompanying outline of a fleet of ships, for the French Navy had recently taken a hammering from the British. Charles was cut dead by offended nobles, but retaliated by sitting for his portrait to Tocque, the current eminent painter. On 30th April the peace preliminaries were agreed to and signed: the situation had now changed. Charles clearly would not be allowed to continue to go openly to court as he had been doing. The French would expect him to realise this. His tactics, if he was going to have any, would have to be prepared.

For a while Charles stubbornly went on insisting that there was many a slip 'twixt cup and lip: only the preliminaries, not the treaty, had been signed. It might never happen. Part of his time he spent drawing up a protest which he formally presented to Louis. For once, his father was in basic agreement and he too protested, though much more as a formality than anything else. Louis dealt delicately with Charles: he proceeded by gentle, subtle hints to show his truculent guest the error of his ways and the correctness of his own behaviour. He was wasting his time. Charles answered boldly that he intended to oppose anything and everything that was said and done at Aix-la-Chapelle and – charmingly – that it was for Louis' own good that he was doing so. There the matter rested until October when the whole treaty was concluded and signed. After that, the fight was on.

Charles' part in the affair that followed was disgraceful. Up to the autumn of 1748 his attitude had been at least defensible: he had come back from an unsuccessful but courageous campaign, expecting to be given another chance by a power who had given him every encouragement. His commitment to those who had died and those who still suffered on his behalf demanded that he should do everything possible to get back to help them in a manner less calculated to risk another débâcle. His energy and determination to this end had been prodigious – it is hard to see what other line he could have followed in the circumstances in which he was placed. His refusal to give up was admirable. But in November 1748, when the peace treaty had been signed, and he was now one puny individual against a combined front of strong countries, his behaviour became hysterical and stupid. No one had expected him to accept the inevitable before it was genuinely inevitable – as James had done – nor was there any reason at all why he should not have tried to make life difficult for the French, but to go on after the Treaty of Aix-la-Chapelle had become a reality was a piece of self-indulgence that had no point. All Europe knew his feelings: he had no need to publicise them. Nor will it do to look for a deep-rooted policy in Charles' silly posturing: there was none. Endearing himself to the English by cocking a snook at the French was entertaining but nothing else. In fact, if that had been Charles' intention, it rebounded horribly later, for though Horace Walpole seemed to be admiring when he said, 'I don't know whether he be a Stuart but I am sure by his extravagance he has proved himself of English extraction!', he then went on to declare 'What a mercy that we had not him here! With a temper so impetuous and obstinate as to provoke a French government when in their power, what would he have done with an English government in his power?' Quite.

Nobody, except Marie-Louise, Princesse de Talmond, had any influence over Charles. She came to know all Charles' adherents and did all in her quite considerable power to help them. In particular she adopted Lady Ogilvy and presented her at court. De Luynes shared her admiration for this pretty nineteen-year-old girl who was now pregnant and desperately wanted to return to Scotland so that if her baby was a son he might one day inherit his father's estates. 'Mme de Talmond presented her because she is a great friend and apart from that because of her connection with Prince Edward.' In other respects, her interference was disapproved of. According to d'Argenson – and it seems proved by her actions – she egged him on. 'The Princesse de Talmond has taken possession of his mind and governs him with folly and fury, though there is not even common-sense in the objects proposed by either of them; an unruly spirit, misplaced haughtiness, and that is all.' Day by day d'Argenson chronicled Charles' refusal to take the hint, and then the direct request, to go. On

21st November, 'The great affair of the day and the most astounding is that of Prince Edward and his firm resistance to leaving France. He says in so many words that he will never leave it alive; he threatens to kill and to kill himself if they force him to it.' On 24th November, 'There is more talk than ever about Prince Edward and the trouble he is giving the King to make him leave the Kingdom ...'

Louis, meanwhile, was going to a great deal of trouble both to find a home for Charles to go to outside France, and to use the most persuasive, respectful means possible to get him to go. His consideration was mistakenly interpreted by Charles as a sign of weakness and he did not hesitate to scorn in the rudest possible way all the emissaries sent to him. The very fact that Louis was so concerned about where he would go once he left French dominions seemed to Charles to indicate a guilty conscience. He never appreciated that it was compassion, not guilt, that motivated Louis. He was sorry for Charles, sorry that he had to be treated like this, but he felt no guilt at all. He knew Charles would never go back to Italy, so he suggested Fribourg in Switzerland. Fribourg was not particularly keen to house Charles, and the British on principle objected, but in any case Charles would not go. The suggestion was an insult. Going to such an unimportant town would be like going to a desert island. Cardinal Tencin got nowhere with his persuasion. Next to try was the Duc de Gesvres, who stood much less chance than Tencin. He too was duly sent packing, in a manner that was widely reported. De Luynes and all the other gossips rubbed their hands with glee: 'M. de Gesvres took a very tender letter from the King himself ... He replied to M. de Gesvres that he knew the king was master of his Kingdom but that he wouldn't get him to leave unless he tore him to pieces. He comes and goes in Paris; he's seen everywhere, parading about.' Meanwhile Charles went about in public more flamboyantly than ever which was an additional embarrassment to Louis, who was daily plagued by the British ambassador to fulfil his obligations under the treaty he had just signed. The Duc de Gesvres was sent again and got the same kind of reception. Louis' sympathy began to evaporate. Obviously something would have to be done, something drastic.

Several courses of action occurred to Louis and he wasted some time following them, achieving nothing except an even greater appreciation of Charles' conceit and obstinacy. It seemed to Louis – himself fatherless and with no experience of the pitfalls of such a relationship – that if you have a truculent young man to deal with you call in parental influence. He therefore sent a special messenger to Rome asking James to help. Perhaps if he had read the bitter letters James had been writing for the last two years he would not have bothered. James' reaction was predictable – he was shocked, ashamed, but helpless. He sent a letter telling Charles to do what he was told but never even expected it to have any effect. It didn't. Next it occurred to Louis – not without prompting – that if a father's influence was nil, a mistress might count for more. He knew perfectly well that the Princesse de Talmond encouraged Charles and that he appeared to depend heavily upon her. He therefore let it be known that if she continued with her active encouragement she might find herself banished to some very nasty place indeed – somewhere where she would find no society, no fashion, no opera, no anything. All Paris enjoyed the scene that ensued and for the first time an element of ridicule entered the descriptions. 'Prince Edward, who was in the habit of going often to Mme de Talmond's, was very surprised, several days ago, to find her out at a time when she was usually in. He insisted on being admitted at least to the garden; The porter went on refusing; finally, as a compromise, one of his men was allowed in and the door closed on Edward himself. The prince's valet went to find M. de Talmond, who said Mme de Talmond would be very annoyed not to have had the honour of receiving the Prince but that the door would not be opened. M. de Talmond came to his wife's house, which he hardly ever did; he was told the door was barred to Prince Edward. Mme de Talmond was furious and tried to go, a few days afterwards, to the Prince's house to apologise for what had happened.' Unfortunately Louis miscalculated: his threat certainly scared the Princess into closing her doors to Charles (if only temporarily) but it didn't dishearten Charles. On the contrary, it made him more determined than ever, more sure that all these tricks betokened a chance that Louis might yield.

There was one last meeting with the poor Duc de Gesvres, on 1st December. D'Argenson says: 'The Prince Edward received him bravely his hand on the hilt of his sword, and told him he would not go. The Duc found his antechamber full of guns, sabres and machinery as if prepared for a long siege...' The Duc went through the motions of reasoning with Charles who replied, at his most arrogant, that in future he would deal only with the King himself and not his representatives. The Duc pointed out that as Charles no longer came to court that would be impossible unless the King came to him. Charles said fine, and added, 'I have nothing further to say than what I have said already – pardon me, I have some business,' and with that he left the room.

On Sunday 8th December Louis signed the order for Charles' arrest. On Wednesday it was carried out at the Opera House, the whole process having in itself an air of comic opera. Charles and all Paris knew what was coming – there had been no attempt to keep it secret. Perhaps Louis hoped that forewarning Charles would make him decide to run while he still had time, but if so it was a forlorn hope. Charles might not face his fate at Culloden, but he had every intention of facing it in Paris. There is no doubt he wanted to be arrested in the full public glare, whereupon he imagined an outcry so loud and clear that Louis would be forced to climb down and apologise and make amends. Charles looked forward to what he imagined was going to be his finest hour. He dressed with special care that evening and made his way slowly in his carriage through the streets to the Opera House, where incredible preparations had been made for his reception. All the gates and doors of the building were guarded, the courtyard outside was full of soldiers, and inside the corridors were guarded too. Quite why there was such a large force is difficult to see – perhaps the authorities expected Charles to fight with the strength of twenty men, perhaps they expected loyal Highlanders to leap to his protection crying claymore, perhaps they anticipated a mob reaction which was not to come for another forty years. In any event, they were disappointed. As Charles stepped from his carriage he was seized by six soldiers and carried before M. de Vaudreuil who was in charge of the operation. He said, 'Monseigneur, I arrest you in the name of the King my master.' Charles replied the manner was a little too violent, but he did not attempt to struggle. He was searched for weapons and then the Major solemnly produced thirty-six ells of black silk ribbon to tie him up with. At this Charles remonstrated: he would give his word not to try to escape or hurt anyone. But the Major said orders were orders – Charles must be bound. They proceeded to truss him up like an oversize turkey which put Charles into a rage. If there was one thing he could not bear it was having his word doubted, and if there was another it was being exposed to ridicule. Both having happened he seems to have been incapable of speech. He said nothing at all as he was carried to the waiting coach. This was later described as acting with 'dignity and composure' but these were the very qualities Charles felt robbed of. Nothing had turned out as he had expected. His majestic presence hadn't prevented anyone laying a finger on him, his plight hadn't softened any hearts. Too late he saw that all his behaviour had brought upon him was exposure to the most utter humiliation. Meanwhile, at Versailles, Louis relaxed and enjoyed a comedy called *La Mère Coquette* in which Madame de Pompadour played the minor role of Laurette. All the important ministers were there and it took on the air of a celebration.

Charles was taken to Vincennes and his companions – less fortunate –

to the Bastille. Altogether, there were thirty-two of them, including a servant of Madame de Talmond, who wrote with cutting sarcasm to the authorities: 'You can, Monsieur, have the Te Deum sung, the victories of the King have reached their zenith, but as the imprisonment of my lackey cannot add to his laurels will you please send him back to me?' At Vincennes Charles was kept in solitary confinement, except for Neil Maceachain, for four days. According to d'Argenson, he quickly overcame his initial gloom – as Neil had seen him do before – and was reported in good spirits. On the 13th, '... he is gay ... and playing at battledore and shuttlecock. He jokes with the officers who guard him day and night, and has requested that they be not changed; he asks them news of the opera, and how Jeliotte sings.' Doubtless it also drifted through to him how all Paris rang with the scandal of his arrest and how strong feeling against the King for permitting this action was. The Dauphin himself was reputed to be disgusted, and d'Argenson considered it amounted to 'an everlasting stain on France; it will put us in line with Cromwell'. There were placards everywhere making fun of Louis and his ministers. One lampoon said:

> O Louis! Vos sujets de douleurs abattus
> Respectent Edouard captif et sans couronne.
> Il est roi dans les fers, qu'êtes vous sur le trône?
> J'ai vu tomber le sceptre aux pieds de Pompadour
> Mais fut-il relevé par les mains de l'Amour?

But placards hurt no one (though the police lost no time tearing them down). Louis had undoubtedly won: Charles had to get out. He was obliged to give his word to do this before he was allowed to leave his place of imprisonment. The pretence was over: he was homeless, unless he chose to go to Rome which he had sworn he would never do; he was virtually penniless after his months of high spending in Paris with no prospect of any income; and there was nothing at all on the horizon.

On 12th December Charles had brought himself to write a letter of abject apology.

My Brother and Cousin,
    I cannot tell you how worried I have been all this time that it has been impossible to explain directly to either you or your Ministers my thoughts; I have too much confidence in your goodness to believe that you could doubt for one moment my feelings and my undying devotion to your sacred person; I hope to be able to prove this one day, and in the meantime I am ready to leave this country immediately, as you wish; I have the honour to be –
                                                                        Charles P.R.

Louis was mollified. Two officers would accompany Charles on his journey, during which he was to go neither to Paris nor to Lyon. Money and post-horses would be provided.

Charles saw the new year in – 1749 – and celebrated his twenty-ninth birthday at Avignon. He had gone first to Fontainebleau – Madame de Talmond tried in vain to get access to him here – from his prison, where a fever gave him a brief breathing space, enough time to decide that short of Rome, Avignon was the only place he could go. There, in the heart of France though it was papal territory, there was still a Jacobite nucleus to welcome him. He arrived at seven o'clock in the morning on 27th December and, as his host William Murray wrote, 'I was never more surprised than to see him at my bedside, after they had told me that an Irish officer wanted to speak to me. He arrived, disguised in ane uniform of Irland's regiment, accompanyed only by Mr. Sheridan and one officer of the same regiment of which H.R.H. wore the uniform, but with no servant.' He was in perfect health after his ordeal, as he himself wrote to his father on 1st January: 'I arrived here on Friday last, and am in perfect good health, notwithstanding the unheard-of barbarous and inhuman treatment I met with.' For a while, no one had any objections to Charles staying in Avignon, but as he well knew, they would come. He had no intention of waiting till he was kicked out, nor was he prepared to let Europe imagine he was down, out and beaten. To everyone's amazement, he rode out of Avignon at the end of February, with only Henry Goring (one of the most faithful members of his household since his boyhood), and three servants, destination unknown.

CHAPTER SEVENTEEN

The Elusive Prince

It was clear, when Charles left Avignon in February 1749, that he was going to spend the rest of his life escaping reality. He was determined not to accept the inevitable, and by his refusal he demonstrated both the strength and weakness of his character. His strength lay in his tenacity, his weakness in his pride.

His behaviour from this point on looked to the rest of Europe like a game – to some harmless and even amusing, to others dangerous and to be feared. Biographers have written ever since of Charles playing it with gusto and enjoyment, yet it seems so obvious that he was in the grip of genuine paranoia. The disguises that he took to – an endless succession of assorted uniforms, and wigs – were not adopted in any spirit of festivity. His incognito was no joke. Charles believed that his life and especially his liberty were in danger. He did not disappear just to annoy his father and Louis XV, nor on a kind of holiday to give himself something to do, but because he thought it was necessary. Everyone was after him. The occasional actual description of someone supposedly sent to assassinate him was certainly frightening enough: '... one Grossert, collector of the customs at Alloa, hath left the country with intentions to assassinate the Prince. He is a middle-aged man, about five foot ten inches high, well made, of a black complexion, and pitted with smallpox, his eyebrows large and black, inclining to lean rather than fat.' These strays apart, it was Charles' special fear that the French would grab him and ship him to Italy where he would be doomed to live out his days in the old Palazzo Muti. That, more than assassination, was the fate he could not bear.

He left Avignon without any plans for his future except, Micawber-like, hoping and believing that something would turn up. De Luynes wrote: 'It is definite that the Pretender left on Monday or Tuesday night in the first week of Lent. Nobody knows if he has gone to Rome, Boulogne or Fribourg. It is believed that the vice-legate told him he couldn't stay any longer at Avignon.' Those who were interested in him did him the compliment of believing that he had some cunning plot afoot and persisted in regarding his disappearance as sinister. Charles had vanished once before and turned up at the head of an army. Might he not do it again? Regardless of the impracticability at that point in time, he was suspected of being capable of anything. Horace Walpole might be writing confidently that Jacobitism was quite dead but there were others who thought differently, or at least did not want Charles to be given the opportunity to try again. The English Government was always eager to know Charles' whereabouts and its ambassadors never gave up making offers to have him arrested. Sir Charles Hanbury Williams wrote from Dresden: '... for a small sum of money I will undertake to find a Pole who will engage to seize upon his person in any part of Poland and carry him to any port in the North that his Majesty should appoint. I have had offers of this sort already made me ... I am convinced it is very practicable.' Lord Hynford was equally eager to oblige when he wrote from Moscow: 'I am sorry that the Russian troops are not now in Poland for otherwise I believe it would have been an easy matter to prevail upon this Court to catch this young knight errant and to send him to Siberia where he would not have been anymore heard of.' General Bulkeley, a Jacobite who lived in Paris, managed to get a message through to Charles eventually, telling him how angry Louis XV was at his leaving Avignon and if he was found in France (which was suspected) he would be forcibly conducted to Rome. Since his household had been left at Avignon in charge of John Stafford and Michael Sheridan, two servants of long standing, it was expected that he would at some point return there, so he was warned that all the approaches in and out of Avignon were being watched. The French no longer trusted him and intended to teach him another lesson.

No W. B. Blaikie has appeared to chart minutely where Charles went each day after he started his wanderings, but such an itinerary would in any case have only a geographical interest. Charles' movements were haphazard, governed by whatever his current obsession was. He covered enormous distances, which of course agreed with him, sometimes only to turn round and cover them again. There were no Highlanders around to arrange his route and provide him with shelter and what food they could, so travelling was an expensive business. It was natural that the first contact Charles should make should be for financial reasons, and this was twofold. On the one hand he had left Stafford and Sheridan back in Avignon with all his worldly goods, and on the other he had the family banker Waters in Paris. The letters he wrote to both of them kept people in touch with him in the vaguest possible way. His fear of detection would not allow him to sign his name or date his letters. Often these missives were written in invisible ink and in disguised hands even worse than Charles' own. The names he did sign at the end only added to the confusion for they changed with bewildering rapidity and it was like receiving anonymous letters which, as Stafford and Sheridan complained, were difficult to accept as trustworthy, particularly when they contained important instructions. What credit could be given to Wm. Bidle, Button, Bidolphe, Burton, Le Croi, Douglas, Doson, Drumless, Forde or Ford, George, Johnson (Wm. and J.), Mildmay, Renfru and Thompson when they never proved their identity? In addition, Charles had a bad habit when he had grown bored with one name of not simply dropping it but giving it to someone else whom he did not want to refer directly to. Stafford and Sheridan needed all the peace Avignon afforded to decipher these epistles.

It was assumed that what Charles must be about was another campaign to Scotland. What else had all his energies been devoted to? It occurred to no one that there had been a violent change in Charles' attitude, though the first place he turned up in ought to have been sufficient indication that a campaign was not imminent. In April, he wrote to his distracted father that he was in Venice. By the time he actually wrote everyone knew he was in Venice. He announced it was the next best place, now that France was out of the question, for him to further his interests. What he meant by this piece of enigmatic nonsense James could not decide, but he was further irritated to find that far from maintaining his precious incognito Charles was actually flaunting his identity and publicly enjoying himself. He had travelled to Venice via Strasbourg, not daring as yet to go into France from which he and his followers were 'banished ... and mose of crisendom for being honest men you shou'd not be surprised at the desier I have of meeting you, there are in reality few that such as us cou'd inhabit ...' Venice, in any case, was no go. Charles was asked to leave. It was obvious that far from wanting to use Venice as any centre of operations, he had simply wanted to settle there. The Nuncio at least let him have a passport to enable him to travel in the Holy Roman Empire – and with it a new name, one Monsieur de Villelongue of Sweden. The passport in his pocket, Charles set off again. The wandering life, after four short months, had begun to pall, but he still would neither settle in Italy nor go to Fribourg. Nevertheless, the endless nagging from his father and older Jacobites to be sensible and accept one or the other was beginning to get him down. He needed comfort and approval. There was only one place he knew where to find both and that was Paris, the city full of women who doted on him. There, he was missed – a little of the salt had gone out of their lives, even de Luynes noting regretfully: 'There is little news of Prince Edward.' Irresistibly, Charles was drawn towards Paris, excited by the genuine danger involved. No test moving through Germany disguised – but what a test to move about Paris!

He appeared in the French capital in the autumn of 1749 and was instantly hidden by two women, who had been his friends without ever being his mistresses, in the convent they lived in. This convent was the Convent of St Joseph in the rue Dominique, founded by Madame de Montespan after her days as Louis XIV's favourite were over. Though basically a religious establishment it also acted as a kind of exclusive club for well-born ladies who wanted to live under some sort of chaperonage and yet retain their independence. They did not necessarily live there permanently but could have a room there and live there for months at a time. The pair who sheltered Charles were sisters – Madame de Vassé and Mademoiselle Ferrand. They belonged to the Flora Macdonald mould rather than that of the Princesse de Talmond – who immediately renewed her affair with Charles and was a frequent visitor. His persona must have appeared quite different to his two hostesses. They saw him as all charm, always polite and chivalrous, and interested in good conversation. They had been his entrée into the salon life that intelligent eighteenth-century ladies so revelled in, a world where ideas and theories were gravely put forward and discussed instead of tittle-tattle and gossip. The Princesse had been a part of this world, but never to the extent of these two sisters who did not balance it with the kind of gay social life she did. On the contrary, they led a comparatively cloistered existence – suitably enough – and their sole pleasures would seem to have been intellectual ones. Quite what they saw in Charles is difficult to fathom – he must have revealed a facet of himself to them that he hid from everyone else, or perhaps nobody else ever did him the honour of supposing he had a mind worth bothering about. He seems to have been able to hold his own in this rarefied company and to have responded to them. It was the ideal female relationship – he was admired by the sisters and admired them with no nasty physical connection. They found his affair with the Princesse hard to put up with – after a first rapturous reunion they soon fell to quarrelling and fighting which dangerously disturbed the peace of the convent. Why they put up with it is a mystery – probably because they were proud of not censuring Charles' behaviour.

Charles lived in Paris intermittently for the next two years, taking great care to keep really hidden. Every now and again the risk he ran would terrify him and he would go off for a while to some safer place, but he always came back, in spite of his word of honour given in 1748 never to return. Honour was something he was getting less and less interested in – after all, what had being a man of honour done for him? Influenced by the atmosphere of the convent he began to indulge in rather clichéd philosophy, even to the extent of writing down his reflections for the edification of Mlle Ferrand. He had decided that he believed in Destiny as much as in God, that one should never judge others by oneself, and – a thought he was particularly proud of – weak men should never be told secrets in case they were frightened by them. The implication was that Charles had truly scaring secrets he could tell. His letters to the sisters when he was away from the convent were noticeably better written and spelled and altogether more literate than his burblings to Stafford and Sheridan or his stiff little notes to his father. Sometimes he actually had something interesting to tell them, such as in the autumn when he went to stay on the Princesse de Talmond's estates at Lunéville and observed an aurora borealis. He described his astronomical experience in enthusiastic detail: if only he could have done so at fifteen and had a teacher by him to capitalise his interest.

He also, at this time, began to collect things on a surprisingly large scale and to take a collector's pride in his possessions: the man of action was disappearing as fast as the man of honour. Poor Waters the banker in Paris was inundated with precise instructions as to the care of books and pictures and marble busts. If one book was missing Charles fretted like a regular antiquarian that the set was ruined: 'if an honest man wants sum single Volume it is Very disagreable to lose the Set'. Where exactly all these new treasures were to be stored was never specified. By collecting them Charles might demonstrate the desire for permanency and settling down but he never carried this a stage farther and put down roots in one place long enough to take an interest in property. His only foothold was the house at Avignon (rented) where his 'family' eked out a miserable existence keeping body and soul together and desperately trying to obey Charles' last stern command that 'My Horses must be taken good care of and the greatest Economy to be had in everything'. While they were frantically economising Charles was buying up half the art world, and though he always sent more money to prevent actual starvation he had his priorities more than a little wrong. The trouble was, the household at Avignon were already part of the past and he was not sure if they had any place in the future.

The days spent out of Paris at Lunéville were not all distinguished by happy experiences such as sighting stars. A large part of them was spent drinking and working himself into a rage over people he thought had slighted him. Louis XV had insulted him so he decided he hated all

Kings. His brother had wronged him and his brother was now not only a Cardinal but a priest so he hated all priests. He took to writing little mottos, sort of Christmas cracker stuff:

> To speke to ete
> To think to Drink

was improved to:

> To ete to think
> To Speke to drink.

Speaking and thinking were not nearly as important or time-consuming as eating and drinking, which were now obsessional. His health, which had up until now stood the strain of his way of life – he was always adding a boastful 'my health is perfect' to the end of his letters – now began to crack. He was confined to bed on several occasions and instead of insisting that he was perfectly all right as he had used to do he began to take an interest in his own ailments and to want to doctor himself. With medicine in the state it was at the time he was entitled to think he could do better. He became as fascinated by anatomy as he had been by astronomy, and again the shame was that it only amounted to dabbling. But the fact that he wanted to dabble at all was indicative of his changed attitude towards another campaign – his energies were no longer totally directed towards this to the exclusion of everything else. He might still pretend that he expected to go off at any time to invade England but he did not act as if he believed it. The struggle to reconcile himself to an eternity of the kind of life he was already living was still going on, and while it raged he was an unhappy man.

His father was not unsympathetic, and his sympathy extended as far as offering constructive advice. At the beginning of August 1750 he wrote to Charles agreeing to the renewal of the commission of regency he had asked for: 'for I am sensible that should I have refused to sent it, it might happen to be of great inconvenience to you. But let me recommend to you not to use other people as you do me, by expecting friendship and favors from them while you do all that is necessary to disgust them for you must not expect that any body else will make you the return I do.' But Charles did expect it. He hated James' continual self-righteousness, his incessant harping on what a silly bad boy he was. Probably he would have had more respect for his father if he had been firmer and more authoritative – if he had been refused all favours unless he presented himself in Rome. James' continual kindness and weakness was not good for him and reaped their own inevitable reward. He kept his father firmly in the dark about everything he was doing – he was just someone there to be used, a necessary evil.

There was nothing very much to keep James in the dark about, until the autumn of 1750 when the most extraordinary thing happened – Charles went to London. It was an unexpected event, even to Charles himself. There was no long preparation such as a dangerous mission like this might have called for, nor do any traces of elaborate arrangements survive. One day Charles was killing time at Luneville, the next he was on his way to the capital he had never seen. It was not his own idea, but that of the English Jacobites who had suddenly come to life in the winter of 1749. This short surge of interest was referred to as a revival of Jacobitism, but was nothing of the kind. What happened was that all the elements opposed to King and Government came temporarily together. What the English Jacobites were proposing was a coalition with Frederick Prince of Wales against his father. This was not at all the same thing as a rising against the Hanoverians in general or the Protestant succession in particular, but the mere fact that the English Jacobites were active at all excited Charles. Such a movement in the heart of the kingdom might lead to anything and was exactly what he had always dreamt about. He followed the progress of the 'revival' with interest prior to his own visit.

It began with the speech at Oxford by Dr King, always Jacobite in sympathies. He made clear his views and was enthusiastically applauded. Then later in the year there was an amazing gathering at a race meeting at Lichfield, where a large number of gentlemen spoke very freely of giving support to Charles. But verbal promises had always been cheap – what was surprising was that several were rash enough to give written ones to Charles' agents. Dr King himself said two hundred and seventy-five were willing to give their names. Charles was convinced that his hour – a different kind of hour from anything he had enjoyed before – was now come. He had no intention of going again to Scotland, in spite of a memorial from Lochgarry telling him the time was ripe for vengeance. London had always been his object and now that he was invited he did not hesitate. The invitation does not survive as a document but then the English Jacobites had always been adept at never putting pen to paper. Charles had no gilt-edged card to flash when he arrived – but he seems to have accepted that as part of the risk, though in later years he was very clear that he had indeed been invited, much clearer than he ever was about his trip to Scotland.

The trip was supposed to be one of reconnaissance: there was no question this time of getting into a boat with a handful of men and starting a rising. He was going to meet his English supporters – a pleasure long denied him – and see what was what. Yet if that was all he intended why did Charles' agent in Antwerp suddenly receive an order to collect twenty-six thousand muskets? Did Charles intend to distribute them through the drawing-rooms of London or had he some more useful army in mind? He gave nothing away: the order is there and that is all. His passion for military equipment had carried him away on a flight of fancy. Luckily, such vagueness did not extend to his actual trip. Horace Walpole, that expert on all that was going on in London, never got a sniff of it. He left Antwerp, where he had proceeded in disguise of course, on 12th September 1750, for London accompanied by a Colonel Brett. He was back in Paris on the 24th so his entire stay cannot have been more than a week.

For Charles it proved both an exciting and yet ultimately a disastrous week. He left London knowing how hopeless the situation was – but at least this time he had learnt the lesson without spilling a drop of blood. He was reputed to have stayed in Essex Street in the Strand with Lady Primrose, very heavily incognito. With great daring he walked around the capital he had never seen, like any sightseer, gaping at buildings and well-known landmarks. The Tower in particular fascinated him. He walked round it, with Colonel Brett, and gave it as his considered opinion that it might be possible to blow in one of the gates that he thought looked less stalwart than the rest. Who was going to do the blowing was another question. During the week Charles met the Duke of Beaufort and the Earl of Westmorland and other less exalted English Jacobites. They left him in no doubt that nobody was going to do anything violent – everything was going to be quiet plotting, just as it always had been. Charles must wait and see, must bide his time, must wait for the right moment. Ill-considered action would get them nowhere. Dr King was more brutally discouraging. He had Charles to tea and convinced him of the total lack of support there would be for any kind of armed insurrection. Charles did not know his Englishmen – it was his own fault if he had misinterpreted their invitation. The things they were going to get excited about would not raise a flutter in the heart of a man who had led thousands of Highlanders. Charles saw they were talking about different things – and left.

Before he left, he did at some point during the week do something that was of importance: he formally became a Protestant. Charles later testified that he had done so, though no official announcement was made at the time. It was consistent with his desire to turn his back on the traditional pattern of his family's attempts to restore themselves. He no longer aimed at anything but the support of the English and restoration within the existing legal framework. Whether he ever thought it out like that or not, the fact was that he had waited until after he had failed to regain the throne by conquest – when his religion would not have mattered initially – to decide to try to regain it by accommodating himself to the mould required. But momentous though the decision was in many people's eyes, it would be a mistake to suppose Charles thought of it as momentous. On the contrary, it no longer much mattered to him. Both on the personal and political fronts religion was unimportant. He had always been a practising Catholic but never an ostentatious one. Henry becoming a cardinal was a step he deeply resented and his own conversion had more than a measure of reaction to this in it. Yet Charles was not defiant over his decision. He seems to have thought that he must do anything he could to give himself a better chance, and that was all. It betrayed, rather than cynicism, how low his confidence was, how great the change in him had been.

Charles returned to France, with few any the wiser. He stayed briefly in Paris before going to Lunéville where he once more slumped into an idle existence all the greyer when contrasted with his recent activity. He took out his disappointment on the Princesse de Talmond, who was rapidly becoming a kind of whipping-boy. Why she stood the ill treatment he meted out to her nobody could fathom. Her letters to Charles – which seem often to have been written while they were within the same house – became hysterical as she begged him to be kind to her and reciprocate her love.

> You will not be satisfied unless you Kill me. Let M. tell you in horror about the effect your letter had on me. You call it hardness, The fact That I won't let myself be killed. I wish to see you, but not to keep you up here. That is impossible. I am in a perpetual sweat; I have to be changed every hour. I don't sleep a wink; I have to be watched over and given herb tea, otherwise I fall into a faint. Moreover you do not wish to sleep up here. You will do as you please, but I did not promise to carry out your wishes when they are immoderate. I am dying of anger; you have killed me.

And, a little later:

> If I did not love you so much I would not be so wretched. The sight of me can do you no harm and the sight of you would restore life to me. I am dying. I love you too much and you love me too little. Since I see clearly and with extreme grief That you want to pick a lover's quarrel and set yourself at variance with me – if This is so, Then send me back by bearer all my notes or letters, and never hope to find anyone more passionately devoted, in spite of all The heartbreaks. I have spent a dreadful night.

If he went on like this what was to be done? What indeed. For different reasons, James was obsessed with the same question. On 30th December 1750, he wrote Charles one of his classic letters of fatherly admonition beginning: 'Tomorrow you end your 30th year. May you see many more than double that number, and happier ones that those you have already past. The hardships you have gone through, and do perhaps still undergo, are not small and it is to be hoped they will contribute at last to what they are chiefly directed.' That, of course, was the point: what was Charles' direction, aged thirty, of no fixed address, income unknown?

It was soon plain which direction his father had in mind: marriage. He had, after all, turned to marriage himself at a similar stage in his life. The continuation of the dynasty had seemed not only an inescapable necessity but a political weapon. Surely his son could see it still was? With great urgency James wrote: 'Your giving lawful heirs to the crown will not only be a constant security to your own person, but it will make you more considered and respected abroad, and will undoubtedly give new life and vigour to the cause, and your friends, whose zeal can never be so warm when all their hopes are centred in you alone.' James went on to say that he thought marriage so important that he almost didn't care whom Charles married. His hopes of his advice being taken were slight – 'If this letter has the same fate with many others I have writ to you, I might have saved myself the trouble of writing it.'

Charles' attitude to marriage had always been unconventional in that he never seemed to find it inevitable. Neither did he find it attractive. Whatever the men of Glenmoriston might have had to say about toasts to a black-eyed beauty who was a daughter of France, nobody's name had ever been seriously linked with Charles and, more important, his total lack of wenching had not gone unnoticed. It was all very well for him to say all that could wait, but would any normal man in his twenties have forsworn attendant pleasures while he waited? It was in a way a relief to James to hear of the liaison with the Princesse de Talmond – at least it proved Charles was capable, even if he had discovered his capabilities late. But marriage was still another matter. Charles began, after his return from Scotland, to make various fatuous suggestions as to who he might marry. One minute it was the Czarina, the next an already married German princess. As James acidly commented when Charles gaily proposed the first, 'What hopes can you have that a simple and blunt proposal of marriage to the czarina ... can succeed at a time she is linked with the Elector of Hanover ...' The whole question of marriage was quite difficult enough without Charles wasting time on impossibilities. He would have to lower his sights, and even then there were not many kings or princes willing to risk incurring the disfavour of England by allying themselves with the Stuarts. But the point was, Charles did not care. Thirty did not seem very old to him. His experience of women had not led him to look kindly on being tied to one for life. He also felt it would be a strategic mistake to marry at that point in time when not even he himself could pretend his prospects were good. To hell with heirs who might have a better chance: it was himself he was interested in. There was not a scrap of self-sacrifice in Charles' make-up.

Meanwhile, he carried on with his reading. What he thought of *Tom Jones* he never recorded but perhaps his choice of titles when he had finished that weighty tome indicates he found it somewhat lacking: how about *The Nun in a Chemise* or *The Brothel* or *The Art of Love in Six Cantos*? Could Fielding compete? He read them in French, and beside them his one book in English at the time – *The Present Situation in England* – must have been dull. Apart from reading, drinking and quarrelling with Marie-Louise, Charles was as usual occupied with plots and schemes for restoration. There were always plots about, but to his credit – or perhaps simply a sign of new cynicism – he paid them little attention. On the contrary, he was more and more attracted to the pressures that could be exerted through diplomatic channels – which would have amazed his poor father. He had got it into his head that the Earl Marischal could help if he wanted. All the pointed rebuffs he had had from this gentleman only seemed to convince him that he did have power. It had excited Charles when the old Jacobite was appointed to the post of ambassador in Paris by Frederick of Prussia. In England, Newcastle shared his interest, saying that the Earl's appointment was 'to encourage the Jacobite party that we may apprehend disturbances from them if a rupture should ensue in consequences of the measures we are taking abroad'. Charles wrote the Earl a sycophantic letter in June 1751 and sent it with Goring – who risked the Bastille every time he entered Paris. 'You know the value I have for an honest man,' he wrote, 'and how glad I would be that such a one was able, or had occasion of shewing himself effectually now for the relief of his King and country. I now charge Col. Goring who will deliver you this, to shew you the powers I thought fit to give him, and to consult with you as to the best method of effectuating his message, as also of what might be attempted at the Court of Prussia, or any other except that of France, their unworthy proceedings rendering them not fit to be trusted. I hope you are persuaded of the true friendship I have for you and the pleasure I would feel to prove it. My health is perfect, and remain your sincere friend.'

The Earl Marischal could be forgiven for not knowing what on earth

Charles was on about. He proved himself worthy of his diplomatic calling by refusing to meet Charles but agreeing to meet Goring. The meeting took place in the Jardin des Tuileries at night in tremendous and rather ridiculous secrecy – quite enough to embarrass both participants who had little idea what to say to each other. The outcome of the meeting so desired by Charles was a further voyage – to Sweden. Sweden had always been a 'fringe' Jacobite country, not to be looked to as hopefully as France or Spain but with definite possibilities. Charles had instructed Goring to go there after his meeting with the Earl Marischal but why the meeting was so essential is a mystery. The Earl was relieved to see the back of the Prince's emissary.

CHAPTER EIGHTEEN

Plots and Affairs

In spite of the lack of cooperation from the Earl, Charles was more cheerful as 1752 opened than he had been for some time. He had spent most of 1751 building up a fine wine cellar, doing more reading and travelling backwards and forwards between Lorraine and Paris. It had not added up to much. It had, in fact, been a bad year: money had been a problem, Mlle Ferrand had died, Stafford and Sheridan bothered him with problems about the Avignon household – quite justifiably but Charles did not think so. The only concrete thing to come out of 1751 was the acquisition of a house in Ghent. Charles had begun to feel down-at-heel and persecuted. Then, to rescue his ego, 1752 brought in the first promising-looking plot to restore his family that there had been for a long time and Charles could not help but be excited. He was also nervous and in the end frightened. He was not by nature good at plotting, lacking both the necessary patience and administrative ability, but in 1752 he made a gigantic effort to overcome his shortcomings, though it taxed his resources to the full. The trouble was, Charles always saw things as elementary. In London he had an adherent, Alexander Murray, who had lately shown his Jacobite zeal by refusing to kneel to ask for pardon to the House of Commons, where he had been brought on a charge of violence during the elections. Murray was well connected – his brother was Lord Elibank, one of those careful English Jacobites who managed to stay on the right side of the line wherever it was drawn. As Horace Walpole put it: 'Both were such active Jacobites that if the Pretender had succeeded they would have produced many witnesses to testify their great zeal for him; both so cautious, that no witnesses of active treason could be produced by the Government against them.' Murray fled to France in November 1751 and soon made himself known to Charles, and convinced him that a blow could be struck for him – arranged by Murray – in London, backed by a simultaneous rising in Scotland and the landing of a Swedish force there headed by the Earl Marischal's brother. It all looked beautifully simple, but was as full of flaws as all other plots had been.

To start with, Charles, who had after 1745 joined his father in insisting that there must be foreign backing, over-estimated the interest shown by Frederick of Prussia. That Frederick *was* interested is undeniable, but it was in the way Louis XV had been interested. He wrote to the Earl Marischal: 'It will be for my interest to encourage them in their design under hand and without being observed. You will agree with me that the state of European affairs does not permit me to declare myself openly.' Charles had a healthy respect for the Prussian King who he agreed was 'a clever man' but he does not seem to have thought this cleverness might extend to behaving exactly as the French King had done. The plotting continued throughout 1752, with Murray returning to London supposedly to see to the details in November. It extended into 1753 without any definite date being fixed for the actual rising, and the longer it all took the farther removed Charles became from it all. Murray was doing what he liked without definite instructions while Archibald Cameron was supposed to be organising the Scottish end and Charles fixing the foreign support.

It was all a mess, but before the end came it had whipped Charles into a new fever of expectation. It was in this mood of exhilaration that in the spring of 1752 he took the extraordinary step of sending for Clementina Walkinshaw to join him at Ghent. No one seems to have found this event as remarkable as it surely was, perhaps because it took place at a time when the Elibank plot fills the stage. Quite apart from the timing, the basis for any attachment between Charles and Clementina was so slight – ten days at Bannockburn in 1746 and that was all. There is not a trace of any kind of communication between them in the intervening years. If Charles had indeed exacted a promise that Clementina would come if he called, it seems clear enough why he had never done so – he had been far too busy with the Princesse de Talmond. But what had Clementina been doing, marooned like some Lady of Shalott waiting for this call that never came?

For six years she had stayed where she was, then one of her uncles obtained for her a place as a canoness in one of the Noble Chapters in the Low Countries. Competition to get into these Chapters was fierce, so Clementina had done well for herself. Yet this move was not as straight-forward as it seemed, for the minute Clementina arrived at Dunkirk we find her writing to John O'Sullivan. According to O'Sullivan, who was delighted to be thus employed as a go-between having somewhat faded into the background of Charles' life, 'she gave me to understand, yt if she had no account from yu, yt her intention was to go into a Convente & expres'd to me yt she was not very oppulante'. This makes it look as though Clementina was trying a last, if improbably belated, throw – more or less casting herself at Charles' feet before disappearing into a convent. But what was strange was that Charles had also written to O'Sullivan, apparently independently, apparently at the same time. The letters in the Stuart Papers on this subject are out of order and undated in the main, but one dated 29th May 1752 makes it clear that O'Sullivan at least thought his new popularity an amazing coincidence – 'Nothing in life cou'd surprise me more than the sight of Your Royal Highness Lettre.' It is in this letter that he tells Charles that Clementina has written to him and that he will carry out Charles' instructions regarding her, which were to pass on some money and await instructions.

Whatever the circumstances, Charles opened the renewed relationship with a letter couched in the most unloverlike terms imaginable. Clementina could never argue that he had left her with any illusions. Their reunion was to be absolutely secret, like everything else in his life at the time, and 'neither Sir John or anybody whatsoever must know the least thing about you or what passes between us under pain of incurring forever my displeasure'.

Charles would rather have used Goring, whom he had come to rely on where delicate negotiations were in the offing, but Goring would have nothing to do with Charles' latest whim and was not afraid to say so, which made Charles all the more determined. Goring's objections were nothing to do with Clementina personally – his fear was that, because of her sister's position as housekeeper to the Princess of Wales, she might be some kind of government plant. The idea intoxicated rather than repelled Charles, and he went straight ahead with his plan to meet Clementina in Paris.

They met in Paris in the summer of 1752 and proceeded to Ghent where they set up house together. Clementina did not demand marriage and Charles did not offer it, but they assumed the rôles of husband and wife from the beginning and he was happy to bestow upon her all his aliases. She had hardly changed at all – he had changed markedly. She was still the same rather plain, quiet, respectable Scottish miss, utterly unlike the vivacious, beautiful, intelligent women of the world that Charles had come to know. He seems to have taken a kind of pride in her very ordinariness, making no attempt to persuade her to alter. Her constancy pleased him above all else, since by now he distrusted even those who were most faithful to him. Her greatest attraction was her unquestioning, undemanding loyalty: he called and she came, on his terms. If she had attempted to play her cards better that fact alone might have persuaded him to defy everyone – which he would have enjoyed – and marry her. But Clementina was no schemer. There is no explanation for her behaviour other than genuine love. It was a love which withstood the shock of seeing a Charles considerably altered from the young gallant of 1746. It was not simply a matter of appearance, though that was marked enough – Charles was not yet fat and repulsive, but six years' drinking and living an irregular lazy life had made his complexion and figure less than perfect. Clementina quickly adjusted to this. What was harder to adjust to was the change in his personality. It was, after all, a personality she had done no more than glimpse, but she could not fail to have been impressed by his apparent idealism, courage and dedication. She cannot have been with him more than a few weeks before she became aware that she was living with a very different man – one who had moods of black depression during which he was often violent, was unreasonable, selfish and irritable and less frequently gay and considerate. But Clementina had made her bed and needed no one to tell her that she would have to lie on it.

For the first year, while the Elibank plot was still in the offing, they were comparatively happy. Pickle, the spy, who started his government activities about this time, admitted that they appeared very content, and went about in public with every sign of devotion. That in itself was an achievement, for up to this time the joys of domestic bliss were unknown to Charles. When Clementina became pregnant at the beginning of 1753 he was delighted and squired her everywhere with touching concern. He was by then thirty-two, without any issue, legitimate or otherwise, so it was a good advertisement. In October 1753 a daughter, Charlotte, was born at Liège and registered there with fictitious parents. Almost from that point on Charles' and Clementina's relationship deteriorated. It was nothing to do either with the strain of parenthood or the fact that it was a girl instead of a boy, but more the breakdown of the false hopes that had buoyed Charles up for the last two years. In March 1753 Archibald Cameron had been arrested and in June executed on the '45 charge. His death killed the Elibank plot. It might not have done so if Charles had not at the same time realised that his Prussian hopes were as remote as his French ones. He would have been furious if he had known that Marischal had written to Frederick in May: 'The Prince's position, coupled with an intrepidity which never lets him doubt where he desires, causes others to form projects for him which he is always ready to execute.' Once the sheer futility of his recent schemes hit him everything went sour. In addition, Charles began to worry that his own life was in danger and whereas before he had scorned warnings to be careful he now used them as an excuse to go on the run again. He left Clementina and her new-born daughter for a while and scurried between a series of German towns, for ever on the lookout for hired assassins. When his self-stimulated panic had subsided he returned to Liège and his family responsibilities. Among these, he did not count writing to his father, who complained bitterly: 'I am entire stranger to all his affairs and all that relates to him, and I should not so much know he were alive did I not hear from second and third hands that those who have the same share in his confidence say he is in good health; for it is now more than two years since he was writ at all here.'

Things were at a very low ebb. The new year seemed always to be a bad time for Charles these days. Hardly was he back from his sojourn in seedy hotels before he quarrelled with Clementina. The quarrels were mainly about money. In a letter Charles showed how arrogant he had always been in this respect. He had asked a supporter for money: 'however I was extremely scandalised not to have received any since I thought fit to Call for it, it is strange, such proceedings.' Charles' supplies – always erratic – had run out again and though lack of money never worried him, other people's worry irritated him intensely. Clementina had never exactly lived in the lap of luxury, but nor had she been used to hardship, which was what she was now enduring. Charles had had years of keeping creditors happy, but Clementina, with a tiny baby to think about, was driven demented by the demands made on her. Charles had no sympathy. They shouted at each other in public and their scenes were widely reported. In November 1753, less than a month after Charlotte's birth, Charles could write to Goring with supreme callousness that not only was he going to discard all his papist servants at Avignon but 'My mistress had behaved so unworthily that she has put me out of patience and as she is a Papist too, I discard her also!!! P.S. She told me she had friends that would maintain her, so that after such a declaration, and other impertinences, makes me abandon her. I hereby desire you to find out who her friends are that she may be delivered into their hands. Daniel is charged to conduct her to Paris.'

But Clementina had no intention of being thrown over – she clung to Charles like a leech, unwilling to admit that she had made the most colossal mistake. Somewhere inside this bad-tempered, cruel monster was the man she had given up everything for, the man she loved. If he now seemed to hate her, he appeared to love his child, and that was her one weapon: if he wanted Charlotte he must keep her. So the three of them went to Paris where they continued their noisy rows. They had one particularly ugly fight in a café which caught everyone's attention, so much so that Waters wrote to Charles that John O'Sullivan had witnessed this disgraceful episode in the Bois de Boulogne and that his reputation was suffering. Reputation was something Charles was almost past caring about. He was unhappy in Paris: 'the terrible situation I am in for want of an abode, and ye impossibility of my staying here, ye Bad Blood I make in this Abominable Country, not being able to Breath as much as ye fresh aire without greatest apprehension.' He spent his time moaning about money, or that other people who ought to be glad to give it to him were not coughing up, and consoling himself with ordering more costly trinkets like a watch and a microscope. Clothes were a consolation. As if Stafford and Sheridan did not have enough worries, he wrote saying he wanted them to send – from what he imagined as an inexhaustible supply – shirts, stockings, stocks, handkerchiefs, lace, and 'Iff you have by you any Fans or Ribens (I do not mean ye Green and Blue) make a little Box of them apart (as they are counterband)'.

Those nearest to him, apart from Clementina, were aware that some kind of Rubicon had been passed. None saw this more clearly and with greater sadness than Henry Goring, who for the past eight years had been Charles' almost inseparable companion, performing for his sake endless feats of endurance. He had travelled the length and breadth of Europe on his master's errands, suffered imprisonment in the Bastille, and never once complained. But he had done all this to serve a man he respected and honoured who he thought had a purpose in life. That man seemed to have gone. 'I have twice, sir, been turned off like a common footman,' wrote poor Goring, 'with most opprobrious language, without money or cloaths … No, sir, princes are never friends, it would be too much to expect, but I did believe till now that they had humanity enough to reward good services.' Goring remonstrated with Charles to mend his ways, to lead a sober respectable life, but Charles flew into a rage as he did at all personal criticism. He would live his life precisely as he wanted. Goring was left with no alternative. 'I, with your leave, Sir, shall retire and spend the rest of my life in serving God,' he wrote, 'and wishing you all prosperity since I unfortunately cannot be for the future of any use to you.' (The rest of Goring's life proved to be short – he died the next year.) Charles affected not to care and busied himself with another move. He told Waters 'as I do not find ye Air here agrees with me in the least, am resolved to quit this cursed country in a few days'. He quit it for new territory – Basle, in Switzerland.

It was a strange choice to make. Basle was a small, rather genteel town with a small closed society of its own into which 'Dr Thompson' and his wife and child could not easily be absorbed. It was not the sort of place a man with no money and many creditors should go. If Charles had imagined the simple life in a Swiss canton would cost him a fraction of what it had cost him in Paris, he was soon disillusioned. Basle was hideously expensive. Within days of arriving he was sending off an urgent request for twelve thousand livres to Waters. Furthermore, it was boring, however much Charles might go on about the air. He missed his 'nusepapers' and set about having his favourite gazettes sent to him. Only Clementina, who joined him a few weeks later, was glad to be there, with some sort of permanency, glad to see an end to the bumping about in broken-down carriages which was so hard on a toddler. But she congratulated herself too early – Charles began to go off on little 'business' trips to some unspecified destination like a seedy commercial traveller while Clementina was left to manage as best she could. Sympathy for her was widespread in Basle, where the solid burghers had noted the beatings and ill-treatment that she received. Charles was known as a bad husband, strange for an English doctor. Charles was expert at leaving others to manage while he had a good time – Stafford and Sheridan in Avignon could have taught Clementina a thing or two. Their latest plea for money resulted in instructions to sell 'Kitchen, butlery, Tables, spare Beds and Bedding but not the Sheets'. Meanwhile Charles was in Paris at the carnival, his fears of imprisonment or assassination quite forgotten. He was approached, while he was there, by many who wanted him to cast Clementina off. For some time various English Jacobites had been trying to bargain with him: they would give him money if he would get rid of Clementina. Charles refused. Whereas before he had boasted he was throwing his mistress aside he now clung to her obstinately because he would not be dictated to. It was none of their business. He might beat and bully the unfortunate woman but she was his and he could do what he liked with her. He wrote: 'whether I have a cook or a cook-maid in my private house at present should, to a person who had no passion, be a matter of moonshine.' They were interfering busybodies. Nobody was going to bring any pressure to bear in his private life – it did not harm his family's or his country's interests.

Charles had never been good at initiating things, though he often looked the originator of schemes. Now, as 1755 ended, he was more than ever struggling to keep his head above the water of debt and disappointment. He did it with a flourish, but fooled nobody, least of all his father, to whom Charles was always forced to turn when things got tight. For the next ten years, when his father was ill and tired, Charles exploited him mercilessly, larding the exploitation over with sweet words. He repeatedly promised to return home if James would send the money, then when the money arrived (as it always did) he spent it. When James was doing him a favour, Charles disguised it as a favour *he* was doing his father – such as sending the servants he could not afford to keep to Rome as a gift to James. His valet-de-chambre Morrison would be a priceless asset for 'he shaves and combs a wig perfectly'. James was not appreciative, having long passed the stage of caring about a perfectly combed wig. He replied tartly: 'When you recommended to me ... several of your servants whom you had dismissed, I should not have imagined that you would have sent any of them here without waiting for my answer.' But he let them stay a while then gave them their fare back to France. Charles had pulled that one too often.

James was thoroughly depressed by his elder son – never more so than in 1755. Like all indulgent fathers, he had always known that one day he would have to pay the price of his tenderness. Charles had had his finest hour. For ten years he had done nothing to justify his promise. In a letter to Edgar, which James had read, he could see how Charles' mind worked and it did not please him: '... my situation is such that I have nothing to say but imprecations against the fatality of being born in such a detestable age ... The unworthy behaviour of certain ministers the 10th December 1748 has put it out of my power to settling any where without honor or interest being at stake.' James was perhaps the last person near to Charles to acknowledge that he had gone so badly astray that there was little hope for him. What distressed James particularly was that his son as a man had developed so unexpectedly into an unpleasant character he could not be proud of. But James had love and faith: he believed that Charles simply needed direction, a direction he could give, to be put right again. If only he would come home the old Charles could be reclaimed. But he would not come and from a distance James felt helpless. What agitated him even more was his growing suspicion that his son did not realise what was happening on the European scene sufficiently to take advantage of it. How could he, flitting as he did from Switzerland to Flanders, in touch with nobody that mattered and totally submerged in piddling affairs? James, sitting tight in Rome attending to his vast correspondence, as he had done now for forty years, saw very clearly which way the wind was blowing. A new war had broken out, the Seven Years War, between France and England, and as ever in such a situation there was hope for the Jacobites in general and Charles in particular. What alarmed James was that not only was Charles not behaving as a respectable candidate for the throne of England ought, but he was not even on speaking terms with the French King. It was obvious he must make his own private peace with France as quickly as possible and tidy up his personal life, part of which must include marriage and legitimate heirs. James wrote urgently: 'For ... whatever may be their aversion to the Hanover Family, is it to be imagined that the people of England would run the risque of restoring a Prince whose family ended in himself?' Later, he became almost hysterical writing (when his previous letter produced no satisfaction), 'My Dear Son, Your honor, your interest every thing that can be dear to man is at stake in this important conjuncture, Act at least your part as a true Patriot, a dutiful son and a man of honour and sense; If you are in a lethargy rise out of it, if you are not show it by your action ...'

It was a challenge, but Charles ignored it. He wanted everything on a plate: if either the English demanded him or the French asked him to head a force, he would consider it, but nothing less. His old, ailing father would have made a better job of appearing keen and willing. Charles read the newspaper reports of the various battles but with complete detachment. He was more interested in moving house again, this time to near the town of Bouillon where he had spent such happy times with his cousin the Duc de Bouillon. It was a château, the Château de Carlsbourg. It was here, at the end of 1758, that Charles had the immense satisfaction of receiving overtures from the French, for whom the war was not going well. Proudly, he refused to see the two cardinals sent to negotiate with him: if France, who had so wronged him, wanted to make use of him again they must be prepared to grovel much more thoroughly. They must also be prepared to show their hand first: when twenty-five thousand troops were ready and waiting, then and only then would Charles meet to talk terms.

It was heady stuff, but Charles, significantly, was less affected than Jacobites throughout Europe. He did not really believe anything was going to happen and furthermore there is even a tone to his letters in 1759 that suggests he was not sure he wanted it to happen anyway, except that it would solve his money worries. If he had actually been called to action – if those hordes of troops had materialised before his eyes – it would have been a struggle to lift up his sword and charge forward. His physical condition was poor, his ailments small but numerous. He could, perhaps, have been transformed if someone had taken him in hand, but who was going to do that? Those about him encouraged him so that their own lazy life could continue. Clementina had no influence at all. Occasionally a visitor like Andrew Lumisden, his father's assistant secretary, would have a good effect but it was always brief. Charles did not want to reform, and no one could convince him that it was worth his while.

He did, however, make one effort, when the bait seemed big enough. The Duc de Choiseul asked, very respectfully, for a meeting. Now Choiseul was an important man, one who had had nothing to do with Charles' disgrace of 1748, and Charles could not resist being courted. In February 1759 he went to Paris – officially, with a passport – to Choiseul's house. Unfortunately he arrived drunk, but the French all behaved like perfect gentlemen and pretended he was not. At least Charles could carry his drink well enough to take in the news that Louis XV was prepared to give him troops and ships, and that when they were given Jacobite plans on the home front should be revealed. All was graciousness. It was only when Charles was back at Bouillon that he realised he hadn't done so well as he thought: where *were* all the troops and ships? It was still all words. In a rage he looked round for something or someone to take the blame, and hit on the idea that it had all happened because he was only a prince, not a king. His father must abdicate, then he could enter into negotiations properly. He would have status and no one would be able to trifle with him. Once he had got hold of this idea Charles pushed it with all the mistaken enthusiasm he was capable of. But James proved surprisingly stubborn: he would not abdicate, not yet. If his family was restored, through Charles' efforts, then he would be pleased to, but not now, not in exile, in favour of a son who did not know how to behave. It was stalemate.

Curiously, Charles seemed to accept this without resistance. He did not reply to letters from Rome because he had piles and couldn't sit up. He lay there reading the newspapers and dealing with the usual apologetic complaints from the household he still maintained at Avignon. All the time he lolled there other people busied themselves on his behalf and he let them get on with it. Solemnly, arrangements for the embarkation of troops were made while Charles read that the French had been defeated by Ferdinand of Brunswick, and arrangements for his own embarkation supposedly proceeded while he ordered a new vest. It was all play-acting, and none knew it better than Charles. In September Quebec fell to the English and Alexander Murray prophesied a Jacobite Christmas feast in London. The French were anxious to send an expedition to Ireland with Charles at its head, but as usual Charles steadfastly refused to have anything to do with expeditions to anywhere but England.

No French invasion took place, to Ireland or any other part of the British Isles: Charles had been right to be sceptical. He was given credit for being farsighted and wise, but one cannot help thinking that indolence played a large part. He no longer wanted to campaign – anything that was difficult was out. As he grew older he became more rather than less arrogant and it was sad to see his energy simply run away instead of maturing into an inner strength. The new cynical shrewd Charles was more of a realist but less attractive as such. Moreover, he only used his recently discovered perception on certain occasions, when it suited his purpose. The insight he applied to his political life was entirely lacking in his personal one. In 1760 he was going to be forty and he had neither home, income, wife or family. He was entering middle age firmly determined never to come to terms with it.

CHAPTER NINETEEN

'Buiried Alive'

Clementina was well aware of this. She had now spent eight years in Charles' company, eight extremely miserable years. Her daughter Charlotte was seven and her infancy and childhood had been punctuated by the endless rows and fights that filled her parents' life. It could not, Clementina felt, go on: what she had endured herself could not be permanently inflicted on her daughter. Charles was fond of her – there are endless testimonies to his affection – but what did this amount to ? Sitting her on his knee and lavishing endearments upon her, that was all. He never thought of Charlotte's future, beyond recommending her to the care of others if he died. He made no provision for her education or comfort, he never bothered to write to her during his frequent absences. It was no kind of life for a child, still less for a young girl. Something had to be done and Clementina was prepared to do it. She had been in touch with James who had promised to maintain her if she left Charles for good and resided in a convent. In July 1760 that is what she did. It is unlikely she hoped such a move would bring Charles to his senses – she knew, on the contrary, that he would rejoice. The break was meant to be final.

Once she had reluctantly made her mind up, Clementina left Charles with a good deal of apprehension, not to say terror. He was a very possessive man and the loss of his only child would enrage him. She also knew that though he might beat and abuse her he would instantly claim her as his own once she left him. Her departure had therefore to be planned with the utmost secrecy, rather as Henry had planned his so many years before. She could not afford to tell anyone, for though there were many among Charles' servants who sympathised with her he had always commanded total loyalty. On 20th July she dressed Charlotte and packed their clothes and hired a coach which took her from Bouillon to Paris. From there she entered a convent at Meaux and James forthwith supported her.

Charles' reaction to her flight was exactly as Clementina had known it would be. The letter she left behind – one of the few of hers that exist – did not help matters. She wrote:

Sir,
　Your Royalle Highness cannot be surprised at my having taken my partty when you consider the repeated bad treatment I have matte with these eight years past, and the dealy risque of loossing my life, not been able to bear any longer such hardships, my health been altered by them has obliged me at last to take this Desperate step of removing from your Royalle Highness with my child, which nothing but the fear of my life would ever have made me undertake any thing without your knowledge. Your Royalle Highness is to great and just when you refflect, not to think that you have push'd me to the greatest extremitie and that there is no one women in the world that would have suffer'd so long as what I have done, however it shall never hinder me from having for your Royalle persone all the attachment and respect and I hope in time coming by my conduct to merit your protection and friendship for me and my child, I put myself under the care of providence, which I hope wont abandone me as my intentions are honest and that I will never doe a dirty action for the whole world. I quite my dearest prince with the greatest regreat and shalle always be miserable if I don't hear of his welfair and happiness. May God Almighty bless and preserve him and prospere all his undertakings which is the ernest wish of one how will be till Death, my dearest Prince
　　　　　　Your most faithful and most obedient Humble Servant
　　　　　　　　　Clementina Walkinshaw

P.S. There is one thing I must assure your R.H. that you may not put the blame on innocent people, that there is not one soul, either in the house or out of it that knew or has given me smalest help in this undertaking, not anybody that ever you knew or saw.

Charles remained untouched by the extreme pathos of such a letter and his anger grew instead of abating. He lost no time in informing the police and having Clementina's and Charlotte's descriptions circulated. They were not flattering: 'the mother is aged about 40, fair, average height, complexion marred by red blemishes, thin faced. The child is about 7, with white blonde hair, a round plain face, fairly big eyes, slightly flat nose, rather well built and strong for her age.' There was no mention of the mark Charles had once threatened to put on Charlotte so presumably he never got round to actually branding her as his. A search was duly made, but no clues found. Charles' rage was succeeded by grief – he cried as well as stormed and swore he would not shave until his precious daughter was returned to him. He was convinced that in spite of her protestations, Clementina was part of a conspiracy – someone had induced her to leave in order to get the child and use her as a weapon against him. When Charles learnt James had been partly in the know everything fell into place for him. 'It was,' wrote James nervously, 'many months before I had undoubted information of her desire to leave you, to satisfy her own conscience in the first place, and to stop the mouths of those to whom she knew she was obnoxious and suspected, and lastly to be able to give her Daughter in a Convent a Christian and good Education: And it is very true that I did what I could to encourage her to endeavour to obtain your permission and consent to leave you, tho I could not disapprove, much less oppose so reasonable and pious desires.'

By the end of August Charles had made himself ill with drowning his sorrows. His friends watched with distress: 'the Prince is no better and thinks he will die if his little daughter does not come back to him.' Charlotte did not come back – though Charles tried to hire a suitable servant to look after her when she did – but her father did not die. He remained shut up refusing to see anyone. Meanwhile, Clementina, safe in her convent, wrote to him very sorrowfully, saying she had done what she had done because there had been no alternative and she had her child to think of. 'You pushed me to the greatest extremity and even despair as I was always in perpetual dread of my life from your violent passions.' Charles, deep in the grip of the paranoia that had started so long ago, could only find his mistress' message menacing. As he saw it, there was only one solution: total isolation. He wrote no letters and replied to none and saw only his closest friends, none of whom had any influence over him. It was no good James telling him he was putting himself first and not thinking of his duty, nor was it any good trying to rouse his compassion – a quality Charles had always been short of. 'If you make no reply to this letter,' James wrote at the start of 1762 when he considered his son had had quite long enough to recover, 'I shall take it for granted that in your present situation you are not only buiried alive, as you really are, but in effect you are dead and insensible for everything.'

'Buiried alive – dead and insensible for everything' – they were ironic words from a man himself on the edge of death and weary of the work he never gave up. But Charles was not quite moribund – one thing did arouse his attention and interest and that was his coming day as King of England, if only in Rome. The titular title was attractive and he wanted to enjoy it to the full. It is nauseating to find him negotiating for these honours without any sympathy to spare for a father who had not yet given them up. Others noticed his eagerness and shook their heads – at forty-two all their once brave prince could do was wait to step into a dead man's shoes. Those kindly disposed made excuses for him – it was all the hardships he had endured that made him like this. They looked back to the months of lying in sodden heather and found their explanations there. Those who were not his friends laid the blame on drink. What caused friend and foe alike a feeling of disappointment was that Charles still did not seem beyond redemption. Always, there was the feeling that he still had it in him to be rescued from the wreck he was making of himself but there was no one to do the rescuing, nor any need for him in the world at large. In England, George III, born and bred in London, had succeeded his grandfather and was more English than Charles could ever hope to be. The country flourished, there was no discontent for the Stuarts to feed on, nobody was alive who could remember a Stuart on the throne. In Scotland, a new generation had grown up free from the clan system and though hatred of the English lived on, stronger than ever, rebellion in favour of the Stuarts was not the automatic alternative. Charles, even then, was becoming more a legend than a reality.

Charles was not immune to these changes, nor did he try to pretend his position was other than it was – he was beyond that. He clung to his claim to his father's title because there was nothing else to look forward to. He never quite got to the stage of actually spurning anyone who thought they might be able to help him on to the throne, but he only paid lip-service to an idea too deep-rooted ever to relinquish. But his passion for secrecy began to abate – there no longer seemed much point in disguising his identity when he was about to blossom forth as King. James, however, took his time dying. In February 1764, Lumisden informed Charles that his father was seriously ill and could not last long. Others wrote and told him the same, in reproving tones. Clearly, they all thought Charles should be at his father's side. He never went – not through any sinister motive or callousness but partly because he thought he had plenty of time and partly because it was all too much effort. He continued to act as though he was about to go at any minute.

While James hung on and Charles waited, an interesting development took place for observers of the family scene: Henry successfully re-established contact with his brother. While Charles had been wandering round Europe getting more and more tatty at the edges in every sense, Henry had been doing very nicely indeed for himself. He was by this time a church dignitary of some standing, one who had collected a large number of lucrative benefits and lived in style. Not only was he rich, his opinion counted for something in papal circles. Henry enjoyed this.

He also enjoyed his popularity among the local people, especially those who lived on his estate at Frascati where he had a house of great beauty and magnificence. He had made the right decision in life and was disposed to be magnanimous towards a brother who had not. In fact, Henry had always wanted to maintain cordial relations – it was Charles who had rebuffed his occasional overtures during the last twenty years. His elder brother's bitterness and the strength of his enmity had surprised Henry, who at all times felt kindly towards him. This kindliness was not as trouble-free as one might imagine, for Henry had good reason to resent Charles' attitude if he had wished. It was he who had had to live with their ailing father all these years and bear the brunt of all his worries and whims. James pined for the son far away rather than appreciated the son at hand. But Henry, apart from the odd row soon smoothed over, accepted his position cheerfully and far from running Charles down, which would have been only too easy, he remained his champion.

In February 1765 Charles received a letter from Henry in which he said 'Among the misfortunes of our family I can not but consider as the greatest of them all the Fatal at least apparent disunion of two Brothers that has render'd them for so many Years past so useless to one another. This is indeed a very great misfortune, but of such a nature that it depends in reality on us two to put a Speedy remedy to it. I pray God he may by his Infinite Mercy make you see the importance of a remedy to so great an Evil in the same light he makes me See it myself ...' Charles, typically, did not reply. Apart from being ungracious, it was also very stupid and shortsighted of him, showing, for anyone who doubted it, that he did not understand the current political situation in Rome. The truth was, Charles was going to need all Henry's influence desperately. Not just the Pope had changed since Charles had been in Rome, but the Papacy itself and the position of the Papal States. His Holiness might not be able, when James died, to accord the same honours to Charles III as he had to James III. He might not even dare to acknowledge him as Charles III at all. On 2nd April Henry wrote again, and at last, in October, Charles answered.

His answer was business-like and to the point. Wasting no time on pleasantries beyond a perfunctory 'Dear Brother', Charles launched into what amounted to a series of orders for Henry. His brother's sole function was to see that the Pope promised now to recognise him as King when their father was dead. If Henry was appalled at the crudeness of this self-interest he did not show it. He too thought Charles should be given the same titles as his father, not just because they were his but because he was fussy about status himself. He had valued being a King's son. He would value being a King's brother equally. Nevertheless, Charles had to be told a thing or too. Delicately, Henry embarked on the unenviable task. He explained to his brother that it was impossible either for him or their father to exact the promise Charles wanted, much though they both desired it. The Stuarts would always be welcome in Rome, they could always live there with impunity, but his Holiness could not give any further guarantees at this point in time. Charles replied Henry must try harder. Henry did, without result. It was not just a case of politics, for there were several other difficulties in the way. For one, Charles' religion. Since 1750 Charles had been an avowed Protestant. He was just as willing to become an avowed Catholic again but as Henry explained it was not quite as simple as that. Some way would have to be found in which Charles could be received back into the true Church without exposing either himself or that venerable institution to ridicule. It would be best if it could be done quietly with just Charles and the Pope involved. And that meant Charles coming to Rome, at once, before his father died.

Henry's point was a good one and told more with Charles than any amount of pleading from his father. As a matter of policy he ought indeed to be in Rome behaving like the heir presumptive instead of in Paris, out of touch with what was happening. Miracles, Henry felt, could be wrought just by Charles being about, paying his respects daily. It would be difficult, Henry argued, if the Pope had publicly treated Charles as heir not to treat him as King when the time came. Furthermore, Henry could not really act successfully as intermediary because he did not really know what Charles was prepared to accept. Slowly, Charles began to prepare for the return he had put off for so long. Henry was pleased, but at the same time naturally apprehensive. He worried about the problems Charles' return would give rise to. It was not just a matter of personalities – though Henry's memories weren't exactly sunny ones – but of more materialistic considerations. Charles did not know what to expect. The Palazzo Muti had changed since he had seen it. There had never been any degree of opulence about it, but now there was obvious neglect and poverty. The furniture was shabby and dilapidated, no decorating had been done for more than forty years for James had had neither the inclination nor the resources to keep up appearances. Furthermore, though it was the only home Charles had to come to, it was not actually his for it was not his father's. The Stuarts had only had it as a grace-and-favour residence. True, Henry had his own establishments, but did he want to share them with Charles? He rather thought not.

James continued to die by inches. When Charles left Bouillon on 30th December 1765, his father had rallied again and he had every expectation of seeing him – though that was not the reason he finally went. He had never returned any answer to James' pleas, 'I am all yours' and, 'Is it possible you would rather be a vagabond on the face of the earth than return to a father who is all love and tenderness for you?' On 2nd January, while he was still journeying through France, Lumisden wrote to tell him his father had after all died: 'Sire, prostrated at your Majestys feet, I most himbly beg leave to condole with you on the death of your royal father of blessed memory, and at the same time to congratulate you on your accession to the throne.' Charles replied, to his brother, referring to their father's death as 'this melancholy event' and then moving swiftly on to say, 'Have nothing more to add but to express the inexpressable impatience I have to embrace a Brother that is so dear to me, so remain your loving Brother Charles R.' Then he jolted on, through Germany and northern Italy, basking in his newly acquired status. The weather was cold, the winds bitter, but Charles' sensibilities were dulled. Grief that should have prostrated him left him untouched.

In Rome, while the new King hurried towards his phantom Kingdom, the old one lay in state on a bed of cloth-of-gold. Neither of his sons had been present at his death – Charles because he was travelling, Henry because he simply could not bear to watch – but he had not died alone. Always a good man, generous and just, James was surrounded by friends and servants who genuinely loved and mourned him. But that had given him no comfort. He died distressed and miserable, worried about what would happen to his family and its Cause after his death. His unhappiness was more than just that of a parent longing to be physically reunited with a child – though to hear, see and touch his dearest Carluccio would have given him the greatest joy possible. But the real agony for James was the realisation that Charles would not carry on the fight, now that it had long ceased to be literally that, as he had done. His son's drinking and brawling, his laziness, his treatment of his mistress – all these were minor hurts compared to the greater one of not doing his Duty. James' only hope had been a chance to reclaim the Charles he was sure was still there beneath all the bluster and to do that he needed him at his side. It was a chance he never got.

The funeral of James III, titular King of England, was a splendid affair. It was a pity Charles missed it. After five days' lying-in-state – which rather gives the lie to Mann's sneer that 'The Romans were vastly impatient to bury him that their theaters might be opened' – he was carried to St Peter's in a procession which included twenty cardinals. All along the route people lined the streets as a thousand wax tapers burned brightly in the fierce wind marking the way. The Pope gave the oration and five hundred clergy attended. They all knew they were burying more than a man and Henry, watching, was filled with the greatest trepidation. The reign of Charles III had begun: or had it?

PART V

The End 1766-1788

CHAPTER TWENTY

Queen of Hearts

When Charles entered Italy after twenty-two years' absence, he did not know that his fate, to which he looked forward so eagerly, had already been decided. All he was coming back for, the only thing he had swallowed his pride to get, had already been taken away. There was no title of King awaiting him.

Immediately after James' death, Henry had had an interview with the Pope, Clement XIII. He begged him to acknowledge Charles as King, and was supported by the French ambassador. The Pope was doubtful, as he had consistently been, and summoned his cardinals to advise him. Henry was hopeful, in view of the open French support he had received, but he did not know that the French Government had already assured England that no matter if appearances made it look otherwise, they would acknowledge only George III and had told the Pope so. Given such a clear line, the Pope had no hesitation: Charles could not be given the title and honours he desired. Sir Horace Mann, the English ambassador in Florence, was triumphant, though he declared 'I have as much compassion for the young man as anybody.' The point was, 'He is rich and if he is capable of being in any degree happy the being deprived at Rome of a title which was denied to his father in every other part of the Globe ought not to make him otherwise.' Henry had the unenviable task of breaking this news to his brother. At first, he tried to stall, urging Charles to remain at Bologna for the time being, but when he heard Charles would not stand for any delay there was nothing he could do but put a good face on it and prepare to welcome him.

For all Henry's strenuous efforts, it was a dismal welcome. One coach awaited him: Henry's. There were no cheering crowds, no flowers, no cardinals lined up to pay their respects, no sign at all that Charles was anything but another middle-aged tourist come to see Rome, of which there were a multitude. Rome took its lead from the Pope at all times and not even curiosity could persuade the inhabitants to go publicly against it. Henry got out and embraced his brother affectionately in a manner that recalled 1746, and then put him into his coach and drove him to the Palazzo Muti. Along the way he explained a few facts of his new life to Charles, who was predictably furious and reacted characteristically. If he was not going to be received as King he would rather be plain Mr Douglas, his favourite alias. Unfortunately an alias discarded is not so easily resumed. On not very much reflection Charles realised this and did the only thing possible – stayed at the Palazzo Muti and pretended things were other than they were.

The first year Charles spent back in Rome was a hard one with few bright spots in it. If he had ever doubted the power of the Pope, it was now brought home to him most forcefully how mistaken he had been. Without the Pope's blessing, Charles could not be received into society. He was faceless, with no position or status. People avoided him because they did not know what to call him so as not to incur either his wrath or the Pope's. So Charles was lonely and morose, as well as bitter. He drank no more than usual, but this was sufficient to shock Henry who made constant references to that nasty bottle killing him. He himself did his best by his brother. He gave him money, consoled him with little treats like putting him on his right-hand side when they went for drives (which a cardinal was only supposed to do for a king) and above all by inviting him often to Frascati. Here, not far from Albano where they had spent their boyhood summers, Charles lay in the sun and was momentarily cheered. But never for long. Always there was the return to Rome and the life described in this letter:

> I have at last seen – in his own house; as for his person it is rather handsome, his face ruddy and full of pimples. He looks good-natured, and was overjoyed to see me; nothing could be more affectionately gracious. I cannot answer for his cleverness, for he appeared to be absorbed in melancholy thoughts, a good deal of distraction in his conversation, and frequent brown studies. I had time to examine him for he kept me hours and hours. He has all the reason in the world to be melancholy, for there is not a soul goes near him, not knowing what to call him. He told me time lay heavy upon him. I said I supposed he read a good deal. He made no answer. He depends entirely for his subsistence upon his brother whom he never loved, much less now, he having brought him into the scrape.

The last judgment was unfair but reflected the sympathy onlookers were nearly always prepared to give to the undeserving Charles. Whatever else had deserted him his charm had not. But of what use was charm in his situation? Charles was not enjoying himself, even though his financial worries were for the time being eased and he could lie in comfort.

Comfort was suddenly not as congenial as he had spent the last ten years thinking it would be, nor was it free from minor irritations. Though James had died a richer man than anyone had thought he was, and Charles had inherited it all, this by no means gave him an unlimited supply of money. His was very much a fixed income that diminished by definition all the time, especially with the fairly heavy demands Charles lost no time in making on it. What annoyed him intensely was the general assumption made by many of his companions of the '45 that he had really 'come into his own' and that now was the time to dun him for old debts and remind him of old promises. Whereas James had dealt with each suitor on his merits, investigating claims with genuine anxiety and a great sense of responsibility, Charles would have no truck with them. He made no attempt to distinguish between the truly impoverished with claims on him, and those who simply were trying it on. Thus Lord Elcho, who could well afford to do without his fifteen hundred guineas, and Jenny Cameron, who could not, were both sent packing with a flea in their ear. Charles was not greedy but he was intensely suspicious of suggestions that he had been the cause of anyone's misfortune and therefore was responsible for them. That he denied: everybody, in his eyes, had always been a free agent. Blame was repugnant to him. Those who needed money because of the direct repercussions of the '45 would have done better to think of some other reason if they hoped to get money from Charles.

It was natural that with an easier, more regular life, his bad habits curtailed in so far as it was possible by the anxious attentions of his brother and those who had been his father's servants, Charles' health should improve, in spite of the Siberian winter of 1767 and the influenza epidemic that followed in the summer. With this improvement came a return of some of his customary energy that had for so long been lacking. The problem was, how to use it? Charles had not the freedom of movement to embark on the hectic social life available, and suddenly he found that it was rather more attractive than he had at first thought. He was by nature a gregarious fellow, unlike his father, and it was no good pretending that he was going to be quite happy sitting, as James had done, answering letters for the rest of his days. It was only sensible for Charles to realise that if he was going to carve out any kind of life for himself in Rome, he would have to make his peace with the Pope. After a year he was ready to do so, to Henry's delighted relief.

It was an awkward moment for Charles and it was entirely in character that he should try to make out that he was doing the Pope a favour instead of vice versa. There is always something splendid, if not admirable, in someone who is a consistent rebel and sticks to his principles, however mistaken, but equally there is no one more pathetic than a rebel who will not admit he is beaten. Charles was beaten, on this the last of the small points of pride he had clung to so stubbornly, but he would not admit it. It would have caused him the greatest mortification if he had known how near he came to being refused an audience at all. The Pope acquainted the English ambassador at Florence, Mann, with the news of Charles' visit and asked him to approve the manner in which Charles would be received. Presumably, if the English Government through Sir Horace had objected enough, Charles might not even have been received. As it was, the reception was a modest affair. Henry took Charles, but was ushered in on his own while his brother waited in an anteroom. When Charles was at last shown in he was announced as 'the brother of the Cardinal of York' – enough to have made any rebel turn on his heel and stalk out. But Charles stayed where he was and chatted away to Clement XIII who, now that the unpleasant formalities were over, was more than willing to be pleasant. Though he was not asked to sit during the visit, Charles left with the impression that he had been a hit. 'God be praised,' wrote Henry, 'last Saturday evening, after a good deal of battleying upon very trifling circumstances, I carried my brother to the Pope privately, as a private nobleman ... the visit went much better than I expected, the Pope was extremely well satisfied and my brother seemed well enough content.'

The way was now open for Charles to be received into a society which he entered with some enthusiasm. Years of absence from such a concourse had not diminished his talent for shining in it. He realised at once his curiosity value and was content to cash in on it, trying hard to maintain the air of mystery that his years of incognito had given him. It was a return to his youth, when every English visitor had done his best to get a glimpse of the young Stuart princes. He found the state of Roman society and its occupations very much as they had been twenty years before and for a while he enjoyed his return to it. A sense of purpose, however vague or unrealised, had always been essential to his well-being. After 1767 he had no such morale-booster. All that lay ahead was old age and loneliness, and Charles found neither attractive. The sheer monotony of his days, now that his physical condition did not permit him to ride and hunt as he had once done, depressed him. New diversions were essential and Charles cast about trying in vain to find them.

He was watched by his father's old servants with the greatest sadness. Men like Andrew Lumisden, who had served James well and valued him as a man not just a master, were sickened by the disintegration of Charles as a person and his total lack of application to what his father had seen as a job. Lumisden had the courage, together with a few others, to try to remonstrate with his new King. He did so out of love, knowing full well Charles' opinion of anyone who thwarted him. When he was drunk, they tried to make him stay at home till he recovered. When he was ill, they nursed him devotedly and tried to make him convalesce sensibly. But Charles was determined to have his own way and to see in this solicitude the most evil of motives. Inevitably, in one of his drunken rages, the clash came and Charles dismissed Lumisden and company with all the imperiousness of which he was capable. The circumstances of the row were widely reported and sent back to Scotland in this version:

John Hay, Andrew Lumisden and Captain Urquhart were dismist for a real act of disobedience. It was true indeed that the King had been in use for some time past to call frequently for t'other glass of wine at dinner and supper, not from any liking to liquor, but like one absent in mind, when he met with other things that vex'd him, as too often was the case. That one day at dinner he had done so till he was somewhat intoxicated, and in that condition proposed going to an oratorio in the afternoon when they absolutely refused to attend him. Yea, he went into his coach and they would by no means go into it, upon which he returned to his apartments and dismist them. In a day or two he sent for them to return to their duty, but they happening to consult with the Cardinal of York, he advised them absolutely not to return; which counsel they took, and he put four Italians into their places as persons more fit for his purposes and designs; the principal one of whom was very fit to be about a great personage, having been bred up at the Court of Modena. He now enjoys more ease and quiet than formerly, and has never been seen concerned in the least with liquor since that event, which has been happily attended with one good effect, to make him think very seriously upon what had happened; and that no man could be of a more firm and determined resolution when once formed than he was known to be.

Quite what Henry was doing advising Lumisden and company not to go back to Charles it is hard to fathom, for he knew perfectly well how indispensable they were to him. Perhaps he thought Charles should simply be allowed to go his own way and that any pretensions – which Lumisden fervently encouraged – to anything more elevated should be discouraged. The four Italians saw their job differently: here was a prematurely old man who had to be kept clean, neat and sober in public. Nothing else was expected of them and they performed their job admirably by a combination of cajolery and tact. From 1767 to 1770, Charles lived in Rome like an old horse put out to grass. He might boast in the occasional letter he wrote of the next rising 'coming like a thunderbolt' but he would have been the most horrified if it had. But then, when he was fifty, Charles' life suddenly changed direction in that satisfyingly abrupt way it always had.

As always, the suddenness was preceded by a long period leading up to it: the event that surprised everyone only looked sudden. It gave Charles a great deal of pleasure concealing what was afoot from everyone – to have something to be secret about, to need ciphers and codes to discuss it, to come and go mysteriously was pure bliss and had a rejuvenating effect. In the summer of 1770 Charles went to Pisa for a course at the baths there. He was glad to go anywhere for a bit of variety. On his way he diverted himself by calling in at Florence, where his arrival embarrassed the Grand Duke and delighted everyone else. He then went on to Pisa, took the cure, found it dull and returned to Florence where he was fêted everywhere he went. Henry was furious that he should be so childish as to stay where his host did not welcome him and wrote urging him to go to Pisa again. Rather to his surprise, Charles agreed. He returned to Pisa – and vanished. Horace Mann in Florence was agog. Where had he gone? To Poland, to try to get that crown? Surely, surely not to Scotland – the idea was preposterous.

It was, but the truth was almost as ridiculous and certainly of better gossip value. Charles had gone to Paris to fix up the details of his wedding. The negotiations had opened with a letter from the Duke of Fitzjames to Charles telling him that France would like him to marry a carefully selected bride in return for a pension of forty thousand crowns, and of course the bride. The offer was made with some trepidation, for a younger Charles had refused most arrogantly much, much better offers. The French knew it was impossible to disguise the measure of insult in their new approach but they were banking on four years in a political void making Charles eager for anything that looked like enhancing his importance. Their calculations were correct. Charles knew perfectly well that all the French wanted was to ensure that the Stuart claim with its nuisance value did not die out. He was willing to fit in with their schemes not just because it would indeed put him at least temporarily in the limelight but also because he genuinely had been giving serious thoughts to marriage himself. While his father had been alive he had always resisted the idea most strenuously, but now he saw it as a proposition not to be dismissed out of hand. He would never marry, as James had done, out of a sense of duty. Nor, really, did he crave heirs, in spite of his reputed love of children. His only child Charlotte had never received any sign that he cared about her and he seems to have been able to consign her to oblivion long after he could reasonably have established the contact she showed herself eager to make. The pull to marriage for Charles at this late date was more that of companionship and status. While he was a dashing, handsome young man in demand such considerations carried no weight, but he had had time in the last four years to see that a bachelor of fifty was not fortunately placed. Women as sexual objects had never interested him, but women as adornments and keepers of his comforts now seemed eminently desirable. He didn't care whom he married – what he wanted was a new adventure without any effort and France obligingly provided him with it.

It had been a struggle for the French to find a suitable bride since there were obvious difficulties on both sides. Charles was no great catch, but on the other hand he himself wanted something that could at least be dressed up as a catch. The searching through the minor princesses of Europe was as much for a compliant not to say desperate father as for a candidate. In the end, they found a mother, not a father. The Princess Gustavus Adolphus of Stolberg-Gedern, formerly Countess of Horn, was a widow with four daughters. Her husband had been a colonel in the Imperial Army and was killed at the Battle of Leuthen. The Princess was given a generous pension by Maria-Theresa, and furthermore a place in one of the Lay Chapters in the Austrian Netherlands was offered to any of her four daughters. The eldest daughter was duly placed at Mons, where, from the age of six, she had spent the rest of her life. It was this girl, Louise, who was selected to be Charles' bride.

Her lineage was impressive enough on both sides – there was nothing Charles could complain about on that score unless he wanted only the daughter of a crowned King. She even had a connection, through her mother, with the Bruces of Scotland, of which much could be made. Born on 20th September 1752, she was baptised at Mons with the names Louise Maximiliana Caroline Emmanuel. As it turned out, convent life was not as unendurable for Louise as it might have been for any other young girl, especially a convent of such an exclusive nature where social life was simply rarefied rather than restricted. Nor did she miss any close family life or lavish maternal love – Elizabeth, her mother, had little time for either. Intelligent, even serious, Louise responded well to study and shone at the arts in which young ladies at the time were proficient. She liked reading, could play several instruments and sing with more than average ability. She had a healthy contempt for the standard of education in the convent, where, she swore, 'I learned nothing'. She was no blue-stocking, also liking to have a good time if in a somewhat limited sense. It must have been this side of her, and perhaps an element of frustration common to most girls of the time, that led her to accept with alacrity the offer of marriage to Charles. Certainly, it was not hers to accept – her mother's consent was the deciding factor – but it will not do to represent Louise as anything but willing. She was no sacrificial lamb. There is no doubt that Louise was nicely positioned to have got out of the deal if she had wanted to, for with the Empress as her patroness – and the Empress was not told of what was planned – she could have successfully appealed to her. Her eagerness to oblige France was based on a desire to escape her lot, congenial though she found it, and also to be Queen, if only a queen of sorts.

Louise's consent was very important. Charles laid down no stipulations apart from his bride being suitable and willing. He did not want any woman forced into marriage with him – such a thing would have been unendurable to his pride. Louise's pedigree and her eagerness mattered more than her dowry or looks. Teenage blondes had never been in Charles' line anyway. Naturally, a girl of nineteen who had had a very sheltered life did not have the knowledge or experience to assess what was a complex situation, but nevertheless Louise's consent had been given in full possession of the facts: that she chose to interpret them as she did was her affair. But she did know Charles' age, that he was a dispossessed monarch not an actual one, and his history.

There was, in fact, nothing so very dreadful to know about Charles. His chances of coming into his own were remote but Louise ought to have been able to work that out for herself if she was really so intelligent and well-informed. He drank, but so did many other men, and that was his only declared vice. Nobody could tell her horrific stories about him – there had been none to tell since Clementina Walkinshaw went out of his life. As a man the female letter-writers of the day found him still charming and attractive. There was nothing gross or revolting about either his appearance or behaviour unless one counted his bouts of maudlin tears or outbreaks of rage. Nobody whitewashed Charles for Louise for he did not need whitewashing. By eighteenth-century standards hers was a free and even a good choice.

Once both parties agreed, no time was lost. Louise and her mother left Belgium for Paris in great secrecy and the marriage took place by proxy on 28th March 1772 under the watchful eye of the Duke of Fitzjames. His son was married to Louise's younger sister Caroline which made it almost a family affair. Immediately afterwards, Louise set off on the long, perilous journey to Italy. She undertook the prospect very coolly with no apparent regrets for what she left behind. Her mother went with her and their escort was Colonel Ryan. First they went to Venice, then took a ship for Ancona, Louise's first experience of the sea. It took her till 11th April to reach Bologna. At Loreto she was met by Lord Caryll and five servants in the crimson liveries of England, which pleased her very much. Meanwhile, Charles had set off for Rome where, for the last few months, he had been leading an exemplary existence in preparation for his new rôle. His eagerness to reform was touching. Not only did he not drink so much, but he made great attempts to smarten himself up and to get rid of the pimples that had spoiled his complexion for some time. He felt healthier, fitter and more optimistic than he had done for years. Rather touchingly, he was anxious that everything should be as perfect as possible for his bride and paid great attention to all the minor details of the ceremony. On 17th April Louise and Charles met for the first time at Macerata. Charles was reported as delighted with his bride's appearance as his father had been with his mother's, which is surprising considering his taste up to then. Louise was a doll-like figure, ornately dressed so that she could hardly move, her hair in complicated rolls and waves and her cheeks sporting carefully applied rouge. They were married at once, despite the fact that it was Good Friday, in accordance with Louise's mother's stipulation. It was a small, modest wedding. The ceremony was performed by the Bishop of the Province and attended by the servants of bride and groom as well as a few local gentry. Charles added a nice touch of sentiment by writing a couplet for the ring:

> This crown is due to you by me
> And none can love you more than me

The ring itself was a splendid turquoise.

For the next two days the newly-married pair were fêted by the people of the province. Two big receptions were given on the Saturday and Sunday evenings, when foreign artists played and sang. The refreshments on both occasions were 'sumptuous and abundant'. Louise and Charles both enjoyed the merry-making, especially the music, and to keen-eyed observers seemed well content with each other. It was easy for those who knew Charles to tell that he was quite transformed; not so easy, even for her own ladies, to tell with Louise, who had a lot of the stoic about her and never displayed what she was feeling. On the Sunday evening, the royal pair distributed money among the local populace who seem to have discovered a genuine affection for their visitors in a remarkably short time. On 19th April they left for Rome. Neither of them could wait to get there. Charles relished the thought of everyone's astonishment, especially brother Henry's, and hoped that such public support from France would make the Pope at last acknowledge him. Louise, for her part, longed to see the city itself where she was prepared to be a regular culture vulture and longed, too, to be installed in her Palace and assume her duties as Queen. They were both very happy as they journeyed through Italy and the sunny spring weather perfectly complemented their exuberant mood.

Their entry into Rome was every bit as splendid as Charles had hoped and helped to banish the memory of his own depressing arrival in 1766.

> Their entry into Rome was as follows, first four couriers, the chevaliers post-chaise, then the Princess's coach-and-six, followed by two other post chaises, the chevalier and the Princess in their coach, followed by the coaches-and-six with his attendants. The confluence of the people was surprising at the cavalcade. The Cardinal of York paid a visit to the Princess the next morning, had a conference with her for an hour, and made her a present of a gold snuff-box set with diamonds of great value. But what shall I tell you? The outside, beautiful as it was, was nothing in comparison of the beauty within. Oh! my dear Lord! it contained an order upon his banker to pay her down 40,000 Roman crowns ... What think you of this affair? She is pretty and young, he strong and vigorous. They may produce a race of pretenders that will never finish which the French will be always playing upon every quarrel. May they increase fruitfully.

The reaction was just as Charles had hoped – for the first time for years he had created a sensation and he enjoyed being back in the public eye. He had also been prepared to enjoy Henry's discomfiture, but his brother had a dignity he himself lacked. There was never anything petty about Henry. He held his own counsel and appeared to accept the *fait accompli* graciously. Henry, never very perceptive where women were concerned, had actually been genuinely impressed by Louise: 'He was delighted to perceive in the youthful Princess all those good qualities wherewith rumour had endowed her, and particularly was he pleased with her great charm of manner and her intellectual attainments, for which the excellent education given her by her parents was responsible. She treated him on an equal footing and with every mark of respect and affection.' His gesture to Louise was a piece of theatrical expertise worthy of Charles himself – and indeed, though pleased, Charles was a little piqued at the good it did Henry in everyone's eyes. When all the fuss was over, it was clear that, fun and goods apart, Charles had not really played such a master stroke after all. There was a new Pope, but he proved as obdurate as the last and Charles' marriage did not gain him the status he so desired. Only confirmed Jacobites saw his act as politically of the greatest importance – Bishop Gordon and his friends were in a state of euphoria, in spite of the fact that the Hanoverians had never sat more firmly on the throne and there was not the slightest trace of any movement either at home or abroad to exploit Charles' supposedly daring challenge.

CHAPTER TWENTY-ONE
Florence and Failure

For a while, Charles' life continued to take a turn for the better, at least superficially, and his adherents could stop being ashamed of him. The present and future were now as interesting as the past, though he could not quite relinquish his ingrained habit of reminiscing about the '45. Louise got to know every favourite story within a very short time. She also got to know that the people about Charles, both old friends and passing visitors, encouraged him to drone on like this about his exploits. What sickened her most was his failure to see that he was being humoured. She managed, however, not to show her boredom and, increasingly, her disgust. Once she had accepted that she was Queen only in the shabby Palazzo Muti, she came to terms with her situation much more quickly and less regretfully than Clementina Sobieski had done before her. Instead of sulking or sinking into a depression, the practical Louise set about transforming her home. The difference was noticed immediately and Charles basked in the compliments his wife earned. Louise was born to command and found the organisation of a household an easy thing. Playing hostess came easily to her, and though they went out to the theatre every evening rather than entertained she did hold several receptions which were a great success. All Rome thought Charles had done very well indeed for himself, and when the writer Bonstetten christened Louise 'The Queen of Hearts' there were few who disagreed. His description makes Charles sound a lucky man: 'The Queen of Hearts when I knew her in Rome was of medium height, she had dark blue eyes, a slightly turned up nose, and the complexion of an English girl. Her expression was bright and piquant, and at the same time so sympathetic that she turned all heads.'

But Louise was not just a pretty face. Rather to Charles' alarm, even though he was proud of her, she began to want to single out the philosophers and artists in Rome in order to talk to them. Good conversation was something she let it be known that she esteemed. Once, Charles would have found in this an echo of his own keenness twenty years ago in France and joined his young wife in her efforts to lift their minds on to a more elevated plane, but now he lacked the necessary concentration. He liked to be entertained rather than stimulated. So Louise held her salons and Charles witnessed rather than participated. Those who attended, drawn by Louise's twin charms, were punctilious in paying their respects to him. He preferred going to the opera, or to the amusing evenings arranged by the ambassadors in the city, but he had no actual objections to Louise's gatherings of distinguished intellectuals. Some of them, like Cordara who had written Latin verses on the '45, he welcomed.

In the middle of his new-found happiness Charles spared no thoughts for those who were miserable. The first summer of his marriage was marred by the arrival in Rome of Clementina Walkinshaw and her daughter Charlotte. Charles was livid. He considered it the height of insolence to appear like that just after his marriage – it was unseemly, unkind and even ungrateful. The pathos of such a visit at such a time was lost on him. He could not even begin to imagine the desperation that had driven poor Clementina to such drastic measures. She had caused him no bother for twelve years, eking out a meagre living on the small pension that first James, then Henry, then Charles himself, had granted her. She had obediently and obligingly signed a declaration saying she had never been married to Charles when it was required of her. She had encouraged her daughter to write to her father in the most affectionate terms without passing on to her any bitterness. All this had seemed endurable until Charles married, and then Clementina must have felt tired of her subservience. She went to Rome not to protest against the marriage, which would have been quite useless, but to try to get some kind of new deal for herself and Charlotte, then nearing twenty and with the bleakest of futures. Charles refused to see her, or to have anything to do with her. Through intermediaries it was intimated to Charlotte that a place could be found for her in her father's household, but not for her mother, not ever. To her credit, Charlotte refused the shoddy offer, and returned to Paris with her much wronged mother. From here she continued to bombard her father with obsequious but accusing letters that had no effect whatsoever.

What Louise thought of all this goes unrecorded, but she probably found the whole subject of children too painful to want to hear about her husband's only offspring. She knew perfectly well that her marriage was principally to produce an heir, and no heir had arrived. She was subjected to constant scrutiny by eager Jacobites, but there was never a sign in spite of several actual announcements made by those reputedly in the know. The first, which percolated to the remotest parts of Scotland, came on Easter Eve 1773, and others followed. Since Louise showed no signs of distress and Charles every sign of being hopeful, the gossip continued. It was lucky for Charles that he had Charlotte to his credit for this prevented the rumours that he was infertile from gaining much credence. The charge of impotence had to do instead. But there is no doubt that Charles was certainly capable of the sexual act, and that his marriage had been consummated, or else Louise would have used the fact later. Neither, at this stage, made any disclosures about their love life. Both seemed content to be discreet, and wait.

While they waited, their marriage began to sour. It was too much to hope that Charles could be permanently reformed when, in essence, his life had not changed. True, the comforts of an attractive home life and an attractive young wife were steadying influences and he certainly continued to *look* better, but he still had no conception of how to execute his arduous role as titular King. Louise was not the girl to show him the way, having very little knowledge of what it was all about. Her husband's obsession with protocol and the recognition of his title actually found an answering chord in her own make-up – it was one aspect of Charles' character that she did not find in the least absurd. She was right behind him when he decided to leave Rome on the approach of the Jubilee of the Pope because he would not be treated as King of England at the ceremonies involved. In August 1774 they left the Palazzo Muti and took a villa between Pisa and Parma; then in October they moved on to Florence for the winter, intending to buy a house and settle there permanently – until they went to St James's, that is.

Florence was a more sophisticated town than Rome, inhabited by a set of aristocratic émigrés as well as the local nobility. It was presided over by the Grand Duke Leopold, a man of great vitality and forceful ideas who imposed the strictest of rules. He was no friend to Charles, but he allowed his arrival to pass without comment though without Ducal hospitality. Others were not so backward. Prince Corsini, of that same family that had shown such kindness to Charles on his northern tour forty years before, came forward and offered Charles a palace near one of the gates of the town, if he would be gracious enough to accept. Charles fell over himself to do so. Apart from the snub given him by the Duke – though he could not have expected anything else since he had always made his attitude clear – Charles found an old problem that had not troubled him for some time rearing its ugly head – money. He and Louise had got through an amazing amount in two years, and Charles himself had watched James' store dwindle for much longer. He badly

needed a new source of income and so, without any embarrassment whatever, he began to apply to the only likely contributors he could think of.
Hardly had he arrived in Florence before he was writing to the Comte
de Vergennes to ask him to intercede on his behalf with Louis XVI.
Actually, said Charles, the King's dear respected grandfather had just
been about to give Charles a pension when he unfortunately died. Such a
pity. Perhaps Louis XVI would like to carry on with the good work?

It took the Comte till January to reply, and his reply was not helpful.
Nothing loath, Louise took up the job. She wrote in May 1775 asking,
politely, for the pension that had been promised her on her marriage to
the tune of sixty thousand livres. The pension was promised and Louise
dutifully wrote to thank the Comte – but she was premature. No money
arrived. Charles was furious but there was nothing he could do. He had
also approached Spain, but with no result. So he and Louise began to
live a precarious existence, depending on what was left of James' money
and what Henry gave them. Their plight was not exactly heartbreaking
for it was the result of carelessness and bad management.

Lack of money did not prevent them, however, from buying, in 1777,
the Palazzo Guadagni, in the street San Sebastiano. It could not have
been more different from the Palazzo Muti which had been in the heart
of Rome, situated as it was on the outskirts of the town in a quiet
thoroughfare with a good view of the surrounding countryside. Charles
took great pleasure in his new acquisition. It was his first real home, the
first he had purchased himself and was prepared to settle down in, and
he felt possessive about it. Every detail took his attention, from the
weathercock (on which he had his Royal coat of arms printed) to the
staircase, over which he had inscribed CAROLUS NATUS 1720 M. BRIT. ET
HIBERNIAE REX FIDEI DEFENSOR 1766. There was a garden which he
decorated with statues of gods and goddesses and had laid out with
gravel walks so that he could stroll there whatever the weather. Doubtless
he intended Louise to stroll with him, but increasingly Louise rebelled
and wanted to do something else. Louise did not like Florence and prided
herself on being a cut above the Florentines. 'You want to hear the life I
lead?' she wrote in 1774. 'It would be dismal for anybody but myself.
I spend the whole morning in reading. Then I dress quickly and go for a
walk. I have always people to dinner and if there is no Opera in the
evening I go to the Casino dei Nobili and withdraw thence at nine o'clock.
Then I write to my friends, to whom I consecrate the closing hours of
the day ... I should like to cross the Alps, for Italian society bores me.
The Florentines are unsympathetic and provincial and scandal is their
sole topic of conversation.' Nor did the climate please her any better.

'We are perishing in the heat,' she wrote in July 1775. 'We are positively roasting. We go out walking and get bored, and that is no relief. Ah! If we could but dwell in your mountains how nice it would be!'

There were plenty of acute observers in Florence to carry on where those of Rome and Paris had left off, and none of Charles' and Louise's ups and downs went unrecorded. Horace Mann filled his letters to Horace Walpole with accounts of the Pretender's scandalous behaviour. Hardly had they arrived before he was writing with glee of a scene at the opera between Charles and a French officer. There was some kind of collision and Charles was rude. The French officer said he supposed Charles did not realise who he was to which Charles replied, 'Je sais que vous êtes Français et cela suffit' – not bad for a man who had just written a begging letter to the French King. A great deal was always made of Charles' drunkenness partly because, as many have pointed out, it was just about the one vice Italian society did not tolerate. If he had gambled exorbitantly or been unfaithful or done almost anything else to excess his fault would have been regarded with more indulgence. As it was, his was an unfashionable and therefore unforgivable vice. By 1776 Mann's excitement and expectation of scandal had died down to a contemptuous tolerance. 'The Pretender, poor man, behaves well when he is not drunk ... he will not stay at home. He goes every evening to the theatre ... but is frequently obliged by sickness at his stomach to retire to the common and much frequented corridor.' There he vomited, coughed, groaned – but always insisted on going back to his box. How much of the performances he saw was doubtful since he seemed to be asleep most of the time. By 1779 Mann was writing: 'He has a declared Fistula, gt. sores in his legs and is insupportable in stench and temper, neither of which he takes the least pains to disguise to his wife whose beauty is vastly faded of late. She has paid dearly for the dregs of Royalty.' She also paid in another way according to Mann. 'He appears to have a great deal of choler on his breast and stomach which makes him cough at nights and disturbs his rest. However he obliges his wife still to lay in the same bed with him and in every other respect uses her very ill so that her health seems much impaired of late.'

It was, as everyone remarked, no life for a young woman. Charles was rapidly becoming tyrannical and this Louise found harder to bear than the drinking and vomiting. She would have been quite happy to take advantage of the intellectual life Florence offered and let Charles get on with whatever he wanted to do. But this he would not allow. Where he went, Louise must go too, and where she went he would drag himself. If Charles wanted to go for a walk in the boiling heat, Louise had to come. If he wanted to go to bed at six in the morning after being up all night, she had to accompany him. Louise's way of dealing with this state of affairs was not Clementina Walkinshaw's – there were no public brawls or fights. The very thought made her shudder with distaste. But neither was she passive. Instead, she resorted to cold, biting letters. She could wither Charles with a few words when she chose, and she chose more and more often. Her scorn drove Charles to distraction – she made him feel stupid, boorish, disgusting. The Princesse de Talmond had fought with him passionately; Clementina Walkinshaw had fought with him out of love; but Louise fought with real hatred and he could not cope. On every count she was superior. His way of dealing with the situation was to try to keep her prisoner and drink himself to a stupor. Her way was naturally somewhat different.

It was Louise's good luck that she had come to live in a country where unhappy wives had an escape route provided for them which was accepted, if not created, by society. The Italians thought themselves very civilised about love, and since most marriages were made for other reasons they thought it barbaric not to cater for it within the very framework of marriage itself. Affairs were awkward things that often had nasty results. Far better to provide husband and wife with an alternative so that they would not be driven to anything so desperate. There thus had evolved a position known as 'cavaliere servente' or 'cicisbeo'. Recognising that every wife's requirements were different, three kinds of cicisbeo were available. The first was a purely honorary variety: simply a man who was available to squire a lady to the opera or some such social occasion when her husband was not available (he might with perfect impunity be doing the same for somebody else's wife and everyone was happy). This position carried no emotional or sexual overtones. Then there was the man who was a kind of high-class valet, and he carried even fewer. This brand of cavalieri was a permanent companion, turning up first thing in the morning and leaving after supper. He talked to and amused the wife, and did a certain amount of fetching and carrying. Lastly, there was the lover. He was bound to the lady by close ties of either intimate friendship or actual sex. The husband did not object, because there was no disgrace attached – he was not considered 'cuckold'. Quite the reverse – he might be admired as lucky. Furthermore, his marriage was not threatened but rather strengthened.

All Florence expected Louise to take a cicisbeo and were surprised that she resisted for so long. They considered it another proof of her arrogance – part and parcel of her refusal to return the calls of the ladies of Florence because a Queen did not return calls. She had plenty of admirers but discouraged all who had come for anything but stimulating conversation in her salon. To her credit, she never went in search of a cicisbeo, but valued her independence as a woman highly. Louise was nothing if not regal, in this as in all else. Homage was what she craved as much as anything. It was obvious that any suitor would have to be prepared to value Louise as she valued herself and that she would need most careful wooing. She got it.

In the summer of 1776, the year Mann records Charles as reaching a new low in disintegration, there came to Florence a young man called Vittorio Alfieri, son of the Count Antonio Alfieri of Cortemilia in Piedmont. He had had a chequered career as womaniser and playboy, but by this time had discovered his talent for writing and had dedicated himself to developing it. He is supposed to have first seen Louise in an art gallery admiring a portrait of Charles XII of Sweden, and to have forthwith rushed out, dressed up in exactly the same clothes and then spent days prancing up and down outside Louise's window. He never referred to such romantic beginnings later, and since he referred to absolutely everything else it suggests so good a story is not true – but it adequately sums up Alfieri's passionate, flamboyant and impetuous nature. His own account of his infatuation was as follows:

> During the summer of 1776 which I had passed wholly at Florence, I had often observed a very noble and lovely woman, a foreigner of most exalted birth by all accounts. It was impossible not to remark her on meeting her, and and still more impossible was it, on once remarking her, for anybody to find her aught but charming ... The first impression she left on my mind was one of infinite charm. Dark eyes with a sparkle in them and the sweetest of expressions, in addition (that which one rarely sees in combination) to a very fair skin and light-coloured hair, gave a lustre to her beauty which was well-nigh irresistible. She was in her twenty-fifth year, and had a sincere taste for all art and literature; she possessed a disposition that was pure gold; yet despite her abundant gifts she was rendered miserable by the most distressing troubles at home. How could I ever face such a tower of virtue?

Never mind the tower of virtue, what about Charles? Once he'd decided that his vow to have nothing more to do with women must in this case be broken, Alfieri had to decide whether he was also going to take on this unattractive husband, well-known to be extraordinarily jealous. It was a daunting prospect but the lure of Louise was strong enough. Entry into Louise's household was easy enough with Alfieri's intellectual leanings, but he hesitated. Deciding to make one last stand, he abruptly left Florence and went back to Piedmont, but the following autumn found him in Florence again, his mind made up. A friend took him to Louise's house and introduced him. He was immediately overcome with admiration and hurried off to Rome to try to regain control of himself. When he returned in the spring of 1778 his decision had been made: Louise was irresistible. What intrigued him was the nature of his feelings towards her: 'In my three earlier intrigues I had not been moved by any passion of the intellect, whilst in this last case the passions of the mind and heart were commingled and equalised, producing thus a feeling less fiery and impetuous, but deeper, profound and more lasting.'

Accordingly, Alfieri began to play court in the rarefied atmosphere of Louise's salon. He was a welcome visitor, for not only was he young and handsome but he had travelled and already had some plays and poems to his credit, which had gained some attention. Since most members of Louise's salon only talked about writing, a real live writer who had had a play performed was quite a catch. It was his talent that captured Louise's attention first. She was thrilled at the idea of actually helping a poet to create, and from being one among many at her salons, Alfieri began to come along on his own at other times of the day so that they could work together – he writing, she inspiring. What added charm to this set-up was Charles' willing acquiescence. He, too, liked Alfieri, and found it most agreeable falling asleep to the strains of the poet's 'Maria Stuarda' which he was engaged on. He thought it showed good taste to be writing about one of his ancestors. So the ménage à trois was established and for the time being everyone was happy. Since Charles was always present, he had no worries that there might be more in this than the muse warranted. It all seemed to him a harmless way of keeping Louise happy.

Naturally, Louise and Alfieri thought a little differently, but for two years they made no attempt to break out of this frustrating situation. They both found Charles utterly repugnant but Alfieri at least found some relief in thinking of poetic images to express his disgust. In the 'Maria Stuarda' that Charles so approved of there was a passage that would have enraged him:

> ... O despicable race,
> Yea, thou wilt one day see thine end. O Thou
> Last off-shoot of it, will the sword destroy thee?
> No, not a hand is vile enough to deign
> To soil itself with blood like thine; thy life
> Will pass in one long slothful sleep, while he
> Who'll hold thy throne will not thy foeman be.
> The battle field will be the table; thou
> In drunken revels wilt the memory drown
> Of thy unmerited, untasted reign.

It was a little hard, considering Charles was so hospitable. So, too, was the picture of Louise, 'like some trapped dove in vain for mercy pleading', and as 'a damask rose, pure, fresh and blooming crushed in the fingers of a filthy clown'.

If Charles was a filthy clown – and certainly there were other testimonies to him having become a dirty old man – he certainly didn't crush Louise. Unpleasant though her plight was, she wasn't nearly as fragile as Alfieri liked to represent. On the contrary, there was a steel-like quality about Louise which enabled her to calculate what was best for her even in the middle of her first love. Leaving Charles would serve no purpose. She would at once put herself in the wrong and be for ever an outcast in the society she loved. Furthermore, there were practical considerations such as money – Louise had no money. Alfieri had but she did not relish the thought of being his kept woman – it would ruin their hitherto beautiful relationship. At the back of Louise's mind there was also the thought that Charles might at any minute die. She had had this thought as early as 1775, writing in a letter: 'Almost, yes, almost two days ago I saw the moment when I was to become mistress of my own fate. Death and disease, the foes of mortals, danced over the head of my Lord and master; but thank God, his hour was not yet come!' Whatever sincerity there had been in her hope was now gone. She wanted Charles to die and miraculously solve everything. There was no question of her seeing that he led a quiet, peaceful life, no thought of trying to divert him from the drink that did so much harm. Louise didn't deliberately try to bring about a stroke that would finish Charles off, but she did nothing to curb her own hard tongue.

It was in any case useless sitting about waiting for Charles to die – he was tough underneath all his ailments and with a strong will to live whatever his circumstances. Alfieri got fed up long before Louise and urged her to leave him so they could get on with their life's work together, but she wouldn't. The tension of it all made her ill but still she searched for a way out that would exonerate her from all blame. It came on St Andrew's Day, 30th November 1780. This was always a great day for Charles, who wallowed in sentiment at a great feast and drank himself to a standstill at the bitterness of his memories. He staggered from the table, anxiously but indulgently watched by his servants, and went to Louise's bedroom where he assaulted her. Her screams brought those who hovered around the door rushing in, and they forced him away – but not before at least a dozen people had seen Louise had been indeed attacked. There was no mention of what had provoked the attack, though everyone agreed it was in excess of Charles' usual frolics. Nor was there any mention of why, knowing the state he would be in, Louise had not taken elementary measures to protect herself. But the point was, the facts were inescapable. She had been brutally attacked. It did not need much encouragement to make everyone believe her life was in danger – which indeed it may well have been if she had chosen. It was up to Louise to make capital out of this before it was forgotten. Shrewdly, Louise realised that she might as well start at the top – through Alfieri, she appealed to the Grand Duke to help her escape the tyranny to which she was being subjected. Her petition was sympathetically received and, assured of ducal protection, the pair now began to plan the details of her escape.

The only problem the two had to encounter was of ditching Charles at the last minute, and in this they were aided by his lack of mobility. There was no question of escaping from the Palazzo itself, for Charles watched Louise night and day and was still her inseparable companion. Whatever he was, he was not stupid and she did not even try to go out on her own. Above all else, she knew Charles loved outings, so she and Alfieri planned a drive to a nearby convent to see the embroidery for which these particular nuns were famous. They did not actually suggest it themselves, but let the idea come from a friend, a certain Mme Orlandini, when she and her 'cavaliere servente' were dining with them. Charles fancied the trip – anything to break the monotony of his day and fill in time till the theatre opened – so off they all went. When they got to the Convent of the White Nuns in the Via del Mandorlo, Louise and Mme Orlandini got out first escorted by her cavaliere, and before Charles had heaved himself out they were already inside the convent and the door was closed. Charles lumbered after them and knocked at the door. After a great deal of hammering and shouting a grille in the door opened, and a voice told him that his wife Louise had sought and had been given protection under the auspices of the Grand Duchess.

It was astounding that Charles' precarious health stood up to such a public shock and the fact that he did not immediately have a heart attack showed the strength of his constitution. As usual at these kind of moments in his life, rage, followed instantly by a desire for revenge, possessed him long before any sense of loss and grief. When he had finished yelling and screaming, Charles hurried back to his house and attempted to bring the whole weight of his kingly authority to bear. Alfieri had been nowhere about, but Charles was not simple – he knew Louise had not retired into a convent for love of the religious life or just to get away from him. The thought that he had been tricked was unbearable, as also was any sugges-tion that Louise and Alfieri might be together. No virtuous husband ever had anything on Charles – his moral indignation knew no bounds, even though his wife had as yet done nothing even remotely immoral.

For once, Charles took to his correspondence with zest – letters flew to the Grand Duke, then the Pope. Getting no answer from these worthy personages – which immediately made it clear to Charles that they must all be in the plot together – he appealed to the learned Monsignore Antonio Martini as the most distinguished local churchman he could think of. Martini's embarrassment was total, as he explained later to Henry: 'The Signor Comte d'Albany has implored me several times to come to see him at his palace, and has even himself struggled to reach my own house more than once in order to consult with me, so that at last I felt bound, out of mere civility to pay him my respects in person. The motive of his anxiety to meet me was explained by himself the very moment I entered his cabinet, and this motive was his fixed desire to start an action here for the restoration, as he terms it, of his lady consort. I did and said all I could to calm his fury but to no purpose.' He went on to say that he would do whatever the Cardinal advised.

Henry now assumed a position of great importance in the melodrama, and his attitude was vital. The main point he had to consider was, what was to be done with Louise? She was his brother's lawful wife. There was no question of divorce. Therefore what Henry decided to do was to make it quite plain to his sister-in-law that though he was sympathetic she must at some point return to Charles – a reformed Charles of course. He was firm about this, and even hopeful of success, completely failing to realise that there was another person to be taken into consideration: Alfieri. He wrote to Louise, telling her to come to Rome where a place would be found for her in a convent, but adding 'I implore you never let others know that you do not intend to return to your husband; do not fear that unless a miracle takes place I should ever advise such a step, but as we may in all reverence believe that what has happened was intended by Providence to show the world that your actions were inspired by a wish to lead a higher life, so we may also hope that He wished by the same means to convert my brother.' He could not have got Louise, let alone Charles, more wrong.

Louise's self-control at this time seemed all the more remarkable contrasted with Charles' total lack of any whatsoever. She knew that at all costs she must keep Alfieri away until her position was secure – there must be no trace of a love affair or her powerful allies Henry and the Pope would desert her. She must concentrate on modesty and beg for their humble guidance and meanwhile lead a life of irreproachable and uncontestable virtue. It was not congenial to her, but she persevered and succeeded in her object. Charles fumed helplessly at the public sympathy she was gaining and retaliated with petty gestures like refusing to let her have her clothes. He knew that all Florence knew Louise was only biding her time before letting Alfieri join her, but nobody would take his side. And he did have a side – he would never have denied that there had been occasions in his married life when his behaviour towards his wife had been less than gentlemanly, but what he felt the world would not take into consideration was that there had also been occasions when Louise had not behaved like a lady. Everyone knew Charles at his worst – they had, unfortunately, seen him in action – but did they know Louise? His way of attacking her was so obvious, hers so subtle. Furthermore, she was his lawful wife and Charles felt that whatever he had done did not invalidate that contract. Everyone knew his rages never lasted long. He was willing to try again, but nobody would give him a chance. Never, ever, had he felt more wronged.

While his anger cooled into misery, Louise was resigning herself to an obligatory year or so in another convent. At least the Ursuline convent in Rome would be preferable to her first refuge. As Henry pointed out, 'French is spoken, and you will enjoy the society of many distinguished nuns'. If Louise's heart sank at the promise of such a treat, she did not show it. Gratefully, she accepted the offer. The only problem was going to be getting out of Florence, for she feared that the minute she set foot out of her present convent Charles was quite capable of having her bound hand and foot and carried to him whatever the Pope or Henry said. More plans would have to be made and the utmost secrecy imposed.

CHAPTER TWENTY-TWO
Count of Albany

Towards the end of December, Louise set out for Rome with an escort of armed servants to meet any attack Charles might make, but in the event her journey proved peaceful. She arrived at the Ursuline convent in Rome and was given the same room Charles' mother had had during her period of refuge. Alfieri did not come with her, in accordance with Louise's instructions to keep away, but finding Florence intolerable without her he went to Naples the following month. Within three months, Louise had stopped being grateful for peace and quiet and desperately wanted to get out of the convent. In April she wrote to Henry: 'You would think me bad tempered but I am only out of spirits and have such headaches that I can hardly speak.' There was only one cure for this nervous tension – removal from the convent. Though it puzzled Henry that his sister-in-law could not be as happy as his mother in similar circumstances, he was quite willing to try to think of a more congenial arrangement. Eventually, it was agreed that Louise could move to her brother-in-law's palace, the Cancellaria, which he rarely used since he spent most of his time in Frascati. To Louise's delighted relief, she was allowed to move into a second-floor apartment there and immediately her life took a turn for the better. Situated as she was, it was plain to anyone who had not previously been fully aware of it that she was under the patronage of a Cardinal and, by implication, of the Pope. This gave her a social clearing that as a woman living apart from her husband she might not otherwise have had. It also gave Alfieri an ease of access for which he had been waiting. By May the two were seeing each other regularly – he took an apartment not far away – and appearing together in Rome.

Charles, when he heard all this, came nearer to that fatal stroke for which Louise had looked in vain than he had ever been. Even though the new development was broken to him very gently by John Stuart, the one faithful servant left to him, it induced a state of permanent hysteria.

His apoplectic fits grew more numerous and his days were considered numbered. What strength he had was spent, during his lucid periods, in writing letters to Henry and the Pope pointing out how they were being duped, or in meetings with Prince Corsini and the Archbishop of Florence during which petitions were drawn up to the same purpose. The injustice of it all obsessed Charles. If Louise, like Clementina Walkinshaw, had retired to a convent and *suffered*, he could perhaps have accepted his lot, but that she should be having her cake and eating it was unbearable. Equally unbearable was Henry's complicity. Charles was reduced to writing pathetic begging letters when his normal tirades failed, full of earnest expressions of concern for his dear brother's health. Nothing irked him more than having to crawl to his younger brother. Furthermore, not only his heart but his pocket had been affected, making peace with Henry essential. The Pope had given half Charles' papal allowance to Louise and he was in dire straits, which everyone noticed. 'The diminution of Count Albany's income has obliged him lately to make a reformation in his family; he has totally altered his way of living and behaves in every respect with proper decency,' wrote Mann. This decency was more debilitating than all the riotous living in the world. Charles eked out a miserable existence, plagued by plans for revenge that could never materialise, without comforts of any kind.

Louise had not entirely banished him from her mind, try though she might. The fact was, by simply being alive he had the upper hand even if it gave him no pleasure. His small meannesses, which one would have thought she could have comfortably allowed him, irked her. He would not send her some books she wanted, and when Henry wrote asking for them she rejoiced that 'the letter you wrote to the King is admirable, and if you will excuse the expression, it is full of malice; I think on reading it he will be at his wits' ends'. Knowing, as she did, how much she and Alfieri were getting away with, it was her constant worry that Henry might at any minute be enlightened. Her main task, therefore, was constantly to ingratiate herself with him. He believed in her integrity and she bent over backwards to sustain this belief. Her endless letters to him are often witty, always lively, but their tone remained respectful. She also carefully introduced Alfieri to him – sending him with a copy of Virgil that she had noticed his fine library was without – so that he too could take the opportunity to make a good impression.

For two years, all went well. While Charles declined, Louise flourished. Rome had never been more congenial, for Pope Pius VI saw it as his duty to make it once more the centre of liberal arts. Artists, actors, singers, sculptors, writers – all were welcomed and encouraged as never before.

Louise and Alfieri were in their element. Their greatest moment came at the performance of Alfieri's tragedy *Antigone* at the Spanish Embassy in November 1782 when the whole of Roman society flocked to see it. Louise made a triumphant entry wearing both the Sobieski and Stuart jewels – Charles gnashed his teeth at the effrontery – and for Alfieri it was a night of glory. A reception was held afterwards of the greatest splendour where the compliments were directed not only towards Alfieri for his achievement but towards Louise who was credited with the inspiration behind it. What heightened everyone's interest in the pair was the knowledge that they were rocking one of society's established customs at its foundations. Alfieri was Louise's cavaliere servente in the fullest sense of the term, yet the very position was dependent on there being a husband around who gave sanction to it. Could he be a cavaliere when Louise was separated from Charles and he disapproved? It was commonly thought to be a dangerous game they were playing and they all relished it, most of all because they thought it could not last.

In March 1783, Charles suddenly became very ill indeed, ill enough to be considered at death's door. At sixty-three he had painfully swollen legs and difficulty with his breathing as well as other assorted maladies. He made his last wishes known and received the sacrament. Told of this, Henry could not fail to go to Florence – though it was not lost on him that Charles had failed, in similar circumstances and with a greater obligation, to come to their father. However, Henry was a Prince of the Church and knew his duty. Off he went to find his brother very much better and apparently playing the game their father had played for ten years. But having come to bury Charles, Henry could not leave without seeing him alive, however embarrassing he felt the interview would be. The convalescent Charles, impressively pale and weak with the last sacrament still fresh on his lips, shook Henry. It was not the brother he had known. Lying there, quite sober and speaking with the greatest sincerity and calm, Charles seemed to him a solemn figure. What he had to say was even more grave. Henry, listening to the accusations he had already heard so many times in letters, suddenly was willing to give them credence. In addition, he was in Florence, and in Florence Charles could produce plenty of witnesses to testify that Louise and Alfieri enjoyed an illicit relationship. Once convinced that he had been duped, Henry, a man slow to anger, worked himself into a fury all the worse through being tinged with shame. He hated to be made a fool of, and it now seemed to him crystal clear that he must have been the laughing-stock of Rome for some time. This made him uncharacteristically vindictive. It was not sufficient to put a stop to Louise and Alfieri's liaison – he wanted the man hounded and Louise publicly shamed. Alfieri was ordered to quit Papal territory and all Rome was informed of what Charles had told him about Louise – which was nothing they did not know anyway but nevertheless found enjoyable. Alfieri behaved with dignity, protesting his innocence but leaving at once, and Louise did not lose her head, informing Henry that 'your wish is fulfilled and your advice followed'. This quiet compliance, plus Louise's gentle rebuke that he could have doubted her, had the effect of totally confusing Henry. Louise and Alfieri had not run off together, perhaps he had been mistaken? Charles, for his part, was satisfied: the idyll had been shattered and his own virtue vindicated. For a while, he fed on the news from Rome and felt better.

But the drama was not yet over. The lovers were parted, and utterly miserable, but Louise had not been returned to him. She, for her part, was on the verge of a breakdown. Alfieri had gone and she did not dare to follow him for the same reasons that had always restrained her: she would become a penniless outcast. A visit from her mother, come to persuade her rather late in the day to go back to Charles, did nothing to help. She filled her time writing frank letters to Gori, Alfieri's friend, to whom she poured out her undoubted agony. 'If only you realised how miserable and depressed I am! It seems to me that my load of wretchedness increases daily. I do not know how I am to exist without the Friend. I meditate self-destruction. I do nothing but weep, nor can I ever think upon him save with utter torment.' Thoughts of Charles' death fascinated her: 'Who knows what will be the end of this Man? This Man in Florence who has been ill so long a time? He seems to me to be formed of iron to destroy us. You will tell me, to reassure me, that he cannot last long; but I see matters clearly. I don't suppose this last illness has given him a fresh lease of life, but I do think he can hold out very easily for a year or two longer. Of course he may at any moment succumb to the gout in his chest. What a brutal thing it is to expect one's happiness through another's death! O God it degrades the soul! Yet none the less I cannot refrain from this desire.' The desire was never fulfilled: 'That Man does not seem likely to pass away. His legs are become useless yet he survives despite his malady.' The thought of being doomed for ever to live apart from Alfieri (who was comforting himself by travelling and buying horses) demented her. 'I have a fixed horror of my life, which is so firmly rooted in my mind that I ask myself now and again "Why am I alive? What am I doing here?"' The only point to life was the thought of being reunited with Alfieri. 'But then I know I must guard my life for his sake so as some day to render him happy. Thus I am doing all that is possible. I take exercise on horse-back. I go early to bed; I am careful of myself.

But my heart is sore stricken and I am scarcely alive, but rather drag along my wretched existence, which I cannot endure much longer. One way or another it must come to an end. Life is but a burden to which I am no wise attached.'

Charles, if he had known of these outpourings, must have been satisfied. Louise was more than paying for anything she had ever done to him. But though he knew she was now separated from her lover and discredited with Henry and the Pope (though he had no idea how quickly her good conduct was reclaiming her position) it brought him no peace of mind. All he did was mope in his palace, thinking back on all the opportunities life had cheated him of, and never quite relinquishing the idea that Louise would come back, penitent. Mann wrote that he had told the visiting Chevalier des Tours: '… he would not again be the tool of France, and that whatsoever might happen nothing less than a solemn invitation from Gt. Britain like that to King William, accompanied by a body of 70 or 80,000 men from France should engage him to move a step. The Chevalier added that the Pretender was not so weak as to flatter himself that anything of that nature would ever happen but that at all events he is so infirm that he is quite unable to perform any long journey.' Nor did he have a son to do it for him – not that Charles would ever have got much vicarious pleasure out of a son doing what he could not do.

So there they were, a miserable pair, Charles in Florence and Louise in the hills behind Rome, and there they would doubtless have stayed till his death but for the fortunate and kindly intervention of a third person, King Gustavus III of Sweden. The King, in the winter of 1783, met Charles at Pisa where he had gone for another course of baths after an exhausting summer during which he had tired himself far beyond his limits. The trouble was, his victory over Louise, plus his long, abstemious convalescence, had made him feel so much better that he had promptly tried to put the clock back and do all the things he had always loved. He had joined in all the local summer festivals, he had danced and feasted and even opened fêtes. The result was total collapse which all the baths in the world were not going to cure. Gustavus was shocked by his appearance, and the kind of life he was leading. Another Swede recorded at the time: 'The Count of Albany … is decrepit and bent; he walks with great difficulty, and so impaired is his memory that he repeats himself every quarter of an hour.' Alone among contemporary observers, Gustavus' pity was untouched by contempt – many commented on Charles' state, but few paused to feel any kind of true compassion, perhaps because they were too near him. They had seen Charles go to pieces gradually, they had seen how much he was to blame himself. Gustavus, coming as a visitor, could not reconcile this broken-down old man with the image he had always had, nor could he accept that royalty could sink so low. Sympathy was something Charles had once scorned, but now he craved it. With Gustavus' encouragement, out came the long saga of all his troubles. Gustavus listened to the tale of woe and disentangling the strands felt Charles' troubles fell into two main categories: domestic and financial. He felt that there was something he could do about both.

For an eighteenth-century king, this Swede was a remarkably down-to-earth and sensible man. He first of all made it quite clear to Charles that if any help was to be forthcoming, he must first of all help himself. In short, he must give up all those fantasies to which he had clung for so long. It only harmed his interests to maintain his pretensions to the throne of England. There was such a thing as facing facts, however much in the right one knew oneself to be. Nobody disputed the Stuarts' claim in theory, but in fact it was a thing of the past. Charles must acquire dignity in defeat. Nobody would respect him until he acknowledged he was beaten, that he was now an old, sick man who had suffered many reversals of fortune and now accepted his lot, however unjust. Other people had been trying to tell Charles this for years, but he was stubborn. He knew the truth perfectly well but appearances were all: the next campaign *had* to be round the corner. Now Gustavus managed what others had not, either because he was more tactful and eloquent or because Charles was more tired than he had cared to admit. In any case, he promised to conform.

Gustavus first of all dealt with money. He wrote to Louis XVI. Charles himself had only just written that September and if he showed Gustavus a copy it must have made him wince, for in it Charles had claimed that now was the moment to attack England and put him on the throne. Furthermore, he had signed himself 'Charles R.'. The tone of this letter was precisely what Gustavus claimed did Charles irreparable harm. His own letter was quite different. He described Charles' condition and then simply asked for money to help him. It was by no means a begging letter, for its tone was peremptory, but it asked for money out of true charity and as one king with a sense of Royal solidarity to another. He also wrote to Charles III of Spain, who immediately coughed up to the tune of one thousand piastres a year. All this was gratifying, but Gustavus knew – and made sure that Charles knew – that any financial settlements as far as France at least was concerned were inextricably bound up with his marital difficulties.

It was not a job anyone would relish – organising a Royal Whip Round for Impoverished Stuarts was child's play by comparison. It also involved meeting all the parties concerned, and that meant going to Rome. However, Gustavus was going to Rome anyway on his interrupted tour, and he was not the man to shirk an embarrassing situation. Nor was he a fool, for he took the precaution of obtaining from Charles permission to negotiate on his behalf. Once in Rome, Gustavus cleverly kept his distance from Henry and Louise, managing everything in writing. What he was proposing was a legal separation – nothing else would in fact do. He was careful to report back to Charles at every step. When he received promising noises from Louise, he wrote to Charles outlining the separation and waited for the following reply before proceeding any further:

> Monsieur le Comte – I cannot sufficiently express my thanks for your communication of the 24th March. I leave myself entirely in your hands, for it would be impossible for me to find anyone to whom I could better confide my honour and my interests. I beg you to end this affair as soon as possible. I quite concur in total separation from my wife and hope she will no longer bear my name. With renewed sentiments of sincere gratitude and friendship I remain your true friend
>
> C. D'Albanie.

Gustavus was gratified to see that Charles R. had disappeared for good, and also that Charles was beginning to see that what he had formerly thought of as a climbing-down on his part was more a casting-off. This he obviously rather liked: as long as he could take a high moral tone and gain practical advantages, the slur to his honour was bearable. It was typical that he should care more about Louise not bearing his name than anything else.

In fact, Gustavus had anticipated more trouble than there actually was. Louise was by this time so desperate that money, which might have proved a major stumbling-block, was of relative unimportance. She was prepared to sacrifice undoubted rights. She wrote to Henry with enthusiasm of what Gustavus had proposed: 'I lend myself the more readily to it, as I hope thereby to prove that I am very far from seizing on the fortune of your Brother, as he declares, and it is without any regret that I now restore him not only the 1000 ecus that you pay me, but also the 3000 which by my marriage settlement constitute my pin money. And I agree equally that he should take back his diamonds from Rome.' She could hardly have been more accommodating. All she kept was the money due to her from France under her marriage contract which was always supposed to have been her personal property anyway.

Although there was really no need, Charles had drawn up a rather magnificent document to legalise his separation, which he was by now not only reconciled to but actually revelling in. Gustavus cannot have approved of its extravagant language, but he let it go.

> We, Charles, legitimate King of Gt. Britain, on the representations made to Us by Louise-Caroline-Maximilienne-Emmanuele, Princess of Stolberg, that for sound reasons she wished to reside at a distance separated from Our person; that circumstances as well as Our common misfortunes have rendered this event useful and necessary for Us both; and in consideration of all the arguments she has adduced to Us, We declare by these presents that We freely and voluntarily give Our consent to this separation and that We do permit her to live from henceforth in Rome, or in any town she may consider most convenient, such being Our pleasure. Given and sealed with the seal of Our arms in Our Palace at Florence, April 3 1784.

It was a pretty nauseating manifesto but Louise was too relieved to be annoyed. She found it in her to hope, 'May Heaven grant him some measure of repose and content in his old age!' Henry was not so amenable. In fact, his reaction struck the one discordant note in the proceedings. What irked him was Louise's willingness to give to Charles what he gave to her. In a sniffy letter he wrote: '... I can never approve of a separation, whose sole aim is interest. I cannot, and ought not, to interfere in any arrangements you two may devise together, but I bid you remember that everything you have received from Cantini (my steward) since you have resided in my palace of the Cancellaria has come from *myself*; and that the said Cantini has my orders to pay it to you so long as you live with me. It is a piece of insolence therefore on my brother's part, this disposing of money which is mine, as though it were his own, and without my knowledge, so that I feel compelled to acquaint him with my own opinion of his conduct in the matter. And I beg you once for all, my very dear sister, not to annoy me further on this point ...' His dear sister did her best to soothe Henry, for though she had no more actual need of him Louise was always diplomatic. Her letter to him was all the same pure humbug – she in fact despised Henry from this point onwards, if not always. Later, she was to write of him: 'he is very whimsical and very dull and he bores every one he meets ... he belongs to a race of amphibious creatures who are intended to be *seen from a distance* but whom an evil chance has brought close to our eyes.'

However, the much ruffled Henry could not prevent the deal going through. It is nice to record that both Louise and Charles showed a fitting sense of gratitude. Louise wrote, '... he acted as a friend as well as a relation', and Charles, 'I cannot sufficiently express my thanks ... it would be impossible to find anyone to whom I could better confide my honour and interests.' Gustavus was simply pleased to have been of help.

He wrote from Paris that summer to Louise that 'I shall deem myself happy, if I have been of any service in softening your lot. I consider you can rest quite easy, Madame, as to your brother-in-law's attitude in this affair. Matters are now well advanced and they cannot be put back.'

Louise was still by no means free to do as she liked, but her position was much easier. Though obliged to reside in the Papal states under the Pope's chaperonage, she obtained permission quite easily to go on a holiday, which no one denied she badly needed. She went to Baden, in Switzerland, and from there to Colmar on the Rhine where Alfieri at last joined her: 'On the seventeenth day of August, 1784, at eight in the morning, at the inn of the Two Keys in Colmar, I met Her and fell speechless from plentitude of my joy.' They stayed together for two months, then separated once more, Louise to winter in Bologna and Alfieri to Pisa. Louise was still insisting on the greatest circumspection rather to Alfieri's bewilderment. She never forgot that she was lucky to enjoy the freedom she had and must not spoil her good fortune by trying to grab more. Charles, after all, was still alive: they were only separated, not divorced.

CHAPTER TWENTY-THREE

A Long Time Dying

Meanwhile, in Florence, Charles found himself more comfortably off than he had been for years, yet he was no more contented. The fight with Louise that had dragged on for so long might in one way have exhausted him but in another it had provided the salt in his life. Now that his marriage was officially over and the dust had settled down, what was he left with? The same dreary life he had led for ten years. Eating and drinking were the only things that filled in his day until the theatres opened. His position in the sophisticated society of Florence had always been precarious, but now he was becoming unacceptable to the vast majority of people. Furthermore, the company and attentions of Gustavus had made him feel the lack afterwards. He was surrounded, in Florence, by a household of servants and inferiors. There were no friends that really deserved the name. Louise's caustic pen put it rather well when she wrote to Henry about this time: 'As to your Brother, nothing surprises me in his behaviour. I know him so well that I consider him capable of going to any length of absurdity. I was cognisant of all his late nonsense in Florence and surrounded by Irish friends he will go on thus, and even make these people baronets. I assure you, my dear Brother, that it will only be with his last breath that he will cease to commit follies.'

But it was actually under the influence of what he thought was his last breath that Charles, back in 1783, had had an idea that was to make his last days pleasanter. When he thought he was dying, he made a will in favour of Charlotte, his daughter by Clementina Walkinshaw, whom he had never even bothered to legitimise. Once recovered, instead of revoking the will he let it stand and seems to have thought more kindly of the daughter he had so neglected. With the official separation from Louise ratified, and Gustavus departed, his life sank back into the doldrums and the notion of seeing his only child began to obsess him. It was pure sentiment and self-interest on Charles' part, for there had never been any contact between Charlotte and himself that he might wish to revive.

Nor did he in any sense know the daughter he was now prepared to drool over. Her letters, on the contrary, had revealed over the years exactly the kind of personality Charles loathed. She was always such a very humble, very unhappy person, casting, by implication, blame on her father. Charles liked cheerful, jolly people. It was hardly surprising that he never replied to letters that ran, 'It is for the third time that Pouponne, that once much loved child and who had done nothing to lose that love, still flatters herself that she is dear to you ... the only treasure worthy of Pouponne's ambition is the heart of her Papa', or, 'O my august papa, o, my King, remember the laws of blood and nature ... Is it possible, my august papa, that your Majesty made me come into this world only to be unhappy and to lead such a deplorable and unfortunate existence?' Well, yes, it was, but Charles did not like to be reminded of the fact. Without any apparent scruples at all, he prepared to legitimise Charlotte and summon her to his side. It never entered his head that she would be other than delighted and flattered and would rush to his lonely side.

In the event, his estimate was correct, though Charlotte had her motives for coming. She had had an unenviable life with enough traumas in it to keep a psychiatrist happy for years. How much she remembered of her first (formative?) seven years trailing round Europe with her unhappy mother in the wake of her restless father is hard to estimate. Observers said Charles always made a fuss of her when he was around, that he liked to have her on his knee and sing to her and buy her presents, so any memories were probably happy and vague. But from the year that her mother fled with her to a convent Charlotte could remember very well indeed what life had been like. For a start, it had been poverty-stricken. Paris during the last quarter of the eighteenth century was one of the most expensive places in the world to live, and the pension allowed to Clementina and her daughter did not increase proportionally. They always had a struggle to feed and clothe themselves, never mind permit themselves any luxuries.

Added to the harsh economic reality of Charlotte's situation was also the realisation that her father had virtually abandoned her and that her mother was a ruined woman. Clementina was too wretched ever to provide any lightening of the load, and another, less resilient daughter would have crumbled under the pressure. But Charlotte was a sturdy, sterling character who plugged away at nagging her father without seeming to be in the least affected. She more than made the best of a bad job, grabbing every little social opportunity that came her way. She got out and about, leaving her mother to her weeping, and though she was never going to be the toast of any town she did not go unnoticed. She seemed able to accept what other girls might have found an insoluble riddle – that her father was a brute but a man to honour. She took a pride in her ancestry and never missed a chance to refer to it. The unfortunate visit to Rome when Charles had just married Louise did not rankle, though the treatment she had received had been monstrous. So too had Charles' command in 1775 that she was never to marry. His own marriage was at that time turning sour and he was intent on guarding his sole offspring jealously. She was by this time twenty-two years old, when marriage prospects might be considered to be at their height, but she never flinched from the vindictiveness of such an order.

Charlotte never openly defied her father. She had a strong streak of common sense and saw no point in provoking trouble. Instead, she led a secret life with the knowledge if not the approval of her mother. She was no beauty, and possessed little of the famous Stuart charm, but she was pleasant and eager to please. Furthermore, she had a certain curiosity value which she was not slow to cash in on. Since marriage was much too complicated a business to envisage while her father lived, Charlotte opted for the next best thing and became the mistress of the Prince de Rohan, Archbishop of Bordeaux. Her mother could hardly object to such an illicit relationship. Still living officially in the convent at Meaux, Charlotte moved in and out often enough to have a stable affair with her elderly lover, and finally bore him three children. The first two were girls, born in 1780 and 1782, and then the third was a boy, Charles (of course), born in 1784. Naturally, Charlotte had not been able to entirely conceal her productivity, but she was very careful not to openly acknowledge her children or their father. He was always 'mon ami' and the children 'mes fleurs'.

It was ironic that just when she had carved some kind of tolerable niche for herself, Charlotte should receive the call for which she had been prepared so long. Apart from the news of the will, which legitimised her, there was then the good news that France had ratified it and the prospect of rapid outward improvement in her status. Charlotte enjoyed this enormously, though 'mes fleurs' promised to be an unexpected complication at just the wrong moment. She now had a title – Duchess of Albany – and this brought with it the privilege of sitting on a stool at the feet of the Queen of France, Marie-Antoinette. Like Charles and Louise, Charlotte adored the empty trappings of monarchy: they were never a mockery to her. The only fly in the ointment was the continued silence towards her mother. Knowing her as she did as a sad, worn-out, pathetic creature Charlotte must have wondered what on earth she could have done so many years ago to merit such persistent coldness. She herself was always faithful to her mother, seeing no contradiction in her parallel pursuit of her father. Charlotte was nothing if not dogged and stubborn and it seemed to her that in the end they were both bound to win. She was, after all, her father's sole heir, and he was an old man near to death, as had been recently proved. Though she had no indication that her father would send for her, the will in her favour must have made her anticipate other overtures. There was never any doubt that she would go, leaving her mother, 'mon ami' and 'mes fleurs' behind. It would have been foolish not to. Charles would die soon and if she wanted to benefit she had to be dutiful. Clementina agreed. They both looked upon it as a short-term venture, not having the experience of Louise.

The Act legitimising Charlotte was registered with the permission of the French King and Parliament and shortly afterwards Charles wrote to her asking her to come to Florence and live with him. The speed with which she replied suggests Charlotte was prepared. She set off towards the end of September, only just recovered from the birth of her son. Before she left, she made arrangements for the care of her children and promised to write not only to Clementina but to 'mon ami' – but he was not to write to her because it would be too risky. It was clearly understood that she would prepare the way for Clementina to join her and they expected to see each other in the not too distant future.

In Florence, Charles was again roused from the apathy into which his ordinary life tended to plunge him. He looked forward immensely to having a woman about the place to make him more comfortable and cheerful, especially a woman who presented no difficulties. There was a good deal of bustle in the Palazzo as he did his best to brighten it up with new furniture and décor in honour of the new arrival, and he enjoyed giving the necessary orders. Not only his household but Florentine society in general were a little bewildered by all this fuss. Charles had never, until this time, admitted having a daughter. She was a shadowy, not quite respectable figure lurking in his background and any mention of her had always enraged him. Now she emerged as a very great lady indeed and they were all at a loss. Charles, as ever when he made a gesture, made it in style, unbothered by any appearance of inconsistency. He never did anything by halves – the volte-face always had to be total. Tarting his house up was not enough – he had to send to Rome for his mother's jewels and his share of the family silver.

Charlotte arrived in Florence on 5th October 1784, and according to Mann her arrival 'occasioned some little bustle in town'. Everyone wanted to take a look at her. Those who succeeded were disappointed, for 'she is a tall, robust woman of very dark complexion and coarse-grained skin, with more of masculine boldness than feminine modesty or elegance'. But the ladies who came in droves to her front door to leave their cards were delighted to have their calls returned. The new Duchess of Albany evidently did not insist on the Royal status the Countess of the same name had claimed. She was friendly and accommodating and they liked her for it, even if she lacked the style for which they were always looking. The Palazzo became a livelier place under her direction: 'private balls, three times a week consisting of eight or ten ladies, at which he [Charles] assists, though he drowses most of the time'. On the whole, Florence applauded.

So too did Charles. He had no objections whatsoever to being in the hands of this capable, bossy woman. The important thing about Charlotte as far as Charles was concerned was that she was subservient in everything that mattered – that is, trivialities. She ran him and his affairs but always deferred to him. His loyalty was so completely won that he was determined to redress what he considered a disgraceful slight to her (forgetting all his slights of past years), and also force others to perform the about-turn he had done himself. The object of this attack was Henry. Charlotte had not been long in her father's house before she realised how important his brother was and what antagonism existed between them. The trouble was, Henry would not welcome Charlotte to the family fold. Charles had written to him in November that 'I wish to inform you that my dearest daughter, having been recognised by myself, by France, and by the Pope, is from now Royal Highness, and as such must be recognised by you, and wherever she goes. I do not wish to dispute any of your own rights as you are my brother they cannot be discussed, but I must beg you not to dispute those of my dear child: the fact of her being my child ought to make her sacred to you.'

If Henry frothed at the mouth on receipt of this epistle, he could be forgiven. With a gigantic effort of will he restrained himself from replying at all and resolved to have nothing to do with Charlotte, however much it annoyed Charles. She could sort things out for herself – which she did. Not a bit put out by Henry's attitude, Charlotte busied herself becoming familiar with all her father's business. The first thing she discovered during this searching examination was that she had in one sense jumped out of the frying pan into the fire: Charles' financial troubles were strongly reminiscent of those her mother had had all her life. He might live sumptuously, whereas they had lived frugally, he might own a Palazzo whereas they had sheltered in a convent, but his supply of ready cash was limited and worry about where the next lot was coming from ever present.

There was, of course, an essential difference, and that was Charles' assumption that he was entitled to enjoy the fruits of the earth and someone would always see he did. There was no humiliation or embarrassment in his financial negotiations. Nevertheless, when Charlotte arrived on the scene, money was in short supply, and she set herself, expert that she was, to make sure that all available sources were tapped and all commitments kept up. Inevitably, this involved Henry, the only rich member of the family. Not at all put off by Henry's coldness towards her, Charlotte began to write him 'business' letters. She wrote, with some cunning, 'I have taken care to hide from the King that I am in correspondence with your Royal Highness; in order to be of greater service to him I thought it necesssary to make a mystery of what is a great pleasure to myself.' With less insight, she included in the business letters criticisms of Louise, which quite undid any of the good her earnest book-keeping might have done. Henry had been involved once in Charles' domestic scene, he did not want to be involved again. But his steward always replied to Charlotte and she chose to interpret that as a sign that she was slowly winning her uncle round.

It was all hard work – no one could grudge Charlotte her dinners and balls. Looking after her father was an exhausting business since he had never learnt to live within his own physical limits. Charlotte fancied herself as a bit of an expert on medical matters, rather as Charles himself had done in his time, but doctoring her father proved too much for her. His legs seemed to be permanently swollen, his blood pressure high, and his breathing difficult. He complained all the time how awful he felt, which Charlotte felt showed a lack of courage. Often, she felt like complaining herself for already the intermittent stomach cramps that were to grow increasingly severe were beginning to bother her. She dosed herself ceaselessly but only time ever made them stop. Nevertheless, she was still a comparatively young woman and could take pleasure, in spite of her ailments, in ordering two dozen pairs of leather shoes at a time and having dresses made by the local seamstress.

It was not a bad life, though it had its unpleasant side – Charlotte was literally nurse to her father – and on the whole preferable to life in the convent at Meaux. Except, of course, that she missed her mother, 'mon ami', and 'mes fleurs'. Charlotte wrote almost daily to Clementina, filling her in on every tiny detail of her life, which in one way was gratifying but in another meant putting up with many moans. Her letters were full of references to 'mes petites fleurs' who Clementina was to make sure were well watered and tended every day. She spoke constantly of hoping to see them before they grew much higher, and of them not forgetting her.

She wrote also to 'mon ami', letters into a void for she kept up her ban on him replying. It was widely rumoured in Florence that Charles intended to find another ami for her: 'he proposes to marry her to a Florentine Cavalier if one good enough can be found'. None ever was, perhaps not entirely to Charlotte's sorrow.

Charlotte's letters also contained, very soon after she arrived in Florence, messages from Charles to Clementina – verbal ones, generously translated on to paper by Charlotte. She had not forgotten, in the gay social whirl she found herself in, her mission in coming at all. She spoke often of her mother to her father, at first needing great daring to do so, and then, as Charles grew used to it as harmless prattle, with greater frequency and less restraint. She was not so optimistic as to hope that more than thirty years' resentment could be broken down in a few weeks, but she hoped that from the odd, careless, fond word he might move on to more formal greetings and perhaps even to putting pen to paper himself. After all, as Charlotte was quick to realise and play upon, Clementina was more than willing to be the prostrate penitent, an attitude Charles had always liked. She included with pleasure the amiable messages Charles sent and was encouraged by her progress.

She was cheered, too, by her progress in another project, equally dear to her heart: the winning over of Henry. Throughout 1785 Charlotte had kept up her 'business' letters, completely unflattened by the lack of personal response from Henry. Then, in October, she heard that on his annual visit to the provinces under his jurisdiction Henry would be visiting nearby Perugia. Immediately, Charlotte urged her father to accompany her there and when he refused with all the force of which he was still capable, she went on her own. Once there, she sent him a note saying who she was and asking to be allowed to come and pay her respects to him. Henry was highly embarrassed and even indignant, suspecting that she had deliberately put him in this awkward position in order to put him further in the wrong. Perugia was a small town. It could not contain two such august persons as the Cardinal of York and the Duchess of Albany without everyone knowing they were both there. Refusing to see his niece would mean a public rebuff. Accordingly, Henry had to swallow his annoyance and agree to see this woman who had been nagging him by letter so long. It was a meeting he dreaded, but in the event it seems to have gone off rather well. Perhaps Charlotte's very lack of charm, wit or beauty endeared her to her uncle, or perhaps he simply reckoned that she was obviously harmless. To her delight, he agreed to recognise her as his legitimate niece and to be reconciled yet again to his brother.

These concessions represented a considerable triumph for Charlotte, which she quite appreciated though she did not expect her father to. They also opened the way for her to urge Henry to help her move her father back to Rome for the winter. Florentine winters were, she argued, notoriously cold. Henry might have replied, with justice, that so were Roman ones, but instead he graciously fell in with her desire. He would make all the necessary arrangements for his brother and his niece to come to Rome. Charlotte's thanks were heartfelt. She genuinely felt a move south would benefit her father's health, but quite apart from that she also felt that to be in Rome was to be in the power-house itself. All the arguments Henry had used twenty years before to persuade Charles to come to Rome before his father died were now Charlotte's. She would be near Henry and near the Pope, fount of many pensions.

On 1st December 1785, Charles and Charlotte began their move to Rome, taking eight days over it. Charles was only persuaded to go on the understanding that he would be coming back to Florence in the spring, but Charlotte regarded the move as permanent. They left in some style – a huge fête was given for all the nobility in Florence. Charles stood the journey well and did not seem depressed by memories of the other two returns he had made to Rome. At Viterbo, Henry was there to meet them, to Charlotte's immense gratification. It was quite a little family party that entered Rome on 9th December and Charlotte was in ecstasies over the civility of their reception. Charles was not. The very sight of Rome seemed to put him in a bad temper and it took all Charlotte's tact and patience to make him settle down. Watching her deal with his brother, Henry realised that at last someone had come along who was not afraid of Charles and was prepared to be more masterful. He saw too that Charlotte only succeeded not, as everyone thought, because Charles was old and sick, but because he was fond of her. She was his. He had reviled and ignored her but she had come when he had whistled. In short, Charles trusted Charlotte as he had never trusted anyone before.

His trust was not misplaced. There were those who found it unseemly that an old man like Charles should gad about so much, flitting from opera to opera and party to party. Charlotte, it was suggested, was trying to kill him off. But in fact nothing could have been further from the truth. There was nothing Charles would have hated more than to be shut up in some sick-room conserving his strength – he much preferred to live out his last days to the full and go with a bang rather than a whimper. He was one of those who would never accept that death was not only inevitable but indeed just round the corner. Sentiments such as the Earl

Marischal had expressed before his death in 1778 – 'he wished he were among the Eskimo for they knock old men on the head' – were never his. Charlotte helped him face his ailments much better than Louise had ever done: whereas she had cringed every time he had to be removed to the corridor of a theatre to be sick, Charlotte wasn't in the least worried. The physical unpleasantness of her father she faced with the greatest aplomb. Furthermore, far from wanting him to die, she desperately wanted him to live a few more years yet, since she had by no means tidied up all the loose financial ends that would give her security when he did die.

Meanwhile, Charlotte became one of the accepted sights of Rome. Henry offered her the family jewels, which she accepted eagerly and wore whether or not the occasion was suitable. She was keen to assume the position she thought she merited as her father's daughter, and entertained on a scale their income did not warrant – with the thorough approval of Charles himself. She gave evening parties to which guests of high rank were pleased to come and hear the good music she made sure was offered. Charles would be propped up on a couch, half asleep, beaming with pleasure at the assembled throng, with Charlotte fussing about him putting his wig straight when it slipped and watching over his glass. She was an indulgent nurse. She gave dinners for such eminent personages as the ambassador and ambassadress of Venice, and travelled to other people's dinners in a splendid coach emblazoned with the letters C.R. When the Duke and Duchess of Gloucester came to Rome, Charlotte was thrilled to be presented to them, seeing nothing inconsistent with such a meeting and her use of the title 'La Pretendente'.

In one respect only was Charlotte like Louise, and that was in the seriousness with which she played the Royalty game. She saw that the servants at the Palazzo Muti wore royal liveries and that within the confines of their home she and Charles were addressed as Majesty and Highness. Not, of course, that this ever got her anywhere, for as the 'Diario di Roma' observed: 'She aspired to the title of La Pretendente for the sake of the rights she could in that case have claimed, had there been a favourable chance, for the throne of England. As far as the Papal Court was concerned, nothing was done to encourage any pretensions on this point, and in Rome they enjoyed no other considerations than those generally shown to strangers of distinction.' Nevertheless, father and daughter were both popular and in the summer when they went to Albano there was a regular stream of visitors to the Savelli Palace to amuse them.

But by 1787, by the time he had been back in Rome two years, Charles was past amusing. He would lie on a sofa in one of the high, spacious rooms, fondling a lap dog to which he had become very attached, and oblivious to most of what was going on around him. It was Charlotte who needed distracting, for her own health and spirits were beginning to flag. Her digestion seemed to be permanently at fault and she was never without pains in her stomach. She seems to have gone on trying to cure herself without consulting any doctors, and finding relief only through cataloguing her ailments for her mother. Her letters to Clementina became increasingly depressed – her little flowers would have grown and not recognise her, even if she should ever see them again, which she was beginning to doubt; her friend would have found solace elsewhere. She longed for her mother to join her, and Clementina in a city on the very brink of revolution longed to go. But in spite of an actual letter written by Charles himself in 1787 to Clementina, there seemed little chance of their hopes being realised. Her father could not have been more fond of her, showing – before he slipped into that state of semi-consciousness from which he was never to recover – every possible mark of respect. Similarly, her uncle Henry also seems to have recognised her virtues and been on good terms with her, but Charlotte still did not dare risk imperiling her own position by actually sending for her mother. She began, instead, to cling to the belief that her father already had one foot in the grave, which indeed he had, but as Louise could have told her he showed a marked resistance to putting the other in to join it. But Charlotte did not have such a long wait. They returned from Albano to Rome in the autumn of 1787 and on 7th January Charles had an attack of apoplexy from which he recovered only to find himself partially paralysed. The fits continued, his strength ebbed, and on 30th January 1788 he finally died.

His body was carried on a litter to Frascati. There, in Henry's cathedral, he lay in royal robes, with the crown of Great Britain on his head, the sceptre in his hand, the great seal on his finger, the sword by his side, plastered with the medals and decorations that had been his ancestors'. His coffin bore the inscription CAROLUS III MAGNAE BRITANNIAE REX. Henry celebrated High Mass before a distinguished congregation. He thought he had done his brother more than justice but Charles would have felt cheated of the honours accorded to his father – he would have wanted St Peter's and the Pope and a slow procession through the crowded streets of Rome, not what amounted to a quiet country funeral. But then that was his problem – a constant feeling that he had been cheated that pursued him to the death. Yet, in another way, Henry did not fail him. Though now, if ever, was the time for all pretence to cease, Henry proved himself every bit as determined as Charles had ever been to be recognised as King. No sooner was his brother dead than he assumed the title Henry IX, gave orders that he should be addressed as 'Your Majesty', changed the ducal coronet on his arms and seals into a royal crown, and coined money and medals in his name. He then published a protestation saying that with his brother's death the Stuart rights to the throne of England were his, but that 'owing to critical circumstances' he would go on using the title Cardinal Duke of York. It was very wise of him.

CONCLUSION

As soon as Charles was dead, the world seemed to forget the years since 1745. So determined were his faithful followers – now very long in the tooth themselves – to enshrine his memory in glory that they succeeded to the extent of making many believe that Charles Edward Stuart died a gallant brave, instead of a diseased old man. The forty-three years after 1745 did not fit in with the legend, so they were dispensed with. Charles became one of the immortal young. His beauty, his bravery and his daring were all that were remembered.

There seems nothing more pointless than to speculate on whether Charles would have made a 'good' King. As A. J. P. Taylor cuttingly remarked: 'They were all good Kings – George IV who was mad was a good King, Queen Victoria, a silly old woman one wouldn't employ as a cook – she was a good Queen.' The term had become meaningless by the time Charles Edward was born. What is much more interesting, if speculation of such a kind can ever be interesting, is whether Charles could ever have become a 'good' man, for he certainly ended up very far from being one. The years after 1745 show him disintegrating fast as an admirable person not because he was either weak or wicked but because failure was totally unacceptable to him. Failure soured him, failure panicked him, failure pushed him into actions which in his successful days he would have been bitterly ashamed of. Yet inability to cope with failure is not necessarily a despicable thing: what was despicable was continuing not to be able to cope with it *after* he had given up trying. Until 1750, Charles tried to justify the faith that was placed in him. From 1745 to 1750 he tried desperately hard to redress the balance with everything against him; after 1750, he gave up, became bitter and spoiled, yet still would not acknowledge his defeat. If it were not for those five years, one would be safe in saying Charles Edward Stuart as a man was lucky to be obscured by his legend.

After 1745, Charles, in retrospect, was of no political importance.

Thus veils are drawn, eyes are averted and a general shuddering of distaste has always pervaded the historians' world at the very mention of him. This is a pity, for though politically unimportant he is still of interest as a human being and, more than that, as a historical figure toppled from his pinnacle. Should he have come to gain the throne, his faults would have been minutely catalogued and his success blamed for them. But here was a man pushed off the stage of history, and history has no further interest in him. What happens when a man is crushed is of no interest because history has no time for him. And yet, in the story, the complete story, of what happened to Charles Edward Stuart is all of human life.

Charles, like very many people, was one of those men who were made for things to go right. As long as things went right, he blossomed. When fortune favoured him all his good points were enhanced and his bad diminished – which is not always the case. In some men success and prosperity can be their ruin: prosperity can turn confidence into arrogance, kindness into indulgence, charm into hypocrisy; determination becomes selfishness, popularity produces vanity, an easy life makes for sloth and laziness, bravery disappears when there is no call for it and indifference takes its place. Until the retreat from Derby, when the upswing in his life's graph went as high as it would ever go, Charles' character was never more truly tested and found sound. He did not have it easy, but he pushed his way on, remaining uncorrupted in the process. The retreat, much more than Culloden, did for Charles. His character could not take a retreat. Culloden and the return to France only accelerated a process that had already begun: Charles had lost faith in himself. Everything that was bad and weak in him came to the fore. He neither matured nor mellowed as the years went on but rotted. Failure and disappointment ruined him more than any battle, whereas in the case of his father they had produced dignity. Charles' undoing was not drink, but failure. As a success, he would have gone from strength to strength. Success would not have spoiled or ruined him, but made him.

To meet, Charles seems to have been disarming to the end of his life. As a youth, only the Earl Marischal found him less than charming. As an old man, even spotty and bloated, there are plenty of tributes to his attractive personality. In Scotland during the '45 his progress was like that of a present-day pop star – the girls flocked to see him and stayed to try to get locks of his hair or threads from his coat. He dealt with this uncritical adulation with the greatest patience, not just because he loved it – many pop stars love the fan worship but are rude and boorish in return – but because he had this perhaps laughable but nevertheless sincere conception of duty to 'my people'. As time went on, Charles became removed from 'the people', but it was through circumstances, not choice. His care for them and anxiety that the poorest of them should be treated well was genuine if despotic. Many, many remembered him for his personal kindness. This contrasts oddly with his extreme cruelty to certain individuals, notably Clementina Walkinshaw and Henry Goring. They both served him well and he cast them both off with contempt. There are other instances of less-well-known servants receiving equally brutal treatment for no apparent reason – though to the hundred or so he employed in his 'family' during his life he was mostly considerate and loyal. Why Charles singled out certain people to exclude from his generally chivalrous behaviour is not obvious, but it was probably that, in knowing him better than most, they exceeded what he considered the bounds of familiarity. They tried to direct him, and that he would never stand for. Unquestioning obedience and worship were always Charles' demands. Telling him home truths was a luxury nobody was ever permitted.

Similarly, loving Charles had its conditions. Without a doubt, he never loved anyone in the full, rounded meaning of the word, nor did he ever have a satisfactory, fulfilling personal relationship with any adult, man or woman. The sterility of his emotional life is perhaps the greatest surprise the study of it holds. As a child, he loved his father and his brother and his love was amply returned, so that although his love for his mother was more complex he had a sound enough basis on which to build his affections later in life. But he never did. He always preferred men to women but there is only the most circumstantial of evidence to show he had homosexual leanings and he never selected any one man for close friendship. In particular, he never had any close friends of his own rank and age. Francis Strickland seems to have been suspected by James of having had more than one kind of bad influence on Charles, but there is nothing in either contemporary accounts or the Stuart papers to indicate he was right. Charles' intimates were always older men who were subservient to him, like John O'Sullivan. None of the Scots nobility attracted him, though the French he had more affinity with. There are letters to him from some of his French cousins that suggest a fairly close liking, but nothing conclusive. Certainly, after Henry Goring left him, Charles had to depend on servants for friendship. He went for nearly forty years without a close companion of any kind, unless one counts Louise whom he so quickly grew to hate. This might not have mattered if Charles had been, like his father, a solitary, private kind of person, but he was on the contrary gregarious and sociable by nature.

His attitude towards women as a species was romantic. His mother had been a lady one treated with respect, who disliked noise or violence of any sort, whom one felt privileged to serve. She had at all times to be handled gently, as though she might break. When Charles grew up he began by treating all women like this. He was polite, full of small, meaningless attentions, gravely concerned for their welfare. He never flirted, was never vulgar or lewd, sought rather to keep them at a distance rather than touch them. (The distance between subject and sovereign would have suited Charles exactly.) This deference towards women caught people's notice very early. Long before the Edinburgh papers picked it up and commented on it, others had marked his absence of either affairs or general whoring. Reasons were rarely offered – it was all a puzzle. Partly it may have been slow development on Charles' part, partly that he attached some kind of mystical significance to women because of his mother and was afraid of them. He himself, when challenged with what was considered insulting neglect, said that he had no time for women yet – affairs of state must come first. The simple answer may have been the true one, for when Charles did have time, when his hopes of another campaign seemed far off and time hung on his hands, then he began to have mistresses. Once introduced to a passionate sex life, he showed no great appetite for it: he stuck to the Princesse de Talmond and she had no serious rivals. An ugly side to Charles' nature immediately revealed itself: as a lover he could write lavish letters and bandy compliments with the best, but it released a brutal streak in him. The only women he was ever seriously involved with, whose lover he was – Princesse de Talmond, Clementina Walkinshaw and Louise de Stolberg – all literally bore the marks of his affection. He liked to beat his women, to fight with them, to injure them. Drink was not the only explanation. The trouble was, he needed something or someone to use as an outlet for his frustrations and his women served. All his anger that things had gone so wrong was vented on them. The Princesse de Talmond chose him, and Louise was chosen for him, but the only time Charles ever chose a woman for himself, Clementina Walkinshaw, he chose her because he thought he could do what he liked with her. To say he liked to be master is to put it mildly: he absolutely had to be the totally dominant partner. Since such an attitude doomed Charles' love life to failure, he was left only with filial love, and that he need never have done without. He withdrew from his father's love through pique and he never did a more stupid thing. Simply, James' love was a gift Charles could not afford to be without because no one else who knew him so thoroughly offered it to him. His rejection of his father's love was one of the saddest aspects of his character. It left a gap that was never filled. Even when cordial relations were resumed with Henry, love did not come into it. Henry had escaped from Charles' clutches in 1748 unworried about any love he might lose, such had been the quality of it since his brother returned. When Charlotte appeared on the scene, Charles had appeared to 'love' her. He found a freedom in loving a child that he had never known, and to be demonstrative gave him great pleasure. Doubtless Charlotte reciprocated, as small children mostly do towards anyone who blatantly adores them, so Charles got some pale shadow of real emotional involvement. But it disappeared with Charlotte's physical disappearance, never to be regained. By the time they met again it was too late to know love of any kind – or only of the most undemanding nature. Charles never knew what it was to love deeply and be deeply loved and it was a lack he felt.

Intellectually, Charles was not the fool he has often been made out to be. Much has been made of his bad spelling and handwriting and not enough of what he actually wrote. His childhood letters are always produced with a flourish to show how badly educated he was at eight or nine, but if they are compared with those of such an acknowledged clever boy as Horace Walpole they stand comparison very well. It is later that the faults seem more glaring, for whereas Horace overcame his bad spelling Charles never did. Even then, his spelling is not uniformly bad – he tends to misspell simple words but get more complicated ones right. Furthermore, his letters – except when he was being deliberately curt and non-communicative – are extremely fluent and coherent and even witty. They also have an energy and enthusiasm about them that make them entertaining – reading most of Charles' longer letters is no chore. His education was not so much neglected, either, as misguided. Charles had no love of learning by rote, of accepting other people's ideas and discoveries, but he did have a curiosity which was never tapped. Had he had his Fénelon much might have been made of him, for it was his truculent attitude and his teachers' dogmatic conventional approach rather than the faultiness of his mental equipment that prevented his learning. His native wit was in fact always sharp enough to get him by even in the most august academic company. Furthermore, he had a lively interest in people of all kinds that bespoke an intelligent appreciation of what they had to offer. He liked to chat people up and listened avidly to what they had to tell him so that the level of his general knowledge was good. His talents extended only as far as music, but nobody who could perform as well as he was said to could be judged lacking sensitivity. Far from being some kind of illiterate thickhead who knew nothing about anything and could hardly put two words together, Charles was highly intelligent, observant and, when it suited him, thoughtful. To complain that he was uneducated was true only in the formal sense and is as of much value as despising a man as stupid because he has no degree, or uneducated because he has never taken an examination. Sustained study and application were foreign to Charles' youthful nature and he missed most of what we mean by education because of it, but the use of the word 'uneducated' implies more than was true.

If Charles has gone down, however accidentally, as stupid, he has suffered even more from being classified as politically an imbecile, the tool or dupe of other people's ambitions. Nobody has ever given him any credit for having even a modicum of political awareness, which is grossly unfair. Charles was always interested in what was going on in the world – he was brought up to be. Talk in James' household was always of 'world' affairs and Charles and Henry would have been strange children not to be affected by such an atmosphere. The comings and goings of visitors from all parts of Europe made them aware from the very first that there was a world wider than Rome. Certainly, their view of politics was heavily prejudiced but it could hardly have been otherwise. They heard the story of how their grandfather lost the throne before they learnt to read. They saw the Hanoverians as wicked ogres who would get their deserts in the end and themselves as rightful deliverers. They understood the power of France and how much hung on French decisions, they knew the importance of the Pope and were glad to have him as their friend. Of the internal state of England, their Kingdom, they knew only what their visitors from there told them and this was usually not so much the truth as what their father wanted to hear. So, as a King's son, even a titular King's son, Charles was well-informed, within certain limits. His main difficulty, as he grew up, was his inability to understand the European scene as a whole. It was an ability few had. When Charles left Rome in 1744 he knew only that France was supreme, that England needed him, and that England was France's enemy. It was an elementary viewpoint, but it rapidly expanded to a more sophisticated one. Charles was not slow to learn that things were not all they might seem. After the fiasco of the 1744 expedition he never trusted France again. He went further than James had ever dared: not only did he never trust France, he saw clearly that he was being exploited by her and was not content to think that was either necessary or irreversible. But he lacked the skill and acumen to manipulate such powerful interests: he could not see how to make her do otherwise. Diplomacy of such a high order was not Charles' forte. As far as his own people were concerned, Charles was suspicious of them all. He could not sift true accounts from exaggerated and became confused when he tried. After the '45 he was a good deal more perceptive but never really separated man from motive. A man with better judgment might have been able to exploit his own value better – but it would have been difficult. Charles always counted on retaining the same importance in the eyes of contemporary statesmen after '45 as before it. This was a fatal mistake. He had written himself and his cause off. No amount of effort on his part could counter-balance that. This he only saw much later in his life, but even if he had seen it in 1746 – and he was not alone in not doing so – to accept it would have been as impossible as it would have been politically wise.

Charles made his own decision not to accept the inevitable in 1748 and the rest of his life was doubly miserable because of it.

Nothing could be more false than the assumption that Charles was 'manipulated' by his advisers and friends. The only manipulation that went on was very much behind the scenes in 1745, and it was of such a devious nature that he could be forgiven for not recognising it. But as far as making decisions went, Charles made his own – regrettably. He could be advised, persuaded or overruled but never duped. Even when he had very little idea what was going on, he would decide what to do. Nor did he make decisions lightly, but worried over them, desperately wanting to behave in a responsible fashion according to his own lights – and, moreover, to be *seen* to behave so. At Derby, Charles made the decision to let others make the decision, a policy he followed throughout the rest of his campaign, only snatching back the initiative at Culloden. Culloden was Charles' decision – never had he shown more clearly and tragically how much better it would have been not to make his own mind up. Casting around for others to blame is a pointless exercise. Because Sheridan wrote many of his proclamations and manifestos it was believed by many – even James – that he had Charles under his thumb, but as Sheridan's own letters show nothing could have been further from the truth. His pupil was still as headstrong and self-willed as ever. When Charles sent for Sheridan it was not because he wanted a stronger person with him but on the contrary, because he wanted a weaker, and a skivvy at that. Sheridan would do what he was told. Similarly, so would O'Sullivan. Both he and Kelly may have seen their master's weaknesses and known how to exploit them, but fundamentally they were both afraid of over-stepping the mark. They trod carefully at all times and back-pedalled at the slightest sign of Charles' anger or disapproval. They told him what they thought he wanted to hear, urged him on the way they thought he had shown he wanted to go. They were never in the least dominant. Charles seems at several points to have felt the lack of a faithful, well-informed, trustworthy adviser, and if only Lord George Murray had been different temperamentally he might have found him. But nobody ever came along. Not until he was old and ill did Charlotte gain an ascendancy that no one else ever had.

There remains the question of why Charles did what he did in the first place. Why, if he was not really wanted, did he go off to Scotland in the first place in 1745? Why cause so much harm? Why try to persist in the same ruinous cause when the harm had been done? Much can be made of the absurdity of the whole Stuart set-up and what seems the obvious futility and waste of Charles' attempt to regain the throne. One can only say, to those who despise him for bashing his own and others' heads against a stone wall, that contemporaries did not see it that way at all. It was fully understood, then, that if Charles Edward Stuart had any spunk at all he must carry on the family tradition and try for restoration. No one, throughout his childhood and youth, thought he could do otherwise. It was simply a question of time and opportunity, which is why he was always watched like a hawk and every movement was suspect. In those twenty years of growing up all Europe took the Stuarts seriously: their scorn was saved for the Hanoverians. Nobody, in 1745, made the mistake of despising his attempt, but either shook in their shoes or watched with consuming self-interest. His whole life, his very *raison d'être*, was wrapped up in it – nobody blamed him then, as they do now, for making it, however much his enemy they were. Nor did Charles do what he did simply for the glamour and glory. He enjoyed both, but he was inspired by duty, dedication and a belief in his family's divine right to the throne. He felt himself to represent Right as opposed to Wrong. His sincerity was never in doubt. Not all would-be conquerors go forward in the name of Justice: the Stuarts did. Charles had no desire to rape, loot, kill or terrorise: he thought he went as a deliverer from oppression and intended no oppression himself. There was about him at the time a kind of purity that stands out amid all the heaps of broken virtues and the stench of decay that surrounded him in the end.

After the '45, historians have found it hard to forgive the waste Charles made of the rest of his life. He was propelled first of all by a genuine desire to try again and a conviction that it was possible, then by sheer cussedness and finally by habit. Every principle he had ever had he stood on its head. People suspected first that he did not care about the holocaust that engulfed Scotland at and after Culloden, and then that he cared too much and had gone mad because of it. Neither was true. Charles certainly cared about the blood bath he left behind but what he would never do was accept the blame for it. Anyone who suggested to him that it was, ultimately, his responsibility was a brave man. He would not have it that men had followed him because he led, but that he had led because they followed. The suggestion that men had been *forced* to follow him drove him wild, and even when he was forced, confronted with the evidence, to admit this might be true he argued they were merely misguided and were shown the way by their chiefs: that was not forcing. His sympathy, his tears, were endless, but guilt was unknown to him. When, in later years, memories made him weep it was the happy memories, the good times had by all, the splendour of it all that made him weep, not the tragedy. He sobbed because he wanted to be back there, not because he wished it had never happened. If he was haunted it was by nostalgia, not grief.

If nobody influenced Charles to any great extent, he himself influenced the fates of others. His story is inextricably bound up with many people. When he died, many of them still lived on in his shadow. Henry did not die until 1807 and saw in his turn some of the misfortune that Charles had experienced. In 1798 the invasion of Italy by Napoleon affected even rural Frascati where Henry had retreated in panic. He had for some time before that been feeling the pinch – the French Revolution lost him some rich livings; then the Court of Spain stopped a lucrative pension; then the Pope used the Stuart family jewels to pay Napoleon to keep out of the Papal states. Forced to flee from Frascati, to his intense distress, Henry arrived in Padua almost as much the beggar his brother had been. It would have amused Charles to see that Henry did not show the same resourcefulness in poverty as he had done himself. Eventually, moved by his plight, Cardinal Borgia appealed to the English Government on his behalf and George III, showing a spirit of magnanimity or gratitude, whichever way one looks at it, offered him a pension of four thousand pounds a year. Henry accepted gratefully – enough to make his father turn in his grave. He was, at the last, under no illusions, even token ones. He went back quietly to Frascati, which gave him as much pain as pleasure for the French troops had sacked his palace and plundered his treasures. Here he died, a sad and lonely man, his only relief that he had a roof over his head in the place where his greatest happiness had been. In his will he left Louise, who had spent many years privately vilifying him, a picture and a gold watch. Magnanimity was always one of his better points.

Charlotte was not lucky enough to get even so much out of life. When Charles died, it seemed that at last all the waiting had been worthwhile, all the subterfuge justified. Paris with her mother, 'mon ami' and 'mes fleurs' awaited her. She sent to Florence for Charles' will, knowing that he had made her his sole heir. Unfortunately his fortune was by then not so considerable and he had left certain legacies to be paid, so Charlotte, not quite the woman of substance she had expected to be, had to delay her departure to enter into some bartering with Henry. She swapped the Crown Jewels in return for hard cash – the allowance made to Henry by the Apostolic Chamber. She had Charles' valuables that remained in his house in Florence brought to Rome and prominently displayed as her own. Perhaps she hoped to sell them before she left. In the event, she never did leave. Her father had died in 1788 in January; by June, when all the ends had been tied up, Charlotte was in acute pain and incapable of anything so arduous as travelling to Paris. Nor was it any good going on doctoring herself. In November 1789 she was operated on, but the cancer in her liver was too far advanced for even the most drastic surgery to be of any use. She died soon after, with no one to love or care for her other than servants. Her end, like her life, seems harder and crueller than any of the other characters in this drama. She put in such a long, dreary apprenticeship for happiness that it seems unbelievable she was allowed none. Strangely, she left everything to Henry, who at the time had absolutely no need of it, on the sole condition that her mother's pension was continued. No more adequate provision was made for Clementina, who by this time found the same pension laughably inadequate even for her simple needs. Nor was any mention made of 'the little flowers'. Perhaps Charlotte did not believe that her mother and her children would ever receive anything she left them, or perhaps when she made her will she felt indebted to Henry. Nevertheless, it seems puzzling.

The death of her daughter in her hour of triumph, as it were, was another blow to Clementina, who was by now used to them. The last years of her life proved even harder than the ones that had gone before. Though she survived the French Revolution – at the cost of watching many who had befriended her die – she was in want so great that it made Henry's need seem nothing. In 1800 a letter written in January by Thomas Coutts found its way to an unnamed minister in England describing the pitiful condition of Clementina. It acknowledges that as the late Pretender's mistress she has no real claim on Hanoverian charity, but suggests that all the same it is a disgrace that the daughter of such a well-known, well-established Scottish family should be allowed to die like this. The letter is marked 'For attention' but if the attention was ever given it was decided to give no practical help. Clementina finally died in 1802, of what sounds like malnutrition, after a long, grey, singularly joyless life. To the bitter end she is said always to have spoken of the man who ruined her with respect and affection.

Alone of the women in his life, Charles' wife came off well from her encounter with him. Louise was in Paris with Alfieri, enjoying herself immensely, when she heard of her husband's death. Surprisingly, in spite of her often repeated sentiments on the subject, Alfieri testified that she was visibly moved by the news and remained upset for some time. He found this as irritating as everyone else found it unlikely. Not unnaturally, everyone expected the famous pair would be married without delay. The fact that they did not caused excited speculation. They went on living apparently separate lives for some years, before finally moving into the same house. Even then, they did not marry. The explanation may have been financial – by marrying Louise would forfeit her right to her French and Papal pensions – but more probably it was a fear of ruining what they had. Alfieri had always denounced marriage, and Louise had found she got along very well without it. They were daringly ahead of their times in some ways, and proud of it. There may also have been, on Louise's part, just a slight lessening of the ardour which had once possessed her, so that, now free, she did not want to tie herself again to any man. But she stayed with Alfieri. In 1791 they both went to England where she was actually presented to Queen Caroline by the Countess of Aylesbury under her maiden name of Princess of Stolberg. No thoughts of her tea service with the Royal coat of arms on back home, or the liveries of her servants there, seem to have troubled her. Nor did she find England, towards which she had once looked with such longing, specially attractive. She and Alfieri toured parts of the country – though they never got as far as Scotland which was their intention – and she spoke with distaste of '... the coal smoke, the constant absence of sunshine, the heavy food and drink' which 'make movement a necessity'. England was equally unimpressed by her, Horace W. recording: 'Well! I have seen Madame D'Albany who has not a ray of royalty about her. She has good eyes and teeth; but I think can have had no more beauty than remains except youth. She is civil and easy, but German and ordinary.' On their return to Paris soon after, Louise and Alfieri were almost caught by the revolutionaries but got out just in time, escaping through the barricades to Florence. Here Louise lived until 1824, a little disillusioned by life but comparatively content even after the death of Alfieri in 1805. Actually she got no great pleasure out of the rest of her life, writing in a jaundiced way: 'I thought that after my husband's death I should continue in peace and happiness, when lo, the Revolution, which has turned my life into a perpetual state of anxiety as to my safety and my means of existence. So you see there is no hope of a real state of peace.' She had other friends, notably Fabre the painter, and was a patron of artists and writers, a veritable grande dame. Unlike Charles, she professed herself ready to die long before she actually did: 'I do not fear Death, but regard it with calmness; and instead of clinging the more to life as I grow older, I find myself growing each day more detached from it. The world is to me no more than a magic lantern. I watch it pass, as I sit at the window.' It was a long show – this was written in 1801 and she did not die until 1824.

Scotland today is, on the whole, ashamed of Charles Edward Stuart. Scots speak of him either contemptuously or apologetically: most of them are eager to let you know that they have not been taken in, that they know perfectly well the famous Bonnie Prince was just an Italian adventurer whom their ancestors in a mad moment of recklessness followed to their deaths. He is something of an embarrassment to men who pride themselves on being realists. Only ladies in Highland Industry shops speak of him with any affection, which seems appropriate since all Charles bequeathed to Scotland that was of any benefit was a tourist industry. He achieved nothing of lasting importance, left nothing behind him to be remembered by except one bloody battle. The wonder is that he is remembered at all. What keeps his memory alive is the bitterness that still exists between England and Scotland. It is a bitterness, a hatred, an enmity that was always there. Charles, because he used this, has become inextricably linked with it. He was Scotland's last hope, a hope which, since it came after the Union was firmly cemented, was always forlorn. Yet Charles was no Scot, no nationalist. The only throne he was interested in was the throne of Great Britain. Had he succeeded, Scotland would have claimed him as their own, but might have had a rude awakening. As it was, he became their own private personal tragedy.

Charles himself was a tragedy, of a common enough kind. Full of promise in his youth, he never matured or developed but stayed forever an arrested adolescent. He never for one moment showed any signs of true greatness. He was liked, loved, adored but rarely respected. Many who perpetuate the legend would like Charles to have been killed at Culloden, preferably leading a heroic charge, dying if possible on the end of Cumberland's bayonet. All heroes need a battlefield death if their reputation is to be above reproach. The years after 1746 – all forty-two of them – are awkward: it is hard to keep up the myth of a brave gallant in those circumstances. And yet those years that are so often hidden or glossed over, those years containing not a single commendable act, those years full of actions that make depressing reading – they are more truly Charles than any that went before. A man under pressure is revealed.

Each man's pressure varies. Charles' pressure was failure. Charles after Culloden is the true man.

Charles of the legend is a sickly creature, the real Charles at least human and not too terrible a character. Charles himself, of course, would have been delighted by his legend – nothing would have given him greater satisfaction. For one who failed so completely in life, there has been no more convincing success in death: Long Live Bonnie Prince Charlie?

Author's Note

The main source for the information in this book has been the microfilmed edition (MIC150) of the Windsor Stuart Papers. These start at Volume 5, September 1715, and finish as far as Charles is concerned with Volume 514. Contained in these volumes are 1,962 letters written by Charles, the first appearing in Volume 83. The period of the '45 – 24th June 1745 to 20th October 1746 – produces only 16 letters. The bulk of the correspondence comes afterwards. I have not thought it necessary to give exact references for these letters since in the later part of the book this would have meant more references than text. This is not meant to be a work of reference, nor an original thesis, and I felt that as long as any interested reader was shown, in general, where to find the material I found, that was sufficient. It would, in any case, have been pointless giving detailed references for with microfilms the whole volume has to be run through.

Charles' letters have never been edited – nor, indeed, have the volumes after 1716. Several people have printed his letters in appendix form to their books and these are invaluable time-savers. Browne, in particular, prints many letters from the Stuart Papers, and can be heavily relied upon.

I have given, in a separate bibliography, a list of many secondary sources that I may not have actually used but found interesting, together with the primary sources included in these reference notes. This is purely for the reader's convenience.

References

INTRODUCTION: FLIGHT INTO EXILE

Details of James Francis' birth

BROWN, Beatrice Curtis, *The Letters of Queen Anne* (Geoffrey Bles, London 1935)

MARLBOROUGH, Sarah, Duchess of, *An Account of the Conduct of the Dowager Duchess of Marlborough*, ed. Hooke (1742)

OMAN, Carola, *Mary of Modena* (Hodder & Stoughton, London 1962)

1708 Campaign

FORBIN, Comte de, *Mémoires* (Amsterdam 1730)

SINCLAIR-STEVENSON, Christopher, *Inglorious Rebellion: The Jacobite risings of 1708, 1715, 1719* (Hamish Hamilton, London 1971)

DANGEAU, Marquis de, *Journal de la Cour de Louis XIV* (Paris 1807)

1715 Campaign

BERWICK, Duke of, *Mémoires du Maréchal de Berwick* (Paris 1780)

H.M.C. Vols. 1 and 2

MAHON, Lord, *History of England from the Peace of Utrecht to the Peace of Aix-la-Chapelle* (London 1836): see Appendix for James' letters

Avignon

H.M.C. Vol. 2

Marriage to Clementina

H.M.C. Vol. 6

GILBERT, Sir John T., *Narratives of the Detention, Liberation & Marriage of Maria Clementina Sobieska styled Queen of Great Britain & Ireland by Sir Charles Wogan and Others* (Dublin 1894)

FLOOD, J. M., *The Life of Chevalier Charles Wogan* (Talbot Press, Dublin 1922)

CHAPTER ONE: ROME

Life in Rome

TAYLER, H., *The Jacobite Court at Rome in 1719* (Scot. Hist. Soc. 1938)
British Museum Pamphlet, 'An English Traveller at Rome' (1721)
MONTAGU, Lady Mary Wortley, *Letters and Works*, 2 vols. (1861)
VITELLESCHI, Marchesa, *A Court in Exile*, Vol. 1
THOMSON, Mrs Katherine, *Memoirs of the Jacobites*, Appendix to Vol. iii

Birth of Charles

W.S.P., Vol. 50

CHAPTER TWO: 'THIS PRETTY YOUNG PRINCE'

Charles' early childhood

W.S.P., Vols. 60, 61, 62

Quarrel between James and Clementina

W.S.P., Vol. 64: John Hay's letters
LOCKHART, George, of Carnwath, *Memoirs concerning the Affairs of Scotland*
W.S.P., Vol. 87: James' letters
POLLNITZ, Baron de, *Memoirs* (London 1745)

Charles' education

FÉNELON, François Salignac de la Motte, *Lettres*, ed. John McEwen (1964)
W.S.P., Vols. 129–168: these contain Charles' early letters, James' replies, and Murray's and Sheridan's correspondence with James on the subject

CHAPTER THREE: APPRENTICE TO A CAUSE

Gaeta

W.S.P., Vol. 172

Tour of N. Italy

W.S.P., Vol. 198

Background to '45

BLAIKIE, W. B., *Origins of the '45* (1916)
FORBES, Duncan, *The Culloden Papers* (1815)

BROUGHTON, John Murray of, *Memorials*, ed. R. Fitzroy Bell (Scot. Hist. Soc. 1898)

ELCHO, David, *A short account of the Affairs of Scotland*, ed. Hon. Evan Charteris (1907)

BROWNE, James, *A History of the Highlands and of the Highland Clans*, 4 vols. (2nd edn. 1845)

CHAPTER FOUR: LESSON IN PATIENCE

Charles' journey to France

W.S.P., Vol. 256

TAYLER, H., *A Jacobite Miscellany* (Roxburgh Club 1948): Sheridan's account of escape from Rome

Failure of 1744 expedition and aftermath

W.S.P., Vols. 257–66

TAYLER, A. and H., *1745 and After* (Thomas Nelson, London 1938): O'Sullivan's narrative

HAYES, Richard, *Biographical Dictionary of Irishmen in France* (M. H. Gill, Dublin 1949)

ARGENSON, Marquis d', *Journals and Memoirs*, ed. E. J. B. Rathery

MARVILLE, *Lettres de M. de Marville au Ministre Maurepas*, Vol. 2

Walsh and slave-trade

THOMAS, Professor H., *Observer* Supplement, 17th October 1965

CHAPTER FIVE: VOYAGE TO SCOTLAND

Journey to Scotland

TAYLER, A. and H., *op. cit.*: O'Sullivan's narrative

CHAMBERS, R., *Jacobite Memoirs of the Rebellion of 1745:* for narratives of Aeneas Macdonald and Duncan Cameron

TAYLER, H., *A Jacobite Miscellany:* narrative of John Macdonald.

TRÉMOILLE, Duc de, *A Royalist Family Irish and French (1689–1789) and Prince Charles Edward*, trans. A. G. Murray Macgregor (1904): for journal of *Le Du Teillay*

W.S.P., Vols. 266 and 267

Arrival in Scotland

Above narratives

FORBES, Revd Robert, *Lyon in Mourning*, 3 vols., ed. Henry Paton (Scot. Hist. Soc. 1859)

FORBES, Duncan, *op. cit.*

CHAPTER SIX: THE FIRST VICTORY

Glenfinnan to Edinburgh

BROUGHTON, John Murray of, *Memorials*
COPE Report – *The Report of the Proceedings and Opinion of the Board of Officers in the Examination into the Conduct, Behaviour and Proceedings of Lieut.-Gen. Sir John Cope* (London 1749)
MARCHANT, John, *History of the Present Rebellion*
JOHNSTONE, Chevalier de, *Memoirs of the Rebellion in Scotland in 1745 and 1746* (2nd edn. 1821)
MOUNSEY, George C., *Authentic Account of the Occupation of Carlisle in 1745* (1846): for news of Charles' progress in England

Lord George Murray's support

Atholl papers as printed in:
DUKE, Winifred, *Lord George Murray and the '45*
TOMASSON, K., *The Jacobite General* (W. Blackwood, Edinburgh 1958)

Condition of Scotland

BURT, Edward, *Letters from a Gentleman in the North of Scotland* (5th edn. 1818)
CUNNINGHAM, Audrey, *The Loyal Clans* (Cambridge University Press 1932)

Capture of Edinburgh

HOME, John, *The History of the Rebellion in Scotland* (1882)
BROWNE, James, *op. cit.*
DODDRIDGE, Dr Philip, *Some Remarkable Passages in the Life of the Hon. Col. James Gardiner* (1747)
TAYLER, H., *A Jacobite Miscellany:* for Whig girl's letter

Prestonpans

MAXWELL, James, of Kirkconnell, *Narrative of Charles Prince of Wales' Expedition to Scotland in the Year 1745* (Maitland Club 1841)
MCNEILL, P., *Prestonpans and Vicinity*
DODDRIDGE, Dr Philip, *op. cit.*
BROWNE, James, *op. cit.*
COPE Report

CHAPTERS SEVEN and EIGHT: EDINBURGH and MARCH INTO ENGLAND . . .

Charles in Edinburgh

ELCHO, David, *op. cit.*
HOME, John, *op. cit.*
W.S.P., Vol. 269: Charles' letters
FORBES, Duncan, *op. cit.*
MAXWELL, James, *op. cit.*

March into England

MURRAY, Lord George, 'Marches of the Highland Army', in *Jacobite Memoirs* . . . by Chambers, *op. cit.*
ELCHO, David, *op. cit.*

Taking of Carlisle

MOUNSEY, George C., *op. cit.*
HUGHES, Edward, 'Fleming-Senhouse Papers', ed. for Cumberland Record Series II
WILLIAMSON, George, Diary (unpublished manuscript, copy in Carlisle Record Office)

March South

TAYLER, A. and H., *op. cit.*: O'Sullivan's narrative
DANIEL, John, 'Progress', in *Origins of the '45* by W. B. Blaikie
MURRAY, Lord George, *op. cit.*

Derby

EARDLEY-SIMPSON, *Derby and the '45:* extracts from letters
ELCHO, David, *op. cit.*
MAXWELL, James, *op. cit.*
TAYLER, A. and H., *op. cit:* O'Sullivan's narrative
MURRAY, Lord George, *op. cit.*

CHAPTERS NINE and TEN: . . . AND BACK TO SCOTLAND and FALKIRK AND RETREAT

Retreat to Scotland

MOUNSEY, George C., *op. cit.*
TAYLER, A. and H., *op. cit.*: O'Sullivan's narrative
MAXWELL, James, *op. cit.*

ELCHO, David, *op. cit.*
WILLIAMSON, George, *op. cit.*

Stay in Glasgow

BROWNE, James, *op. cit.*, Vol. III

Falkirk

TOMASSON, K. and BUIST, F., *Battles of the '45* (Batsford, London 1962): includes Hawley's letters
HOME, John, *op. cit.*
BROWNE, James, *op. cit.*, Vol. III, Appendix: for Charles' and Sheridan's letters
MURRAY, Lord George, *op. cit.*
TAYLER, A. and H., *op. cit.:* O'Sullivan's narrative

Loss of Prince Charles

GIBSON, John, *Ships of the '45* (Hutchinson, London 1967)

Duke of Cumberland

CHARTERIS, Hon. Evan, *William Augustus, Duke of Cumberland 1721–48*
HENDERSON, Andrew, *The Life of the Duke of Cumberland* (1766)

CHAPTER ELEVEN: CULLODEN

Culloden

PREBBLE, John, *Culloden* (Secker & Warburg, London 1961)

Flight of Charles

BLAIKIE, W. B., *Itinerary of Prince Charles Edward Stuart* (Scot. Hist. Soc. 1897): includes Lord George Murray's and Charles' letters
W.S.P., Vol. 273: James' letters

CHAPTERS TWELVE and THIRTEEN: ON THE ISLANDS and HIDE-AND-SEEK

Charles' wanderings

BLAIKIE, W. B., *Itinerary . . . :* includes Lochgarry's narrative
TAYLER, A. and H., *op. cit.:* O'Sullivan's narrative
FORBES, Revd Robert, *op. cit.*
CAMERON, Dr, *Two Accounts of Escape of Prince Charles Edward*, ed. H. Tayler (Oxford University Press 1951)
GIBSON, John, *op. cit.:* for French attempts at rescue

CHAPTER FOURTEEN: PRISONERS AND MARTYRS

Prisoners

SETON and ARNOT, *Prisoners of the '45*
PREBBLE, John, *op. cit.*
FORBES, Revd Robert, *op. cit.*

Trials

CLARKE, Baron, Notebook (original manuscript in possession of Tullie House, Carlisle)

Condition of Scotland after '45

ALBEMARLE, Earl of, *The Albemarle Papers*, ed. Charles Sanford Terry (New Spalding Club 1902)
FORBES, Duncan, *op. cit.*

CHAPTER FIFTEEN: A HERO

Arrival and reception in France

LUYNES, Duc de, *Les Mémoires du Duc de Luynes sur la Cour de Louis XV (1735–58)*, Vols. VII and VIII
BROWNE, James, *op. cit.*, Appendixes to Vols. III and IV: for letters between Charles, James and Henry

Spain

W.S.P., Vols. 277–283

CHAPTER SIXTEEN: DISGRACE AND EXPULSION

Liaison with Princesse de Talmond

LUYNES, Duc de, *op. cit.*
ARGENSON, Marquis d', *op. cit.*
W.S.P., Vol. 316: for Princesse's letters

Henry

LUYNES, Duc de, *op. cit.*
ARGENSON, Marquis d', *op. cit.*
W.S.P., Vols. 284 and 285

Treaty of Aix-la-Chapelle

BROWNE, James, *op. cit.*, Vol. III, Appendix

CHAPTER SEVENTEEN: THE ELUSIVE PRINCE

Wanderings 1748–1752

BROWNE, James, *op. cit.*, Vol. III, Appendix to Vol. IV
LANG, Andrew, *Pickle the Spy*
POLNAY, Peter de, *Death of a Legend* (1952)

Expedition to London

KING, Dr W., *Political and Literary Anecdotes of His Own Times* (London 1819)
FORBES, Revd Robert, *op. cit.*, Vol. iii
JONES, G. H., *Main Stream of Jacobitism* (Oxford University Press 1954)

Negotiations with Marischal

BROWNE, James, *op. cit.*, Vol. III and Appendix to Vol. IV
TAYLER, H., 'Jacobite Epilogue'

CHAPTERS EIGHTEEN and NINETEEN: PLOTS AND AFFAIRS and 'BUIRIED ALIVE'

Elibank Plot

PETRIE, Sir Charles, *The Jacobite Movement*
JONES, G. H., *op. cit.*
FORBES, Revd Robert, *op. cit.*: for Dr Cameron's death

Clementina Walkinshaw

TAYLER, H., *Prince Charlie's Daughter* (London 1950)
LANG, Andrew, *op. cit.*
W.S.P., Vol. 351

Charles' life till 1766

W.S.P., Vols. 351–420
LANG, Andrew, *op. cit.*
LANG, Andrew, *Companions of Pickle*

CHAPTER TWENTY: QUEEN OF HEARTS

Charles' return to Rome

MANN, Horace, *Letters to Horace Walpole*
SHIELD, A., *Henry Stuart, Cardinal of York*
VITELLESCHI, Marchesa, *op. cit.*, Vol. II

Quarrel with father's servants

FORBES, Revd Robert, *op. cit.*, Vol. iii
VITELLESCHI, Marchesa, *op. cit.*

Marriage to Louise

LEE, Vernon, *The Countess of Albany* (John Lane, The Bodley Head, London 1909)
VAUGHAN, H. M., *The Last Stuart Queen*
VITELLESCHI, Marchesa, *op. cit.:* for account of ceremony from contemporary archives

CHAPTERS TWENTY-ONE AND TWENTY-TWO: FLORENCE AND FAILURE and COUNT OF ALBANY

Life in Florence

MANN, Horace, *op. cit.*
LEE, Vaughan, *op. cit.:* Louise's letters quoted
VITELLESCHI, Marchesa, *op. cit.:* Alfieri's letters quoted
MAHON, Lord, *Decline of the Last Stuarts: Extracts from the Despatches of British Envoys to the Secretary of State*

Break with Louise

As above plus:
W.S.P., Vol. 507

CHAPTER TWENTY-THREE: A LONG TIME DYING

Charlotte

W.S.P., Vols. 507–514
TAYLER, H., *Prince Charlie's Daughter:* extracts from letters to mother included
MANN, Horace, *op. cit.*

Death of Charles

FORBES, Revd Robert, *op. cit.*
VITELLESCHI, Marchesa, *op. cit.*
W.S.P., Vol. 514

Selected Bibliography

This is arranged according to subject and provides general reading as well as information on specific topics.

Background to Charles' birth

BERWICK, Duke of, *Mémoires du Maréchal de Berwick* (Paris 1780)

BOSQ DE BEAUMONT, G. de, *La Cour des Stuarts à St Germain-en-Laye 1698–1718* (Emile Paul 1912)

BROWN, Beatrice Curtis, *The Letters of Queen Anne* (Geoffrey Bles, London 1935)

BURNET, Gilbert, Bishop of Salisbury, *History of His Own Times*, Vol. VI (1823)

CAMPANA DE CAVELLI, Marchesa, *Les derniers Stuarts à St Germain-en-Laye 1698–1718*, 2 vols. (Emile Paul 1912)

CLARENDON, Henry, Earl of, *Diary 1687–90*

FLOOD, J. M., *The Life of Chevalier Charles Wogan* (Talbot Press, Dublin 1922)

FORBIN, Comte de, *Mémoires* (Amsterdam 1730)

FULLER, William, *A Brief Discovery* (London 1696)

GILBERT, Sir John T., *Narratives of the Detention, Liberation & Marriage of Maria Clementina Sobieska styled Queen of Great Britain & Ireland by Sir Charles Wogan and Others* (Dublin 1894)

GREEN, D., *Queen Anne*

HAILE, M., *James Francis Edward, The Old Chevalier*

JONES, G. H., *Main Stream of Jacobitism* (Oxford University Press 1954)

LA FAYETTE, Marie Motier, Comtesse de, *Mémoires de la Cour de France 1688–89*

MAHON, Lord, *History of England from the Peace of Utrecht to the Peace o, Aix-la-Chapelle* (London 1836)

MARLBOROUGH, Sarah, Duchess of, *An Account of the Conduct of the Dowager Duchess of Marlborough*, ed. Hooke (1742)

MILLER, Peggy, *James* (Allen & Unwin, London 1972)

——, *A Wife for the Pretender* (Allen & Unwin, London 1965)

OMAN, Carola, *Mary of Modena* (Hodder & Stoughton, London 1962)

RANKINE, Alexander, *Memoirs of the Chevalier St George* (1702)

SÉVIGNÉ, Mme de, *Lettres* (Edition Lefèvre, Paris 1943)

SINCLAIR-STEVENSON, Christopher, *Inglorious Rebellion: The Jacobite risings of 1708, 1715, 1719* (Hamish Hamilton, London 1971)

Rome and Italy in the eighteenth century

ANDRIEUX, Maurice, *Daily Life in Papal Rome in the 18th Century* (Allen & Unwin, London 1968)

DORAN, J., *Mann and Manners at Florence 1740–86* (1876)

MONTAGU, Lady Mary Wortley, *Letters and Works*, 2 vols. (1861)

TAYLER, H., *The Jacobite Court at Rome in 1719* (Scot. Hist. Soc. 1938)

VAUSSARD, M. R. J. A. A., *Daily Life in 18th-century Italy* (Allen & Unwin, London 1968)

VITELLESCHI, Marchesa, *A Court in Exile*, 2 vols.

The 1745 Rebellion: contemporary narratives

BOYSE, Samuel, *An Impartial History of the late Rebellion* (1748)

BROUGHTON, John Murray of, *Memorials*, ed. R. Fitzroy Bell (Scot. Hist. Soc. 1898)

GRAHAM, Dugald, *An Impartial History of the Rise, Progress & Extinction of the late Rebellion*

HENDERSON, Andrew, *The History of the Rebellion* (1753)

HUGHES, Michael, *A Plain Narrative* (1746)

JOHNSTONE, Chevalier de, *A Memoir of the '45* (1820)

MARCHANT, John, *The History of the Present Rebellion* (1746)

MAXWELL, James, of Kirkconnell, *Narrative of Charles Prince of Wales' Expedition to Scotland in the Year 1745* (Maitland Club 1841)

RAY, James, *A Complete History of the Rebellion* (1752)

VEZZOSI, Michele, *Young Juba; or the History of the Young Chevalier* (1748)

1745

BLAIKIE, W. B., *Origins of the '45* (1916)

——, *Itinerary of Prince Charles Edward Stuart* (Scot. Hist. Soc. 1897)

BROWNE, James, *A History of the Highlands and the Highland Clans* 4 vols., (2nd edn. 1845).

CADELL, Sir Robert, *Sir John Cope*

CHAMBERS, R., *History of the Rebellion*

——, *Jacobite Memoirs of the Rebellion of 1745*

CHARTERIS, Hon. Evan, *William Augustus, Duke of Cumberland 1721–48*

COPE, Report: *The Report of the Proceedings and Opinion of the Board of Officers in the Examination into the Conduct, Behaviour and Proceedings of Lieut.-Gen. Sir John Cope* (London 1749)

CUNNINGHAM, Andrew, *The Loyal Clans* (Cambridge University Press, 1932)

DODDRIDGE, Dr Philip, *Some Remarkable Passages in the Life of the Hon. Col. James Gardiner* (1747)

DUKE, Winifred, *Prince Charles Edward and the '45* (Robert Hale, London 1939)

——, *The Rash Adventurer* (Robert Hale, London 1952)

——, *In the Steps of Bonnie Prince Charlie* (Rich & Cowan, London 1953)

——, *Lord George Murray and the '45* (1938)

EARDLEY-SIMPSON, *Derby and the '45*

ELCHO, David, *A short account of the Affairs of Scotland*, ed. Hon. Evan Charteris (1907)

FORBES, Duncan, *The Culloden Papers* (1815)

FORBES, J. Macbeth, *Jacobite Gleanings*

FORBES, Revd Robert, *Lyon in Mourning*, 3 vols., ed. Henry Paton (Scots. Hist. Soc. 1859)

FORTESCUE, Sir J., *History of the British Army* (Macmillan, London)

GIBSON, John, *Ships of the '45* (Hutchinson, London 1967)

GRANT, Mrs Anne, *Letters concerning Highland Affairs*

HENDERSON, Andrew, *The Life of the Duke of Cumberland* (1766)

HEWINS, The *Whitefoord Papers*

HOME, John, *The History of the Rebellion in Scotland* (1882)

JARVIS, *Collected Papers of the Jacobite Risings*, 2 vols. (Manchester University Press)

LANG, Andrew, *Prince Charles Edward* (Longman, London 1900)

——, *A History of Scotland*, Vol. IV

MAHON, Lord, *The Forty-Five*

MOUNSEY, George C., *Authentic Account of the Occupation of Carlisle in 1745* (1846)

PETRIE, Charles, *The Jacobite Movement* (Eyre & Spottiswoode, London 1959)

PREBBLE, John, *Culloden* (Secker & Warburg, London 1961)

SETON and ARNOT, *Prisoners of the '45*

TAYLER, A. and H., *1745 and After* (Thomas Nelson, London 1938)

TAYLER, H., *A Jacobite Miscellany* (Roxburgh Club 1948)

——, *Jacobite Epilogue*

TERRY, Charles Sanford, *The Forty Five* (Cambridge University Press, 1922)

THOMSON, Mrs K., *Memoirs of the Jacobites*

TOMASSON, K., *The Jacobite General*

TOMASSON, K., and BUIST, F., *Battles of the '45* (Batsford, London 1962)

Unprinted manuscripts

CLARK, Baron, Notebook (Carlisle Library)

WILLIAMSON, George, Curate of Arthuret, Diary (Carlisle Castle)

Relating to Charles after 1745

KING, W., *Political and Literary Anecdotes of his Own Times*

LANG, Andrew, *Pickle the Spy*

———, *The Companions of Pickle*

LEE, Vernon, *The Countess of Albany* (John Lane, The Bodley Head, London 1909)

LUYNES, Duc de, *Les Mémoires du Duc de Luynes sur la Cour de Louis XV (1735–58)*, Vols. VII, VIII, IX

MAHON, Lord, *Decline of the Last Stuarts: Extracts from the Despatches of British Envoys to the Secretary of State*

MARVILLE, M., *Lettres de M. de Marville au Ministre Maurepas*

POLNAY, Peter de, *Death of a Legend* (1952)

RATHERY, E. J. B., *Journals and Memoirs of Marquis d'Argenson*

SHIELD, A., *Henry Stuart, Cardinal of York*

SKEET, F. J. A., *The Life and Letters of HRH Charlotte Stuart, Duchess of Albany* (Eyre & Spottiswoode, London 1933)

TAYLER, H., *Prince Charlie's Daughter*

VAUGHAN, H. M., *The Last Stuart Queen*

General books for eighteenth-century background

ANDERSON, M. S., *18th Century Europe 1713–89* (Oxford University Press, 1966)

RUDÉ, George, *Paris and London in the Eighteenth Century*

FEILING, K., *The Second Tory Party 1714–1832* (Macmillan, London 1938)

HAYES, Richard, *Biographical Dictionary of Irishmen in France* (M. H. Gill, Dublin 1949)

LOUGH, John, *Introduction to 18th-century France*

MATHIESON, W. L., *Scotland and the Union 1695–1747* (Jackson, Glasgow 1905)

MITCHISON, R., *A History of Scotland* (Methuen, London 1970)

PLUMB, J. H., *The First Four Georges* (Batsford, London 1956)

RUDE,   , *Paris and London in the eighteenth century*

WALPOLE, Horace, *Letters of Horace Walpole*, 13 vols., ed. Toynbee (Oxford University Press)

WILLIAMS, B. *The Whig Supremacy*, Vol. 11 of *Oxford History of England* (Oxford University Press, 1962)

Complete Lives of Charles

LANG, Andrew, *Prince Charles Edward* (Longman, London 1900)
This is by far the best. Nothing before or since matches it, in spite of much new information that has come to light. The only others with any claims to being complete are:

EWALD, 4 vols.

NORRIE, 4 vols.

Index

The best in biography from Panther Books

John Brooke
King George III   £1.95 ☐

J Bryan III and Charles J V Murphy
The Windsor Story   £2.95 ☐

Margaret Forster
The Rash Adventurer   £1.25 ☐

Antonia Fraser
Mary Queen of Scots   £3.95 ☐
Cromwell: Our Chief of Men   £3.95 ☐

Eric Linklater
The Prince in the Heather   £2.50 ☐

Henri Troyat
Catherine the Great   £2.95 ☐

Sir Arthur Bryant
Samuel Pepys: The Man in the Making   £3.95 ☐
Samuel Pepys: The Years of Peril   £3.95 ☐

To order direct from the publisher just tick the titles you want
and fill in the order form.   **GB181**

All these books are available at your local bookshop or newsagent, or can be ordered direct from the publisher..

To order direct from the publisher just tick the titles you want and fill in the form below.

Name _____

Address _____

_____

Send to:
Panther Cash Sales
PO Box 11, Falmouth, Cornwall TR10 9EN.

Please enclose remittance to the value of the cover price plus:

UK 45p for the first book, 20p for the second book plus 14p per copy for each additional book ordered to a maximum charge of £1.63.

BFPO and Eire 45p for the first book, 20p for the second book plus 14p per copy for the next 7 books, thereafter 8p per book.

Overseas 75p for the first book and 21p for each additional book.